To my Star.
Arletta

in honor of the labours
of Chuck Ketchum

-Ken op Styczynski
July 2019/4019

Western New York Lodge of Research: Books of Transactions 1983-2013

Western New York Lodge of Research
Books of Transactions 1983–2013

Compiled and Edited by Ken JP Stuczynski
Published by

cyphrGlyffe

An Imprint of
Amorphous Publishing Guild, Buffalo, NY USA
Amporphous.Press/cyphrGlyffe
©2019

To all those who seek and share Light

Contents

The Morgan Affair, Why?

Second Book of Transactions

Third Book of Transactions

Editor's Preface

The Western New York Lodge of Research F.&A.M. No.9007 is a chartered Lodge of the Grand Lodge F.&A.M. of the State of New York. Constitutionally, it is a peculiar entity—we do not confer degrees, nor pay *per capita* to Grand Lodge, as you must already be a Mason in good standing to belong. We have a Charter like any other Lodge, by-laws, regular and summoned communications, and affiliations from members of other jurisdictions. There are few Research Lodges in New York—and not a significantly large number in the whole world—but we are presently more active than most in our jurisdiction, and (in my opinion) could realistically aspire to become noteworthy among the intelligentsia of global Freemasonry.

In one Masonic sense, it is more of a Lodge than most—nearly without fail, the Master's obligation to provide some program of instruction is fulfilled, whereas the average Lodge of our time neglects this most central and ancient of charges. That is why we like to say, "All Lodges should be a Lodge of Research".

But not all are impressed. There are those who do not consider us a "real" Lodge, and the tale passed to me was that it was a long, uphill battle to receive our Dispensation for just that reason all those years ago. I have been told there were times of little activity between early years and ones more recent, but this is all second-hand history to me. Petitioning to affiliate in 2012, immediately after I was raised to the Sublime Degree, I found the Lodge to be quite industrious and fruitful.

In fact, I was prompted to enter the Masonic Brotherhood on two fronts—my wife's lifelong desire to join the Order of the Eastern Star, and an interest in the work of the this local Research Lodge. I had started writing my "Arabic Cyphre Hypothesis" (the last article in this book) even before my Initiation, and happily offered it as my first Masonic presentation. The inspiration to write it—and to explore Freemasonry itself—was a late-night discussion with a business associate, Brother (now Worshipful) Mark Robson. He quickly become a mentor, inspiration, and friend.

Other narratives aside, he and I were shortly thereafter tasked to create *Volume* 3 of the *Book of Transactions*. I was eager to work, but didn't have the personal relationships (yet) to corral content from the files of the various Brothers. Therefore, he handled the acquisitions, and with editorial suggestions from a few reviewing Brothers, I organized, edited, and had it printed. The design and form of this volume was modelled after *Volume 2*. Whereas the second volume had Vitruvian Man on the cover and a world map on the back, I chose a chart of historical Arabic numerals and a map of England, to match some of the content of the third volume.

It was not long thereafter a desire arose to republish earlier works. There was no compiling to do, save converting to digital text two book-sized, spiral-bound works, namely *Works Under Dispensation* and *First Book of Transactions*. I combined them into a single volume similar in size and design to the other two, with a faded-edge cover and a map of Erie County on the back.

My thinking regarding the hue of these softcover volumes (back and front) was that the oldest ought to be grey, and the third volume shifting the hue toward peach-pink from the sepia-tan of the second volume. A fourth volume (and so on) could be a pastel further down the spectrum, for a pleasing view of the growing collection on a shelf.

The quest to create a fourth *Book of Transactions* held a challenge—there were too few publishable works by more than one or two authors. This is still the case for now. Presentations were many and excellent, but only recorded in notes and slideshows, if that. And as we are running out of copies of some of the existing volumes, I advocated for the creation of a reprint of it all in what is now this composite tome. The Brethren agreed.

This also gave me the freedom of an updated style and format, as it need not conform to existing volumes. Having edited all of the works at this time except the second volume, it was a quick start, slowed only by the repeated passing through of the whole book to improve consistency in form and style. The details of these style choices, inclusion or exclusion of material, and other editing decisions, can be found in the back matter under "About the Editing of this Book".

At this time, I must interject my personal thanks and appreciation to Brother (Dr.) Mark Donnelly, whose publishing experience is proving invaluable to a quality completion of this work. Publishing tools and tutorials are everywhere, but true mentoring is rare and dear. What I am learning in this project may carry me from a wishful, fledgling publisher to lands unimagined.

Further publications of the Western New York Lodge of Research will likely appear, but this is meant to stand alone as an anthology, not a series of periodicals (such as the "*Short Talk Bulletins*" of the Masonic Service Association of North America). Other research Lodges have regularly periodic publications and different rules about what is published or republished. Though we may be inspired by the fruits of their labors, we are not attempting to emulate or replicate such models. These works are a natural culmination of many individual's efforts, through times of vibrancy and latency, notes preserved and speeches lost, and the scholastic peculiarities that arise when affording a voice to Brethren of wildly diverse interests and education.

The final product here is meant to give witness to all the works previously published, in a hardcover, dignified form that will be proudly touched by the hands of our members, warmly received by seekers, and cherished by those who come after us. It is a memorial to all those who, in this time and place, were willing to shine a light upon knowledge, apply reason, and let fly imagination. May we find ourselves, in another thirty years, the proud inheritors of these values, and benefactors of the same unto new generations.

Wor. Ken JP Stuczynski
Editor, Books of Transactions
24 March 2019

From the East: The Master's Message

It is an honor and a privilege to be sitting the East at the time of the publishing of this anthology of some of the written works of the Brothers of the Western New York Lodge of Research No.9007. Many more stimulating presentations have been made in a format not lending it to publication. No matter whether written and read, slide show or powerpoint, lively and informative discussions follow. The subjects vary, but cover a wide range of topics of interest to most Master Masons.

Our membership has grown from the original 25 charter members in 1982 to over 70 at this time. Some new members are coming from outside Western New York and even some from out of state. Any Master Mason is welcome to join. A large portion of the membership are Worshipfuls, Very Worshipfuls, Right Worshipfuls, and Most Worshipfuls. However, any Master Mason interested in the acquisition of knowledge and the dispensing of it to other Masons will find us a friendly and supportive group.

This anthology is a consolidation of three books of transactions which will enable the reader an opportunity to learn from past presenters, some of whom are no longer with us.

I wish to thank Worshipful Kenneth Stuczynski for taking on the task of editing and arranging the publication of this volume. I would also like to thank those who assisted him and those who made it all possible by sharing their research and thoughts in writing.

Fraternally,
RW *David Bindig*
Master, 2018–2019

Masonic Truths—A Disclaimer

No one owns Freemasonry; we all contribute and draw, without any formal account or tally made, from the fonts of knowledge given us by our forebears and each other. We are all entitled to a voice sovereign onto ourselves, to have an opinion of our own, and beg a gentle tolerance to respectfully write upon the opinions of others, however we may differ in belief.

As an institution, Freemasonry is perhaps the purest in intent and form, in that it does not exist save within and between the hearts of Men. Authority is derived from consent as sure as submission to its universally-accepted ideals—as each conscience sees them—is obsessively preserved within the bounds of the individual's free will and accord. We share Landmarks, or notions of them, that we know not fully from whence they came, but it is in how we best work and agree that they are realized. They do not bind us with arbitrary rules, but are forcibly recommended so that we may learn, amidst bonds of Brotherhood, the virtues of Natural Law.

Therefore, it would be a disservice for any writer or speaker, no matter how learned or scholarly, to assert truths as definitive and "Masonic" in the same breath. It only follows then that the reader should equally avoid the notion that anything written here is official Masonic dogma, as there simply is no such thing.

This does not mean there is no Truth, or that the substitute for it we find in the limited media of language and pulp, cannot be found here. As writers and editors we have a profound responsibility to introduce the reader, second-hand at best, to whatever truth we can find along our own journeys. It is my hope the acquaintance made will be a pleasant one, and you may find what you seek in a form that is useful to you.

– The Editor

WORKS UNDER DISPENSATION

{The introduction content here is taken from the 2014 republication of the First Book of Transactions / Works Under Dispensation. The original Works Under Dispensation was published in 2008, and included the summonses for the meetings, the promotion of "Workshop Seminars", a directory of members (active and corresponding), and the bylaws. Only the last of these is published here, as an appendix at the end of this book. There was also a work not herein contained, an abridged version of a work regarding "The Lodge Historian" by Charles F. Grimwood of the Research Lodge, Heritage Lodge No.730 AF&AM of Canada in the Province of Ontario.}

From the East: The Master's Message

It was March 14, 1982 when Brothers started meeting for the purpose of a Masonic Research and Study Group. Dispensation from the Grand Lodge F.& A.M. of the State of New York was granted October 9, 1982 for the

'Western New York Lodge of Research' to formally meet. The Charter from the Grand Lodge F.& A.M. of the State of New York was granted to the 'Western New York Lodge Of Research No.9007' on March 23rd, 1984 by MW Ernest Leonardi.

In the early days, Brothers came together for workshops designed to promote Masonic Research as it pertained to Western New York Masonry and share on various topics. Over time, meeting agendas focused more on Discussion Groups. Today, meetings are held on a monthly basis with the Lodge dark over the summer months. Discussion Groups on Masonically connected topics are the focus of most meetings, with three tiled communications for the purpose of constitutional business.

Meetings in 1982 were in the homes of Brothers and transitioned over time to Masonic buildings. Today the Western New York Lodge of Research No.9007 meets for discussion groups at the Western New York Masonic Service Bureau and tiled meetings at the Cheektowaga Masonic Center.

Activity and growth in the Western New York Lodge of Research No.9007 has been strong over the years as Brothers are looking for more light. Brothers are questioning Masonry and how it has fit, is fitting and will fit into our lives. Passionate research is being done by our Brethren to find answers to those questions and coming back to the Western New York Lodge of Research No.9007 with their findings.

As the Western New York Lodge of Research No.9007 celebrates our thirtieth anniversary there is a great demand for the materials previously presented and published. We are herein republishing together the original 'WESTERN NY LODGE OF RESEARCH UNDER DISPENSATION' and 'WESTERN NY LODGE OF RESEARCH F.& A.M. FIRST TRANSACTION' books.

I must extend my gratitude and thanks to Bro. Ken Stuczynski and all the Brothers of the Western New York Lodge of Research No.9007: Brother Stuczynski for his countless efforts in reformatting the original books of transaction for this volume; the Brethren for their continued commitment and passion to Masonic education which is driving and will continue to drive our Lodge of Research.

Fraternally,
RW Robert Drzewucki
Master, 2013-2014

Introduction and Disclaimer

It is my pleasure to present this republication of the first "Book of Transactions" and articles published under dispensation by the Western New York Lodge of Research. These articles represent the earliest presentations given by our Brethren, between the years 1983 and 1990.

Only nominal editing has been done, mostly for consistency of notations, typographic errors, and the occasional confusing breach of clear punctuation. Except for the "Brief History", articles are listed in their original order. Individual copyrights are maintained by their authors and are used here with permission or reasonable assumption thereof.

As with most written works of Brethren within the Fraternity, the ideas and opinions presented here are that of their respective authors. They do not necessarily reflect the position of the Grand Lodge of the State of New York or other Masons in general.

Though laden with researched facts, the articles are open to the interpretation of both writer and reader. Within the Lodge of Research, we explore, debate, and encourage each other to draw our own (often contrasting) conclusions. We encourage you to do the same.

We wish you the benefits of speculation on these topics and the desire to seek further Light, herein and in all things.

Submitted 23 April 2014,
Bro. Kenneth JP Stuczynski
Editor

A Brief History on the Organization of Western New York Lodge of Research

{From the 2008 publication of "Western New York Lodge of Research Under Dispensation", the section referencing up to 1982 originally from a communication in January 1983.}

It was nearing the end of 1981, when a small group of interested Masons got together to discuss the possibility of forming a Masonic Research and Study Group. Several meetings were held in private homes, although the first informal meeting was held at Buffalo Temple, after the Ceremony of Investiture of Masters-Elect. A notice of invitation to join the group was placed in the Masonic News, in which several brother Masons applied. The Buffalo Consistory also offered the use of their Cathedral for their meetings and gave them permission to utilize their library.

A petition to form a Study and Research Lodge in Western New York was submitted to then Grand Master MW Bruce Widger on April 12, 1982. He replied on May 9, 1982, to acknowledge receipt of the petition and to inform the brothers that he had forwarded it onto the Grand Secretary who would discuss it with the new Grand Master.

At the Erie County Warden's Seminar a small group of members met with the new Grand Master, MW Ernest Leonardi, to discuss their petition. He told them to send a letter to him with all the particulars and that they would hear from him within the month. On October 9, 1982 they forwarded a letter to him, and true to his word, they received their Dispensation on October 21, 1982, under the name WESTERN NEW YORK LODGE OF RESEARCH, with Wor. Alan G. Fowler, Master; Brother Melvin H. Levy, Senior Warden and Wor. Charles L. Ketchum, Jr., Junior Warden.

A set of By-Laws were drawn up, several designs for a seal and logo were presented for approval and petitions for membership were printed for distribution.

Preparations were in progress for the official presentation of their Dispensation. Commander-in-Chief Ill. Harold L. Aldrich gave them permission to hold a meeting at the Scottish Rite Cathedral on December 6, 1982. RW Robert H. Bahn, DDGM of the 3rd Erie District, presented their Dispensation, assisted by RW Chester Buck, Grand Director of Ceremonies.

It was nearing the end of 1982, and the members which started as a small number of interested Masons grew to 21 founding members that signed the original petition.

The members then started to invite other interested Master Masons to affiliate with their Lodge. Petitions were made available from all the members, and petitions were also being circulated to the Erie District Lodges for brothers interested in becoming Charter Members of the new Western New York Lodge of Research.

Western New York Lodge of Research received their Charter on May 3, 1983.

This was the Beginning!!

The Logo / Seal

During the planning stage of our Lodge, the organizers felt a need for a Logo or Seal. Some designs are shown below. Numbers 1, 3, and 5 were designed by Bro. Charles L. Ketchum, Jr., with the use of his computer, while numbers 2 and 4 were designed by Bro. David W. Jamison.

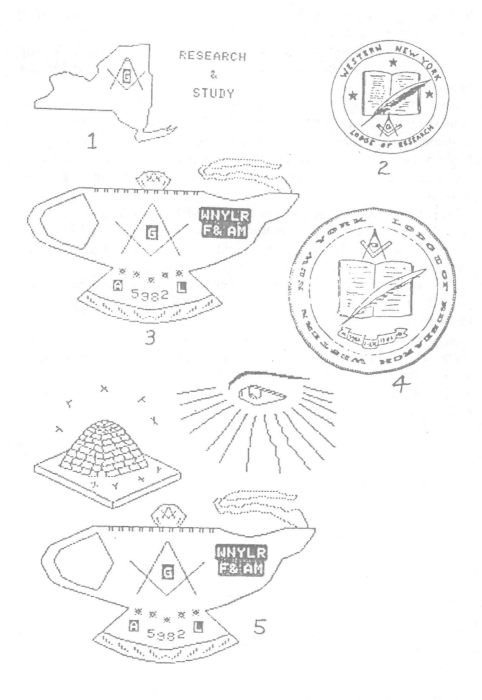

No.1: This design was used as the logo on top of the petition for membership of our study group, before we received our Dispensation to

form a Lodge. The Brethren using these petitions became the Founding Members of Western New York Lodge of Research.

No.3: After receiving our Dispensation we used this design at the top of the petition. The Brothers using this petition became our Charter Members.

No.5: This group was designed on Brother Ketchum's computer, more of an oddity than a logo. It does have meaning though. The All Seeing Eye to guide us, the Beehive to remind us to work industriously, aided by the Lamp of Learning. The majority of the members thought that the use of the lamp of learning had been overused, so we went to Brother Jamison's designs.

No.2: This was the first design presented by Bro. Jamison and was accepted by the membership with some minor changes.

No.4: At present, this is the design that is being used, but has not been finalized. The changes still to be made are as follows:

(1)   Western New York Lodge of Research around the side will be pushed up the sides a little bit and the letters F.& A.M. will be placed on the bottom edge;

(2)   F.& A.M. will be removed from the ribbon;

(3)   Three stars will be placed on the design. One on each side of the book and one below the book;

(4)   Then maybe a small lamp of learning on the ribbon in place of F.& A.M.

The Charter

The WNY Lodge of Research was presented its Charter by Grand Master MW Ernest Leonardi (right).

The Second Masonic Research Lodge in New York State, and the 68th in the World, was formally recognized when Western New York Lodge of Research was formally presented with their Charter by MW Ernest Leonardi, Grand Master of Masons in the State of New York, on Friday Evening, March 23, 1984. The Ceremony took place in Highland Masonic Temple, 2456 Main Street, Buffalo, NY. RW Edward G. Eschner acted as the Grand Marshall for the occasion.

Preceding the Ceremonies, in the Banquet Hall of Highland Temple, a Roast Beef Dinner was served by the members of Tyrian Chapter No.610, O.E.S.

Honored guests besides the Grand Master were RW Calvin G. Bond, Deputy Grand Master, RW Edward G. Eschner, Past Senior Grand Warden, RW Paul O'Neill, Past Junior Grand Warden, RW R. Kerford Wilson, Trustee of the Masonic Home at Utica, NY, RW Louis Schmidt, Karl H. Buehrig, Howard E. Fritsch, Arnold R. Doster, Kenneth Perry, Joseph F. Walkowiak, and H. Curtiss Buffum.

Following the Charter Presentation, the Officers of the Lodge were installed into office by RW Julius S. Hilczmayer assisted by RW Albert E. Hemstreet as Marshal. The installing staff were the members of the Past

District Deputy Grand Master's Association led by their President RW Paul R. Leberman.

The officers of the Lodge were: MasterMaster, Alan G. Fowler; Senior Warden, Charles L. Ketchum, Jr.; Junior Warden, Don C. Markham; Treasurer, Eugene E. Compton; Secretary, John Borycki; Chaplain, John P. Fulciniti; Senior Deacon, David W. Jamison; Junior Deacon, Joseph E. Smeller, Jr.; Senior Master of Ceremony, Herman Black; Junior Master of Ceremony, Stuart M. Farmer; Steward, Jack Jensen; Steward, Frederick W. Leisinger, Jr.; Marshal, Max Winklhofer; Tiler, David L. Beu and three Trustees, LaVerne S. Lamkin, One Year, L. Edward Newman Two Years and George E. Strebel, Three Years.

After the Installation of Officers, the Lodge was presented Aprons & Jewels by Wallace J. Dietz on behalf of Fortune Lodge No.788 of North Collins, NY and Jewels of the Lodge by Harold Eichelberger on behalf of Queen City Lodge No.358.

The Early History of Freemasonry in Erie County, New York State

By RW Charles L. Ketchum, Jr.

{This paper was presented at Western New York Lodge of Research UD F. & A.M. on February 7, 1983 by Wor. Charles L. Ketchum, Jr., Junior Warden of the Lodge. A special thank you was given to the many Lodge Secretaries, Historians and Worshipful Masters, who were kind enough to send Wor. Ketchum information about their Lodge History. Those Histories helped in the preparation of this paper.}

Freemasonry came to Erie County when the early settlers, many of them Masons, felt it was necessary to form a Masonic Lodge in their village. For unexplained reasons, efforts to establish a Lodge did not come easy.

WESTERN STAR LODGE NO. 239

The first petition to form a Lodge in Erie County, was dated, December 10, 1807. It was properly drawn up and forwarded to the Grand Lodge of the State of New York, requesting a warrant to establish a Lodge in what was from 1801 to about 1812 known as the Village of New Amsterdam, now Buffalo.

The following names were attached to the petition: Brothers, Zenas Barker, proposed as Worshipful master; Cyrenius Chapin, Senior Warden; Frederick Miller, Junior Warden; Philo Andrews, Apollos Hitchcock, Erastus Granger, Joseph Landon, Benjamin Caryl, Edmund Raymond, Rowland Cotton and Benjamin Hodge.

WESTERN STAR LODGE was the name chosen by the Brethren, and they would hold their meetings in the home of Zenas Barker, located in the Town of Clarence. The petitioners stated that it was extremely difficult for them to attend a Lodge meeting, as the nearest Lodge was sixty miles away.

In September of 1808, their petition was endorsed by Genesee Lodge

No 130, which was located in the Town of Hartford, Ontario County, at the time.

No action was ever taken upon the first petition, so finally, about four years later, a second petition dated, January 6, 1812, was drawn up. WESTERN STAR LODGE was again chosen for the name of their Lodge, but the meeting place was changed to the home of Brother Joseph Landon, which was located in the Village of New Amsterdam, in the Township of Buffalo. This time the petitioners claimed that there was no Lodge within forty miles of their homes.

The second petition bears the endorsement of Olive Branch Lodge No.215, located in Batavia at that time. The document was dated January 16, 1812, and was signed by their Worshipful Master, Wor. Richard Smith and Bro. Isaiah Babcock, Secretary of the Lodge.

MW DeWitt Clinton, Grand master of Masons in the State of New York, granted a Dispensation to the Lodge on January 31, 1812, for a period of two years. The Grand Secretary RW John Wells issued the Dispensation on February 6, 1812; on March 10, 1812, WESTERN STAR LODGE was instituted by Bro. Herman B. Potter.

The Officers installed were:

Brothers, Zenas Parker, Worshipful master; Cyrenius Chapin, Senior Warden; Frederick Miller, Junior Warden; Abel M. Grosvenor, Treasurer; Judge Charles Townsend, Secretary; Nehemiah Seelye and Daniel Bristol, Deacons; Ralph M. Pomeroy and Raphael Cook, Stewards; and Rowland Cotton, Tiler.

About a year later a petition was forwarded to the Grand Lodge, for a Charter, dated June 15, 1813, in the Village of Buffalo. It stated therein that several of the petitioners had previously applied for a Dispensation to establish a Lodge in the Village, and that they had enclosed the usual fee, but unfortunately the letter and the money were lost.

A second petition for a Warrant was sent to the Grand Lodge about four years later, and a Dispensation to establish a Lodge was then granted by the Grand Master, on February 12, 1812. Since that time, they had assembled and conducted the business of Freemasons and conferred the three degrees of masonry, according to the best of their abilities, and now they wished to obtain a Charter.

The following names were attached to the petition: Brothers Benjamin Caryl, proposed as Worshipful Master; Herman B. Potter, Senior Warden; Oliver Forward, Junior Warden; Frederick Miller, Joshua Lovejoy, Thomas Atkins, Joseph Hershey, Sylvester Clark, Asa P. Harris, Nehemiah Seelye, Benjamin Hodge, Joseph Still, Judge Charles Townsend, Jonas Harrison,

Joseph Trowbridge, Benjamin Enos, Ralph M. Pomeroy, Cornelius Davenport, Zenas W. Barker, Joseph Landon, Willard Smith and Asa Coltrin.

The petition for their Charter was laid before the Grand Lodge, on December 7, 1814, by MW DeWitt Clinton. He informed the Grand Lodge that the brethren had applied for a Dispensation on two separate occasions: the first was received on March 1, 1809 and the second on March 4, 1812. They now pray that their Charter be granted and their dues under Dispensation, which they had been working under, might be relinquished in consequences of the great losses the members had sustained by destruction of the Village of Buffalo, having been burned by the British and Indians on December 30, 1813. It was unanimously resolved, "that a Warrant do issue to the said Brethren and that all dues Under the Dispensation be relinquished".

The Lodge received its Charter, dated December 24, 1814, and was assigned the number "239" on the Grand Lodge Register. Therefore the first Masonic Lodge in Buffalo and the County of Erie was WESTERN STAR LODGE No.239.

WEST ORB OF LIGHT LODGE.

The next petition for a Lodge to be located in Erie County, came from the Town of Willink. The document was without a date and was signed by the following: Brothers John Carpenter, Seth Abbott, Calvin Clifford, John Strong, John Cole, Eames Merriam, Parmilee Allen and William Warren.

The Lodge was to be named, WEST ORB OF LIGHT LODGE. Bro. Isaac Phelps, Jr. was to be their first Worshipful Master; Bro. Benjamin Enos, Senior Warden; and Bro. James Stevens, Junior Warden. The Petition was recommended by Western Star Lodge No.239, on January 20, 1815. But for some reason it never went into operation.

BLAZING STAR LODGE No.294

A new petition for a Lodge to be located in the Town of Willink was drawn up and dated May 19, 1816, recommended by Brothers Isaac Phelps, Jr., as their first Worshipful Master, Hawxhurst Addington, Senior Warden, and James Stevens, Junior Warden. Among the signers of the petition appear the names of Brothers Benjamin McKay, Harry B. Stevens, William A. Burt, William Warren, David Norton and Seth Abbott. Several of the names were identical with those attached to the petition for the Lodge "West Orb of Light Lodge". The petition was recommended by Western Star Lodge No.239, on February 5, 1817.

BLAZING STAR LODGE received the number "294", and the Charter was dated July 31, 1817. An endorsement on the petition, made by the Grand Secretary, RW Elias Hicks reads as follows:

> "This Warrant was granted on a former petition, on December 6, 1815, but was never taken out; $30.00 was then received by J. Wells Esq., who has paid the same to me".

We must note that RW John Wells was the Grand Secretary at the time when "West Orb of Light Lodge" petitioned for a Lodge.

There is no doubt that the petition referred to upon which the $30.00 fee was paid and endorsed as having been received was that of "West Orb of Light Lodge". Therefore, I conclude that possibly due to the poor mail service at that time, the communication from Grand Lodge was never received by the Brethren, so in due time they drew up a second petition changing the desired name to "BLAZING STAR LODGE". Whatever the reason, BLAZING STAR LODGE No.294 became the second oldest Lodge in Erie County.

SARDINIA LODGE No.342

SARDINIA LODGE No.342 was located in the Town of Sardinia, County of Erie. The Grand Lodge granted their Charter on March 6, 1822. Wor. David Bigelow was their first Worshipful master, along with Bro. Elihu Rice, Senior Warden and Bro. Silas Parker, Junior Warden.

CONCORD LODGE No.346.

CONCORD LODGE No.346 was located in the Town of Concord, County of Erie. The background of their beginning is not complete, but is rather interesting. On December 27, 1821, the Brethren of the Town of Concord sent a request to Blazing Star Lodge No.294 for a recommendation to form a new Lodge. This request was carried on foot by Bro. Comfort Knapp from Concord to Aurora. Their petition was granted by the Grand Lodge on June 7, 1822, and their Charter was granted on June 8, 1822. Brother Comfort Knapp was to be installed as their first Worshipful master, with Bro. Ira hall as Senior Warden and Bro. Archibald Griffiths as Junior Warden.

CENTRE LODGE No 356.

If you thought the earlier Lodges had a problem with communicating with Grand Lodge, this one takes all the honors.

A petition for Dispensation to establish a Lodge in the Town of Clarence was drawn up and dated January 31, 1814. The name chosen for the Lodge was CENTRE LODGE and was recommended by Olive Branch Lodge No.215, which was located at that time in Batavia. Among the signers of the petition appeared the names of Brothers Asa Harris, William K. Stewart and others, recommending Bro. Archibald S. Clark to be their first Worshipful Master, Bro. John Hastings as Senior Warden, and Bro. James Baldwin as Junior Warden.

By a misapprehension, the Grand Secretary RW John Wells supposed that this petition was superseded by the Warrant issued to Western Star Lodge No.239 on December 24, 1814. Waiting patiently for an answer until May 31, 1817, the petitioners dispatched a letter of inquiry, the reply to which stated the above-mentioned supposition and was forwarded to them on June 9, 1817—which did not seem to have reached its destination. The petitioners were evidently models of patience and perseverance, for again they waited until October 22, 1822, when another effort was made to ascertain the fate of their petition. An answer to this letter dated November 1, 1822, advising them to re-petition for a Dispensation, finally reached them. A new petition was drawn up, dated November 16, 1822, and was recommended by Western Star Lodge No.239. Grand Lodge finally granted their Dispensation. On March 6, 1823, they received their Charter, which registered the Lodge in the name of CENTRE LODGE No.356, to be located in the Town of Clarence, in the County of Erie. Wor. Frederick Sheldon was their First Worshipful Master, with Bro. Benjamin Bevins as Senior Warden and Bro. Elisha Baldwin as Junior Warden.

LIVINGSTON LODGE No.416.

At the Fourth Annual Communication of Grand Lodge, on June 1, 1825, a Charter was granted to the Brethren in the Town of Boston. Brother Comfort Knapp, son of the first Worshipful master of Concord Lodge No.346, would be Worshipful Master, with Bro. John Brooks as Senior Warden, and Bro. Hiram Knapp as Junior Warden. The Lodge would hold their meetings in the Town of Boston, in he County of Erie, and was registered in the name of LIVINGSTON LODGE No.416. The Lodge was constituted and officers installed on December 22, 1825, by Wor. John

Wadsworth, Past Master of Blazing Star Lodge No.294 in the Town of Aurora.

As you noticed, there was a close tie between LIVINGSTON LODGE No.416 and Concord Lodge No.346 because of Father and Son, but I discovered an interesting fact while reading through some of the Lodge Histories of Erie County. The story begins during the Anti-Masonic period, when all Lodges in Erie County, including Concord Lodge No.346 and Livingston Lodge No.416, ceased their labors. One of the members of Living Stone Lodge No.255 attended a lecture back in the early 1950s. He related that an elderly speaker said that his Father had told him of attending Lodge meetings during the Anti-Masonic period, at irregular intervals and at different meeting places each time, and in many cases they were held on moonlit nights, out of doors, on hill tops in Boston and Concord. Through the tireless efforts of men like these Masonry survived, although they were Brethren without a Chartered Lodge.

It is also interesting to note that many members of LIVINGSTON LODGE No.416, including Wor. Comfort Knapp, their first Worshipful Master, were Charter Members of Living Stone Lodge No.255.

AMHERST LODGE No.429

AMHERST LODGE No.429, also received their Charter at the Fourth Annual Communication of the Grand Lodge, on June 1, 1825. The names that were entered on the Charter were Brothers Frederick S. Sheldon, Worshipful Master, Job Beston, Senior Warden, and Ebenezer A. Lester, Junior Warden, who were authorized to hold a Lodge meeting in the Town of Amherst, in the County of Erie.

HAMBURG UNION STORE LODGE No.434.

Along with Livingston Lodge No.416, Amherst Lodge No.429, and others, the Brethren of HAMBURG STORE LODGE No.434 received their Charter at the Fourth Annual Communication of Grand Lodge, on June 1, 1825. Brother Cushion Swift was named Worshipful Master with Bro. Edmund S. Stevens as Senior Warden, and Bro. Mason Young as Junior Warden. The Lodge would be located in the Town of Hamburg, in the County of Erie.

PORTER LODGE

A petition for Dispensation to form a Lodge in Black Rock, in the County of Erie, to be known as PORTER LODGE, was dated November 12, 1823, and is on file in the archives of Grand Lodge. Brother James L. Barton was to be their first Worshipful Master, with Bro. Nathaniel K. Olmstead as Senior Warden, and Bro. Nathaniel G. Reynolds as Junior Warden. The following names were attached to the petition: Brothers Lewis G. Hoffman, John D. Harty, William Burt, Adam Gray, Ethan Allen and Donald Fraser.

The petition was recommended by Western Star Lodge No.239, on November 15, 1823. The Grand Lodge seems to have taken no action on this petition.

BARTON LODGE No.442.

A second petition for a Dispensation to form a Lodge in Black Rock, in the County of Erie, to be known as BARTON LODGE, bears the date of May 5, 1823. It recommended Bro. James L. Barton to be their first Worshipful Master, with Bro. Nathaniel G. Reynolds as Senior Warden, and Bro. James McKnight as Junior Warden.

The names of the petitioners include: Brothers Lewis G. Hoffman, John D. Hardy, Ethan Allen, Henry Potter, Sheldon Thompson, James Tisdale, D.S. Davidson and Nathaniel Fills.

The petition was recommended by Western Star Lodge No.239 on May 5, 1824, and on June 6, 1825, Grand Lodge granted a Charter to BARTON LODGE No.442. Brother Robert McPherson became the Secretary and Bro. Sheldon Thompson the Treasurer.

PORTER LODGE VERSUS BARTON LODGE No.442.

A question arises—why did BARTON LODGE receive a Charter and not PORTER LODGE? It seems that there might have been two groups working towards a Dispensation at the same time, not knowing of the other's intentions, or there may have been a difference of opinions on how a new Lodge should be established, its name and/or Officers etc.. I do not know what the real reason was, so lets compare the differences.

BARTON LODGE drew up their petition six months previous to that of PORTER LODGE; PORTER LODGE received a recommendation from

WESTERN STAR LODGE No.239, six months previous to that of BARTON LODGE.

The name of Brother James L. Barton for Worshipful master appears on both petitions, and a number of the names are identical on both petitions.

BARTON LODGE"s recommendation from WESTERN STAR LODGE No.239 included the endorsement, "That all former recommendations for a Lodge at Black Rock be recalled".

Although the above does not fully explain the reason for the two petitions, it does show that the Brethren of WESTERN STAR LODGE No.239 chose the petitioners of BARTON LODGE.

THE ANTI-MASONIC PERIOD

Up to this time, the Lodges in Erie County were progressing under favorable conditions and on the membership rolls were registered a large number of highly respectable and intelligent citizens. This growth increased the jealousy and ill feeling of the Anti-Masons. The sudden disappearance of William Morgan on the 12th day of September, 1826, who was reported to have been drowned by Masons in the Niagara River, led to hostile demonstrations. Unfortunately for the Masonic Fraternity, nothing definite could be discovered as to the fate of this individual.

The adversaries of Masonry, under the control of designing leaders, were not slow in making use of the rumor of Morgan's murder to fan the spark into a flame. Anti-Masonry swept over the land like a whirlwind, shaking the Fraternity to it's foundation. Manipulating by skilful but unscrupulous positions, the Anti-Masonic faction increased in strength and power, and forced many Lodges to discontinue their labors.

Finally, in the year 1843, the Anti-Masonic Party lost its political power—Anti-Masonry died, but Masonry survived. All efforts to drag it into the dust and cast suspicions on its aims were in vain. During the Anti-Masonic period, all the Lodges in Erie County ceased their labors, but the revival of Masonry gave new life to the Fraternity. The old members, with undiminished love for the Craft in their hearts, talked freely about renewing their membership in the Fraternity, and proceeded to draw up a petition to form a new Lodge in Buffalo.

HIRAM LODGE No.105

The petition drawn up by these Brethren was circulated throughout the community in November of 1844. Thirty-two of these local Brethren eagerly attached their signatures to the document, including the following: Brothers Henry B. Myer, Selah Barnard, Nelson Randall, James Forestall, Horatio G. Gates, Orman Butler, Thomas J. Winslow, John A. Weimer, Robert Russell, Charles S. Pierce, John McPherson, Miles Jones, Nehemiah Case, Abner Cutler, Joseph A. Cameron, Daniel M. Seaver, Charles Radcliffe, Solomon Drullard, Elijah D. Effner, Benjamin H. Austin, Thomas Muller, George Case. Levi Allen, Christian Heistend, Cornelius A. Waldron, Benjamin Bidwell, Isaac W. Newkirk, Merlin Camp, Stephan Powers, David C. Sough, Joseph Dorr and Darius Smith.

The Grand Lodge granted a Dispensation on January 31, 1845, for the formation of HIRAM LODGE, which was received with joy by the Brethren. Their first informal meeting was held on Friday, February 14, 1845. Brother Henry B. Myer, who had been named Worshipful Master of the Lodge, presided on the occasion.

At the first formal meeting of the Lodge Under Dispensation, on February 28, 1845 a petition for membership was presented from Horatio Warren, who became their fist initiate, and who subsequently became a Charter Member and Worshipful Master in 1853 of WASHINGTON LODGE No.240.

At the Communication on March 7, 1845, Worshipful Henry B. Myer introduced Bro. Dr. Clark to the members of the Lodge, who in turn presented the Lodge with the jewels of WESTERN STAR LODGE No.239, except for the Square and Compasses which had been lost. The Brethren of the Lodge were very pleased with the gift, and after thanking Bro. Clark, agreed that a new Square and Compasses be procured to replace the missing ones, as they saw the need of having a new set of jewels in use.

In 1852, a Brother from Buffalo, visiting in Detroit, found the two missing jewels. These jewels were surrendered by the Lodge in Detroit to HIRAM LODGE after a formal resolution was sent to the Lodge in Detroit on June 2, 1852. The jewels have the inscription on them, "Presented by M∴W∴ DeWitt Clinton to WESTERN STAR LODGE No.239".

The Dispensation, which expired by limitation with the session of Grand Lodge in June 1845, was extended by the Grand Master, MW Alexander H. Robertson, to October 20, 1845. At the Communication on December 19, 1845, the Worshipful Master announced that their Charter from Grand Lodge had been received, being dated December 5, 1845. The Lodge was registered on the rolls of Grand Lodge as HIRAM LODGE No.105, and would become the oldest present day Lodge in Erie County.

At the December 26, 1845 meeting, the following Brethren were elected and became the first Officers of HIRAM LODGE No.105: Brother Henry B. Myer, Worshipful Master; Nelson Randall, Senior Warden; Charles S. Pierce, Junior Warden; Robert Russell, Treasurer; and Stephen Powers, Secretary.

On January 1, 1846, the Lodge was constituted and the Officers were installed including the following appointed officers: Brother Carlos Cobb, Senior Deacon; James McCredie, Junior Deacon; Miles Jones and Charles Pickering Stewards; and James Forestall, Tiler.

At that time the Lodge was holding their meetings on the fourth floor of the building at 219 Main Street, but as membership in the Lodge increased, it became evident that more spacious quarters for the Lodge were required. On October 23, 1846, a resolution was adopted to rent a room on the third floor of Brother Nehemiah Case's building on the corner of Washington and Exchange Streets at $150.00 per year. This building soon became the Masonic Temple, and was occupied by the majority of the Masonic bodies of Buffalo.

HIRAM LODGE No.105 had the privilege of endorsing many new Lodges in the early years, which included: CONCORDIA LODGE No.143, ERIE LODGE No.161, WASHINGTON LODGE No.240 and PARISH LODGE No.292.

REFERENCES

Smith, H. Perry. *History of the City of Buffalo and Erie County*. (Syracuse, NY: D Mason & Co., 1884) Vol. 1 pg. 12; Vol. 2 pp. 351-367

Freemasonry and Roman Catholicism

Wor. Rev. Don C. Markham

{Editor's Note: This paper was republished by Educational Lodge No.1002 AF&AM of St. Paul Minnesota in December 1988 (Bulletin No.107)}

The relationship between Freemasonry and the Roman Catholic Church has been the subject of much writing throughout the years. Indeed, for many years there was an active program against the Fraternity carried on by the Church and there were voluminous writings produced. The situation changed somewhat drastically in 1974, and much of the anti-Masonic writing has ceased/replaced by a policy of "peaceful coexistence." Any accurate consideration of the relationship between Freemasonry and Roman Catholicism, therefore, must be covered in three areas: the attitude of the Church prior to 1974, the attitude of the Church since 1974, and the attitude of the Fraternity towards the Church.

As Freemasonry spread from England to the European continent in the early years of the Eighteenth Century, it attracted the attention of the rulers of many nations. As a "secret society," some feared that it would be the vehicle whereby conspiratorial plotting might take place against the Church and the State. Because of this fear, the Fraternity was "officially" condemned by the Church in1738, when Pope Clement XII issued the Papal Bull entitled 'In Eminenti'. This Bull consisted for the most part of a rather condemnation of the "secrecy" of the Fraternity.

The issuance of this particular Papal Bull has perplexed Masonic Historians for many years for several reasons. The first thing about it that is confusing is the fact that, in the Bull, there appears more of a denial of the right of men to engage in voluntary associations, regardless of what these voluntary associations might be, rather than a condemnation of the actual institution. No charges, other than secrecy, are laid against the organization. No mention is made of its identity or what it might have stood for, its teachings, or its requirements. Harry L. Haywood, a noted Masonic writer and clergyman, points out:

He (Clement) himself meant by "secrecy" a fact of his own which had for him an immediate urgency: his own local priests were not permitted in the Lodges, he himself was not permitted to enter them, and his own orders had no authority in them. His successors did not have any of his own private reasons for resenting this "secrecy," but turned it into an abstract and general charge, and averred that secrecy in associations of men is in itself anti-Christian, unlawful, and immoral. [1]

However, even though the attitude held by Haywood may be at least partly true, it was not until a few years ago that a truly "reasonable" explanation for this Bull appeared. A French Roman Catholic Mason writer made a study of the Bull and its language, together with the political implications of the period, and came up with an extremely plausible and cogent explanation of it.

Alec Mellor considers that there were two motives behind the issuance of the Bull, 'In Eminenti'. The first is the obvious and stated motive, "secrecy," and this grew out of the fear that, as a secret society, the Freemasons were "political conspirators." The second motive, Mellor feels, was referred to in the Bull as "and for other just and reasonable causes known to ourselves." This enigmatic statement would indicate that the real motive was something in the nature of a "State secret" which could not then be made known. Mellor considers that the "real reason" might have been the influence of the "Old Pretender" who was attempting to gain support of the Papacy for the restoration of the Catholic monarchy in England. Just prior to the acceptance of the Bull, an English Lodge in Florence was closed. Mellor notes that this particular Lodge was a "hotbed of Hanoverian supporters and one of its most influential members, Baron Stosch, was one of Sir Robert Walpole's spies." [2] This is supported by a statement from another Roman Catholic writer, who, in writing about the issuance of 'In Eminenti' stated that it was written "in response to a particular situation in the city of Florence but was addressed to the entire Catholic population and so was, at least in principal, general in scope." [3] The absence of any Masonic documents in the Stuart Papers at Windsor, together with the reference in a study of some documents that have been preserved from this period referring to the fact that "the Master of the Lodge, Lord Winton known as a Jacobite refugee, was half mad, an incessant source of trouble to the Old Pretender, and who was constantly quarreling with his Wardens" [4] leads Mellor to state, "can it not be supposed that it was the Old Pretender himself who persuaded the Pope to close this Lodge, especially as it used to receive double agents as visitors?" [5] In addition to the above, Mellor summarizes his argument in the following statement:

Many years later after the Convention of Wilhelmsbad (1782), the court counselor Waechter was sent to Rome by the leaders of the

Strict Observance to ask Prince Charles Edward, who was by then an old man, whether the famous 'Unknown Superiors' actually were the Stuarts, the letter replied that he knew nothing about the matter, that he had wanted to become a Freemason when he was young but that his father (the Old Pretender) had forbidden him to do so. If we take this conjunction with the fact that the Old Pretender handed over to Cardinal Corsini, nephew to and minister of Pope Clement XII, piles of documents he had sent from St. Germain, things become clearer. It becomes easier to understand why no Masonic Papers remained among the Stuart Papers in Windsor and we can get an inkling of what probably happened. After having got the Pope to close the Lodge, the Chevalier St. George brought his support to the Holy Office in view of the 'fulmination' by means of the Bull 'In Eminenti'. This second motive for condemnation had to remain secret. Had it been divulged, the last chance of the restoration of a Catholic King to the throne of England would have been compromised. That is the probable explanation of the phrase in the Bull: 'Aliisque justis ac ration-abilibus causis Nobis notis' (and for other just and reasonable causes known to Us). [6]

These arguments are further supported by the fact that there was no definition of Freemasonry, as such, in the wording of the Bull, and, as Mellor points out "When the Roman Catholic Church condemns a heresy it always starts by defining it, if only to enable the faithful to understand." [7] Neither the rituals nor "Anderson's Constitutions" are even mentioned or banned. Mellor also states that Freemasonry, at that time, was far from being anti-Catholic. In fact, Thomas, Duke of Norfolk and a Roman Catholic, was Grand Master in 1730-31. [8] Furthermore, in 1776, Pope Pius VI drew up a list of the 'errors of the 18th Century' in his Bull, 'Inscrutabili'. It did not contain a word about Freemasonry. [9]]

In 1751, Clement's successor, Pope Benedict XIV became the next Pope to issue a condemnation of the Fraternity. This was in the nature of a confirmation of the Bull, 'In Eminenti', by the issuance of his own Bull, 'Providas'. [10] Father Robert Crooker, Professor of Canon Law at St. Michael's College in Toronto, states that this was "in response to another local situation in Naples." [11]

Mellor also makes note of the fact, that:

An erudite Jesuit Priest, Father J. Ferrer Benimelli... expressed the opinion that yet another motive was added to the official ones; certain slanderers had insinuated that the Pope himself had belonged to the Lodge when he was young! [12]

This doubtless did have an influence upon the issuance of that particular Bull.

To better understand and appreciate the workings of the Church in this particular period, it helps to know the historical context. Mellor mentions the fact that in the 18th Century, Papal Bulls "had to be ratified by the Catholic States before they became mandatory." [13] This was so that the governments of these States would be obligated to utilize the secular arm in the enforcement of the Bulls. This explains, in part, why these two Bulls, 'In Eminento' and 'Providas', were not as widely enforced in the 18th Century as one would think they might be. The primary enforcement took place in Spain and Portugal where the Inquisition held sway. England, Ireland, Scotland, France and Germany were among thoso areas where the Fraternity was relatively uninfluenced by the Bulls, 'In Eminenti' and 'Providas', at the time of their issuance. There were many members of the Fraternity who were Roman Catholic, and as Mellor remarks concerning the situation in France at that time, "Numerous Priests and even Bishops became members of the craft." [14]

In Italy, itself, there did not exist a full and complete acceptance or enforcement of these Bulls. In fact, in 1786, a priest, Father Isidoro Bianchi, wrote a pamphlet bearing the title 'Dell Instituto dei veri Liberi Muratori' or 'Of the Institute of the true Free Masons', and in its preface makes the following statement:

> As all men ought to make up one family, know ouch other as Brothers, love each other reciprocally without distinction of rank, power, strength, climate or opinion and form a unique society with solid and incontestable principles such as those which unite and bind the Freemasons, it, therefore, must not seem surprising that a man who has had the chance to belong to their Order, may nonetheless speak with some precision and truth of their very respectable Institution. [15]

Father Bianchi displays a great understanding and appreciation of the Fraternity and it is interesting to note his constant reference to "true" Freemasons. Because of the time when this pamphlet was written, he must have become familiar with some of the "spurious" Masonic groups, which were causing great difficulty in Europe, hence his emphasis. The marvel is that he was able to differentiate between the two, for most clerics of the period were not. In fact, in referring to the two Papal Bulls of the Eighteenth Century that had to do with the Fraternity, he stated:

> Being as, however, the true Freemasons Society is neither contrary to the well-being of the republic nor opposed to religion as it has been shown, it follows that the serious anathemas expressed in the two Bulls are not meant to be against it. They do not nor cannot concern their wise Institution. The condemnation presumes the

crime. The crime is dependent upon clear proof. The guilty must be convinced and the sentence cannot fall on the innocent. [16]

Father Bianchi also makes reference to the fact that in many nations, the Fraternity has been encouraged and protected, citing as examples the Kingdom of Prussia, Sweden, Denmark, Holland, England, nearly all of the German States, France, and in some parts of Italy. He further cites an edict of the Emperor of Italy, which states:

> On the contrary, when these Lodges will be put on a new footing, they will be exempt, forever, from any further persecution, search or investigation and may freely hold their meetings; and indeed, in this way, this Society to which many Gentlemen well known to me, belong, may make itself really useful to humanity and science; but at the time, all spurious Lodges and secret reunions which have caused much inconvenience, will be forever abolished and strictly forbidden. [17]

Further, in relating the purposes and principles of the Fraternity, Father Bianchi brings out the fact that "true" Freemasonry is a help, rather than a hindrance, to religion and he does so in these words:

> But if there exists a Society such as the one we are speaking of, which far from deviating from the sacred doctrine, adopts it as the basis of its duties, is it not true then that in this case, religion comes to be more solidly fortified and is not the practice of its law, counsel, and prescription made easier? [18]

In many ways the situation in the Eighteenth Century was one of confusion and misunderstanding concerning the aims and purposes of the Fraternity, As Mellor argues, the Bull issued by Clement and confirmed by Benedict was probably politically inspired. It never did condemn the Fraternity other than its "secrecy." And, of this "secrecy," Father Bianchi writes:

> Now, those who condemn this Society because it religiously observes secrets, fall in that coarse error of the fool who condemns the regularity in the design of a building. These kind of secrets cannot be made respectable other than under the obligation of silence and an oath of secrecy. They cease to be mysteries as soon as they are divulged to the ears of the profane world. [19]

He goes on to give instances from the Church Fathers and from the Scriptures relative to the practices of early Christianity with its "mysteries and secrets" and reiterates many of his comments about the basic worth and value of fraternity as a human society.

Inasmuch as the writing of Father Bianchi was in the latter part of the Eighteenth Century and the Papal Bulls were issued in the second quarter of that century, it would be well to consider briefly what had transpired in the intervening years. In Bavaria, a professor of natural and canon law at Ingolstadt University by the name of Adam Weishaupt, gathered about himself a group of young students who would meet at his home and discuss philosophic subjects. This group came to be called the "Society of Enlightened Ones" or "The llluminati." Weishaupt was a cosmopolitan and liberal for his times and was opposed to the bigotry and superstition of the established Church. As an anti-clerical movement, the "llluminati" became a political force. Joining the Masonic Fraternity in 1777, Weishaupt tried to incorporate the "llluminati" into Masonry. [20] He did not succeed, but the fact that he was a Freemason and attempted to subvert the Craft for his own purposes caused many outside the Craft to connect the two widely-differing groups into one. The "llluminati," therefore, must be considered as one of the principal "spurious" Masonic groups to which Father Bianchi referred. Because the average person equated the two, it was the aim of Father Bianchi to differentiate between the two by his insistence upon "true" Freemasonry in his definition and in his writings.

One other concern of the Eighteenth Century Roman Catholic reaction to the Fraternity must necessarily be the mention of the intense persecution which it evolved in Spain and Portugal, primarily. In these two countries, the Fraternity was literally destroyed and its adherents were punished, tortured, and frequently killed by the forces of the Inquisition. It was not even safe for a "sojourner" from another country if he happened to be a member of the Fraternity. Such persecutions are recounted in some of the histories of the Fraternity and the most notable is in a book which enjoyed wide circulation in England in the Eighteenth Century, entitled, 'The Sufferings of John Coustos. for Free-Masonry, and for His refusing to turn Roman Catholic, in the Inquisition at Lisbon', "Where he was sentenc'd, during Four Years, to the Galley; and afterwards releas'd from thence by the gracious Interposition of his present Majestic King George II." This book, which was published in 1746, enjoyed wide circulation and, although John Coustos was only one of the many who were thus victims of the horrors of the Inquisition, he was one of the few survivors to write about it. The book being published in 1746, it was doubtless used as propaganda to help defeat the Jacobite cause in that same year.

The Roman Catholic persecution of the fraternity during the Eighteenth Century was varied in scope and intensity according to the locations involved, and was dependent upon the attitude and cooperation of the reigning civil powers in that area. Basically, the only areas wherein the Papal Bulls were enforced were the predominantly Catholic-oriented countries of Spain, Portugal, and Poland. Mellor closes the section of his article dealing with the Eighteenth Century by stating, "Up to the end of the Eighteenth Century the two Papal Bulls formed a complete whole. Their motives remained peculiar to the period in which they were issued." [21]

The next phase of the Roman Catholic attack on the Fraternity began in 1821 and continued up until 1902, taking the form of Papal Bulls, Encyclicals, and Apostolic Letters.

- Pius VII: 13 September 1821, "Ecclesiam"
- Leo XII: 13 March 1825, "Quo Graviora"
- Pius VIII: 24 March 1829, "Tradita"
- Pius IX: 9 November 1846, "Qui Pluribus"; 25 November 1865, "Multiplies Inter"; 12 November 1869, "Apostolicae Sedis"; 21 November 1873, "Etsi Multa"
- Leo XIII: 20 April 1884, "Humanum Genus"; 20 June 1894, "Praeclara"; 18 March 1902, "Annum Ingressi" [22]

Father Crooker states that, in regard to these, Pius VII's main point was that the same condemnations applied to the rising group known as the "Carbonari" who were becoming a strongly anti-Papal, political group in Italy, and that Leo XII repeated this condemnation in his writing. [23] Writings of Pius VIII and Gregory XVI in 1829 and 1832 denounce the Fraternity and its influence. Pius VIII refers to the "imminent peril arising from Masonic influences in the schools and colleges," [24] and Gregory XVI compares Secret Societies to a sink in which "are congregated and intermingles all the sacrileges, infamy, and blasphemy which may be contained in the most abominable heresies." [25] Throughout the reign of Pius IX there appear a number of condemnations of the Fraternity. For the most part, they are related to the political movement in Italy which ultimately led to the dissolution of the Papal States and the fact that many of the leaders of that movement, i.e., Cavour, Garibaldi, and Mazzini, were Masons. One must also consider that Pius IX was the one who formulated the doctrine of Papal Infallibility and also was vehemently opposed to almost everything that was American or English, where Freemasonry was strongest. Haywood refers to the fact that:

... in 1864, he issued his now famous 'Syllabus', or catena of 'condemned propositions'...; in it he has brought together into a single document the many opinions, theories, commands, and denunciations which he had scattered through his numerous Allocutions, Bulls, Encyclicals, and Apostolical Letters over a period of eighteen years and by so doing made them at one stroke, and unexpectedly, official doctrine which every Roman Catholic in the world was expected to obey; and since among the "condemned propositions" were such doctrines as that people have a right to think for themselves; to have free public schools; the legitimacy of marriage in Protestant Countries; freedom of worship; separation of Church and State; and other such doctrines and principles as belong to modern, free peoples, the 'Syllabus' spread consternation everywhere; and among Roman Catholics in democratic countries continues to be an embarrassment... [26]

In his last writing on the subject, 'Etsi Multa', he pointed out the fact that it was not the Masonic body in Europe alone that is referred to, but also the "Masonic associations in America and in whatever part of the world they may be." [27] This had far-reaching implications, for previously the Papal Decrees had been considered as applicable to those Masonic groups which were anti-clerical or which were political—now they encompassed the world. The result was widespread dimitting of many Roman Catholic Freemasons in Ireland, England, France and America, for they could no longer, in good conscience, belong to a proscribed organization.

The primary objection to any of the proscribed organizations at that time, seemed to be their "secrecy." Time and time again the issue of "secrecy" was brought to the fore in the writings and deliberations of the church. A writer on this subject of the church and its secrecy, as well as its attitude towards secrecy, as observed that:

By the Nineteenth Century, when secrecy reached its height, Catholicism had suffered centuries of Protestant incursion and resulting persecution, then (it suffered from) the ravings of skepticism, which had led to severe repression on the church in France. The powerful Masons were campaigning against Catholicism. New scientific and intellectual developments seemed to threaten the foundations of the faith. [28]

Much of the problem extant between the Church and the Fraternity was largely due to a misunderstanding of the nature of "true" Freemasonry. "Irregular," "Spurious," or "Clandestine" Freemasonry such as existed in many areas on the European continent at that time, was indeed, guilty of offences against both Church and State, and the Roman Catholic hierarchy "tarred all with the same brush." Mellor states of this period that, "as from the middle of the Nineteenth Century it is not an exaggeration to state that the salient point of Italian politics was the war against Catholicism directly led by the Lodges." [29] This was a war against Papal control and was waged by elements within Italy who used the Lodges as places for their conspiratorial activities–thus betraying the basic principles of the Fraternity itself. That these Lodges were not recognized as "regular" by the majority of the Grand Jurisdictions was not understood by the Papacy, and the natural consequence was the prohibitions and the proscriptions against the Fraternity, per se. In reference to this same period in France, Mellor states:

> In France the successive anti-clerical governments persecuted the religious congregations. In 1877 the Grand Orient of France deleted from its Constitution all reference to the Great Architect of the Universe and the Grand Lodge of England immediately withdrew its recognition, a decision very easy to understand. [30]

Mellor also gives two reasons why the Papacy made no distinction between regular Freemasonry and the organizations which were "spurious." (1) There were few Catholics in England and of that number probably none were members of the Fraternity; and (2) Regular Freemasonry was unknown in the Latin countries–all that existed were the "spurious" varieties. [31]

While Mellor's reasoning is probably sound, one might yet wonder how the Papacy was unaware of the fact that Lord Ripon, Grand Master of the Grand Lodge of England, had resigned his office as Grand Master when he became a member of the Roman Catholic Church in 1874. [32] The fact is, however, they probably were aware of the nature of the differences between "regular" and "spurious" Lodges, but because of their long-standing antipathy towards the Fraternity because of its secrecy and oaths, they chose not to make any distinction. After all, such condemnations had been a part of Roman Catholic policy since 1738, and as Ostling notes:

> The major factor in the Papal condemnations was the opinion that various organizations were opposed to both Church and State. But secrecy was also a factor. Canon law indicates that the problem was not secrecy per se, but secrecy which was maintained in the face of rightful inquires of the Church and State authorities. [33]

One may further note that, both in 1843 and 1884 assemblies of U.S. Bishops at Baltimore came out with statements against the "secrecy" of organizations with the comment that "secrecy by itself is a presumption against an organization." [34] It is also noted by Ostling that "the Catholic

Church has a well-established teaching against secrecy, not only in public institutions, but in private organizations." [35]

In 1884, the anti-Masonic campaign of the Church took on new leadership and new direction. Probably as a direct result of the waning power of the Papacy in governmental affairs and the rapid growth of the attitudes of separation of Church and State in various parts of the world, Pope Leo XIII, in an attempt to reestablish the dominion and control of the Papacy, issued the Encyclical Letter which bore the title, 'Humanum Genus'. This was the most serious condemnation of the Fraternity which was ever published by the Church. In it the Fraternity was defined as being an "anti-Christian sect," which placed it, in their eyes, in direct competition with Christianity. The Encyclical covers many pages and is the broadest, most definitive, anti-Masonic statement ever produced by the Roman Catholic Church. It is also anti-ecumenical, for by its wording, the world is divided into two forces—the Church (Roman Catholic) and the forces of Satan (everyone else, including Protestants) and indicates that the two must ever be in constant conflict. The attitude conveyed in the wording of this Encyclical is that any opposition to any policy or program of the Roman Catholic Church is, in actuality, the work of Satan. This includes any type of democratic government, separation of Church and State, public education, taxation of religious properties, and freedom of speech. The Fraternity is seen as being "anti-Catholic" and its broad tolerance is explained away in these words:

> If the sect does not openly require its members to throw away the doctrines of Catholic Faith, this tolerance, far from injuring the Masonic schemes is useful to them. Because this is, first, an easy way to deceive the simple and unwise ones and it is contributing to proselytize. By opening their gates to persons of every creed they promote, in fact, the great modem error of religious indifference and of the parity of all worships; the best way to annihilate every religion, especially the Catholic, which, being the only true one, cannot be joined with others without enormous injustice. [36]

In defining of Freemasonry as a "sect" by this Encyclical has given rise to a multiplicity of anti-Masonic writings from the pens of a great many authors since 1884. The term "sect" refers to Freemasonry as a religion, and, as such, places it is competition with every organized Church. Author after author has, since that time, followed this line of attack.

Shortly after the proclamation of the Encyclical, Albert Pike, Sovereign Grand Commander of the Southern Masonic Jurisdiction of the Scottish Rite, published an answer to it—and his choice of words and method of response were almost as narrow and bigoted as the words of the

Encyclical. All it succeeded in doing was to fan the flames of hatred so that they burned all the brighter. By reciting a long list of abuses of the Roman Catholic Church and recounting the horrendous work of the Inquisition, Pike did a great disservice to the Fraternity. At one point he states:

> Thus this letter, beginning "Humanum Genus," The Human Race, is not only an open declaration against Freemasonry, ... THIS ENCYCLICAL LETTER IS A DECLARATION OF WAR AGAINST THE HUMAN RACE. [37]

The bitterness might be justifiable in one sense, for the Encyclical was an unprovoked attack upon the Fraternity, yet it is true that when an argument gets to the bitter stage, both sides are apt to get careless with the truth. So, in another sense, it was only adding fuel to a fire already burning brightly. At another point in the reply, in reference to the policy of the Roman Church in some South American Countries, and in particular to the actions and activities of the "soldiers of Catholicism," the Jesuits, Pike stated:

> Thus it menaces the public peace in those countries, inciting revolt and insurrection and assassination, and makes the Lord's Prayer the patent of an Inquisitor, and the Sermon on the Mount a warrant for murder. [38]

Both the Encyclical, which attacked the Fraternity and all Democratic Institutions, and Pike's response, which was equally as bigoted in wording, are indicative of the strong feelings of the times in which they were written. Unfortunately, while the one precipitated the continued attacks against the Fraternity since that time, the other did nothing to help the situation, but merely added more fuel to the fires of opposition. Proponents of prejudice have utilized both to their own selfish advantage ever since.

One of the leading writers in the Roman Catholic attack on the Fraternity since the publication of 'Humanum Genus', was Arthur Preuss who's book, A Study in American Freemasonry, was first published in 1908. This was reprinted many times and, for years, was the standard work against the Fraternity. Primarily utilizing the writings of Mackay and Pike, Preuss attempted to show the "truth" of the accusations made in the Encyclical. Being out of the Roman Catholic tradition where one has "authoritarian statements" in abundance, Preuss was unable to understand or appreciate the fact that no one has the right to speak "ex cathedra" for the Fraternity—that the views of individual writers, however popular they may be or however often they may be reprinted, are their own. Preuss constantly spoke of "exoteric" and "Esoteric" Masonry, and was of the firm conviction that the average member of the American Lodges was not "in the know" when it came to the true aims and purposes of the Fraternity. Also, Preuss was unable to distinguish between the fact that there were "sectional" differences because of the particular fears and prejudices of the writers in those areas. Somewhat of his entire attitude is reflected in the concluding paragraph of his book, which reads:

> As for us Catholics, if we remain longer in ignorance of the true character and aims of American esoteric Freemasonry, and neglect to take the proper precautions, in obedience to the oft-repeated warning of our Holy Mother the Church, it will serve us right if the Masons succeed in obtaining the balance of power in the United States, as they hold it to-day in France, and treat us in America as our poor brethren are treated in that beautiful but unfortunate land. [39]

During the reign of Benedict XV, the discipline of the Catholic Church was gathered in the Code of Canon Law, adopted in 1917, and canon 2335 of that document reads:

Those who join the Masonic sect, or other association of the same sort that plot against the Church or against the legitimate civil powers, thereby incur an excommunication simply reserved to the Apostolic See. [40]

During the period from 1917 to 1974, one could hardly find a 'literature rack' in a Roman Catholic Church which did not display at least one pamphlet against the Fraternity and membership therein. Published by such groups as Radio Replies Press, Liguorian Pamphlet Office of the Redemptorist Fathers, Claretian Publications, The Paulist Press, Catholic Truth Society, or Bruce Publishing Company, to name just a few, these pamphlets bore a variety of titles and subjects all having to do with the fact that Freemasonry is a competing religion and a political and moral threat to the Church and to humanity.

In 1958, William J. Whalen's book. *Christianity and American Freemasonry*, appeared under the imprint of the Bruce Publishing Company in Milwaukee, and, using the same techniques and attitudes of Preuss, renewed the attack on the Fraternity. Whalen does make a very good point in his preface when he makes the statement: "If there is one secret in Masonry it is that there are no Masonic secrets." [41] His book, however, is much more objective in some areas that Preuss, but continues on the same line and follows the definition of the Fraternity as given in 'Humanum Genus', a full translation of which appears as the appendix to his work. On one of the concluding pages of his book, Whalen states:

Although we believe that Masonry ultimately undermines the Christian basis of society, propagates an insidious religion of naturalism and the spirit of religious indifference, administers an immoral oath, and often engages in or tolerates anti-clericalism, we have a Christian Obligation to love Masons. When we deny the compatibility Of the Lodge and the Christian Faith we do not question the sincerity of Protestant Masons but their consistency. [42]

The inability to look upon the Fraternity as a fraternity, rather than a religion is characteristic of the arguments and attitude of the entire Roman Catholic position prior to 1974, and virtually all of their official and unofficial publications represent this attitude and view. In reference to the information and attitudes about the Fraternity as understood by the Roman Catholic Church, Father Crooker in his speech stated:

Much of the "information" seems to come from ex-Masons; no matter how sincere they may be, I wonder if their interpretations are more trustworthy than, for example, those of ex-Catholics about *my* religious beliefs and practices! [43]

Father Crooker continues in his consideration of the relationship between the Fraternity and the Church by stating his opinion that most of the objections to Masonry are to be found in two areas, the religious one of "sect," and "to the religious implications which the Popes saw—or thought they saw—in matters of social and political policy." [44] He refers to the problems inherent in the struggles for Italian unification and comments, "In fact it was only when that struggle became fierce that prohibitions of Masonry were effectively promulgated and enforced by Catholic Bishops of other countries where Masons and Catholics previously lived in relative harmony." [45]

In 1974, a great change took place in the relationships between Freemasonry and Roman Catholicism. In that year, one of Pope Paul VI's principal officers, Cardinal Seper, head of the Vatican Office for the Doctrine of the Faith, wrote a letter to Cardinal Krol of Philadelphia in which he indicated that the provisions of Canon 2335 do not necessarily prohibit membership in the Fraternity in the U.S. In reference to this, Father Crooker states: "While insisting that the Canon is still in force, the letter explained that if the Lodges do not in fact correspond to its description, then it does not apply to them!" [46] This means, of course, if the Lodges in question are not anti-clerical or anti-government.

The common interpretation of this law currently allows for Roman Catholic membership and participation in the Fraternity except in the

Southern Masonic Jurisdiction of the Scottish Rite, because of its "anti-Catholic" attitudes.

Since 1974, a large number of Roman Catholics have petitioned and been initiated into the Masonic Fraternity. Many are now in positions of leadership in many local Lodges. They have neither renounced nor become indifferent to their Church or its activities, but one the whole, have become even I bit more active than they previously were. In the Western New York area, there have been several, in recent years, who have served as Masters of their particular symbolic Lodges and who have also become active in both the York and Scottish Rites. Some are, in addition, also active in the Knights of Columbus. Referring to the whole idea of Roman Catholics within the Masonic Fraternity, Alec Mellor, a French Roman Catholic Mason, concluded an article which he wrote by stating:

> There must be room in the world of the future for "THE ROMAN CATHOLIC FREEMASON." What must he be?... Masonry, if he rightly understands the Art, must make him a better Roman Catholic, and his own religion, if he practices it, and upholds it as his duty, must make him a better Mason. [47]

With these words, Mellor has really hit at the meaning of it all. An active churchman, when he becomes a member of the Fraternity, usually continues to be an active member of his Church. The Fraternity does not interfere with such activity, nor does it intend to do so. The Fraternity does not compete with religion or with the religious beliefs and practices of any of its members. What they do is truly up to them and their own responsibility.

Since 1974, there has indeed been a notable change in Roman Catholic attitudes and policies towards the Fraternity and its members, both Catholic and non-Catholic. The former displays of anti-Masonic literature once so prevalent in the literature racks of Churches have now disappeared, their places having been taken by pamphlets which are less hostile. Father John A. O'Brien, of Notre Dame University, is the author of one such pamphlet, entitled, "Catholics and Masons: Now Good Friends," which is commonly seen. Supreme Knight John McDivitt of the Knights of Columbus, a member of years ago, ordered all publications of an anti-Masonic nature withdrawn from circulation. [48] Roman Catholic leaders now share platforms with Masonic speakers on civic and community occasions without rancor and hostility in many parts of the country, and cooperation in community affairs has become a commonplace thing to the benefit of all.

Once in a while, however, something happens to stir up feelings. In March of 1981, a news release from the Vatican Office of the Doctrine of the Faith proclaimed that Canon 2335 was still in effect, and had not been changed. Jumped on by the media and prefaced with lines like, "Vatican Outlaws Masons," this naturally caused much confusion and excitement, particularly among men who had, in good faith, joined the Fraternity. Upon contacting the Diocese of Buffalo in this regard, the following letter was received by me, dated March 4, 1981:

"I am pleased to enclose two articles which appeared in the National Catholic News Service today. I think that they more clearly explain the statements from the Congregation for the Doctrine of the Faith than the secular press did." [49] These two news articles are really no more than as affirmation that Canon 2335 is still in effect with regard to those Masonic groups which are anti-Catholic. Otherwise, the 1974 decision to let it be up to the Bishop in each diocese has not changed.

The Fraternity itself throughout its history has not been anti-Catholic. However, this does not mean that there have not been anti-Catholic Masons. Indeed, there have been those who have been vehemently anti-Catholic in both writing and speech. This is not the 'official' view. Throughout the years there have been a number of men who were both active Roman Catholic and active Masons, and never saw and conflict between the two. Daniel Carrol, brother of the first Roman Catholic Bishop in the United States, was both an active Roman Catholic and an active Mason, and his brother did not "consider the Papal ban applicable to this country until sometime after 1800." [50] In modern times, George M. Cohan was an active Mason and Roman Catholic throughout most of his life and never saw any conflict between the two.

Because of its belief in the necessity for harmony and peace within its Lodge rooms, the Fraternity has not allowed itself to become embroiled in sectarian discussions. Most Lodges, in their investigation of petitioners, should they discern that a petitioner is Roman Catholic, would make sure that the individual knew his own Church's stand concerning the Fraternity, and once that was known, if he still desired to petition the Lodge, would handle it from that point on with little or no comment. As long as a man believes in the existence of a Supreme Being and in the immortality of the soul, his own particular religious persecution is his own business. To be sure, in some communities with strong anti-Catholic feelings, a Roman Catholic petitioner might be black-balled, but in most Lodges, his religious persuasion would make no difference.

We have truly come a long way in our relationships with one another. Hopefully gone forever are the anti-Catholic and anti-Protestant feelings which once polarized communities. For several years now, progress has been made the barriers which once separated Protestant and Catholic have now been torn down, never to be erected again. Masons and Catholics are, as Father O'Brien put it, now good friends in many communities. Indeed, some years before the lowering of the barriers, in some communities the fraternal organizations cooperated on a local level for the good of the community. In Attica, New York, there existed a Tri-fraternal Brotherhood Dinner" for a period of nearly ten years prior to 1974, at which the Masons, Knights of Columbus, and Odd Fellows would gather to honor outstanding workers in the community. For the past several years, Buffalo has been the scene of an "Annual Brotherhood Banquet" sponsored jointly by the Masonic Fraternity and the Knights of Columbus and have utilized this event as a means of raising funds for the Children's Hospital and for the Sheehan Burn Treatment Center. Shriner's parades now often will include marchers from the Knights of Columbus and both will work together at the annual circus to raise funds for the Shrine Crippled Children's Hospitals and Burn Centers.

Where high walls of misunderstanding and intolerance once existed, these have now been replaced by bridges of brotherhood and fellowship. What was only an elusive dream a few short years ago has now truly become a reality in the practice of the principles of brotherhood and understanding between men. It was in 1968 that Father O'Brien, from the University of Notre Dame, called for a church commission to hold dialogues with Masonic leaders that the obstacles to Roman Catholic membership in the Fraternity might be removed. In a speech made before a group of Scottish Rite Masons in Dansville, Illinois, Father O'Brien made the following statement which seems to have since borne fruit:

> We have so much in common—belief in God, immortality, man's moral responsibility for his conduct, religious freedom, the dignity of the human person—that we belong together. [51]

Citations

[1]   Harry L. Haywood, *Freemasonry and Roman Catholicism* (Chicago, Illinois-The Masonic History Co. 1960) p. 22.

[2]   Alec Mellr, *"The Roman Catholic Church and the Craft"* (Ars Quatour Coronatorum"–Vol. 891976) p. 63.

[3]   Robert Crooker, Speech, "*The Roman Catholic Church and Freemasonry*" delivered before Ontario Shores Council, Allied Masonic Degrees, Toronto, Ontario on December 1, 1979

[4]   Mellor, op. cit. p. 63.

[5]   Ibid.

[6]   Ibid.

[7]   Ibid., p. 62.

[8]   Ibid.

[9]   Ibid.

[10]   Ibid., p. 63.

[11]   Crooker, op. cit.

[12]   Mellor, op. cit. p. 63.

[13]   Ibid.

[14]   Ibid., p. 64.

[15]   Isidoro Bianchi. *Dell 'Instituto Dei Veri Liberi Muratori.* Giordano Gamberini, ed. With Translation. (Ravenna, Italy: Longo Editore 1980) p. 89.

[16]   Ibid., p. 120.

[17]   Ibid., p. 119.

[18]   Ibid., p. 94.

[19]   Ibid., p. 100.

[20]   William   R.   Denslow. 10,000   *Famous   Freemasons,* Vol.   IV. (n.p.–Missouri Lodge of Research 1961)

308. 308.

[21]   Mellor

[22]   Ibid.

[23]   Crooker,

[24]   E. Cahill, *Freemasonry and the Anti-Christian Movement.* (Dublin, Ireland–M.H. Gill & Son. Ltd 1952) p. 123.

[25]   Ibid.

[26]   Haywood, op. cit. p. 38.

[27]   Cahill, op. cit. p. 126.

[28]   Richard N. Ostling, *Secrecy in the Church.* (New York–Harper & Row 1974) p. 79.

[29]   Mellor, op. cit. p. 65.

[30]   Ibid.

[31]   Ibid.

[32]   Ibid.

[33]   Ostling, op. cit. p. 123.

[34]   Ibid. p. 124.

[35]   Ibid.

[36]   Haywood, op. cit. p. 86.

[37]   Albert Pike. "A *Reply for the Ancient and Accepted Scottish Rite of Freemasonry to the Letter "Humanum Genus" of Pope Leo XIII."* (n.p.–n.n. 1948) p. 24.

[38]   Ibid., p. 37.

[39]   Arthur Preuss, ed. A *Study in American Freemasonry.* (St Louis, Missouri–B. Herder Book Company 1924) p. 426.

[40]   Crooker, op. cit.

[41]   William J. Whalen. *Christianity and American Freemasonry.* (Milwaukee, Wisconsin–Bruce Pub. Co. 1958) p. vii.

[42]   Ibid., p. 167-168.

[43]   Crooker, op. cit.

[44]   Ibid.

[45]   Ibid.

[46]   Ibid.

[47]   Alec Mellor, "The Roman Catholic Freemason." ("The Royal Arch Mason."–Vol. X. No.9 Spring 1972) p. 269.

[48]   Alphonse Cerza, "*Freemasonry and the Ecumenical Movement.*" ("The Royal Arch Mason."–Vol. IX. No.3. Fall 1967) p. 79.

[49]   Letter from Rev. Robert J. Cunningham, Vice Chancellor, Diocese of Buffalo, N.Y., March 4,1981.

[50]   Whalen, op. cit. p. 103.

[51]   John A. O'Brien, "*Encouraging Words from a Noted Roman Catholic Theologian.*" ("The Royal Arch Mason."–Vol. IX. No.5 Spring 1968) p. 145.

Review prepared by Wor. Charles L. Ketchum, Jr.

RW Rev. Dr. Don C. Markham is to be congratulated on his paper, "Freemasonry and Catholicism." The text is quite complete and to my findings quite accurate, although I take exception to his quote of Alec Mellor, "Mellor mentions the fact that in the 18th Century, Papal Bulls 'had to be ratified by the Catholic States before they became mandatory'." Although the use of the word 'ratified' is correct, I would have stressed the word 'promulgated', after Mellor's quote.

Using one of Right Worshipful Rev. Dr. Markham's references, 'Freemasonry and Roman Catholicism, by H.L. Haywood,' I quote from page 32. "According to an ancient law of the church a Bull is not enforced in a given diocese, district, or country until it is officially promulgated, by which is meant that copies of it are posted, and local means to enforce it are set up; it is not locally enforced otherwise." This promulgation procedure was necessary before ratification could take place.

In the first paragraph of his text, the Rev. Dr. Markham stated, "Any accurate consideration of the relationship between Freemasonry and Roman Catholicism, ... must be covered in three areas: the attitude of the church prior to 1974, the attitude of the church since 1974, and the attitude of the fraternity towards the church." After reading through the manuscript, I found it hard to locate where the areas ended and the next started. The Rev. Dr. could have used separate headings, which would have made it easier to locate these three ideas.

Again I must congratulate R∴W∴ Rev. Dr. Don C. Markham on an excellent paper, which was very easy to read.

APPENDIX—"IN EMINENTI"

Condemnation of the Society, Lodges and Conventicles of LIBERIMURATORI, or Freemasons, under pain of excommunication to be incurred ipso facto, and absolution from it being reserved for the Supreme Pontiff, except at point of death.

Clement, Bishop, Servant of the Servants of God, to all the faithful in Christ, greeting and apostolic benediction.

Placed by the disposition of the divine clemency on the eminent watch-tower of the Apostolate, though with merits undeserving of it, according to the duty of pastoral oversight committed to us, we have with constant and zealous anxiety so far as is descended to us from above, given our attention to those measures by means of which entrance may be closed against errors and vices, and the integrity of orthodox religion may be best preserved, the dangers of disturbances may be expelled, in the present very difficult times, from the whole Catholic world.

It has become known to us, even in truth by public rumor, that great and extensive progress is being made by, and the strength daily increasing of, some Societies, Meetings, Gatherings, Conventicles, or Lodges commonly known as of Liberi Muratori, or Freemasons or some other nomenclature according to difference of language, in which men of any whatsoever religion and sect, content with a certain affection of natural virtue, are associated mutually in a close and exclusive bond in accordance with laws and statutes framed for themselves; and are bound as well by a stringent oath sworn upon the Sacred Volume, as by the imposition of heavy penalties to conceal under inviolable silence, what they secretly do in their meetings.

But since it is the nature of wickedness to betray itself, and to cry aloud so as to reveal itself, hence the aforesaid Societies or Conventicles have excited so strong suspicion in the minds of the faithful that to enroll oneself in these Lodges is quite the same, in the judgment of prudent and virtuous men as to incur the brand of depravity and perverseness, for if they were not acting ill, they would not by any means have such a hatred of the light. And this repute has spread to such a degree that in very many countries the Societies just mentioned have been proscribed, and with foresight banished long since as though hostile to the safety of kingdoms.

We, accordingly, turned over in our mind the very serious injuries which are in the highest degree inflicted by such Societies, or Conventicles not merely on the tranquillity of the temporal state, but also on the spiritual welfare of souls, and perceiving that they are inconsistent alike with civil and canonical sanctions, being taught by the servant, and a prudent ruler of his master's household, to watch that no persons of this kind like thieves break into the house, and like foxes strive to ravage the vineyard, that is to say, thereby pervert the hearts of the simple and privily shoot at the innocent; in order to close the wide road which might be opened thereby for perpetrating iniquity with impunity and for other just and reasonable causes known to ourselves, have determined and decreed that these same Societies, Meetings, Gatherings, Lodges or Conventicles, of Liberi Muratori, or Freemasons, or by whatever other name called, herein acting on the advice of some Venerable Brethren of ours, Cardinals of the Holy Roman Church, and also of our own motion, and from our certain knowledge, and mature deliberation, and in the plenitude of Apostolic Power, should be condemned and prohibited as by this present Constitution we do condemn and prohibit them.

Wherefore we direct the faithful in Christ, all and singly, of whatever status, grade, dignity, and preeminence, whether laics or clerics as well secular as regular, even those worthy of specific and individual mention and expression, strictly and in virtue of holy obedience, that no one, under any pretext or farfetched colour, dare or presume to enter the above mentioned Societies of Liberi Muratori, Freemasons, or otherwise named, or to propagate, foster, and receive them whether in their houses or elsewhere, and conceal them or be present at them, or to afford them the opportunity or facilities for being convened anywhere, or otherwise to render them advice, help or favour, openly or in secret, directly or indirectly, of themselves or through the agency of others in whatever way;

and likewise to exhort, induce, incite or persuade others to be enrolled in, reckoned among, or take part in Societies of this kind, or to aid and foster them in any way whatsoever; but in every particular to abstain utterly as they are in duty bound from the same Societies, Meetings, Assemblies, Gatherings, Lodges or Conventicles, on pain of excommunication to be incurred by all who in the above ways offend—to be incurred ipso facto without any declaration, and that from this excommunication no one, except on the point of death, can obtain benefit of absolution except through Us, or the Roman Pontiff for the time being. Further, it is our will and charge that as well Bishops and higher Prelates, and other local Ordinaries as the deputed Inquisitors of Heretical Depravity everywhere take action and make inquisition against transgressors, of whatever status, grade, condition, order, dignity or eminence they be, and inflict upon them condign punishment, as though strongly suspected of heresy, and exercise constraint upon them. To the above mentioned and any individual of them we grant and impart free power of proceeding against the said transgressors, of making inquisition, of constraining by condign punishment, and of invoking thereupon, if need be, even the aid of the secular arm for that purpose.

It is our will also that exactly the same credit be given to copies of these presents, subscribed by the hand of some public notary, and fortified with the seal of some person placed in ecclesiastical dignity, as would be given to the original documents if exhibited or displayed.

Let it be lawful therefore for no man to infringe this proclamation notifying our declaration, condemnation, charge, prohibition and interdiction, or to act counter to it with reckless daring. But if any one presume to attempt this, let him know that he will incur the wrath of Almighty God, and of the blessed Apostles Peter and Paul.

"Given at Rome in the Basilica of St. Mary the Greater, in the year of our Lord, 1738, on the 28th April, in the 8th year of our Pontificate."

Quoted in H.L. Haywood. *Freemasonry and Roman Catholicism.* (Chicago: The Masonic History Co., 1960) pp. 17-21.

FIRST TRANSACTIONS

{The introduction content from the 2014 republication of the First Book of Transactions / Works Under Dispensation is found at the beginning of the section "Works Under Dispensation". The original work of Volume 1 was published in 2009.}

The Grand Lodge of Israel: The Origins and Development of Freemasonry in the Holy Land

By RW Maurice Solomon

{Original biographical note in 1990:

Right Worshipful Brother MAURICE SOLOMON was born in Glasgow, Scotland, served in the British Army during World War II, and received an honourable discharge with the rank of Captain in 1946. In October of that year he joined Lodge Montefiore No.753 A.F. & A.M. in Glasgow, and is a Life Member. He arrived in Rochester, N.Y., in November 1954, and affiliated with Flower City Lodge No.910, serving as Worshipful Master in 1972.

Since that time, he has had a continuing record of service to the Craft. He was Secretary of the Masters and Wardens Association of Monroe County, Secretary of the School of Lodge Administration, Director of the School of Instruction, and President of the Bureau of Masonic Education. He was also Assistant Grand Lecturer from 1975 until his resignation in 1984. In 1980, he was appointed Grand Representative of the Grand Lodge of Louisiana near the Grand Lodge of New York, which also carried the rank of Past Junior Grand Warden of Louisiana.

In January 1984, he installed his son as Worshipful Master of Flower City Lodge, the first time in that Lodge's history that a son had followed in his father's footsteps by becoming Master.

Rt. Wor. Bro. Solomon is currently serving his second term as President of the Masonic Service Bureau of Rochester, N.Y., and is active with the Tartan Square Club of Rochester, which exemplifies the Ritual as it is practiced in Scotland, for the benefit of Lodges throughout the Monroe and adjoining Districts.

He is a member of the American Lodge of Research, and of Quatuor Coronati Lodge No.2076, London, England.

Editor's note: British spellings and salutation abbreviations have been maintained.}

Forward

This article is not, nor is it in any way intended to be a History of the Grand Lodge of Israel, nor of the events leading to its formation and subsequent progress. It is rather an attempt to chronicle the progress that was made from the time Freemasonry was introduced into what was then Palestine, through the establishment of the Grand Lodge, and its subsequent growth. Since my Mother Lodge is Lodge Montefiore No.753 A.F. & A.M., of Glasgow, Scotland, which played such a crucial role in the erection of the Grand Lodge of Israel, I have for a long time felt a desire to undertake this project, having frequently in mind some of the misleading and inaccurate information that has been published by well-meaning contributors.

In preparing this article, I have relied on my personal experiences, knowledge of some of the events (thanks to my late father-in-law, who, as a Past Master of Lodge Montefiore, was involved in some of the discussions), and have drawn somewhat heavily on information published in various issues of "HABONEH HAHOFSHI," the official magazine of the Grand Lodge of Israel.

I also take this opportunity of publicly acknowledging my gratitude to Rt. Wor. Bro. Gerald Levin, P.M., Secretary of Lodge Montefiore 753, and now Substitute Grand Master of the Grand Lodge of Scotland, for allowing me such generous access to the files in his possession, and to Wor. Bro. Symie Miller, J.P., Past Master of Lodge Montefiore, for his kind permission to use the material. As you will read, Wor. Bro. Miller was one of the key figures in the negotiations which led to the establishment of the Grand Lodge of Israel.

The History

Sacred history informs us that in the fourth year of his reign, King Solomon commenced the erection of a Temple, the curious workmanship of which was calculated to excite the wonder and admiration of all succeeding ages. The Temple was located on Mount Moriah, in the City of Jerusalem, and construction took approximately 7-1/2 years to completion.

The building of King Solomon's Temple plays a most significant role in the teachings and history of Freemasonry, and of all the objects which comprise Masonic symbolism, surely the most cherished is the Holy Temple in Jerusalem. If the Craft were to be divorced from its dependance on the Temple, if we removed from our rituals all reference to the Sacred Edifice, and the legends and traditions so closely connected with it, where would that leave Freemasonry?

It is something of a paradox that non-Operative (or Speculative)

Freemasonry, as we know it today, had its origins in lands far distant from the site of the Temple which serves as the most important Shrine in the Craft. How ironic is it, therefore, that Freemasonry, having found its origins and undergone development in distant lands, should not establish a foothold for itself in its native land until well into the 19th Century, and it is now a fact of Masonic history that the "Cradle of Freemasonry" did not have a Grand Lodge of its own until midway through the 20th Century.

There is some evidence available that Masonic Lodges of some kind existed around the middle of the 19th Century, but these were all formed by groups of Freemasons who found themselves in the Palestine area either on a temporary basis, or on some mission—business, study of an archaeological or religious nature—and these Lodges existed only until such time as their founders completed their respective tours of duty and returned to their native lands.

Such Lodges were mainly of French influence, since the Grand Orient of France was at that time the Supreme Body in that part of the world, although there are some traces of other European, and even British-sponsored Lodges.

One such Lodge was reputed to be Reclamation Lodge, said to have been founded in 1868 by Bro. Robert Morris, which held its first (and possibly only) meeting at the site of King Solomon's Quarries, by candlelight, but following its Gala opening, little else is known.

One Lodge which does merit close attention and consideration began in 1873, when a group of Canadian Brethren petitioned the Grand Lodge of Canada (today the Grand Lodge of Canada in the Province of Ontario) to form a Lodge in Jerusalem. This Lodge was chartered on May 1, 1873, under the name Suleiman al-Muluki (Solomon the King) No.293, and has also been referred to as Royal Solomon Mother Lodge. Records show that this Lodge continued to function until around 1903, after which time there is no information available, and for all practical purposes it is presumed that the Lodge simply ceased to exist. From the historical standpoint, however, it is generally accepted that Lodge Suleiman marked the beginning of symbolic Freemasonry in the Holy Land. {See Appendix A, at end of this article.}

In the meantime, in August 1891, a group of French engineers, who were in Palestine to build the Turkish railway from Jerusalem to Jaffa, founded their own Lodge, naming it "Le Port du Temple du Salomon" (The Gateway to Solomon's Temple) Lodge, under the auspices of the Grand Orient of France, and records show that both Jewish and Arab dignitaries were admitted to membership. In 1906, this Lodge moved to Jaffa, changed its name to L'Aurore (The Dawn), and then to Barkai, working in Hebrew. It is interesting to mention here that, with their membership consisting of Brethren from all three major religious faiths, the first two Masters of the Lodge were Christian Arabs. {See Appendix B, at end of this article.}

(The Grand Orient of France was involved in a dramatic development on September 14, 1877. Having previously, in 1871, abolished the Office of Grand Master, they adopted an amendment to their Constitution, after deliberating for more than a year, which expunged the existence of the Great Architect from their tenets. The Grand Lodge of England, after due consideration, resolved that such an amendment was totally opposed to the traditions and practices of all true and genuine Masons, since belief in the existence of a Supreme Being was always considered to be a Landmark of the Fraternity, and declared that the Grand Orient could no longer be regarded as a Masonic body. Similar action was quickly taken by other Grand Lodges.)

In the years which followed, up to the outbreak of World War I, other Lodges were formed which functioned for a few years, during which time a large number of local residents were initiated. One such Lodge was Carmel Lodge, resurrected by the Grand Lodge of Scotland in 1910. Some of the founders of this Lodge were of the Jewish Faith, and in 1912 one of the Brothers initiated was Shabbatei Levy, later to become the distinguished and highly-respected Mayor of Haifa, and that City's first Honorary Citizen; destiny had also chosen him to become the first-ever Grand Master of the Grand Lodge of Israel in 1953. Carmel Lodge also had the distinction of initiating many Brethren who would later become the founding members, and some Worshipful Masters, of what is now Reuven Lodge No.1.

The outbreak of World War I, and the years that followed, changed forever the whole picture and history of Freemasonry in the Holy Land. With the British Army taking over control of the country from the Turks, and more especially after the capture of Jerusalem by General Allenby, the Masonic influence of the occupying forces soon made itself felt.

Both the Grand Lodges of England and Scotland erected a number of Lodges. One such Lodge was restricted to soldier-Masons with the rank of Sergeant and above, while another consisted only of Senior Officers, although they later admitted and initiated what they chose to call "locals" of British Nationality. One such "local" invited to become a member was an Irish Jew name Isaac Becker, but on learning that membership was restricted to holders of British Passports, he sternly refused to become a member of what he termed "some selective Club" and not a Masonic

Lodge, and he stormed out of the meeting. Bro. Becker was later (1937) to become Worshipful Master of Sharon Lodge No.1387 S.C. (now No.7).

Not to be outdone by all this activity, the Grand Lodge of Egypt (the only one of three such Egyptian bodies to be recognized, the other two being considered clandestine) erected an Arabic-speaking Lodge in Jaffa. They became even more active during the years between the two World Wars, and erected several more Lodges. The Grand Lodge of Scotland, also pursuing a policy of expansion, erected another five Lodges, including the first Lodge under Scottish jurisdiction ever to work in Hebrew.

The 1930's saw the demise of organized Freemasonry in Germany, where the contemptible Hitler chose as his favourite targets Jews and Freemasons (or Freemasons and Jews, if you prefer). The then Grand Master of Germany, Most Worshipful Bro. Leo Mueffelman chose to go into exile with many of his Brethren, taking with him the official Seal of the Grand Lodge, and what more logical (and appropriate) venue for his new home than—Jerusalem. There he founded Ein-Hashiloah Lodge No.26 in 1931.

(Those Freemasons who remained in Germany, forbidden to meet openly, chose a unique method to identify themselves. They wore a forget-me-not in their lapels to show their membership and support for the Craft.)

Grand Master Mueffelman formed 4 German-speaking Lodges (two in Tel-Aviv, one in Jerusalem and one in Haifa). Today there are 6 German-speaking Lodges in the Grand Lodge of Israel, working their own "Schroeder" Ritual.

(The symbolic Grand Lodge of Germany-in-Exile came to a peaceful end in 1949, when they returned the Seal to the Grand Master, the highly-revered Most Worshipful Theodore Vogel.)

The years preceding World War II saw the formation of other Lodges which exist today: Moriah (1928), Hiram (1929), Reuven (1931), Har-Zion (Mt. Zion) (1932), Genossar, Ha-Kokhav (Star), Mizpah and Rashbi (1933), Sharon (1935), and Eliyahu Ha-Navi (Elijah the Prophet) (1936). All of these Lodges, with the exception of Sharon, work in Hebrew, although Eliyah Ha-Navi also works in Arabic. Sharon Lodge works in English.

(Sharon Lodge has had the distinction of providing four Grand Masters of Israel, one of whom, Most Worshipful Max Silverstone, was present at a meeting of the Lodge in Tel-Aviv which I attended in November 1984. I was received most graciously, and during the course of my conversation with Grand Master Silverstone, he asked me to convey his personal and fraternal greetings to Lodge Montefiore No.753, which I was about to visit after an absence of some 30 years.)

The year 1932 brought a most interesting development. In June of that year, seven Lodges petitioned the Grand Lodge of Egypt for the purpose of establishing an independent Grand Lodge, and this suggestion was approved. Bro. Shuqri Houri was elected to become the first Grand Master, but unfortunately he died before he could be installed. A second meeting was convened in December 1932, and at this time Bro. Mark Gorodisky was elected Grand Master.

On January 9, 1933, the Grand Master of Egypt, Most Worshipful Fuad Bey Hussein, accompanied by a large delegation from Egypt, and in the presence of an audience consisting of Jews, Arabs and Christian, formally consecrated the National Grand Lodge of Palestine. Unfortunately for the unity of this Grand Lodge, a number of the Lodges in the country preferred to retain their allegiance to their Mother Grand Lodge, the Grand Lodge of Scotland, and decided to remain outside the framework of the newly-formed National Grand Lodge. As a result, many of the world's Grand Lodges, including Scotland, England and Ireland withheld recognition, a situation which caused some distress, and which in later years was to have some repercussions, as you will read later.

This lack of universal recognition was deeply felt by the National Grand Lodge, but as long as there was disunity with no apparent signs of solidarity, they had to remain content with the "status quo." Between 1933 and 1953, the National Grand Lodge produced ten Grand Masters, each of whom worked tirelessly and diligently to further the cause of Freemasonry throughout the land, and the last of these Grand Masters, the Most Worshipful Dr. Avraham Shaoni, concentrated his efforts on the unification of all the Lodges, and the ultimate establishment of a united all-embracing Grand Lodge.

(Sadly, we understand that today in Egypt, because of the law and restrictive decrees, there is no apparent evidence of the existence of any Masonic Lodges.)

The years immediately following World War II saw a large number of refugees arriving in the country, and special mention must be made of the attention that was devoted to a group of Roumanian Masons, who were particularly embittered, and often skeptical. Working with considerable patience and great diligence, the Masonic Fraternity gradually persuaded these not unwilling brothers to be brought back "into the fold." To allow for their easier absorption, two Roumanian-speaking Lodges were erected, one of which, Hashakhar, still exists in Tel-Aviv.

1948, as the world knows, saw the birth of the State of Israel. With it came the withdrawal of all foreign ("friendly") forces, and as a direct result, most of the Lodges opened by the occupying powers ceased to exist; some moved back to the United Kingdom, but the majority simply returned their Charters. Five Scottish Lodges remained, in Jerusalem, Tel-Aviv and Haifa. It was these Lodges, with their local counterparts from the National Grand Lodge, who were to become instrumental in establishing a united Grand Lodge of Israel. Jordan Lodge, working in Arabic, decided to move to Amman, Transjordan, and Golden Throne, already ensconced in East Jerusalem, were geographically now part of Transjordan.

With the attainment of independence, and their state now in being, many of the Brethren began to feel that now, more than ever, it was necessary to have unification of all the Lodges in the country, with a view to forming an independent and Sovereign Grand Lodge. The five Scottish Lodges already referred to, Holy City 1372, Reuven 1376, Mizpah 1383, Sharon 1387, and Aviv 1397, decided to convene a meeting in 1949, and as a result, a petition was approved and signed by 26 of their combined Past Masters, including, it must be said, a number of Christian Arabs, asking the Grand Lodge of Scotland for permission to form their own Sovereign Grand Lodge of Israel.

In a project such as this, it is not unusual, and always very helpful, to try and obtain assistance from "friends at court." In this, the petitioners were most fortunate, and eminently successful. They sought, and succeeded in receiving the unqualified support and cooperation of the Past Masters of Lodge Montefiore No.753, of Glasgow, Scotland, a group of whom made it their particular business to campaign on their behalf. Of these Past Masters, there was one who, more than any other, literally gave of his all "above and beyond" to further the cause of the applicants. Worshipful Bro. Symie Miller, J.P., joined forces with two former Englishmen now living in Israel, a lawyer name Max Seligman and a Bank Executive named Max Silverstone, each of whom was later to become a Grand Master of Israel. By means of visits to the Grand Lodge of Scotland, continuous correspondence, telephone calls, and trips by Bro. Miller to Israel, they conducted a series of negotiations and discussions in their efforts to achieve their desired goal. In some cases, Wor. Bro. Miller found himself involved in visits of a highly sensitive and secretive nature—some twenty years later U.S. Secretary of State Henry Kissinger conducted a similar type of venture, which was to earn worldwide recognition as "shuttle diplomacy"—but he nevertheless continued to pursue his self-appointed "Labour of Love." {See Appendix C, at end of this article.}

Weeks became months, months became years, and slowly but surely, progress was made, success seemed within reach, and the elusive recognition, so earnestly sought for, was now within grasp.

In the concluding negotiations, several matters of a critical nature had to be resolved. The proposed new Grand Lodge would require a Constitution, but this presented little difficulty. Since the petitioning Lodges had operated under the aegis of the Grand Lodge of Scotland, what was more logical than to draft a Constitution that was based, for the most part, on that of their Mother Grand Lodge? It was also agreed that the five petitioning (and therefore founding) Lodges would, on the creation of the new Grand Lodge, immediately surrender their Charters to the Grand Lodge of Scotland, upon which they would be issued their new Charters by the Grand Lodge of Israel.

There yet remained one final, and delicate matter, to be cleared up. The Grand Lodge of Scotland, quite naturally, was anxious to clarify the status of Golden Throne Lodge No.1344, since their acquiescence was absolutely necessary for unification purposes. It was respectfully pointed out by the authorities in Israel that Golden Throne was geographically situated in what was now the Hashemite Kingdom of Jordan that because of geopolitical reasons, there was neither contact nor the possibility of communication, and that, in any event, their geographical location was not, and could not be considered (at that stage in time) to be a part of the State of Israel, and therefore outwith the jurisdiction of the proposed new Grand Lodge.

The explanation, as logical as it was, proved satisfactory and acceptable to the Grand Lodge of Scotland, and formal approval was now given to the creation of a new Grand Lodge.

(As far as can be ascertained, Golden Throne has now ceased to exist. Of Jordan Lodge, which had been a vibrant and thriving Lodge while working in Jaffa, there is little or no information available. I have the most reliable information that Freemasonry functions today in Jordan, my understanding being that it does so openly, and I am in the process of trying to obtain specific details through personal contacts.) {See Appendix D, at end of this article.}

Elation at the news was short-lived. When word was received by the National Grand Lodge of Palestine (now calling itself the Grand Lodge of Israel) of the decision by the Grand Lodge of Scotland, the consternation that followed brought home in full measure the lack of recognition, and the realization it would be in their best interests not to be left "out in the cold." The member Lodges therefore decided to petition the Grand Lodge of Scotland with a request that they be included in the new Grand Lodge, and be accorded the same consideration and privileges as the petitioning Scottish Lodges.

At this the Grand Lodge of Scotland, not unexpectedly, demurred. After all, they did not recognize the National Grand Lodge (which you will recall had been formed by Egypt) but it was still their ambition to see all the Lodges in the Country unified under the banner of the new Grand Lodge, a desirable goal for the good of Freemasonry as a whole.

So, it was back to the drawing-board and bargaining table. The Grand Master of the National Grand Lodge went to Edinburgh to plead his case with the Grand Lodge of Scotland, while discussions and negotiations continued among the parties in Israel. Finally, agreement was reached, and a resolution was adopted which hopefully would be acceptable to all concerned, and terminate the impasse. The Lodges comprising the National Grand Lodge of Palestine would, on the creation of the Grand Lodge of Israel, immediately surrender their Charters, and that Grand Lodge would voluntarily go into liquidation. The Lodges would, at the same time, submit a formal petition for membership in the new Grand Lodge, which would be approved, and be thereupon issued new Charters. In addition, as a measure of protection, the Master of each Lodge would be required to give an assurance, not only on his own behalf, but that of his Lodge, backed by a solemn obligation, swearing to adhere to the Ancient Landmarks of the Fraternity, and promising to support and maintain the Constitution and Laws of the Grand Lodge of Israel.

It was further agreed that, initially, there would be two joint Grand Secretaries, and two joint Grand Treasurers.

The Grand Lodge of Scotland, having reviewed all the information, now gave complete approval for the erection and consecration of the Grand Lodge of Israel.

For their official Seal, the Grand Lodge chose an interwoven emblem, consisting of the Star of David, the Crescent of Islam, and the Cross of Christianity, representative of all three major Faiths represented in the Country.

Tuesday, October 23, 1953 was a Landmark Date in the history of Freemasonry in the Holy Land. In the morning, all the distinguished guests were received in audience by President Ben-Zvi of Israel. Later that day, a vast assembly, representative of Freemasonry from all over the world, gathered in the Auditorium of the Y.M.C.A. in Jerusalem to witness the historic ceremony. Among the delegations present was one from Lodge Montefiore No.753, and no prouder person than Wor. Bro.

Symie Miller, who was there to witness the fruition of all his devoted labours, and the realization of a "dream."

With all the pomp and pageantry befitting such an occasion, the various delegations entered in procession, with the place of honour being taken by the delegation from the Grand Lodge of Scotland.

Heading the delegation was the Rt. Hon. the Earl of Elgin and Kincardine, Right Worshipful Past Grand Master of the Grand Lodge of Scotland, accompanied by the Grand Secretary, Right Worshipful Dr. Alexander Buchan, the District Superintendent of the Scottish Lodges in the Near East, Rt. Wor. Bro. G. L. C. Colenso-Jones, and Bro. Reuben Cohen, who with the Grand Secretary, were to act as Wardens during the ceremony of Installation.

The brother already chosen to become the Grand Master was Shabbetai Levy, C.B.E., former Mayor of Haifa, and Lord Elgin proceeded to install him in due and ancient form. Who can guess at the feelings and emotions of those present as they heard the Installing Grand Master, as a climax to the ceremony, make the following proclamation:

> In the presence of the Brethren here assembled, I hereby proclaim that there is now erected and consecrated a sovereign Grand Lodge by the name and designation of the Grand Lodge of the State of Israel. From henceforth it is fully empowered to exercise all rights and privileges to the terms of its constitution, and the ancient usages of the Fraternity.

There was a brief moment of silence, to be broken (in traditional Jewish fashion) by a dramatic blast from a Shofar (Ram's Horn)—The Grand Lodge of Israel had come into existence.

Lodge Montefiore, having played so prominent a role in the events culminating in the establishment of the Grand Lodge, now showed its generosity by donating the Regalia, the highlight of which was a magnificent Gold Chain of office for the Grand Master, and consisting of 12 Gold Links, emblematic of the 12 Tribes of Israel, with a centerpiece surmounted by two Tablets of the Law, with the 10 Commandments and a seven-branched Menorah (candlestick). {See Appendix E, at end of this article.}

(In a rare gesture of Goodwill, and in keeping with the spirit of the occasion, special dispensation had been received from both the British Government and Government of Israel to waive all duties and taxes pertaining to the Regalia.)

Immediately after his Installation, Most Worshipful Grand Master Levy performed an act which proved to be a most happy augury for the peace and future of Freemasonry in Israel. He invited Most Worshipful Bro. Dr. Avraham Shaoni, Grand Master of the National Grand Lodge of Palestine (soon to be defunct) to join him, and formally installed him as Immediate Past Grand Master of the Grand Lodge of Israel.

(After only a few months in office, Grand Master Levy resigned early in 1954, and was succeeded by Dr. Shaoni as Grand Master, in which office he did so much to further the interests of the new Grand Lodge.)

As previously arranged, the five founding Lodges, Holy City, Reuven, Mizpah, Sharon and Aviv, surrendered their Charters to the Earl of Elgin, and were then ceremoniously presented with their new Charters. Following this, the Masters of the other Lodges were then admitted, surrendered their Charters, and after taking the formal obligation previously agreed to, were also presented with their new Charters as members of the Grand Lodge of Israel. At the conclusion of the day, there were 31 Constituent Lodges. The Grand Master then formally appointed the Earl of Elgin to be the first Honorary Member of the new Grand Lodge, and presented him with an appropriate Jewel to mark the occasion.

The National Grand Lodge of Palestine voluntarily ceased to exist, as had been previously agreed, and as a result Freemasonry—in the "Cradle of Freemasonry"—had finally become unified.

In his oration, the Rt. Hon. the Earl of Elgin said:

> Today we are taking part in the establishment of the Sovereign Grand Lodge of the State of Israel, founded in accordance with the wish of five Lodges on the Roll of the Grand Lodge of Scotland. These five Lodges—HOLY CITY, REUVEN, MIZPAH, SHARON and AVIV—have today returned their Charters which enabled them to work under that Constitution. As parents of these Lodges, we have a natural regret that five active Daughters should withdraw from our Family household, but we are glad that the withdrawal is occasioned not by inactivity but from an urge on their part for further work and greater responsibilities. We rejoice, therefore, in the birth of the new Sister Lodge. The presence of the Grand Secretary and myself today, accompanied by other Office-Bearers and Brethren, signifies that the Grand Lodge of Scotland approves of the new Grand Lodge, and is anxious to give all possible assistance in bringing it into active fellowship. This is the definite task in which we are engaged today, and which will be completed when the Gavel is handed over to the Most Worshipful Bro. Shabetai Levy.

Since 1953, under the guidance of an enthusiastic, progressive-minded and well-organized administration, Freemasonry in Israel has developed in a manner that could serve as an example for others to copy.

Recognition from the other two Supreme Grand Lodges soon followed, together with other Grand Lodges throughout the world, and today the Grand Lodge of Israel enjoys fraternal relations with almost every Grand Lodge in the world, with the exception of a few of the lesser-known jurisdictions in Latin America.

Including the present incumbent, there have been 20 Grand Masters, and as one might expect, religion knows no bounds; membership consists of Jews, Arabs, Christians, Moslems, Druzes, Armenians, Copts, Greek Orthodox and Bahais. Of the more than 60 Lodges, the majority work in Hebrew, while five work in English, five in Arabic, six in German, one in French, two in Spanish and one in Roumanian. What other Grand Lodge can claim such a cosmopolitan diversity?

The existence of so many Lodges of differing creeds and religions (to be technically correct, all the Lodges are Masonic—it is the membership that differs) points up the spirit of Brotherhood and coexistence which exists in the Grand Lodge of Israel. This coexistence has been demonstrated in many ways, and I would like to give a few examples.

We already have the example of the Roumanians discussed earlier. One of the more interesting—and unique Lodges in the Jurisdiction is Ha-Lapid (in Arabic El Shu'la), The Torch, No.65 working in Arabic in Jerusalem. This is the only Lodge in Israel whose membership comprises not only Brethren of all faiths, but also Arab Moslems who formerly belonged to Jordan Lodges.

As a result of the 1967 (Six-Day) War, which saw the historical unification of Jerusalem, the Grand Lodge of Jordan ordered all its Lodges in the "West Bank" to close down. Many of the Brethren, however, were reluctant to discontinue their Masonic ties, and both eager and anxious to remain in the Craft, sought ways to do so under the very difficult postwar conditions which prevailed.

Some of the English speaking Brethren joined Holy City No.4 in Jerusalem, but to them, this merely represented a partial, temporary solution, feeling that their Masonic future lay in more comprehensive labours, with a greater degree of responsibility. Some of the more active Moslem Brethren decided to meet with their Jewish colleagues, and over a period of time conducted a series of exhaustive negotiations, which resulted in the adoption of a resolution petitioning the Grand Lodge for permission to establish a separate Lodge, which would be able to absorb all the Brethren affected.

There were obviously many difficulties involved, but despite this, the determination of the Brethren overcame all obstacles, and after some highly concentrated efforts, Ha-Lapid Lodge was founded in June 1974, the first of its kind in Israel.

We can also point to the recent establishment (in 1982) of Ra'anana Lodge No.70 (named after its location) and working in English, This Lodge consists primarily of Brethren who immigrated from Zimbabwe, South Africa, and the United Kingdom. They use the South African Ritual. {See Appendix F, at end of this article.}

Let us not forget Lodge of the Holy Land No.50, whose officers consist of the Grand Master and Line Officers from the Grand Lodge, but which meets only on the occasion of a Masonic pilgrimage to Israel. Membership is confined to brethren who are nonresidents of Israel, and as of today, there are well over 400 members, all from Overseas.

In addition to Ra'anana Lodge, the Grand Lodge of Israel has also recently consecrated two other new Lodges, Nazareth No.71, working in Arabic, and La Esperanza No.72 in Haifa, working in Spanish.

This, Brethren, is coexistence, but possibly the greatest example, combined with Pure Brotherhood, surely occurred in 1981, when the Grand Lodge of Israel elected as its Grand Master a Christian Arab from Haifa, the Most Worshipful Jamil Shalhoub. In his address at the installation banquet, Grand Master Shalhoub said:

> I wish to express my thanks and esteem toward my Brethren Freemasons for having chosen me as their Grand Master—a choice differing from its predecessors in that it marks the first time since the inception of the Grand Lodge of the State of Israel, and even prior to this, under the various Lodges functioning, an Arab Brother is being installed in this high and honourable Post. I would wish to extol your pure attributes and adherence to the Principles of our Order, which stand for Brotherhood, Liberty and Equality. The doctrine of Freemasonry is the doctrine of Justice and Truth. By your act, you have confirmed your greatness as a chosen and noble people, adhering to its lofty principles. It is this greatness which has carried us through tests and crises, successes and failures—to emerge even stronger and more solidly founded.

(I had the pleasure and privilege of meeting with Grand Master Shalhoub when I visited the Grand Lodge offices in 1981. He is a frequent and well-known visitor in Toronto, Canada, where his daughter lives, and recently his son-in-law affiliated with Palestine Lodge No.559, G.R.C., Toronto.)

Mention must also be made of the second Masonic Pilgrimage held in Jerusalem in 1976. Addressing the opening ceremony, Sheik Labib Abu-Rukun, Grand Chaplain, speaking in Arabic, told the delegates:

> I am proud to tell you that we, free citizens of Israel, although we

belong to different faiths and religions, have done and shall continue to do our utmost to save our State from dangerous aggressions; we shall defend our State with all our means and possibilities ... As you can see, Israel is a true example of peaceful coexistence between all religions and nations, and Israel can be an example which many States could follow.

The Prime Minister, Yitzhak Rabin, also addressed the assembly:

I know that Jerusalem is, by Masonic tradition, the birthplace of Freemasonry . . . The family of Freemasons is a Brotherhood of decency. You stand for tolerance and equality. You seek to live by the morality of justice, and concern for your fellow men. The world is a better place because of the magnificent selfless work you do ... I share with you the prayer that the individual good you do, day by day, will yet become the universal good of Mankind.

At this same Pilgrimage, the Grand Master was given a special memento of the event by the Grand Lodge of Canada in the Province of Ontario, the presentation being made by the Grand Representative, Right Worshipful Bro. A. Lou Copeland, a Past Master of Palestine Lodge No.559, Toronto, who today is Deputy Grand Master of Canada, and who, God willing, barring some unforeseen development, will in July of this year (1985) be elected and installed as Grand Master of the Grand Lodge of Canada in the Province of Ontario. {See Appendix F, at end of this article.}

As evidence of its progressive-minded ability, two events that occurred in 1984 are noteworthy.

In June, the Grand Lodge of Israel convened a Congress of Grand Representatives. There is little doubt that the work and standing of a Grand Representative, within the framework of Freemasonry, has never been adequately defined. As a consequence, it has become an Office devoid of purpose, and the view is generally held that the appointment of a Grand Representative is only honorary. The Grand Lodge of Israel feels that the Office should be an important link in the chain of our universal Fraternity, thus ensuring closer relations. It deserves to be accorded proper recognition and standing.

(The reader will forgive me if I heartily concur with these sentiments, having held such an appointment for two years.)

To mark the occasion, a Grand Representative's medallion was struck by the Grand Lodge of Israel and presented to each visiting Grand Representative.

Later that same day, June 24th, The Grand Lodge held a Public Installation of its Grand Master and Grand Line Officers at the Tel-Aviv Hilton Hotel. The Grand Master, Most Worshipful Bro. Elly Weiss, presented his Grand Line Officers with suggestions for their consideration, and charged them with the attainment of a streamlined, smoothly-flowing ceremony, from the entrance procession to termination, the overriding consideration being at all times to maintain the dignity of the Fraternity.

The Grand Master himself prepared a leaflet, outlining the meaning of Freemasonry, including its aims, purposes and activities. Great care was taken to present the salient aspects of the Order without revealing, obviously, any of the esoteric work, known only to the Brethren.

The traditional (closed) ceremony having taken place earlier in the day at the Masonic Temple, the public (open) portion was held in the Ballroom of the Hilton Hotel in the evening, in the presence of over 1,000 Brethren and guests from all over the World, including representatives from many Grand Lodges. The event, which was fully covered and reported by TV, radio and the press, was so successfully received that the following day the Grand Lodge office was flooded with calls from well-wishers, all expressing their admiration and offering congratulations, a truly indicative expression of the manner in which the Grand Lodge of Israel is flourishing.

What of the future? From some of the events described in the foregoing, it is evident that the Grand Lodge of Israel is a vibrant organization, dedicated to the highest Principles of the Fraternity, and determined to be a leader in innovations which, while not departing in any way from the established Landmarks of the Order, are nevertheless designed to freshen the outlook on the Craft and promote its objectives by calling on the Order to return to practical Freemasonry, in other words, to engage in Masonic work in the Community, in public life, and in the general environment in which we live.

Part of this philosophy is reflected in the ancient and traditional Tyler's Toast offered in Scottish Lodges, adhered to in Israel, and practiced in full measure as we each go our different ways:

HAPPY TO MEET–SORRY TO PART
HAPPY TO MEET AGAIN.

Appendix A

The exact fate of Royal Solomon Mother Lodge is clarified in the publication, "Whence Came We," produced by a special committee of the Grand Lodge of Canada in the Province of Ontario, appointed by Grand Master Eric W. Nancekevill in 1975.

A group of brethren, spearheaded by Bro. Robert Morris, a Past Grand Master of Kentucky (who was also associated with the formation of Reclamation Lodge already referred to), and Bro. Alexander A. Stevenson, Past Grand Master of the Grand Lodge of Canada, petitioned the Grand Lodge of Canada at the close of 1872 to grant its patronage for the founding of a Lodge bearing the name "Royal Solomon Mother Lodge." Previous applications had already been made to the Grand Lodges of England, Scotland and Ireland, and also to several Grand Lodges in the United States, all without success. No information bearing on these rejected applications was within the knowledge of the Grand Lodge of Canada, and accordingly they approved the formation of the Lodge in 1873, in what was then Palestine, at that time under the rule of the Turkish Empire. The first Master of the Lodge was the same Bro. Robert Morris Because of the great distance from Canada, proper supervision was almost impossible, and many of the Lodge's actions proved to be slipshod, careless, and often grossly unconstitutional. In 1901, the Grand Secretary demanded that the Lodge forward its minute books for examination. The Lodge continued to function, but when the Grand Secretary finally received a copy of the minutes in July 1902, they revealed that the Lodge "from the first meeting had persistently violated the Constitution." In addition, the Grand Secretary received letters from several brethren claiming to have been defrauded by the Lodge, and demanding repayment of money improperly extracted from them. At the Annual Communication of the Grand Lodge of 1902, the recommendation was handed down that the Grand Master be empowered to withdraw or cancel the warrant unless good cause could be shown why that course should not be adopted. The Worshipful Master of Royal Solomon Mother Lodge was ordered to return the warrant, books, papers, seal and other effects. The order was ignored, and the Lodge continued to work, but it was not until 1907 that an official complaint was entered, resulting in the Grand Master cancelling the warrant and notifying all other jurisdictions of his action. In the words of Bro. W. S. Herrington, who was to become Grand Master in 1933, "this was the tragic end of the first attempt of the Grand Lodge of Canada to establish a constituent Lodge in a foreign country."

Appendix B

The correct name of the Lodge "Le Port du Temple de Solomon" was for a long time in question, particularly as to the correct translation from French to English, and in this respect, we must of necessity depend on

French grammar, and then on two pieces of evidence produced by Very Wor. Bro. Baruch Elron, Grand Director of Ceremonies of the Grand Lodge of Israel. The word "Porte" being feminine would be prefixed by "La" and means Door or Gate, whereas Port, being masculine, would of course be prefixed by "Le."

Bro. Elron claims to have in his possession a certificate issued to a Brother Avraham Levy in August 1890, clearly showing the name of the Lodge as "Le Port...," and then in 1982, Bro. Elron, in company with another brother, searching through some relics, discovered a medallion, which after diligent cleaning and polishing, proved to be from "The Port of the Temple of Solomon." This seems effectively to clarify the confusion arising from the correct name of the Lodge.

Appendix C

On Thursday, August 29, 1985 thethe Grand Lodge of Israel bade farewell to Most Wor. Max Seligman, who had regretfully decided, for health and family reasons, to return to the United Kingdom after spending 60 years in the Holy Land, of which 50 had been devoted to the Craft. With the Senior Past Grand Master leaving the jurisdiction, this left Most Wor. Max Silverstone as the Senior resident P.G.M.

Appendix D

An examination of the Lodges registered with the Grand Lodges of England, Scotland and Ireland reveal the existence of only one Lodge, Jordan No.1339, operating under the jurisdiction of the Grand Lodge of Scotland, working in Amman.

Appendix E

In a personal gesture, Bro. Symie Miller presented the Grand Lodge of Israel with a sword for use by the Grand Tyler.

Appendix F

Another Lodge which should be considered especially is Star of Israel No.51, consecrated in May 1961, and operating in Herzlia. The Lodge was formed for the benefit of the many English-speaking visitors who came to the area. They had the misfortune to lose their premises to a fire caused during an electrical storm, and had to move to Tel-Aviv until they could restore their own facilities. Happily, this has been done, and they are not in Herzlia.

Appendix G

On Thursday, July 18, 1985, I had the privilege and pleasure of attending the sessions of the Grand Lodge of Canada in the Province of Ontario, at which time Most Wor. Bro. A. Lou Copeland was elected and formally installed as Grand Master.

The Law Is ...

By RW Charles Kysor

> The plumbline between the loud and angry crowd; who very angry and very loud, say the law is we and the soft idiot who very softly says the law is me.

Unlike a "Perry Mason" story: neither, the Grand Master who intervened in the annual election of a Lodge nor, the Grand Master who entertained the charge, knew what really happened. Certainly, the trial commissioners who decided the cases did not know the facts.

Two years after the actual events, the trial commission, adduced the "facts" from witnesses testifying to conflicting versions of the same events and/or from the written pleadings.

The trial commission has the unpopular duty to guarantee the accused will be presumed innocent until the proctor proves, by a preponderance of the evidence, the accused committed a specific masonic offense.

This paper used an actual case to demonstrate the art of the law. Quotations are from a transcription of the stenographic notes made by a court reported at the trial, or from the formal written pleadings and exhibits.

The dates are omitted, although the sequence of events is the same as the actual events. The names are obviously fictitious. The Worshipful Master, who was the aggressor is named Jubala; and the Senior Warden who met chicanery with lawlessness is call Jubalo.

All Master Masons, including the Grand Masters promise and swear to support the Constitutions of the Grand Lodge of the State of New York, also all laws, rules and edicts of the same. Both Jubala and Jubalo also promised to support the bylaws, rules and regulations of Old Parochial Lodge, so far as the same came to their knowledge.

Old Parochial Lodge, was an old "white tie Lodge." It had been a very large Lodge (1100 Brothers) that owned a five -story building in the middle of the city. It was very proud of its heritage. In the anteroom there were framed pictures of the Past Masters who had been Mayor of the City.

Old Parochial Lodge conducted its affairs by local custom and usage. It even had its own "Hall of Fame." Like many Lodges that owned buildings it had difficulty accepting the fact that the building formerly a source of wealth was now a liability. And, an even more unacceptable fact that membership in Old Parochial Lodge was no longer a great social asset.

One Past District Deputy, when he was a Senior Warden, planning his year as Master, did not plan to appoint either Jubala or Jubalo line officers. The Past Masters of Old Parochial Lodge persuaded him to follow the custom and usage of Old Parochial Lodge that every officer every year progresses to a higher place or station.

The year Jubala was Master, the number of members had dwindled to 750. The stated average attendance on the annual return was 25. Old Parochial Lodge has not been destroyed. No one has successfully played the role of Jubalum. Several of the brethren auditioned for the part when they lost control of their passions and said:

"The Laws of God, the Laws of Man He may keep that will and can; Not I: let God and man decree Laws for themselves and not for me; And if my ways are not as theirs Let them mind their own affairs."

Many of the brethren of Old Parochial Lodge regarded Jubalo, his father, and his two brothers as shysters, and the friend as their dupe. One of the officers said: Jubalo "didn't support the Master as much as I thought he should. He did his job by coming in and left and that's all he was concerned about. As far as ritualistic work, he was great, he's real good, he's got parts in Scottish Rite that's impressive, but when it comes to Lodge visitation or other supporting work, there was no support."

On their side; Jubalo, his father, his two brothers, and his friend thought of themselves as superior masons. "They were damned sick and tired of being referred to as a group,"

The year Jubala was elected Master, there were some votes for Jubalo as the Master instead of Jubala. Jubala was the Senior Warden at the time and was expected to be the Master, and it turned out to be that way.

Jubala and Jubalo brought their family piques and quarrels into the Lodge. The piques and quarrels ripened into hard feelings. The hard feelings culminated on November 8th, when the Worshipful Master, Jubala replaced Jubalo's brother, as the Senior Deacon; Jubalo's friend, as the Tiler; and Jubalo's uncle, as the Marshal.

On November 15th, an extra First Degree was scheduled to allow one of three brothers to catch up with the other two. The Lodge room became charged with emotion when Jubalo's friend objected to the conferral of the extra First Degree.

A Past District Deputy Grand Master, attempting to reduce the tension, announced from the sidelines that the objection did not indicate the candidate would not be initiated. Jubalo's father said to the candidates' father: "I don't know what anyone would have against your son."

Wor. Jubala was not prepared to deal with the objection, so he called the Lodge from labor to refreshment. The Master and the officers went to the Secretary's Office to consult with the Past District Deputy. The Secretary accused the Past District Deputy who attempted to console the father of the candidate of a "conspiracy." The discussion between them was heated and their voices were raised.

The Secretary said the objection was part of a conspiracy to get even with the Master for removing three appointed officers the preceding meeting. Some thought: because Jubalo was not in a tux; and, was familiar with Masonic Law of objections there was a "conspiracy" between the members of the "group."

The afternoon of the degree, Jubalo had testified in federal court at 3:00 o'clock, in a matter important to his business, which had no relation to the Lodge. Jubalo had to drive 70 miles to confer the First Degree at 7:30. Instead of going home, he went to the Lodge, hoping to find a spare tux. None was available, that evening, so Jubalo occupied the station in business clothes.

The minutes do not reflect the violence in the Lodge room on November 15th. The minutes merely report: "The Worshipful Master, honoring the objection, announced the degree will be conferred next week."

On November 22nd, the tempest in the tea pot aspect of the affair became obvious when Jubalo initiated the third brother into Old Parochial Lodge.

The proctor charged: Jubalo's friend objected to the conferral of the degree because he wanted to get even with the Lodge officers.

If you were the trial commission would you find Jubalo's friend guilty of a masonic offense?

The trial commission did not find Jubalo's friend guilty because he exercised his Constitutional right to object to the conferral of the degree. The Worshipful Master was mandated to defer the initiation (Book of Constitution section 356). His reason is immaterial because not even the Grand Master may ask the reason for an objection.

An 1864 treatise on Masonic Jurisprudence by Past Grand Master John Simons said: It is more important that peace and harmony should be preserved in the Lodge, than it is that a candidate should be initiated.

The brethren didn't record all the sordid details of the Lodge's decline. To stimulate attendance Old Parochial Lodge held elections as light entertainment. All officers advanced—everyone knew who was going to be elected—so who cared how the election was conducted?

On December 20th, Jubala's wife drove him to Old Parochial Lodge. Jubala, fatally ill, was determined to preside at the annual election of officers. His choice for each of the elective offices was printed on the ballot distributed to each of the brethren: the Junior Warden for Master; the Senior Deacon appointed on November 8th, for Senior Warden; the Junior Deacon appointed on November 8th, for Junior Warden; a 40 year member of Old Parochial Lodge, a Past Master, incumbent Treasurer, for Treasurer; the incumbent Secretary finishing his 3rd term, a Past Master, for Secretary.

The incumbent Treasurer, a teller, as well as a candidate for Treasurer was frothing at the mouth when Jubalo opposed the nominations. Jubalo's slate was: Jubalo, Senior Warden for Worshipful Master; the Junior Warden for Senior Warden; Jubalo's brother for Junior Warden (he had served as Senior Deacon from January until November); Jubalo's father for Treasurer; the incumbent Secretary for Secretary.

> "There was a lot of confusion with the election. The Worshipful Master announced who had won, he did not announce the number of votes each candidate received."

One of the tellers in a sworn statement sent to the Grand Master said: Jubalo was elected Master; the Junior Warden was elected Senior Warden; and Junior Deacon was elected Junior Warden. The tellers went to Jubala, the Master, because the tellers thought the Senior Deacon should have been elected Junior Warden.

A second teller testified at the trial that Jubalo did nothing wrong at the election. The problem was that the tellers did not follow the law.

The tellers did not announce the results of the election; they deferred to the Master. Jubala announced: a majority of the ballots were cast for Jubalo; Jubalo was declared elected Worshipful Master. He also declared the Junior Warden was elected Senior Warden. The brother, who was appointed Junior Deacon on November 8th, received a majority of the ballots for Junior Warden.

The brother who was appointed Senior Deacon on November 8th received votes for Senior Warden and he also received the votes for Junior Warden.

The tellers thought he should not be out of the line, so they added the votes he received as Senior Warden to the votes he received as Junior Warden. Then, they referred the decision to Jubala, who had nominated him for Senior Warden. Wor. Jubala, fatally ill, declared all the officers, including the "improperly elected" Junior Warden, duly elected.

After the election, Jubalo, his brothers, and his friend went to see the ballots. The Worshipful Master handed the ballots to Jubalo and said the others had no business looking at the ballots.

The Secretary claimed Jabalo's father responded, "If I ever catch you outside the Lodge room, I'm just going to beat the hell out of you."

Jubalo's father contended he was not in the Secretary's office; he was in the hall where he said, "Once you leave the room, I hope you can live with your conscience." Upon the secretary's request, Jubalo's brothers and their friend left the secretary's office. Jubalo went through the ballots, and without saying anything, left the ballots on the desk and walked out.

The proctor charged: Jubalo's group threatened the life of the Worshipful Master.

The only evidence of any threat is the statement of the Secretary that Jubalo's father said: If I even meet you outside the Lodge, etc. The statement is controverted.

On December 21st, the day after Jubalo became Master-elect, he asked the Grand Master to intervene in the election of the Junior Warden of Old Parochial Lodge because the tellers had not correctly counted the ballots for Junior Warden. Even though the Master-Elect studied the Handbook of Masonic Law, he did not file written charges. He made a telephone call to the Grand Master.

The record does not state why the Grand Master declared the election of all officers of Old Parochial Lodge null and void.

The record does show the Grand Master, on the day of the District Investiture service, informed the Past District Deputy Grand Master, that Jubalo, the Master-Elect of Old Parochial Lodge was not to be invested with the Secrets of the Chair. How do you reconcile the Grand Master's action with Section 308 of the Constitution which says: "Previous to his installation the Master-Elect of the Lodge must be put in possession of the secrets of the chair."

The Past District Deputy Grand Master called the incumbent District Deputy Grand Master and informed him of the Grand Master's decision.

Jubalo, unaware of the Grand Master's decision, thinking he was the Master-Elect, went to the investiture service. Imagine his pain, upon being told at the investiture service, by the District Deputy that he could eat dinner, but he could not be invested with the secrets of the chair. The Grand Master had declared his election as Master of Old Parochial Lodge null and void.

On January 3, Jubalo presided at Old Parochial Lodge because Jubala was fatally ill. Again imagine being in the East while the Secretary reads the Grand Master's letter:

> "It is ORDERED that the election of officers, on December 20th, be declared null and void. Also, A DIRECTION by the Grand Master that the new election is to be held at the regular stated communication on January 17th, to be conducted by the District Deputy, Past District Deputy, Staff Officer and Past Grand Steward."

The testimony was sufficiently confusing that the trial commission did not fully comprehend the testimony of the brother, who was elected Senior Warden in the first election, and who was also elected Worshipful Master in the second election.

The most favorable inference the prosecution could make was: the witness did not feel or believe that on January 3rd the statement of Jubalo's friend that if Jubalo were not reelected Worshipful Master, candidates would not be raised the ensuing year. The testimony was controverted by both Jubalo and his friend.

The proctor charged: the night of the installation three of the accused said: "If Jubalo is not elected Worshipful Master, there would be no new members raised."

The trial commissioners held: There is not a scintilla of evidence that Jubalo and his friend made the threat to use the black cube without qualification.

Do you agree with the trial commissioners? If not, is it possible the decision is based in part upon the commissioners dissatisfaction with the prosecution?

The January 17, election results were:

The Junior Warden, Worshipful Master: 61-32-4. The Senior Deacon, Senior Warden The Junior Deacon, Junior Warden The incumbent Treasurer, Treasurer The incumbent Secretary, Secretary

After the election the new Master-Elect said: "Jubalo and his friend repeated the threat that he would not raise a candidate the year he was Master of Old Parochial Lodge."

The Grand Master did not investigate Jubalo's charge until March, after the second election had been held and the officers were subsequently installed. Jubala died the day after his candidates were installed.

The Grand Master requested his Staff Officer to obtain statements from the "other side." One of the six statements sent to the Grand Master was written by the brother, who was elected Senior Warden in the first election, and who was also elected Worshipful Master in the second election.

On the evening of January 3, which was to be our installation of officers... I was approached by (Jubalo's friend) who told me that when the new election was held if (Jubalo) was not elected as he had been in the previous election, that there would be no more members raised in the Lodge.

Of the six statements that were admitted into evidence at the trial, five of the deponents were present and testified. Their statements, including the above, were excluded by the best evidence rule. Their live testimony, subject to cross examination, was held to be better evidence than their written statements.

The sixth statement was excluded because it was based on hearsay evidence. That is evidence based upon what a brother said another brother told him what happened. A summons had been mailed to the sixth affiant at the address supplied by the secretary of the Lodge. It was returned undelivered by the post office. Therefore, the sixth affiant was not served and, may not have known of the trial. Of course, he did not testify.

The Grand Master personally visited Old Parochial Lodge after receiving the six statements. Jubalo and his faction questioned the Grand Master about his failure to punish the persons who conducted the election.

The Grand Master must be concerned with the welfare of the institution called the Grand Lodge of Free & Accepted Masons of the State of New York. When Grand Lodge is not in session he exercises the executive and judicial power of Grand Lodge. The Constitutions do not give the Grand Master legislative power.

The trial commission appointed by the Grand Master was charged to apply the law to one specific set of facts. The application of the law to the facts is an art—not as precise as the measurement of a plumbline, level or square.

An anecdote may illustrate the problem. Last week, a distraught brother came to the Worshipful Master of the Western Lodge of Research and requested a Masonic funeral for his dog Spot. The Master, taken aback explained that the Masonic funeral service is only for Masons and the Western Lodge of Research is for scholars; it certainly was not intended for animals. The distraught brother renewed his plea saying the dog Spot was dearly beloved and would be sorely missed. To perpetuate Spot's memory the brother wanted to establish a $10,000 memorial in the

Western Lodge of Research. Rt. Wor. Jackie Jensen said to the distraught brother: "Why didn't you tell me your dog Spot was a Masonic scholar?"

The Code of Procedure says the primary purpose of Masonic discipline is to preserve the Masonic Institution by the prosecution and punishment of an individual whose acts tend to injure a particular Lodge.

The common law guarantees each brother—particularly those with bad reputations—will not be found guilty unless the Regional Proctor overcomes the presumption of innocence by a preponderance of the evidence.

In my opinion, the trial commission was not concerned with broad matters of policy. It was limited to the issues raised by the complaint and the five answers to the complaint.

The Regional Proctor consumed the first two hours of the trial correcting the Proctor's Complaint to conform the specifications of the complaint to a date an objection was made; to the date a candidate was blackballed in Old Parochial Lodge; the identification of the accused; and that he did not have the written request of the Grand Master for any of the witnesses to discuss any blackball.

The Regional Proctor said he felt a credibility gap was created: by the necessity to correct the Proctor's Complaint; and the witnesses inability to recall dates—even when the minutes of the Lodge were available for reference.

The witnesses were ignorant of almost every fact required to sustain the burden of proof. The witnesses were not prepared. It was obvious the Regional Proctor had not "horse shedded" the witnesses. It was equally obvious that the brethren of Old Parochial Lodge considered the accused guilty of the charges.

This became a real problem because the Regional Proctor had the burden of proof—the burden of proving the acts occurred; the statements were made; and, that the five Masons conspired to damage Old Parochial Lodge. He also bore the burden of overcoming the legal presumption that the accused were innocent until proven guilty. The best witness for the prosecution said, "The problem at Old Parochial Lodge in my estimation came from a personal conflict between Jubala and Jubalo, who are related, and I am led to believe had some personal problems relating to the family which were somehow brought into the Lodge and created problems where neither would do anything to help the other."

In the subsequent trial, the statements sent to the Grand Master were marked Exhibits No.1–No.6 for identification. They were not admitted in evidence, and therefore, the statement in Exhibit No.3 that Jubalo and his friend said on two occasions, "If Jubalo is not elected Master in the second election, you will not raise anyone the year you are Master" could not be considered.

The affiant's testimony at the trial, although controverted by Jubalo and his friend, and not as definite as Exhibit No.3, could have been considered some evidence that at least two of the accused threatened to black ball candidates without regard to qualifications.

On March 6th, the Grand Master asked a former staff officer to meet with Jubalo about the charges against the officers who conducted the regularly scheduled election held on December 20th. Jubalo asked the Grand Master to continue with the charges.

On March 7, the Wor. Master requested Rt. Wor. James to be at Old Parochial as an observer, as there was a ballot coming up. Two of the five accused were not in the Lodge when the petition of the Master's son was rejected. One of Jubalo's brothers quit going to the Lodge because "it is kind of tough to swallow, being accused of certain things on certain days when you're not even there."

On April 17th, two weeks before the end of his term of office, the Grand Master came to the Lodge to address the brethren on the privilege and the obligation of the ballot.

Immediately after the Grand Master's address the petitions of five candidates were presented to the Lodge. The ballot was declared cloudy, before the Grand Master could leave the anteroom. The Grand Master was very upset and a most heated discussion took place in the anteroom between the Grand Master and the accused.

The accused had attended Lodge, that night specifically to discuss the "null and void election" and whether or not the Grand Master intended to punish the officers who had acted improperly. Jubalo wanted to pursue the charges that the tellers did not correctly report the election of the Junior Warden.

The Grand Master did not address their problem. He refused to punish the dead Jubala and the tellers in the election he had declare null and void. The Grand Master was more interested in stopping the black balling of candidates who petitioned Old Parochial Lodge.

The Proctor charged: Accused acting in concert violated Code of Procedure 5A in that they improperly used the black cube as set forth in the Matter of Babylon Lodge.

This is a very difficult charge to prove because there can be "no discussion upon the merits of a petition for initiation, passing, raising, or affiliation" (Section 356, Constitution). The only exception is if the Grand

Master, pursuant to Section 406, directs the brethren to testify in the proceeding for the violation of Section 354 of the Constitution.

The Grand Master did not make the requisite direction. Accordingly, there was no evidence as to how any of the accused "used the black cube."

In the Grand Lodge Proceedings of 1942 Matter of Babylon Lodge, No.793, held that, "The making of the statement followed by the rejection constituted some circumstantial evidence of the commission of the offense, from which a Trial Commission might properly conclude, "if it saw fit," that the offense had been committed (emphasis supplied).

Option No.5 of the Judge Advocate dated February 8,1967 Re: Fallsburgh Lodge No.1122, approves the holding of Babylon but disagrees with that the prosecution must show more than the making of the statement. The Judge Advocate concluded: "The making of the threat to reject candidates, regardless of their qualifications, justifies the prosecution of charges in accordance with the Code of Procedure for the commission of a Masonic offense."

The next Grand Master told his District Deputy to send a written summons to Jubalo, his father, his brothers, and his friend to attend a meeting with the District Officers. The meeting produced some hope of a reconciliation.

At the request of the second Grand Master, the District Deputy called a second private meeting. The tellers the accused wanted present were at the second meeting. The accused believed they were not notified of the second meeting because they were not welcome.

One year later, on April 11th, when the Junior Warden left town, the Old Parochial Lodge Officers asked Jubalo to assume the role of Junior Warden of Old Parochial for the remainder of the year.

The contention of the formerly illegally elected Junior Warden, now Worshipful Master, that Jubalo failed to respond within the prescribed time was controverted. Jubalo said, "I did see him in Consistory. I just assumed everything was okay. Maybe that was an error on my part. Maybe it wasn't."

Jubalo said, "They said they couldn't guarantee I would be elected Worshipful Master the next year. I said, that I could not guarantee that you'd have the support my family and I have given in the past."

A year and a half after the events, the next Grand Master asked that something be done. His staff officer, Rt. Wor. Alfred took that thought as a cue to charge the accused with misconduct. Rt. Wor. Alfred based his charge upon statements given to him through the Lodge. Jubalo's brother stated to Rt. Wor. Alfred that blackballing would continue until the offenders were thrown out of the Lodge.

On May 22nd the Grand Master entertained the complaint. At the same time the Grand Master appointed five Past Masters to hear and determine the charge to be prepared by the Grand Proctor.

On June 10th, the Grand Proctor charged in the complaint:

> "That you and each of you as members of Old Parochial Lodge did individually and in concert with each other in (the incorrect year), engage in an un-masonic conspiracy to destroy, hurt, injure and cause irreparable harm and damage to the welfare, prosperity and good health of said Old Parochial Lodge."

Each of the five accused denied the one charge.

At the trial on November 23rd, the Regional Proctor, amended the specifications previously signed by the Proctor and served upon each of the accused.

The five accused acted on their own behalf. There is no provision to appoint the five accused counsel.

> And how am I to face the odds
> Of man's bedevilment and God's?
> I, a stranger and afraid
> In a world I never made.
> They will be master, right or wrong:
> Though both are foolish, both are strong.

The five trial commissioners unanimously held that the said Jubalo, Jubalo's Father, Jubalo's Brothers and Jubalo's friend: are not guilty by reason of the failure of the complainant to offer a scintilla of admissible evidence to overcome the strong presumption of innocence inherent in Masonic Jurisprudence. In brief, the complainant did not sustain his burden of proof. The complainant's motion to amend the charge and specifications is granted. All other motions are denied.

Questions Raised by the Case

If you were the trial commission, would you have been disturbed by the provision of Section 318 of the Constitutions: "In case the offices of Master and Wardens becomes VACANT, the Grand Master... shall issue a dispensation to the DDGM directing the assembling of the Lodge, the holding of an election to fill the vacancies and the installation of the officers."

The trial commission could find no provision for the Grand Master to create the vacancies by declaring the election of Jubalo as Master of Old Parochial Lodge null and void.

Would you agree the only constitutional power given the Grand Master over subordinate Lodge elections is to grant a dispensation for an election to fill vacancies; and to grant a dispensation when a Lodge may have failed to elect its officers at the proper time?

Old Parochial Lodge has a Charter from the Grand Lodge of New York. Only the landmarks, control the inherent power of a warranted Lodge to elect and install its officers. In the election of its officers, Old Parochial Lodge is entirely uncontrolled, save by its own by laws and the usages of Masonry. The Grand Lodge cannot interfere with the choice by the brethren of persons to fill those offices.

Would you have found as a fact that Jubalo and his friend told the Master-Elect before and after the second election he would not raise a candidate the ensuing year?

If you found Jubalo and his friend made the statement, would you have found the statement sufficient to constitute a Masonic offense?

Do you understand the Roman Catholic Italian boy who introduced a Grand Chaplain to his Roman Catholic Italian mother, as our family Protestant Minister? His mother exclaimed: "What does your family need with a Protestant Minister?" The son replied "Mom, what if they're right?"

In Conclusion do you agree with the poet:

And since my soul we cannot fly
To Saturn nor to Mercury,
Keep we must, if keep we can,
These foreign laws of God and man.

Light on a Dark Subject

By RW Rev. Don C. Markham

{Presented March 29, 1990. Editor's note: The use and capitalization of various racial terms have been preserved and no special meaning is intended or should be construed outside of plain use of such words in context of history and language.}

The consideration of the relationship between Black Freemasonry and Mainline Freemasonry is of paramount importance in this day and age, because the future of the Fraternity is at stake. As we enter upon a new age, some of the old ideas of the relationship between these two entities must be carefully considered. This consideration must necessarily include the objections leveled against the Craft.

First, part of the objection to the fraternity among some religious groups is based upon the fact that these groups object to the "exclusion" of blacks from the fraternity. Second, because of such accusations of "racism" it becomes necessary to look at patterns of black membership in the fraternity. This must be considered in the light of the actual status of blacks in Masonry—both in the "regular" Grand Lodges and in the "African" Grand Lodges.

The question of 'exclusiveness' in regard to blacks and the fraternity was first brought into the anti-Masonic agitations by the evangelist, Charles G. Finney, in 1869. Finney had been an active abolitionist in the years prior to the Civil War. He had been among those religious leaders who were responsible for the translation of religious enthusiasm into social activism in various forms, abolitionism being one such form. In his capacity as a leader at Oberlin College in Ohio he had been responsible for the training of many young evangelists, a number of whom traveled extensively through the south in the immediately post-Civil War Period. [1] Therefore, it was only natural that Finney, in his attack upon the fraternity, should bring up this issue. Referring to the appearance of a statement made by the Grand Lodge of New York and published in the "American Freemason" under the editorship of Robert Morris, in Louisville, Kentucky in 1854, Finney quotes the article extensively in his work.

In essence, the statement adopted by the Grand Lodge of New York in 1854 was that it was not considered proper to initiate into the Lodges persons of the Negro race and that such exclusion was in accordance with Masonic law as well as the ancient charges and regulations. It gave as reasons the fact that it was well-nigh impossible to ascertain the fact of "free-born" in relationship to the Negro, inasmuch as many were yet slaves or had been born in slavery, and also made reference to the fact that "their not being as a race 'persons of good report,' or who can be 'well-recommended' as subjects for initiation." [2] The statement of the Grand Lodge also reflects the prejudicial attitudes of the times in which it was written, for it refers to certain "facts" about the Negro, such as, "depressed social condition," [3] "general want of intelligence," [4] "the impropriety of making them our equals in one place, when from their social condition and the circumstances which everywhere attach to them, we can not do so in others," [5] and "their general positive deficiency of natural endowments." [6]

The comments of Robert Morris, as editor, are of interest for they also reflect the prejudicial attitudes of the South at that time, and conclude with the statement that "the race ought not to amalgamate socially or physically." [7] The editorial comments are followed by the second portion of the article which makes the statement:

> That no person of the Negro race shall be examined or admitted as a visitor of any lodge of Masons under this jurisdiction, if made in an African lodge in North America. Because all such lodges are clandestine and without legal authority. [8]

Finney draws his own conclusion that this is Masonic "benevolence unmasked" [9] and that "a depressed social condition is a bar to admission to this benevolent society." [10] While his point is well-taken in regard to the statements quoted, nevertheless the statements and the interpretation of Finney belong to two vastly-different periods in the history of this Nation, even though they were made only fourteen years apart. In order to adequately understand the statements of Morris and the Grand Lodge of New York and the conclusions which were drawn by Finney, one must look at and consider the circumstances surrounding each.

The world of 1854, when the statements of Morris and the Grand Lodge of New York were made, and 1869, when Finney drew his conclusions, were vastly different. The middle years of the decade of the eighteen-fifties was that period in American history which was marked by sectional rivalry and great political and social tension. The Fugitive Slave Law was in effect. The Underground Railroad was in full operation. Westward expansion had brought into being great tensions—in fact, the passage of the Kansas-Nebraska Act in 1854 was largely responsible for splitting the Democratic Party. Nebraska, formed as a state under this act, "adopted a constitution excluding slavery." [11] Kansas, on the other hand, where the majority opposed slavery, became embroiled in a bitter, bloody conflict marked by civil strife and violence mainly over the issue of slavery. [12] As a historian put it, "perhaps the most significant result of the Kansas-Nebraska Act was the formation of the Republican Party." [13] Attracting anti-slavery Democrats, as well as Free Soilers, the new party had as its chief goal "preventing the extension of slavery to the territories." [14] The split between Northern and Southern Democrats over the entire issue of slavery was a prime factor in the success of the new party and also the Know-Nothing Party in the congressional campaigns of that year. [15] The relative success of the Know-Nothing Party in that period was indicative of a 'paranoia' similar to that which fostered the growth and success of the anti-Masonic movement just twenty years earlier. The growth and prosperity of the Know-Nothing movement caused Abraham Lincoln to write a denunciation of Know-Nothingism in 1855, and in this letter he stated:

> As a nation we began declaring that 'all men are created equal.' We now practically read it, 'All men are created equal except Negroes.' When the Know-Nothings obtain control it will read: "All men are created equal except Negroes, foreigners, and Catholics...[16]

The tensions over slavery were bad enough, but they also penetrated and permeated the whole of society at that time. Churches were splitting over the issue of slavery, and even in the South dissension over the whole issue caused persecution of anyone who dared disagree with the 'system.' Ministers and churches in the South "proved" the legitimacy of slavery on Biblical grounds. Proponents of slavery in the North rallied behind their Southern brethren in the Democratic Party and in some organizations. The fraternity, being a human organization, was subject to similar problems and, because of its landmark "prohibiting political or sectarian discussion within its lodge rooms" came out with the statement quoted by Finney. One must also remember that, at that time, New York City was well-known for its Southern sympathies and that the leaders of the fraternity were doubtless very strongly influenced by their relationships with the South. Slavery was legal at that time, was considered by many to be "morally right," and even the churches disagreed on the subject. To use, therefore, a pre-war document such as this one, was an unfair condemnation of the fraternity. By the time Finney made his statement, the war had been fought, the slaves freed, and the situation had changed drastically.

Another writer who brought up the question of the fraternity's racial "exclusiveness" was William J. Whalen, the noted Roman Catholic opponent of the fraternity. In 1961, he made reference to a situation which had taken place shortly before the turn of the century, stating:

When the Grand Lodge of Washington agreed to extend partial recognition to Negro Masons in that state, every Grand Lodge in the United States and Canada severed fraternal relations with the Washington Grand Lodge. Masonry's attitude toward Negro Americans exposed the Craft's shallow ideas of the brotherhood of man under the fatherhood of God. The lodges reinforce the pattern of racial segregation in this country, particularly in the South, where Masonry might have been a progressive force in this critical area. What is dismaying is that by 1961 not a single lodge in any of the 50 Grand Lodges, North or South, has had the courage to open its doors to Negroes. [17]

The situation with the Grand Lodge of Washington did, indeed, take place, but at a time when the idea of segregation was not considered as abhorrent as today. Granted, it was wrong and should not have taken place, but so are a number of situations both in the South and the North regarding segregation at that time.

Unfortunately it is relatively easy to find "horrible examples" when pursuing any issue, but one must consider them in the light of human feelings and opinions at the time that they occurred—not condemn them sixty years later when feelings had changed. In another place in his book, Whalen also makes the statement in reference to the "powerful Grand Lodges," "they could easily exercise a measure of control over the bigotry of the Southern jurisdiction just as they could lift the bars against Negro members if they wished." [18] Perhaps this could be done, but it would prove nothing. At least in the years since 1896 (the earliest copy at my immediate disposal) the constitution of the Grand Lodge of the State of New York has had no prohibition or even mention of the race of a petitioner. The ancient Landmarks of the order state:

That every candidate for the honors of Freemasonry must be a man, free born, of mature and discreet age, no eunuch, no woman, no immoral or scandalous man, but of good report, having no maim or defect in his body or mind that may render him incapable of learning and practicing the art. [19]

Thus there is no reference to the race or national origin of any petitioner for membership be considered in the same manner, by being referred to an investigating committee which reports back either favorably or unfavorably to the lodge before any ballot may be taken. The constitution also stipulates that no discussion of the merits of any petitioner may take place within the lodge rooms. [20] No individual or outside influence may exercise control over who an individual lodge receives as members. This, too, is the subject of one of the ancient Landmarks of the fraternity, and reads:

> That the right of a Lodge to judge for itself who shall be admitted to initiation or affiliation therein is inherent and indefeasible, not subject to dispensation or legislation of any kind or from any source whatever. [21]

Some Grand Lodges do have black members, some do not—this is a matter for the individual lodge to decide by means of the ballot. There are no restrictions against black members in the majority of the Grand Lodges, but it is up to the local lodge to admit members upon the ballot of the membership in that particular community and after the report of the investigating committee has been made. It cannot be legislated by anyone else.

Both the Grand Lodges of New York and New Jersey have a number of black members. Alpha Lodge No.1167, chartered under the laws of the Grand Lodge of New Jersey in 1872, was the first regular lodge to initiate any number of blacks as members, and gradually became a totally black lodge. Its rights and existence were challenged at first, but it remains a legally constituted and active lodge on the roster of its Grand Lodge. Allied Lodge No.1170, chartered under the Grand Lodge of New York, is an all black lodge and this year (1981) one of its members is serving as the District Deputy Grand Master for the District in which it is located. In addition, there are a number of lodges in many jurisdictions which have blacks as members. Unfortunately, the numbers are small, but they are slowly increasing. One of the problems in truly ascertaining the numbers of black members in individual lodges since the 1870's is that no record of the members of the lodges is kept by race, nor should it be.

When confronting the question of black membership in local lodges, one finds, once more, that easy answers delude the researcher because of the nature of the Masonic Institution. Being a voluntary association, with membership determined by the unanimous ballot of the lodge, there are some areas where blacks would not be admitted owing to the particular prejudices of individual members. Education and the gradual changing of the way in which people think will ultimately result in the elimination of prejudicial acts. This has been the case with many of the churches and it will be the case with the lodge in the course of time. At the present time there are relatively few black members of the lodges, but those who are currently members have done a great deal in helping to break down the bars of prejudice and open the way for others to be admitted.

In many of the foreign Grand Lodges, blacks have been members for many years and members of these Grand Lodges have been received as visitors in quite a number of American lodges. In England, France, and Germany there have been no racial barriers for some time, and as more and more inter-fraternal visitation takes place between these Grand Lodges and the Grand Lodges within the United States, the situation will improve. While the practices of individual lodges have not always upheld the full meaning of the principle of the brotherhood of man under the fatherhood of God, more and more members today are coming around to the acceptance of the black as a member. It will be a long, long time, however, before the provincialism and prejudice extant in some areas of the country is overcome.

Heretofore we have been considering the question of black members in the bodies of mainstream Freemasonry, but another area which must be considered in this study is that of the black Mason in the black lodges. Although there are a number of black Grand Lodges, the only one with any semblance of 'regularity' is the Prince Hall Grand Lodge. Prince Hall Freemasonry is an extremely vital force within the black community throughout the entire world. With its Grand Lodges in most states and many foreign countries, plus a large number of military lodges located on or near various military installations of U. S. Forces throughout the world, together with all the concordant and coordinate bodies which one finds in 'regular' Masonry, the Prince Hall fraternity has done much to elevate the character and influence of the fraternity among the black members of our society.

The issue of the 'regularity' of Prince Hall Freemasonry has been the subject of much controversy and discussion in recent years, and the issue is still unsettled as far as the majority of the fraternity is concerned. This paper is not the place to argue either for or against this, but rather to present the facts as they are. To do this, it becomes necessary to give the reader a few of the facts regarding the Prince Hall group.

In 1775, Prince Hall and fourteen other Negroes were admitted to the Masonic fraternity in Boston, Massachusetts, in a military lodge working under the auspices of the Grand Lodge of Ireland. [22] This military lodge was No.441 on the registry of the Grand Lodge of Ireland and was attached to the 38th Foot (Regiment) which was then stationed at Castle William in the Boston vicinity. The Master of the lodge at that time was Sergeant J. B. Batt of Major Andrew Bruce's Company of the 38th Foot. [23] In his history of this period, Wesley states:

> When the British regiments left Boston on March 17, 1771, a "Permet" was issued by John Batt for them to meet as a lodge, a traditional and established method used by new lodges, to meet, "walk on St. John's Day," "to bury their dead in manner and form." [24]

It was under this "permet" that the functions of the first Negro lodge in the United States began. Authorized to "meet as a lodge" and to engage in customary Masonic activity, "to walk on St. John's Day," and "to bury their dead in manner and form," this was a commonplace idea at that time in history. Wesley gives the date of the actual formation of "African Lodge No.1" as being July 3,1775, and it was doubtlessly done under this "permet." As a regular lodge it thus functioned until 1784 when application was made to the Grand Lodge of England for a Charter. [25] In the meantime, however, Prince Hall had requested and received from John Rowe, Provincial Grand Master of North America, a second "permet." [26] A "permet" in that time would be similar to a "dispensation" of today, and the next logical step was the securing of a Charter. Following the custom of the times, in order to secure such a Charter, one would have to approach one of the three Grand Lodges which operated in the colonies, these being the Grand Lodges of England, Ireland, or Scotland. Inasmuch as John Rowe, Provincial Grand Master of North America, who had issued their "permet" was authorized by the Grand Lodge of England, it was to this body that Prince Hall addressed his request for legality and authorization. On March 2, 1784, Prince Hall wrote a letter to William Moody, Master of Brotherly Love Lodge No.55 in London, requesting his assistance in obtaining the necessary document. [27] Informed of the fact that the Charter had been prepared and awaited the payment of necessary fees, Prince Hall wrote to the Grand Lodge office on June 30, 1784. Prepared and issued under the date of September 29, 1784, the charter was not delivered to Prince Hall and the lodge until April 29, 1787. [28]

Thus, "empowered to do regular Masonic work" African Lodge No.459 came into being and functioned for many years. In the course of time, acting as a "Mother Lodge," African Lodge was responsible for the founding of lodges of Negro Masons in Philadelphia in 1797 and later one in Providence, Rhode Island. [29]

In 1808, these three lodges formed the first Negro Grand Lodge which later adopted the name of its founding father and became the basis of all Prince Hall Grand Lodges in the world. Although criticized by opponents of Negro Masonry, the "regularity" of this is attested to by one of the most outspoken critics of the Negro Mason, Albert Pike, in a letter written by him to John Caldwell in 1875. (This letter is reprinted in full in the Appendix {found at the end of this article}).

From these beginnings, black Masonry in the United States developed side-by-side with the "regular" Grand Lodges composed almost totally of "Caucasians." Although considered by the "regular" Grand Lodges to be "clandestine" or "irregular," most of the argumentation in support of this is based upon arguments which are an attempt to understand the 18th, 19th and 20th Century term and customs. This cannot be done satisfactorily and be faithful to the facts of history. Indeed, one of the most common mistakes of any writer is the tendency and practice of judging the past by the terms of the present. History must be considered in the light of the times in which it took place. Pike, with all his prejudices as a Southerner, was eminently fair in his treatment of the "regularity" of black Masonry.

Like its "Caucasian" counterpart, Black Masonry has developed through the years as a primarily "middle-class phenomenon" and while it draws some from the upper class, the majority of its membership and strength is drawn from the middle class. As such, it has been the subject of two recent sociological studies, one by a Jew and the other by a black woman. In the opening lines of his work, Muraskin states "this is a study of the black middle class, analyzed through one of its oldest social institutions–Prince Hall Freemasonry." [30] Making mention of the fact that the liberal academic community holds the American middle class–both white and black–in contempt, Muraskin asserts the importance of the middle class in both society and history. [31] Indeed, the impact of fraternalism, itself, has been largely ignored in the studies of American society through the ages. Muraskin maintains that "the entire strata of blacks found in Freemasonry–which is representative of the greater black middle class–is ignored." [32] He also is of the opinion that the best way to see the black bourgeoisie is not to concentrate on individual gifted leaders or the small elite group at the top of society, but to do an in-depth study of an institution which involves the middle class, and has picked out Prince Hall Freemasonry for this purpose. He is also of the opinion that utilizing such a group for this purpose will present a more accurate picture of black society, for the spokesmen of Prince Hall Freemasonry are "men who are more in touch with the average black middle class man than are more prominent black leaders." [33] His feeling is that the fraternity has helped immeasurably in the building of community among the black population and that it has also helped to create ties "between the black middle class and its white counterpart," [34] and further, feels that these ties are ideological rather than institutional. [35]

The development of the Prince Hall fraternity has been a strength-giving and inspiring force to the black community. In it are to be found outstanding leaders, both lay and clerical, who have worked unceasingly to build both the institution and the community. The failure of many sociologists and historians to recognize the importance of fraternalism has not deterred Muraskin in his work. Maintaining the position that "Black Freemasonry has been and is a remarkably healthy institution," [36] Muraskin notes that its "greatest numerical growth" has been after and not before the turn of the century. Ignored by many sociologists and historians as being unimportant and uninfluential in modern times, the fact that Muraskin has taken an opposing view is interesting and worth consideration. His assessment of its value and importance in the life of the black community cannot be easily ignored.

Founded in Boston, the Prince Hall fraternity spread throughout many of the Northern States and even into those Southern States which had a large free black population in the years before the Civil War. Following the War, it continued to grow and expand as the Southern States were opened up to organization and social improvement. Muraskin notes that black Masonry was carried by leaders of the Reconstruction movement into the South and that it did so "hand in hand with the black church." [37] Citing as examples such people as Bishop J. W. Hood of the African Methodist Episcopal Zion Church in North Carolina [38] and Pastor Al Stanford of the African Methodist Episcopal Church in Georgia, [39] he shows the intimate connection which existed and still exists between the fraternity and the leaders of the black churches. In fact, Muraskin states that:

> The informal personal links between Masonry and the churches have been maintained not only by the clergymen who are adherents of the Order but by the even larger number of Masons who obtain important lay positions in the churches. It is primarily through noncleric Masons that the most formidable bonds between Masonry and organized religion have been forged. [40]

During the periods of great stress for mainstream or "Caucasian" Freemasonry, such as the anti-Masonic period, the black lodges were relatively uninfluenced and affected. They proceeded to grow slowly and steadily. Much of this may well have been due to the closer connection with the church than existed in mainstream Freemasonry, for much of the persecution of the Craft was inspired by the leadership, both lay and clerical of the extant churches.

The black churches and the black fraternity grew up together and in harmony. The leadership of both was the same throughout the formative years and so, in this intimate connection between the two, there is much less likelihood of polarization and a sense of competition which seems to hover over the mainstream community. Both lodge and church have been actively working in partnership for the good of the black community. Black-oriented organizations and self-help programs have utilized the talents of both and this has contributed to a cohesiveness within the community. Upon questioning one black Mason of high degree concerning the existence of problems or antipathy between the fraternity and the churches, the answer given was that there are no problems. Upon further questioning, it was determined that in his particular church affiliation there was, indeed, no problem. Such however, is not always the case. The Prince Hall fraternity probably draws the greater majority of its membership from those churches with whom no problem or contention exists, so there may, in fact, be no problem. However, some groups which oppose the fraternity among Caucasians would also oppose it among blacks.

One of the biggest problems for the black fraternity in its history has been the struggle for its primary existence and influence in the face of "clandestinism." The rise of other and rival black Grand Lodges has caused no end of grief for the Prince Hall group. With Prince Hall Freemasonry being not only the oldest but the only "regular" Freemasonry among the blacks, the rise of rival groups has threatened their existence in some areas and has led to much misunderstanding of the fraternity. Indeed, the Northern Jurisdiction of the Ancient Accepted Scottish Rite of Freemasonry, Prince Hall Affiliation, has attempted to help its membership combat this situation through the issuance and distribution of a book entitled, "The Prince Hall Counselor", which was an outgrowth of the work of a Commission on Clandestine Masonry which outlined its program and area of activities as follows:

> 1.) To spread among its own members a fair knowledge of the history and regularity of Prince Hall Masonry;
>
> 2.) To Familiarize all regular Masons with the character, purposes and tactics of clandestine Masonry;
>
> 3.) In general, to train Prince Hall bodies in the most effective methods of terminating the existence and spread of such Masonry;

4.) In particular, to outline basic procedures for successful litigation against spurious Masonic organizations. [41]

Called upon many times to "defend its honor" before the courts, the Prince Hall fraternity has been successful in establishing its own "regularity" when compared and contrasted with its opponents. Occasionally its efforts have been helped by the appearance of representatives of the "Caucasian" Grand Lodges to testify in its behalf. For the black Mason, this problem is very real and important and, because of these "competitors" in the community, the Prince Hall fraternity has had to literally fight for its existence.

Although the Prince Hall fraternity is still considered as "clandestine" by the "Caucasian" Grand Lodges, there has been a movement in existence for some years to remove this barrier between the two. The earliest and most notable of these actions was taken by the Grand Lodge of Washington in the latter part of the Nineteenth Century and early years of the Twentieth Century, largely under the leadership and inspiration of William H. Upton, a Past Grand Master of the Grand Lodge of Washington (Caucasian). In a report made to the Grand Lodge in 1899, entitled, "Light on a Dark Subject," Upton presented both the facts for and the arguments against the recognition of the Prince Hall fraternity. This report was later expanded into a book which is of inestimable value to anyone wishing to know the facts. [42] The Grand Lodge voted to recognize the legitimacy and regularity of the Prince Hall brethren, but in the face of tremendous pressure later rescinded the action.

A similar situation took place in the Grand Lodge of Massachusetts in 1947, when a Committee, appointed for the purpose of investigating Prince Hall Masonry, issued a report acknowledging the legitimacy of Prince Hall Masonry. In the motion made by the Chairman of that Committee the following statement appears:

> There exists in the United States a completely organized and functioning Masonic world of which many of us know little, although it descends directly from the Mother Grand Lodge of the world, that of England. [43]

The adoption of the Report of that Committee, in effect, acknowledged the legitimacy of Prince Hall Freemasonry. Unfortunately, however, a year later the action was rescinded as Massachusetts bowed to the pressure exerted upon it by other jurisdictions.

At various times throughout the last hundred years, the subject has been delegated to committees in many of the Grand Lodges and the reports of those committees would be interesting enough to create a book of their own. These investigative actions have not been without effect, however, for they show the fact that attempts are being made to resolve the situation of racial separation in the fraternity. This is illustrated by some of the statements which have been made as a part of the reports of such committees in relatively recent years.

At the Grand Lodge Session in 1977, The Grand Master of the Grand Lodge of Minnesota reported to his Grand Lodge on a meeting held with black leaders in his jurisdiction. In his report, he made reference to the subject as discussed as involving three primary topics and his words on that occasion are worthy of note, for he stated concerning those three topics:

> 1.) Recognition of Prince Hall Masonry as "legitimate." This question of the legitimacy of Prince Hall Masonry appears to me to fall in a grey area. There is no question but that African Lodge No 459 was chartered by the Grand Lodge of England. Some subsequent lineage may have been broken, or was indirect or questionable, because of the practices of the time, but then, the history of recognized Masonry is frequently garbled, too, during that period of time.
> 2.) Problems both organizations would face is getting their members and other Grand Jurisdictions to accept such recognition. Racial prejudice is a two-way street.
> 3.) There would be the problem of having two sovereign Grand Jurisdictions in the same area. The Prince Hall group does not want to "integrate" into our organization and thereby lose its identity. They want "separate but equal" status, acceptance, and visitation rights, but not amalgamation. We wish to maintain our territorial sovereignty, together with the present good relations which we now enjoy with other recognized Masonic Jurisdictions. [44]

The admission by the Grand Master of Minnesota of the fact of the "legitimacy" of the black group's history and the recognition of the problems which both groups faced in resolving the issue, are a beginning of understanding, and in the results of the meeting, the statement appears, "All agreed that this meeting represented the 'first step in a journey of a thousand miles.'" [45] Beginning in 1975 and continuing to the present time, the question of relationships with the black Masons has been a part of the proceedings of each Session of the Grand Lodge of Wisconsin. Reporting in 1975, the Committee to Study Non-recognized Grand Lodges, prefaced its report with a very positive statement relative to the relationship of blacks to mainstream Freemasonry in Wisconsin. This preface was worded as follows:

Our committee understood that we were not required to devote our energies to the issue of blacks as members of Masonic Lodges operating under the jurisdiction of the Grand Lodge of Wisconsin. This is because the Grand Lodge of Wisconsin makes no distinction between men because of the color of the skin, or of their race, or of their creed. Furthermore it would be contrary to the teachings and principles of Freemasonry if the petition of any worthy black applicant made to a constituent lodge of this Grand Lodge were to be denied because of his color or race. [46]

The report of the committee followed, presenting a very accurate synopsis of the history of Prince Hall Freemasonry. No immediate action was taken, but a resolution for the recognition of Prince Hall Freemasonry as legitimate was presented for consideration at the next Grand Lodge Session. In 1976, the group which had presented the resolution withdrew it before a vote could be taken. Since that time, further efforts have been made in the Grand Lodge of Wisconsin towards the resolution of the situation regarding Prince Hall Freemasonry.

At the 1980 session, the Grand Master of the Grand Lodge of Wisconsin presented a rather extensive report relative to the conduct of talks between representatives of Prince Hall and the Grand Lodge of Wisconsin and outlined what progress had been made thus far. He stated that a series of articles concerning the history of Prince Hall Masonry had been printed in the Grand Lodge magazine during the previous year, and that on September 11, 1979, he sent a letter to the Grand Master of Prince Hall Masons in Wisconsin "offering to each constituent lodge in good standing in the Prince Hall Grand Lodge of Wisconsin the opportunity to become a chartered lodge under the Grand Lodge, F. & A.M. of Wisconsin." [47] He also reported that, on September 19, 1979, the Grand Master of the M. W. Prince Hall Grand Lodge of Wisconsin had replied as follows:

> With the understanding that we are in agreement that an appropriately creative arrangement (not to be confused with something inane and simplistic like our complex organization being annexed by yours) is necessary for an indeterminate period of time, pleased be advised that I am prepared to recommend that the M. W. Prince Hall Grand Lodge accept your offer to merge itself with the Grand Lodge, F. & A.M. of Wisconsin. Discussions will be necessary pursuant to working out the details.

There are a number of issues that will need to be examined and attendant problems to be worked out. However, the obstacles are by no means insurmountable and my view is that if we are truly serious about ending the long night of racism that has divided Black and White Masons in

America and in Wisconsin—it can be done in a manner that would be acceptable to Prince Hall Masons as well as the members of your Craft.

Let us meet as soon as practicable and 'reason together' on these great issues. The discussion meetings have been held on a regular basis and the work of ironing out details is progressing in this jurisdiction.

At the 1980 session of the Grand Lodge of Connecticut, the Grand Master reported to the membership relative to a series of informational meetings held between representatives of the Prince Hall Grand Lodge and Grand Lodge, A.F.& A.M. of Connecticut. These informational meetings which originally rejected the policies and attitudes of New Jersey and New York have reversed their positions and entered into fraternal relationships once more, with few exceptions.

The Prince Hall organization is intensely proud of their history and accomplishments and does not seek to lose its "identity" by being assimilated into mainstream Freemasonry. They desire instead acknowledgment as "legitimate" Masons and acceptance as brothers. Loretta Williams in her study on "Black Freemasonry and Middle-Class Realities" refers to the existence of the two organizations, black and white Masons, as being evidence of the process of "pillarization" in our society. The rise of such organizations and institutions, while necessitated by the "caste" system at the time of their founding, has been a focus of development and identity in both communities. The letting down of the bars which have hitherto separated the two has not resulted in the abandonment of the "pillarized" institution, but rather pride has taken over and the institutions continue to exist and prosper as a testimony to their value and importance in society. She feels that "American society can be analyzed in terms of a pillarization process along racial lines having major impact upon all social division." [51] In her discussion of the nature of such "pillarized institutions, she also asks a pertinent question, "Given the continued politicized use of ethnicity, and the increasing self-consciousness of blacks in the past two decades, will pillarized institutions comes to exercise an increasing impact on the continuous structure of interaction in our society? [52] She also makes the statement that "Pillarization implies choice," [53] and that the two Masonic institutions can exist and work side-by-side with each serving the community of those who "choose" to join its ranks. [54]

There is no "easy answer" to the relationship between the Prince Hall organization and mainstream Freemasonry. Any idea of assimilation would effectually destroy the glorious heritage and history of the Prince Hall organization, a history that has been inextricably involved with the religious, social, and political life of the black community in America. Harry Davis, one of the leading historians of Prince Hall Freemasonry, made the suggestion a number of years ago, that:

> Probably the only practical or feasible action at this time is to borrow from the usages of diplomacy and establish and *entente cordiale* between white and colored Masons. This implies mutual respect and consideration between both groups and will not run counter to prejudices or dogmas which may exist in the white Fraternity. In fact, such a status exists today informally in many jurisdictions; it can be accelerated by the conduct of individual Masons. Such a status involves only fraternal cordiality, sympathetic understanding, and tacit recognition of the historic legitimacy of the Prince Hall sodality. It would tend to make American Masonry consistent and would clarify the position of colored Masons in the eyes of puzzled fraters outside of America. [55]

This, then, may be the answer to the problem and bring about a long-needed and awaited truth to the entire idea of fraternalism, wherein all men may truly be recognized as brothers under the fatherhood of God.

While a "separate but equal" status may be abhorrent to some, the rise of Prince Hall Freemasonry is a part of the growing mass of material on black history, and to remove its influence from the black community would be to weaken the cause of brotherhood. Joseph Walkes, Jr., author of a recent history of Prince Hall Freemasonry, closes his book with this statement:

> Whatever is in store for the Masonic fraternity in America in the future and for those who will have to pass judgment on it, the role of the Prince Hall Freemason must be considered as one of the most glorious chapters in the pages of American history. [56]

The idea of the *entente cordiales* leaves both organizations with their identify and integrity intact and yet allows for brotherhood to be practiced in truth and honesty. Further, in recent years, the development of a black nationalistic pride has resulted in the formation of a new organization for research and study within the confines of the Prince Hall organization. Under the leadership of Joseph Walkes, Jr., the Phylaxis Society was born and is growing among the members of the Prince Hall fraternity. Its founder, himself an author, has made a significant contribution to the body of Masonic knowledge with the appearance of his book, entitled, "Black Square and Compass: 200 Years of Prince Hall Freemasonry." Through encouraging historical study and research, the glaring errors of the past may be overcome and the whole fraternity, white and black, will benefit. To assimilate the Prince Hall fraternity into the mass of Freemasonry in America, would be to destroy and annihilate the history of the American black in a particularly important segment of our society. To preserve black identify in Freemasonry, while recognizing social equality within the Craft, will further the cause of brotherhood and understanding.

In effecting this, several events have taken place in the recent past. In November of 1989, the first of what is hoped to be many "Fellowship" Dinners was held in Western New York between members of the Grand Lodge of New York and the Prince Hall Grand Lodge. Both Grand Masters were present on this occasion together with a large number of brethren and ladies from both groups. The beginnings of a bridge of understanding and fellowship took place and this will grow and increase in years to come.

Also, in recent months two Grand Lodges have voted to recognize the Prince Hall Grand Lodges and to allow intervisitation–these being the Grand Lodge of Connecticut and Nebraska. Hopefully, many more will take such action in the future–thus proving the universality of brotherhood and fraternity. So mote it be!

Citations

[1] Whitney R. Cross. *The Burned-over District*. (Ithaca, NY: Cornell University Press 1950) p. 156

[2] Charles G. Finney. *The Character, Claims, and Practical Workings of Freemasonry*. (Cincinnati, Ohio: Western Tract and Book Society 1869) pp. 187-188 passim

[3] Ibid., p. 187

[4] Ibid.

[5] Ibid., p. 188

[6] Ibid.

[7] Ibid., p. 189

[8] Ibid.

[9] Ibid.

[10] Ibid.

[11] Lorman Ratner. *Dialogue In American History*. (New York: Holt, Rinehart and Winston 1972) p.104

[12] Ibid.

[13] Ibid.

[14] Ibid.

[15] Ibid.

[16] Gustavus Myers. *History of Bigotry in the United States*. (NY: Random House 1943) p. 202

[17] William J. Whalen. *Christianity and American Freemasonry.* (Milwaukee, WI: Bruce Publishing Co. 1961) pp. 10-11

[18] Ibid., p. 99

[19] *Book of Constitutions and Code of Procedure of the Grand Lodge of Free and Accepted Masons of the State of New York.* (NY: J. J. Little 1896) p. 90

[20] Ibid., p. 47

[21] Ibid., p. 90

[22] Harold Van Buren Voorhis. *Negro Masonry in the United States.* (New York: Henry Emmerson 1940) p. 10

[23] Voorhis. Op.Cit. p. 10

[24] Charles H. Wesley. *Prince Hall Life and Legacy.* (Washington, DC: United Supreme Council, Southern Jurisdiction, Prince Hall Affiliation 1977) p. 35

[25] Ibid.

[26] Ibid.

[27] Ibid.

[28] Ibid.

[29] William H. Upton. *Negro Masonry.* (Reprint of the ed. Published by the MW Prince Hall Grand Lodge of Mass., Cambridge 1902) (NY: AMS Press Inc. 1975) p. 107

[30] William Alan Muraskin. *Middle-class Blacks in a White Society: Prince Hall Freemasonry in America.* Berkeley, CA: University of California Press 1975) p. 1

[31] Ibid., pp. 1-2 passim

[32] Ibid., p. 7

[33] Ibid.

[34] Ibid., p. 27

[35] Ibid.

[36] Ibid., p. 29

[37] Ibid., p. 38

[38] Ibid.

[39] Ibid., pp. 38-39

[40] Ibid., p. 163

[41] George W, Crawford. *The Prince Hall Counselor.* (n.p.: Prepared and published under the auspices of the Prince Hall Grand Masters' Conference) p. x.

[42] William H. Upton. *Negro Masonry.*

[43] Grand Lodge of Massachusetts. *Negro Freemasonry: A consideration*

of the Subject of Negro Freemasonry by the MW Grand Lodge of Masons in Massachusetts at its Quarterly Communication on March 12, 1947. p. 9

44] Earl K. Dille, ed. *The Masonic Review of Bruce H. Hunt.* (n.p.: Missouri Lodge of Research 1977) Vol. 33, p. 176

[45] Ibid.

[46] Ibid., p. 170

[47] Bruce H. Hunt. A *Masonic Review.* (Springfield, MO: Grand Lodge of Missouri 1981) p. 78c {missing notation in text}

[48] Ibid. {missing notation in text}

[49] Ibid., p. 77c {missing notation in text}

[50] "*The Light.*" (Official Publication of the MW Prince Hall Grand Lodge of F. & A.M. of Pennsylvania–Vol. XXXI, No.1, Spring 1981) pp. 6-7 {missing notation in text}

[51] Loretta J. Williams *Black Freemasonry and Middle-Class Realities.* (Columbia, Missouri: University of Missouri Press 1980) p. 8

[52] Ibid., pp. 8-9

[53] Ibid., p. 131

[54] Ibid., p. 132

[55] Harry E. Davis. A *History of Freemasonry Among Negroes in America.* (n.p.: United Supreme Council, Ancient & Accepted Scottish Rite of Freemasonry, Northern Jurisdiction, USA (Prince Hall Affiliation) Inc, 1979) p.249

[56] Joseph A. Walkes, Jr.. *Black Square and Compass: 200 Years of Prince Hall Freemasonry.* (Richmond, VA: Macoy Publishing and Masonic Supply Company rev. ed. 1981) p. 166

Appendix–Views of Albert Pike

Views of General Albert Pike, Sovereign Grand Commander, Ancient and Accepted Scottish Rite. Alexandria, Virginia, 13 September 1975

My Dear Friend and Brother –

I can see as plainly as you that the Negro question is going to make trouble. There are plenty of regular Negro Masons and Negro Lodges in South America and the West Indies, and our folks only stave off the question by saying that Negro Masons here are clandestine. Prince Hall Lodge was as regular a Lodge as any lodge created by competent authority, and had a perfect right (as other lodges in Europe did) to establish other lodges, making itself a mother Lodge. That's the way the Berlin lodges, Three Globes and Royal York, became Grand Lodges.

The Grand Orient of Haiti is as regular as any other. So is the Grand Orient of the Dominican Republic, which, I dare say, has Negroes in it and Negro Lodges under it.

Again, if the Negro Lodges are not regular, they can easily get regularized. If our Grand Lodges won't recognize Negro Lodges, they have the right to go elsewhere. The Grand Lodge can't say to eight or more Masons, black or white, we will not give you a Charter because you are Negroes, or because you wish to work the Scottish Rite, and you shall not go elsewhere to get one. That latter part is bosh.

Hamburg recognized the Grand Lodges. Yes, and so the German Grand Lodge Confederation is going to do, and so will the Grand Orient of France before Long.

{This was written before the Grand Orient had dispensed with the requirement of a belief in God.–William H. Upton}

Of course, if Negrophily continues to be the religion established by law of your States, there will be before long somewhere a beginning of recognition of Negro Lodges. Then the Royal Arch and Templar bodies of Negroes must be taken in, and Masonry go down to their level. Will your plan work? I think not. I think there is no middle ground between rigid exclusion of Negroes or recognition and affiliation with the whole mass.

If they are not Masons, how do we protect them as such or at all? If they are Masons, how to deny them affiliation or have two supreme powers in one jurisdiction.

I am not inclined to meddle in the matter. I took my obligations to white men, not to Negroes. When I have to accept Negroes as brothers or leave Masonry, I shall leave it.

I am interested to keep the Ancient and Accepted Rite uncontaminated, in our country at least, by the leprosy of Negro association. Our Supreme Council can defend its jurisdiction, and is the lawmaker. There can not be a lawful body of the Rite in our jurisdiction unless it is created by us.

I am not so sure but that, what with immensity of numbers, want of a purpose worth laboring for, general indifference to obligations, pitiful charity and large expenses, fuss, feathers, and fandango, big temples and large debts. Masonry is become a great helpless, inert mass that will some day, before long, topple over, and go under. If you wish it should, I think you can hasten the catastrophe by urging a protectorate of the Negroes. Better let the thing drift. *Apres nous le deluge.*

Truly yours, Albert Pike

Illustrious Comp. John D. Caldwell

{From William H. Upton, *Negro Masonry*, pp. 214-215.}

Mordecai Manuel Noah: Was He a Freemason?

By Bro. Melvin H. Levy
{Presentation delivered September 29, 1986}

Worshipful Master, Brethren and Guests:

This evening, I invite you to join with me in the investigation of whether Mordecai Manuel Noah was or was not a Freemason.

Let us begin with a quick review of his life. He was born on July 19, 1785, in Philadelphia, Pennsylvania, then the capital of the United States, several years after the War for Independence. His life-span covered a critical period in United States history, of sixty-six years.

His father, Manuel Mordecai Noah (circa 1755–1822) was a bankrupt itinerant merchant. After being left an orphan, at an early age, he was raised by his maternal grandfather, Jonas Phillips.

While serving an apprenticeship as a gilder and carver, he managed to attend school for a few hours each day. Being of a studious disposition, he succeeded in educating himself in all manners of learning and became an exceedingly clever writer.

He became a clerk in the United States Treasury, through the assistance of Robert Morris (1734–1806).

He became a Major in the New York Militia.

He began his political career in Philadelphia, in 1808, when he, along with other "Democratic Young Men," supported the Republican candidate James Madison, for President.

A year later, he went to Charleston, where he edited the "City Gazette."

As a "War Hawk," he strongly supported the War of 1812.

In 1813, he was appointed a consul at Tunis, but was recalled two years later, after he was accused of misappropriation of funds, though the charges were later dropped.

On his return to the United States he established himself permanently in New York with the help of an uncle, Naphtali Phillips, publisher of "The National Advocate," which ardently supported the Democratic Party in New York County.

He became the editor of this newspaper in 1817, giving him access to the Tammany Society.

He was appointed High Sheriff in 1822, and two years later was elected Grand Sachem of Tammany.

He later filled the important position of Surveyor of the Port of New York.

When his uncle sold "The National Advocate" in 1824, Noah became the Publisher of "The New York National Advocate."

He broke with Tammany over its opposition to DeWitt Clinton, then Commissioner of Canals, and in 1825 supported Clinton for Governor.

Noah continued to oppose Tammany in the paper he established, "The New York Enquirer," which he published from 1825 to 1829.

He was critical of Andrew Jackson, particularly of his attack on the United States Bank.

He associated himself with the newly-created Whig Party in 1834, and as the publisher and editor of "The Evening Star," a Whig paper, demonstrating anti-immigrant and anti-Catholic biases.

When the Native American Party of 1835 to 1836, the forerunner of the Know-Nothing Party, was created, he was one of its chief supporters.

He also supported the Texas revolt of 1836 against Mexico, and angrily attacked the abolitionist cause.

In 1841, he became an Associate Judge of the New York Court of Sessions.

He was a prolific playwright; many of his plays reflected his patriotic fervor.

Noah's interest in Jewish affairs drew him into activities on behalf of the congregations of Mikvel Israel in Philadelphia, and Sheerith Israel, in New York.

Long taken by the idea of Jewish territorial restoration, Noah was the first to advocate the establishment of a Jewish agricultural settlement.

In 1825, he helped purchase a tract of land on Grand Island, in the Niagara River, near Buffalo, New York, which he named "Ararat," and envisioned as a Jewish colony.

Though the proposal elicited much discussion, the attempt was not a success, and Noah's pretensions as ruler were ridiculed.

After the failure of the Ararat experience, he turned more strongly to the idea of Palestine as a national home for the Jews.

He aided in the establishment of a Jewish College in America.

As the best-known American Jew of his time, Noah delivered in 1840 the principal address at a meeting at B'nai Jeshurum, in New York, protesting the Damascus Affair.

He died in New York City on March 22, 1851.

As you can tell, he had a very active and full life.

Now let us take a closer look at certain parts of his life, in order to see how some well-known Masons may have had an influence on him.

In 1740, the threat of the Spanish coming into St. Augustine from Florida was a real one; the Portuguese Jews were frightened, for the Inquisition was still a reality.

It is true that Jews and Marranos managed to live in or do business with Catholic Mexico, Venezuela, and Cuba, but Jews who had just risked everything to escape from the Portuguese Inquisition had no desire to expose themselves to the very uncertain mercies of Spanish captors.

Among those who fled was Dr. Nunes.

Seventy-eight years later his great-great-great Grandson, Mordecai Manuel Noah, wrote of a member of his family, a grand aunt, who died in this country, that she carried with her to the grave the marks of the cords with which she had been bound to the torture rack.

This family tradition should not be cavalierly dismissed as a typical Noah romancing. As late as the 1770's, while in St. Eustatia, Janet Schaw, a "Lady of Quality," met a victim of the Inquisition so disfigured by torture, that he barely resembled a human being.

Moses Nunez (Menes), the son of Dr. Nunez, was a customs office agent and was on the watch for smuggling. He was certainly no favorite of the colonial merchants, but he was no out-and-out loyalist. In 1775, he took the "Oath" on the New Testament, the "Holy Evangelic of Almighty God."

During the War he served as an Indian agent for the Georgia Revolutionary Forces and when the Whigs had the upper hand, in 1782, he was not detained as a Tory. He was a real Pioneer, who had come into Georgia shortly after Oglethorpe, in July 1733. In the course of the years, he became a man of some wealth, owning property, lands, notes collectable, and slaves. Oglethorpe and Nunez belonged to the same Masonic Lodge, and when the later died, David Montaigut, a gentile friend, who once had been the Speaker of the House of Assembly, preached the funeral sermon.

The first wife of Nunez (her maiden-name was Abrahams) was Jewish. His second "wife" was a mulatto. By his first wife, he had one son and by the second, three sons and one daughter. Nunez made no distinction in his will between his firstborn and the other children, but to protect the quadroons, he emancipated them formally in his will. He also willed to his second wife several of his remaining slaves.

During his lifetime he also saw to it that all his children were given some schooling to judge from the fact that one of them, who qualified as an executor, wrote a good hand.

We know of two sisters of Moses: Esther, a native Georgian, had married a DeLyon; and Zipporah, a young lady, nineteen years of age when she arrived from abroad with her father.

Zipporah had been born in Portugal, a Catholic, and she grew up in this land to marry a rabbi, Mr. Machado, the Hazzan of Sherith Israel. His contemporaries agreed that Zipporah Machado was an unusual woman, charming, cultured and a mistress of six languages. Her charity, which she bestowed as her means permitted, was "unbiased by national or sectarian prejudices."

She was the mother-in-law of a Revolutionary veteran Jonas Phillips, and the great-grandmother of a Commander in the United States Navy Uriah P. Levy, and of a Grand Sachem of Tammany Hall, Mordecai Manuel Noah, all Jews.

Mordecai Manual Noah was the eldest son of Manuel Morducai Noah, of Charleston, South Carolina, a Patriot of the Revolution, and Zipporah Phillips Noah, the daughter of Robert Phillips, of Philadelphia, one of the most prominent patriots of the Revolutionary Period. His father had supported the Revolution with both money and arms. He served in General Washington's army, and a tradition in the Noah family persists to the effect that our first President was a guest at the wedding of Mordecai's parents and signed the wedding document.

In the six decades of the antebellum period, the Jewish experience in America produced many colorful characters. Already their lifestyles resembled those of the Twentieth-Century Jews more than those of the Eighteenth Century.

When Noah was but a child of less than six and a half, his mother died, on November 18, 1792, in Charleston, South Carolina, where she was buried. His father seems to have been stricken with melancholia and, for a long time, to have disappeared. Many years later Noah, while traveling in France, came upon his father. It is believed that a certain amount of Moses' eccentricity may have been derived from the psychology of his father. His dominant qualities seem to have been inherited from his mother's side, which came from the strain of the remarkable Phillips family.

Noah was the son, not of his parents, neither of whom he knew as a child, but of his maternal grandfather, from whom he learned those Franklinian virtues that were to guide him for the rest of his life. In Jonah Phillips, too, was the living source, by example and in the precept of that patriotism for Israel and for America which was to be the dual motif of Noah's career. When receiving his education, his classmates included Stephen Decatur and his brother John, of whom the former subsequently attained eminent distinction for his services to his country in the American Navy.

When young Mordecai, in his determination not to be a burden upon the Phillips household, apprenticed himself until his twenty-first year as a gilder and carver, is not known precisely. That he did, however, we know from his own writings. What time he could rescue from his prentice days, he spent in the Old Franklin Library, and at the Philadelphia theater and with a group of youngsters who yielded themselves gleefully up to amateur theatricals.

In the Library, which was a rendezvous for the political figures of the day, Noah, silently watching as he read, got to know men as well as books. It was here that his earnest studiousness attracted the attention of the officials, and of the gentlemen who foregathered to debate the destinies of a nation. It was here that he was discovered by Robert Morris, who rescued him from his indentures. Morris found his protégée a position as clerk in the office of the only auditor that the United States Treasury of that day could boast.

Noah, as a youngster, was symptomatically drawn to the theater. Drama fascinated him. He read it, followed it, studied it. Shakespeare was a second Bible. The circumstances of his life had been leading him, from the first, toward a psychology of self-dramatization. When, therefore, the necessity of forging a career presented itself, it was an easy transition from strutting upon the scene to the posturing of the politician and the orator. Patriotism, too, was ingrained in him; he was equally sure, then, once he had tried his hand upon the adaptations of foreign plays current in his day, to embark upon a very definite theatrical Americanism.

As playwrights, Jews began to contribute to the American stage in the early Nineteenth Century. Isaac Harby and Mordecai Manuel Noah were prominent among them. Both men wrote conventional melodramas, conspicuously devoid of Jewish subject matter, despite the active involvement of Noah and Harby in Jewish community life. Perhaps they felt that Jewish life was too insubstantial to provide the working basis for a dramatic theme; or perhaps they wished to vie with their contemporaries on more universal ground. Curiously, during the Eighteenth Century, it was only in the writings of non-Jews that Jewish characters appeared.

From boyhood on he was a constant attendant at the Chestnut Street Theater. Early in his life he evinced an enthusiasm for the theater, which was destined to find expression, not only in the authorship of successful stage plays, but in other aspects of his dramatic and varied career.

When a boy, he was a member of a thespian company, he performed the duties of cutting the plays, substituting new passages, casting parts, and writing couplets at the exits. The plays which he wrote were:

- The Fortress of Sorrento
- The Grecian Captive
- The Grand Canal
- Marion, or The Hero of Lake George
- O Yes, or The New Constitution
- She Would be a Soldier
- The Siege of Tripoli
- Paul and Alexis
- Yesef Caramatti

Eleven were produced with great success. Four or five years after he had settled himself in Harrisburg he went to Charleston, South Carolina, where he studied law, at the same time editing the "Charleston City Gazette." Here he had his first experience in the field of journalism, in which he later became a potent leader.

He was recognized as the best "paragrapher" of his day. Many of his writings were of a political nature. From his contributions to various periodicals, and the character and variety of his writings, it is evident that he was one of the shining literary lights of the period. He was the friend of George P. Morris and other unremembered literati of this period. His literary activity won for him an important place in American letters. His writings were tempered with a dignified kindliness and thoughtfulness, indicative of an amiable disposition and good breeding.

During the War of 1812, he advocated War in the columns of his paper, writing many fiery articles over the pen name of "Muley Molak," and in so doing incurred the enmity of the Pacifists. When it was discovered that he was the author of the above articles, he was challenged to duels, in one of which he killed his challenger.

The American generation of the 1820's through the 1840's grew up in freedom and some entered the Arts, the professions and public service, a few with modest success.

Nalphtali Phillips published the semiweekly newspaper "The National Advocate," with Mordecai Manuel Noah as editor. He edited a number of newspapers and attained considerable political influence. His editorials and short articles were so stimulating and enjoyable that they became very popular.

As a writer of essays, he was gifted with a lively style, which abounded in a common sense, calculated appealing to that vast misunderstood class, too frequently described as "average readers." In a collection of his newspaper essays, published in 1845, entitled, "Gleanings From A Gathered Harvest," these characters are markedly displayed. These deal with the large and petty vices of that period, common, indeed, in all latter-day periods of human history, and might well be called "Lessons in Prejudice, Economy and Industry."

At twenty-four he became an editor of a newspaper in Charleston and won a place among the "Young War Hawks," as those who advocated hostilities against England were called. Most important, they did not see eye to eye with the Irish on the view of slavery. When Political leaders like Mordecai Noah gave vent to anti-Irish sentiment, they were no doubt echoing what many Jews had come to feel.

He was a man of pronounced opinion and forceful character, who apparently delighted in controversy. The outspoken political loyalties professed by men like Noah and Belmont were not characteristic of American Jewry.

In contrast to the Federalist Party, local branches of Jeffersonian Persuasion, such as New York City's Tammany, were accessible to Jews. Jews like Mordecai Meyers, Noah Jackson, Mordecai Noah, and Emanuel Hart later assumed leadership roles in it.

Mordecai Noah, the grandest Sachem of them all, edited several newspapers for the Democratic Party, including the important "National Advocate." In turn the Federalists had little to show, but an unconcealed anti-Semitism, which led them to refer to the opposition as "Shylocks," and to label Democratic organs as a "Jew Press" and the principle of the party as "anti-Christian." However, as editor of various newspapers, Noah took an anti-Tammany stance and eventually became a founder of the Whig Party.

A liberation of the franchise in most States preceded Jackson's election. A surge of humanism, reform movements including workingmen's rights to organize, women's rights, penal reform, and absolutionism, was an intrinsic part of the general reform firmament which characterized Jacksonian Democracy. It possessed the earthier aspect of rotation in office, based on the idea that the average man could fill any office in the land. In other words, it was a "Spoils System."

Such measures apparently found favor among Jews whose leadership, such as Reuben and Samuel Etting, Jacob Cohen, Solomon Jacobs, Samuel Mordecai, Joseph Jonas, Emanuel Hart and Mordecai Noah, staunchly supported "King Andrew." But when it came to supporting Jackson's hand-picked successor, Martin Van Buren, there was a parting of the ways.

Mordecai Noah, the most outspoken and best known of the Jewish political leadership, never enjoyed the favor of the "Albany Regency," a reform faction in the Democratic Party headed by Van Buren, which virtually controlled New York State.

During his early years of Tammany, though, Noah was appointed by the State Legislature as High Sheriff of New York. "What a pity," wrote an outraged citizen concerning Sheriff Noah, "that Christians are to be hung by a Jew." "What a pity," replied the Sheriff, "that Christians should have to be hung."

Noah was also appointed to the positions of Associate Judge of the New York Court of Special Sessions and later made a Surveyor of the Port of New York.

During his years in New York he became an officer of the New York Militia, attaining the rank of Major.

Jewish feeling of belonging is reflected in the frequency with which they turned to the government for succor. Usually they solicited positions as consuls, Indian agents, custom inspectors and collectors, treasury agents, auditors, marshals, and agents in foreign ports.

In 1811, Noah received the appointment as American Consul for Riga, Russia, but at that period this post held forth no inducements, because of the commercial obstacles created through the war on the continent, which was then being waged with great vigor. It was the year in which Alexander I had broken the alliance with Napoleon, who from that time on was a constant and powerful foe. Russia was almost incessantly at war, the national debt and the burden of taxation had been augmented, and though Alexander was unmistakably liberal, a consulship in a chaotic country did not appeal to Noah.

In 1813, Madison appointed Mordecai Manuel Noah as Consul to Tunis, in the Barbary States, which was a salaried office and a trust of importance.

President Madison had two years of deliberation, during which time he had ample opportunity for forming a perfect knowledge of the character, claims and qualifications of Major Noah.

Foreigners needed strong protection for they were not very welcome to Mussulmen.

War had been declared against the United States by the Algerians. Mr.

Lear, the American Consul-General, was rudely dismissed, and a vessel from Salem, Massachusetts, was captured and her crew made prisoners. The relations of the United States with the Barbary States were particularly uncertain, and the policies of those regencies were but imperfectly understood in this country.

Noah was instructed to negotiate for the release of these captives and it was determined that he should have entire charge in the Mediterranean. He accepted the appointment. His task was a difficult one, requiring the exercise of shrewd diplomacy and subjecting his person to the riches of Oriental hospitality and possible dangers.

He understood that one of his main functions was the release of the sailors kidnaped by the Algerians and that while the government was to be kept out of view, that any disbursements were to be drawn for on the Department of State. Noah employed Richard R. Keene of Cadiz, Spain, a native of Maryland, who had become a naturalized Spaniard to ransom the captives. He secured the release of two of the crew and four others, reputedly Louisianians. Noah had to come up with more monies than he was authorized to use, but was able to secure their release. When he drew on his government for the money, the draft was not honored.

Instead his commission was revoked, the letter of recall affirming that his Jewishness was deemed to disqualify him for the post and that his handling of monies was in question.

James Monroe stated, in his letter of April, 1815, that

At the time of your appointment as Consul at Tunis, it was not known that the religion which you profess would form any obstacle to the exercise of your consular functions. ... Recent information, however . . . proves that it would produce a very unfavorable effect. ... In consequence of which the President has deemed it expedient to revoke your commission.

Apparently some of Noah's enemies had been at work in Washington.

Noah returned and was quick to protest this discrimination, first in a pamphlet published in Washington, in 1810, and again at length, in his "Travels." He was joined in his protests by a number of prominent American Jews, among them Isaac Harby, then editor of "The Southern Patriot." "When was it discovered that religion disqualified a man from the exercise of his political function?" Harby inquired in a letter to Monroe. "Or has this doctrine ever been known, since the first hour of the establishment of our invaluable Constitution. ... An objection on the score of religion would sound to them (the framers of the Constitution), most monstrous and unnatural. ... They know no religious distinctions. ... One great character of citizenship alone prevails."

In time, however, Noah obtained a clean bill of health in the conduct of his mission, and the sums he advanced in performing it were negotiated.

During his trip, Noah traveled in order to obtain authentic information relative to the situation, character, resources, and numerical force of the Jews in Barbary, many of whom were immigrants from Judea and Egypt.

The only Jewish traveler in those countries, whose works were extant, was a Spaniard, Benjamin of Tudels, who traveled in the Thirteenth Century.

Another reason for his directing his steps towards that quarter of the globe was to visit England, France and Spain, and to faithfully record his observations. He had found that the city of Tunis was filthy in the extreme and by no means a comfortable residence. He was horrified by the poverty and degradation which he witnessed in North Africa and was determined to gather the Jews together and provide them with a "City of Refuge."

Mordecai Manuel Noah made a spectacular Zionist gesture in the New World three quarters of a century before Theodor Hertzl launched the modern Zionist movement in Europe. He attempted to establish a Jewish colony in America as a preliminary to the return of the Jews to Palestine.

Grand Island, the site chosen for his "City of Refuge," was bought by New York State from the Indians in 1813. By 1819, Grand Island was overrun by squatters and poachers, who were stripping the Island of its enormous supply of virgin wood.

Under pressure from local real estate developers, the New York Militia forcibly removed these outlaws and, in 1820, Grand Island, ideally located midway between the shores of Canada and the United States, was subdivided into building lots.

The year 1825 was memorable for Buffalo: the aging General Lafayette visited the village that year; the Erie Canal was opened and linked Buffalo with the chief American Port of entry for immigrants; the three Thayers were hanged for hacking and shooting to death their hard-bitten and ironically named creditor, John Love; and Mordecai Manuel Noah decided to found a haven for the Jews on Grand Island, in the Niagara River.

Five years earlier he had become interested in the Island and introduced a bill to purchase it, in 1810, in the New York legislature, but it never passed. Noah then read in the papers that the State was about to subdivide the Island into farm lots. Without benefit of State legislative support, he began to set his plan in motion. He persuaded a friend, Samuel Leggett, of New York City, to buy 2,555 acres on the Island. Part of this land was at the head of the Island and the remainder was at the center opposite Tonawanda, at the point where the Erie Canal met the Niagara River. In his early enthusiasm, he was not very concerned with the problem of acquiring the rest of the Island. His plan was not quite as commercial as it has sometimes been portrayed. He had chosen a spot which might, with suitable management, have developed into a rival of Buffalo and Black Rock. Capital was needed here at the terminus to exploit the opportunities offered by the newly-opened Erie Canal. The community that Noah envisioned might very well have grown to be a great metropolis, given the impetus of Jewish capital and immigrant brawn.

In the New York City paper the "National Advocate," of which he was editor, he urged the Grand Island project. Other newspapers supported the plan. Even the "Niagara Journal" stated that "the plan would help the Village and would contribute to local prosperity." As plans for the dedication ceremony were reaching a final stage, the "Black Rock Gazette," although noting with surprise "that so few Jews were interested in the venture, hoped to see the Jewish capitalists, merchants, farmers, and mechanics settle in the area." The local newspapers were no doubt prompted a little by self-interest.

Finally, in late August 1825, Mordecai Manuel Noah arrived in Buffalo with "his robes of office and insignia of rank securely packed." He had designed the elaborate costume himself. He was accompanied by A. B. Seixas of New York, who had, since 1820, helped Noah in his scheme. In the Village of 2,500 souls, Noah's only friend was Isaac S. Smith, an acquaintance from his Tunis days. He was ready for the dedication ceremonies that were to climax his dream of the establishment of an American Zion. Unfortunately, natural conditions conspired to frustrate even the dedication ceremony.

Hearing that dedication ceremonies for Noah's would-be Jewish State were to be held on the Island, hundreds of locals, fully expecting a modern-day Moses, with hordes of Jews in tow, lined the shores of the Niagara River in September 1825, in hopes of getting a glimpse of the group's entry into the Promised Land.

One commentator noted that the local spectators brought with them a "supply of cakes and ale, pastries and pies and cold meats, to give the Jews a good stomach for their undertaking."

Bad weather, however, forced a cancellation of the ceremonies, which were moved instead to St. Paul's Episcopal Church, in Buffalo.

Meanwhile, back at St. Paul's Church, the "Masonic and Military" procession had begun. The ceremony was described by an eyewitness,

John C. Lord, a young school teacher who was to become a lawyer and still later an outstanding Presbyterian divine. "It was a strange mixture of Hebrew and Christian Rites." Lewis Allan later commented on the unusual quality of this unique ceremony, which he described as "this strange and remarkable proceeding, so novel as that of laying a foundation for a Jewish City, with its imposing rites and formula, its regal pomp and Jewish ceremony, in a Christian Episcopal Church, with the aid of its authorized rector." It is possible that the rector, Addison Searle, had known Noah during the latter's Tunis mission.

While Noah himself was not troubled by the anomaly of the situation, others were.

"At ten o'clock the military and Masonic companies had lined up before the Masonic Lodge." Within an hour the procession, led by Grand Marshal Colonel Potter on a prancing steed, was moving. "The tramp of soldiery, of National, State and Municipal Officers, advanced to the spot where the corner stone of a new Canaan was to be laid." Behind the band and the vanguard filed Stewards, Apprentices and representatives of their associated crafts, Master Masons, Senior and Junior Deacons, Senior and Junior Wardens, Masters and Past-Masters of Lodges, members of the reverend clergy and more Stewards bearing the symbolic corn, wine, and oil, and a Principal Architect, with Square, Level and Plumb, flanked on either side by a Globe, and backed by a Bible. "There was also in the paradoxical pageantry, a sprinkling of the Chosen People for whom this new Promised Land, this 'Ararat,' had been chosen."

And now all eyes were fixed upon a portly gentlemen of forty, proudly erect of carriage, florid of face, keen of eye, sandy-haired, over fleshy cheeks and an eagle's beak, who strode just ahead of the rear guard of Royal Arch Masons and Knight Templar.

Noah gave a speech which he thought of as the "Jewish Declaration of Independence," where he "reorganized the Nation of Israel, under the direction of the Judges." Noah appointed himself a Judge of Israel. He proposed to "levy a tax of three shekels on each Jew throughout the World for the purpose of financing the Jewish State." Then, in addition to urging all Jews of the World to join him on Grand Island, he also invited the Karachi, Samaritans, Falashas, and even the American Indians, whom he was convinced were the ten lost tribes of Israel.

Upon completion of this ceremony, a large celebration was held at a local tavern, where a "grand salute of twenty-four guns climaxed the affair while a band played a medley of patriotic arias."

As a part of the ceremony, a cornerstone was brought from Cleveland, and Seth Chapin, of Buffalo, cut the stone and inscribed it:

ARARAT
A City of Refuge for the Jews
Founded by MORDECAI MANUEL NOAH
in the Month of Tizri 5586
Sept. 1825 & in the 50th year of American Independence

Noah received far more support in Buffalo than he did in the Jewish community. Ridiculed, denounced, but mostly ignored by Jews, in New York City and in Europe, Noah soon forgot about his Jewish State on Grand Island.

After the grand beginning, Mordecai Manuel Noah packed his robes of office and left Buffalo a day or so later, having never, to the best of anyone's knowledge, set foot on Grand Island.

The cornerstone that was never mounted is all that remains of Noah's grand dream. It is now a prized possession of the Buffalo Historical Society, but it had a strange history and journey before it finally came to rest there. Lewis F. Allen, who came to Buffalo a few years after the dedication ceremony, later recalled that he found the stone "leaning against the foundation of St. Paul's Church, near Pearl Street in Buffalo." He next saw the stone in 1834, "on the lawn in front of the home of General Peter B. Porter at Black Rock." Because Noah had asked him to see that the stone was cared for, Allen transported it to Grand Island, where he had it installed in a shrine so that it could be seen by passengers on passing vessels. Until 1850 it remained enshrined there, but then it was removed to a farm on Grand Island. Later it appeared at the Canadian resort "Sheer Water." It was finally taken to the Buffalo Historical Society on January 2, 1866, where it now stands as a memorial to one man's wild and fruitless dream.

Now as a colonizer, Noah was far behind another American Jew, who from 1843 to 1846, promoted a colonization project at the request of Sam Houston, then President of the Republic of Texas.

He was Henry Castro, scion of a Marrano family, which had found refuge in France, who preferred to call himself Henri Comte de Castro.

Some 5,000 Germans migrated to Texas and settled there as a result of his efforts. Castro County and the quaint little town of Castroville, west of San Antonio, preserve his efforts.

As colonizer, Castro was a success and Noah was a failure. Nevertheless, the muse of history smiles graciously on Noah, and has all but forgotten the "Comte de Castro."

After the project's failure, Noah turned more strongly to the idea of Palestine as a national home for the Jews. He was the first American Zionist, well before the movement had received a name.

In 1824, he stated that "We will return to Zion as we went forth."

In 1837, in his "Discourse on the Evidences of the American Indian Being the Descendants of the Lost Tribes of Israel," Noah returned to the dream of the restoration.

> "The Jewish people must now do something for themselves; they must move onward to the accomplishment of that great event, long promised, long expected . . . under the cooperation and protection of England and France, his re-occupation of Syria ... is at once reasonable and practicable . . . a just, a tolerant and liberal government... will be a bulwark to the interests of England and France . . ."

Seven years later the return to Zion became a subject of a "Discourse on the Restoration of the Jews," delivered at a Tabernacle in New York on October 28, 1844. It was not a "scientific" address, but a Zionist Polemic. The discourse appeals to American Christians to aid in restoring a Jewish State in Zion, and seeks to convince them why it is in their interests as Christians and as Americans to do so.

Noah remained firmly convinced that the land of Israel would one day pass "into the possession of the descendants of Abraham," and that the Jews would take "their rank once more among the nations of the Earth."

Noah meanwhile continued his many endeavors. After joining the Odd Fellows he wrote an article for the "Odd Fellow Offering" in 1851 on Simchat Torah, submitting a chemist's report on imported olive oil, which had been adulterated with lard, also a contemporary volume of recipes, where he sent his own method for making kosher wine.

The intrusion of Jews into American higher education was not a totally new phenomenon. Mordecai Noah was one of the prominent Jews who helped to found the New York University in 1831.

The spiritual energy of American Jews was not expended merely within the framework of the local community. It spilled over into a concern for broader Jewish problems, and its spokesman, in such matters was Mordecai Manuel Noah. In New York, a meeting took place on August 19, 1840, in the B'nai Jesharim Synagogue. After a request to permit its holdings in Shearith Israel had been deeded by the trustees of the premier Jewish Congregation in the New World, a decision against public action in the face of the sinister events in Damascus was discussed. The principal address at the meeting was delivered by Mordecai Manuel Noah, who was generally regarded as the ranking American Jew, and who never hesitated to exhibit the hopes and wrongs of his people to the gaze of the World.

The meeting adopted a resolution calling on President Martin Van Buren for diplomatic intervention in Damascus, and the committee was surprised to learn from Secretary of State John Forseth that such intervention had already taken place.

In 1845, Noah warned that "if marriage between Jews and Gentiles would be permitted, the American Jew would disappear within two or three generations."

He married Rebecca Jackson in 1827 and she produced for him a large family. Her father, Daniel Jackson, was a Mason as well as two of their sons.

Noah was involved in making plans for a Hebrew Hospital, but on the second day of Spring, March 23, 1851, Mordecai Manuel Noah died. He was buried in the 21st Street Burial Ground. In the newspaper announcement of "The Asmonean," it stated:

> Doctors, authors, musicians, comedians, editors, mechanics, professionals and non-professionals; all classes vying with each other in eager desire to offer tribute of respect to the mortal remains of Major Noah, prior to their departure for their final resting place. ... Among the societies represented were the Hebrew Benevolent Society of which the deceased had been President; the German H. H. Society, the H. B. Bachelors Association, the Young Men's H. B. A., the Society of Mutual Love, the Noah Lodge of B'nai Israel, the I. O. B'nai Brith. ... The officers, lay and clerical, and a large body of members from each of the following Synagogues ...

So ended the life of the most eminent Jew, beginning at the end of the "War of Independence," through the "War of 1812," and ending just prior to the "Civil War."

As for the question of whether he was a Mason or not, let me present the following facts.

The following people who affected his life were members of the Masonic Fraternity: his father; his uncle; his father-in-law; at least two of his sons; Robert Morris; James Madison; James Monroe; George Washington; Uriah Levy.

At one of the meetings at a Synagogue he addressed a member as "Brother." This member was listed as being a Mason.

When he was in Tunis, the head of the Pirates was very friendly to him, although he wasn't to any of the other Consuls. Was it because he was Jewish or a member of our Fraternity?

He was a friend of DeWitt Clinton.

He had as an enemy, Martin Van Buren, known as an anti-Mason.

Some of the situations in his plays have Masonic content. Many of the writers he had contact with were active in Masonry.

All the founding members of the New York Whig Party, except Noah, were active in Masonry.

The Priest who officiated at the Ararat ceremony was a Mason.

The Governor of New York, who attended the Ararat ceremony, was a Mason.

It is quite possible that the tavern where the participants met after the Ararat ceremony was also used as a Masonic Temple.

What I have to still find out:

Was Noah made a Mason in New York or Charleston?

Was Tammany Hall powerful enough to have Noah accepted by all classes of people and organizations?

Was it just coincidence that there were so many people who were Masons who took an interest in him?

In the Odd Fellows do they call each other "Brother?"

I personally believe that Mordecai Manuel Noah was a Mason and that the only reasons that it isn't mentioned are: All these novels, books, articles, etc., represent Noah as a Jew; Since he was living during the Morgan Era, which began in 1826, not too many Masons would admit to their membership.

I will continue my investigations into the life and activities or Mordecai Manuel Noah, with the intent to further my light as to any Masonic affiliation.

Bibliography

Makeover, A. B.. *Mordecai M. Noah—His Life and Work—From the Jewish Viewpoint.* New York: Block Publishing Company, 1917.

Harris, Maurice H.. *Modern Jewish History—Illustrated (From the Renaissance to the close of the World War).* New York: Block Publishing Company (Press of Philip Cowan), 1928, copyright 1927.

Goldberg, Isaac. *Major Noah—American-Jewish Pioneer (1785-1851).* Philadelphia, Pennsylvania: The Jewish Publication Society of America, 1936.

Adler, Selig and Connally, Thomas E., *From Ararat to Suburbia* (*The History of the Jewish Community of Buffalo*). Philadelphia, Pennsylvania: The Jewish Publication Society of America, 1960-5721 first edition.

Encyclopedia Judaic, Vol. 12. Jerusalem Ltd., Ketea Publishing House, Fount Printing, 1978.

Severance, Frank H., editor. *The Book of the Museum*. (historical society publication) Buffalo, New York, 1921.

Allen, Lewis F. *The Story of the Tablet of the City of Ararat*.

Karp, Abraham J.. *Haven and Home* (*The History of the Jews in America*). New York: Schocken Books, 1985.

Dimont, Max. *The Jews in America* (*The Roots and Destiny of American Jews*). New York: Simon and Schuster, 1978.

"*The Jewish Standard*". Toronto, Ontario, July 1-14, 1981.

Feingold, Henry L.. *Zion in America* (*The Jewish Experience From Colonial Times to the Present*). The Immigrant Heritage of American Series, Cicyle S. Neidle, editor. New York: Twayne Publications, Inc., 1974.

Marcus, Jacob Radar. *Early American Jewry*, Vol. II. (*The Jews of Pennsylvania and the South 1655-1790*). Philadelphia, Pennsylvania: The Jewish Publication Society of America, 1955.

Learsi, Rufus. *The Jews in America: A History*. Cleveland and New York: The World Publishing Company, 1954 (second printing).

Haggard, Forrest D.. "*The Clergy and the Craft*". Transactions of the Missouri Lodge of Research, Vol. No.27, 1970, The Ovid Bell Press Company, Missouri, Chapter 13, page 96.

"*The Jews of the United States*". New York Times (Library of Jewish Knowledge), editor, Priscilla Fishman, Quadrangle/The New York Times Book Company, 1973.

Goldman, Mark. *High Hopes* (*The Rise and Decline of Buffalo, New York*). Albany, New York: S. U. N. Y. Press, 1983.

Marcus, Jacob Radar. *Memoirs of American Jews 1775-1865*, Vol.I. Philadelphia, Pennsylvania: The Jewish Publication Society of America, 1955.

Smith, H. Perry, editor. "History *of Buffalo and Erie County, With Illustrations:* 1620-1884, *Vol.I.* Syracuse, New York: D. Mason and Company, Publishers, 1884, Chapter XXII, pages 199 and 429-436.

What is Freemasonry? A Collection of Historical Facts

By Wor. Stuart M. Farmer
  {*Presented March 7, 1983*}

Readings at previous educational meetings dealt with the question, "What is Freemasonry?" I wanted more of an answer, and, after much research in Masonic writings on the subject, this paper is the result. In fashioning a satisfactory answer I found it helpful to ask several questions such as, "What was Masonry?", "How old is Masonry?" and "What is the difference?" Let us consider the last question first.

The answer is to be found in the beginning of the middle chamber lecture you recently listened to, wherein you were told that we view Masonry under two denominations (or titles), operative and speculative. By operative Masonry, you were told, we allude to the building of structures such as Homes, Temples, Churches and Cathedrals. Speculative Masonry is a building of character and minds, a shaping of heart and soul, whereby we learn to subdue the passions, act upon the square, and in a similar manner learn to erect that house, not made with hands, wherein our souls shall find rest forever and forever more.

In its beginning, Masonry was a craft or guild of workmen who cherished and preserved the builder's secrets unto themselves, that they might travel and work in foreign lands, receiving Masters wages, that they might be better able to support themselves and families and, (note this next phrase) contribute to the support of distressed Master Masons, their widows and orphans.

The ability to travel freely was from ancient times much sought after, and valued highly by those who had achieved that freedom. It helped to distinguish, the free men from the slaves and serfs of that time. Masonry, the art of building mostly with stone, or stone masonry or stonemasons as they were also called, had from its dimmest conception, apparently two degrees or classifications – the Entered Apprentice and the Fellowcraft. The Entered Apprentice was a callow youth who was indentured for a period of usually seven years of training, working with his hands, during which time his only recompense was his food and lodging with his Fellowcraft instructor.

The Fellowcraft was the same man, no longer a youth and no longer unskilled, but able to teach as he had been taught, to earn his corn, wine and oil, to travel and to care for his own and for his Brother Fellowcrafts. There was no higher classification or degree than fellowcraft at that time, as operative Masters were selected from the Fellowcrafts available for each specific job or building and, on its completion resumed their title of Fellowcraftsmen. With the passing of time and the development of wisdom in other trades and professions such as Doctors, Lawyers, etc., these thinkers of the day began to envy the Masons and to admire the way they cared for each other in times of stress. Many such were admitted to membership in several ancient craft lodges, located in and about London, England, about the year 1712. The following are excerpts from "A History of Freemasonry" by Mackey and Singleton, Volume IV, page 1008.

In the year 1717 we find an operative guild presenting itself in cold simplicity of organization as a body of practical workmen to whom were joined some honorary members, who were not craftsmen, with an imperfect and obsolete system of bylaws, with, but one form of admission, with secrets common to all classes, which were of little or no importance, for the intellectual and Geometrical secrets of a medieval craft had been lost, and finally, with an insignificant and unpolished ritual, a mere catechism for wandering Brethren to test their right to the privileges and hospitality of the Fraternity.

These several Lodges were moved, probably at the urging of their honorary members, to unite with one another in the formation of a Grand Lodge, which had as its first Grand Master, from June 1717 to June 1718, Anthony Sayer, a gentleman.

There were no signs of a contemplated change; his efforts seem to have been directed solely to the strengthening and confirming of the union of the operative lodges by consulting at stated periods with their officers.

From June 1718 to June 1719, George Payne presided over the Craft. Now we discover the first traces of a sentiment tending toward the improvement of the institution. Old Manuscripts and records were anxiously sought for that the ancient usages of the Craft might be learned. In preparing for the future it was expedient to know something of the past.

The result of this collating of old documents was the compilation of the "Charges of a Freemason" which was appended to the first edition of "The Book of Constitutions".

Mackay breaks with Masonic tradition at this point in assigning the authorship to George Payne. A noted antiquary... Thus well fitted by the turn of his mind to such labors. From June 1719 to June 1720 the Grand Master was one Doctor Desaguliers, and his administration is made memorable by the first great change in the system. As previously mentioned, the body of the Craft had always been divided into two classes, apprentices and fellows . . . distinguished by the possession of certain privileges. In lodge however, they assembled together and took counsel together, the fellows being prominent in rank as a class of workmen and in numbers, which suggested to Dr. Desaguliers the advantages that would result from a more distinct separation—not by a recognition of rank—but a separation by granting to each class a peculiar form of initiation with accompanying secrets.

This step was taken by Dr. Desaguliers soon after his installation as Grand Master, the one degree or form of initiation or admission which had hitherto been common to all ranks of craftsmen he modified by confining one part of the apprentices, making it the working degree of the Lodge. Another part he enlarged and improved, transferred to it the most important secret, the Masons Word, and made it a degree to be conferred only on Fellowcrafts, and only in the Grand Lodge. Thus the degree of apprentices thus modified, continued as of old to be conferred on new candidates and in the Lodges. The entered apprentice now ceased to be a youth, but henceforth denoted one who had been initiated into the first degree of Freemasonry, a meaning which it has ever since retained. Dr. Desaguliers, now contemplated a further development of the ritual by the addition of another degree. He had seen that the old operative craft was divided into three classes or ranks of workmen, to the first and second of these classes a degree peculiar to each, but the third and highest class was still without one. To give it perfection it was necessary that a third degree should be invented to be the property of the third degree or Masters. In 1723, Dr. Desaguliers presented the third degree, his most recent invention to Grand Lodge, which body accepted it, introduced it into the ritual and, from that time forth, Ancient Craft Masonry has had three degrees.

The year 1723 then marks the birth of Freemasonry as we know it now, and the death of the operative Masonry, or rather, its absorption which had preceded it. Thus are we left with but one of the original questions: How old is Freemasonry, or how old is Operative Masonry. The answer is simply older than any known records. But an age of roughly 4,000 years has been assigned to it, and while this is 1982 A.D. (the year of our Lord, or *Anno Domini*), it is also Masonically speaking 5982 A.L. (*Anno Lucis*, or in the year of Light). Speaking of the current year, is Speculative

Masonry or Freemasonry still the same as it was back at its birth in 1723? Grudgingly we have to admit to certain small changes, mostly deletions, or substitutions of words which have lost their original meaning. But no institution which rigidly permits no changes or innovations can expect to live, and do we not have hope in the wisdom of future generations, and what knowledge they may bring to light?

Freemasonry today means a universal, world-wide brotherhood composed of men of goodwill, of good character, and of good reputation, who believe in almighty God, and practice the spirit of the universal brotherhood of Man, who are loyal to their country, devoted to the principles of friendship and fellowship, and who aim to be of service to all mankind.

The mission of Masonry is to help build a better world through its particular process of building better men to live in it, by urging the practice of brotherly love for all, charitable relief for those who may be in need, and morality and good citizenship in every community, charity, fraternity, Education, character building and a social organization. That is what we are all committed to, and we invite you to join us, as you are raised to the sublime degree of Master Mason.

Freemasonry is not a secret society, it is not a religious society, it is not politically oriented, it is not a mutual benefit society. Freemasonry is a voluntary society, to which no one is asked to join, and from which any Mason in good standing may withdraw at any time.

The Preservation of Historical Materials

By RW Rev. Don C. Markham
{June 29, 1986}

One of the big problems facing organizations and families who are interested in their past is the preservation of historical materials–particularly documents and photographs. This problem is enhanced by some of the natural dangers which threaten such historical materials.

The biggest danger, of course, is fire. Since such historical materials are extremely combustible, fire is a real threat to their existence. We are all familiar with the notation in many Lodge histories: "Unfortunately the records for this period of time were lost in a fire." With this in mind, therefore, it is necessary for organizations and families to make some arrangements for the preservation of such materials in the event of fire. This might be through storage in a fireproof container such as a safe or a fireproof file. Nothing, however, is really "fireproof"–the best that such things are is "fire-retardant." That is to say that they will withstand certain temperatures for certain periods of time. The intensity of heat and duration of exposure will have a marked effect upon the condition of the materials stored in such surroundings. Paper items packed tightly will rarely be a total loss–the edges may get singed, but unless the heat and flames are extremely intense salvage is possible.

However, tightly packing such materials in an air-tight container such as a safe or fire-proof file brings an additional threat of dampness. Dampness caused by lack of air circulation brings mold and mildew which attack the very fibers of the paper and frequently do more damage than fire. As heat outside a fire-proof container builds up, the moisture contained in the air trapped inside condenses and dampness becomes a great threat. The longer such containers are left before being opened, the greater the danger of mold and mildew. So, it becomes vital to start salvage immediately after such a situation occurs, opening and airing out and drying the materials one hopes to salvage and preserve. One constantly must battle with the forces of natural destruction.

The next most frequent threat to historical materials is water. In addition to the problems of mold and mildew already mentioned, there is an additional threat when paper materials are subjected to inundation. You may recall the floods in the Southern Tier in 1972 which wrought great damage. One of the tragedies of that flood was the loss of much historical material—largely through ignorance. Books that are soaked through must be dried slowly one page at a time. This is tedious work and rarely is effective when large numbers of volumes or documents are involved. The library of the Corning Glass Works was inundated in 1972. Priceless and rare volumes—many are one of a kind—were threatened with total destruction until someone came up with the idea of freezing the books and documents. Freezing helps to remove moisture and also retards development of mold and mildew. Stored thus, the items could be worked on one at a time and consequently loss was kept at a minimum.

Light is also a threat to many items of historical value. We have all seen how sunlight bleaches draperies, carpets, and furniture—it does the same with ink and with photographs. Documents and photographs must be protected from strong light if such fading is to be avoided. Many of the old inks used in writing were herbal inks—made from juices of berries, lampblack, and similar materials. These oxidize upon exposure to light and will frequently fade until they are virtually illegible. Sometimes they can be restored to readable circumstances through infrared photography—but sometimes even this does not work. So, such materials should be stored in acid-free envelopes and other containers which will protect them from natural loss.

Most paper today is pulp-paper as contrasted with rag-paper. Pulp paper contains a great amount of acid which causes the fibers to yellow and become brittle in a relatively short time. Just look at a piece of newspaper that you clipped and kept for a few years and see how brittle it has become. The same is true of any pulp-paper item. Old newspapers from 100 years ago are frequently as bright and pliable as they were when printed because they were printed on rag content papers which retains its character far, far longer than other types. Important documents, therefore, should be written or typed upon at least a 50% rag content paper for preservation.

Newspaper items may best be preserved by copying them with a dry-toner copier on a paper which is at least 50% rag content. They then become much more durable and usable.

Photographs present problems in preservation also. For best results they should be stored in polypropylene envelopes which will not damage their surface. Vinyl will adversely affect the surfaces of the photographs and there will be a certain amount of sticking to the surface. Polypropylene, however, does not have that reaction and may be safely used for photographs and documents of historical interest.

Damaged or torn documents may be repaired through the use of adhesives designed for that purpose. One should consult someone skilled in library preservation for the names of such materials. One thing to avoid, however, is SCOTCH TAPE! This is the worst enemy of the historian or librarian as it destroys virtually all that it touches. The adhesive penetrates the paper and yellows it leaving a residue which breaks down the paper even after the tape has yellowed and fallen off. There is no such thing as a "safe" transparent tape at the present time.

Many people seem to think that the lamination of documents or photographs is a preservative means, but it is NOT! Lamination impregnates the photograph or paper with a material which is capable of destroying that item. The plastic laminate frequently becomes scratched or cloudy and prevents clear view – but the laminate cannot be removed! Any attempt to do so will effectually destroy the photograph or document thus treated, so this means it is to be avoided at all costs.

The hazards of preserving historical materials are great unless one is very much aware of the manner in which it may be safely done. There are people skilled in such work who may be consulted. Some of the means listed may be utilized by anyone, but for specific problems or needs, consult with someone who knows the field—this is absolutely vital, lest valuable historical material for your family or organization be lost through carelessness or wrong use of materials.

THE MORGAN AFFAIR, WHY?

Original Written by LaVerne S. Lamkin, March 1984
Founding member, Western New York Lodge of Research
Edited by Charles L. Ketchum, Jr., September 1997
Founding Member and Worshipful Master, Western New York Lodge of
Research

Original Editing Notes:

In 1985, Wor. LaVerne S. Lamkin, a Charter Member of Western New York Lodge of Research requested RW Charles L. Ketchum, Jr., Worshipful Master of WNYLoR, to publish his Paper, "The Morgan Affair, Why?" in the next bulletin of the Lodge. Time and space was not available, so his paper was not printed. Shortly thereafter Brother Lamkin died. His paper got misplaced and was never published. Brother Ketchum, when rearranging his library in 1997, found the letter of request and paper. He then decided to edit the paper for grammar and accuracy, and add additional information he could find from his own private library. Editing is in bold italic.

{Editor's note: This work cannot be divided into original parts, edits, and additions, without serious distraction. Most of the edits were additions or expansions of historical detail of the places and people contained within the framework of Brother Lamkin's work. Brother Ketchum's words comprise roughly half of the total text found here, and is responsible for most of the data of individual biographies and Lodge histories. Some version with marks indicated as above may be available on request from the Western New York Lodge of Research.

The term "Indian", whether referring to Native Americans or their tribes, has been minimized–but not eliminated or substituted–in this version. The term has socially fallen out of favor since the original writing and publication, and the changes were made out of consideration and respect for the present reader, and in such a way as to maintain accuracy without deviating strongly from the original tenor or meaning.}

The Beginning (Historical Context)

Where else but in Batavia and when better than 1826 could the Morgan Affair have occurred? As a member of society In America's leading city and capital, Joseph Ellicott, with his brothers, sisters and nephews, certainly knew Robert Morris as the financier of our nation. So would be the Brisbanes and Carys. All three families were Episcopalian, a religion long inclined toward Masonry.

In 1788, land speculators Oliver Phelps and Nathaniel Gorham purchased most of the land in New York State, east and west of the Genesee River from Massachusetts. These men agreed to pay $1,000,000.00 for the six million acre territories. Before the two could sell the land, however, they had to find a way to get the title of the land away from the Seneca Indians. They did this in part by giving the Indians $5,000.00 and an annuity of $500.00, for 2.5 million acres east of the Genesee River, and about 2 million acres west of the River. The Senecas kept most of the land west of the Genesee River because they believed the "Great Spirit" had made the river a boundary between them and the white man. Financial problems soon caught up with Phelps and Gorham. In 1790 they had to turn back two thirds of the land west of the River in order to keep the title to the land east of the River.

The bad luck of Phelps and Gorham did not discourage Robert Morris from buying 1 million acres of the land between the Genesee River and Seneca Lake. A few months later, Morris obtained approximately 4 million acres west of the Genesee River from Massachusetts for $333,333.00. At first Morris was very successful in land acquisition, but by 1797 Morris had exceeded his ability to get necessary cash funds and found himself in serious financial straits. Common sense told him to sell it to the only wealthy group of investors in the world, the Holland Land Company who had made them and their nation wealthy owning land over all the world.

Between 1792 and 1793, Morris sold a great bulk of his land to Theophile Cazenove, the representative of the six Dutch banking houses that later organized into the Holland Land Company. By 1797, Cazenove was able to acquire 3.3 million acres of land west of the Genesee River.

Before the Holland Land Company paid for the land in Western New York, they insisted that Morris first get the land rights from the Indians.

Morris agreed promising "That no money will be paid him until the leaders of the tribes of Indians sign an Agreement of Title for the land to be bought." Several years passed due to Indian Wars and British procrastination. The long awaited Treaty meeting began on August 28, 1797. The Indian representatives were Red Jacket, Cornplanter, and Farmer's Brother, who at first refused to sign away the lands. The sessions were stormy and both sides seemed to be reaching a dead end. Morris finally tried a new tactic. A promise of sixty cows won over the Seneca women. Bribery brought support from key Seneca leaders when he offered Red Jacket $600.00, Cornplanter $300.00, Farmer's Brother $100.00, Little Billy $100.00 and Little Beard $50.00. In addition, annuities were granted to Cornplanter for $250.00, Red Jacket $100.00, Farmer's Brother $100.00, Little Billy $100.00 and Captain Pollard $50.00. Thus, the Senecas were persuaded to give up their ancient claims to most of Western New York.

On September 15, 1797, fifty-two Seneca leaders and Thomas Morris, as attorney for his father, Robert, signed the Treaty of Big Tree, at present day Geneseo, New York. The Senecas ended up with $100,000.00 and a little less than 200,000.00 of the original 4 million acres. After the signing of the Treaty of Big Tree, Robert Morris was able to turn over the 3.3 million acres of land to the Holland Land Company.

Early Settlers on the East side of the Hudson River

In 1621, Holland organized the Dutch West India Company. The Company founded New Netherland and made the first settlement, at Fort Orange (Albany), in 1624. In 1625, 150 miles down the Hudson River, the Company built a fort at New Amsterdam (New York City).

One of the more prominent members of the Dutch West India Company, Kiliaen Van Rensselaer, a diamond merchant of Amsterdam, led a faction in the Company which advocated vigorous colonization. He owned three of today's counties and by his Patroon System was successful in encouraging families from Holland to settle on both sides of the Hudson River from Fort Orange south toward New Amsterdam. He chose Roeloff Jans {an ancestor of Bro. Lamkin, original author of this work} to be his representative in America, and Roeloff and his bride, Anneke, came here in 1630 with the first boat load of settlers. Roeloff and Anneke located at Fort Orange and furnished the early settlers with tools, seed and food with which to start their new lives here. With the competent handling of his responsibility, Roeloff was able to send millions of dollars in furs and food products (all wheat had to be milled in the company's mills) back to Holland.

So successful was Roeloff in his management that the Company gave him a farm on the west side of the Broad Way, the only road from New Amsterdam to Fort Orange. The southern boundary of this farm was the northern wall of New Amsterdam and its western side was the Hudson River. Roeloff Jans died at sea in 1637 on one of his yearly trips back to Holland to bring additional settlers to the colony.

The first Dominie (clergyman) of the Dutch Colony also taught school, but the second Dominie, Everadus Bogardus, serving from 1633 to 1647, refused to teach. Bogardus also demanded that the company give him land outside the city where he could establish an estate. This was a farm bordering Roeloff Jan's to the north. Later he entertained some of his wealthier parishioners in his home and got them drunk enough to sign pledges to build him a new and bigger church. He also married the widow Anneke Jans.

Its Charter of Organization stipulated that the Dutch West India Company give a part of its lands around the world to the House of Orange, the rulers of Holland. This resulted in Anneke, the sister of William II of Holland and widow of Roeloff Jans, becoming the wealthiest woman of the world. Outliving Bogardus also, she inherited both farms. With the second conquest of the colony by the English she moved back to her old home in Albany at the corner of State and James Streets where a bank stands today. She is buried in Albany's Pioneer Cemetery, and In the Museum of Art, diagonally across State Street from the Capitol, is a diorama showing that home and also a relief map showing its location. The Colony was renamed for the Duke of York and the Episcopalian Trinity Church was built at the south edge of Anneko's land, opposite today's Wall Street. Anneke's brother's son, William III, by marrying the daughter of James (the Duke of York, who ruled New York for 21 years), also became the King of England for three years.

The Holland Land Company

With their purchase of Western New York from Robert Morris, the Holland Land Company hired Joseph Ellicott in 1797 to survey the 3.3 million acres of company land at $8.00 a day. Given complete authority, he hired about 150 men (surveyors, draftsmen, cooks, ax men and camp keepers). Ellicott immediately prepared for the project by exploring the land for the project ahead. During the fall of 1797, he toured the boundaries, surveyed the southern shore of Lake Ontario to the mouth of the Niagara River, and from the southwest beach of Lake Erie to the western boundary of New York. He also prepared a topographical map of this survey. The great survey started in March of 1798 and was completed in October of 1800 and had cost the Holland Land Company exactly $70,921.69½. On November 1, 1800, in Philadelphia, Joseph Ellicott, and agent-general for the Holland Land Company Paul Busti, came to terms and signed a contract for the position of resident-agent. The first contract was for six years and paid a sliding salary. Ellicott would receive $1,500.00 a year so long as the area under his control remained at 300,000 acres. The annual salary would increase in proportion to the acreage under his control. In addition, he would receive a commission of 5% on all sales under his Jurisdiction. At the date of his retirement, Ellicott was to be given two bonuses from the Company—1,000 acres of land and 1% of all the unsold property under his control. The Company, in return, expected Ellicott to sell the land, to work only for Dutch proprietors, and to enrich the stockholders. The Company would also spend up to $2,500.00 for a residence and an office for Ellicott. During the twenty-four years as resident-agent, Ellicott's contract was renewed several times and the terms revised. In 1810, for example, he received 30,000 acres of land to satisfy his 5 percent commission, and changed the limit of his bonus, to be given him at the time of retirement to 6,000 acres, rather than the original 1% of all unsold property. Ellicott received about $11,500.00 annually for the first 10 years, but dropped to about $7,000.00 for the last 10 years.

Iroquois Indian Chieftains

Joseph Ellicott came to the area in 1797 when the Holland Land Company made its treaty with the Indians, with Red Jacket being the Indians' main spokesman. Red Jacket's brother's granddaughter married William Parker and one of her sons was General Ely Samuel Parker of the Civil War. He was a Mason and also inherited the silver medal George Washington gave Red Jacket and is buried alongside Red Jacket in Forest Lawn Cemetery in Buffalo, New York.

Red Jacket's mother had three husbands. One was his father, one the father of Corn planter who became chief of today's reservation of that name, and the third being the father of Handsome Lake.

Seneca Chief Red Jacket

Red Jacket, often referred to as "The Last of the Senecas," was born at Old-Castle, near Geneva, New York, in 1751; he died at Seneca Village, New York, on January 20, 1830. His Indian name was Sa-go-you-wat ha, meaning "keeper awake." He acquired his more familiar name when he was still a young boy during the time of the Revolution. He distinguished himself by his activity and his intelligence, and attracted the attention of the British officers, who presented him with a scarlet jacket which he took great pride in wearing. When that jacket was worn out, he was given another jacket. Red Jacket continued to wear the same type of coat, until it became a mark of distinction, and he was given the name by which he was best known.

At the early age of seventeen years, Red Jacket attracted the admiration of his tribe by his quickness of feet and his remarkable memory. During the war he was frequently employed as a runner to carry dispatches, and in that context he took little or no part as a warrior; so it appeared he better understood how to rouse his countrymen to war than to lead them to victory. Yes, Red Jacket was not distinguished as a warrior; his true causes, however, of his great influence in his tribe were his talents and the circumstances under which he lived. When the power of his tribe had declined and its distinction was threatened, it was then that Red Jacket stood forward as a patriot, defending his nation with fearless eloquence, and criticizing its enemies in words of fierce insult or bitter sarcasm. He became their counselor, their negotiator, and their orator.

The whole life of the Seneca Chief Red Jacket was spent in hopeless endeavors to preserve the independence of his tribe, and in active opposition to the plans of the benevolent to civilize the Indian way of life. His views remained unchanged and his mental powers unimpaired to the end of his life. The only weakness, into which he permitted himself to fall, was that of intoxication.

Red Jacket changed his place of residence several times, and twice located in what is now West Seneca. One cabin stood near the intersection of Barnsdale Avenue and Mineral Springs Road in Winchester, and the other about 4306 Seneca Street. When he was approaching his last days, he visited his friends at their cabins, and talked with them about the condition of their nation in a most impressive and affecting manner. He then would tell them that he was close to his last days, and his counsels would soon be heard no more. He covered the history of his people from the most remote period to which his knowledge extended, and pointed out, as few could, the wrongs, the privations, and their loss of character which they constituted that history. He would conclude by saying, "I am about to leave you, and when I am gone, and my warnings will be no longer heard, or regarded, the shrewdness and the greed of the white man will prevail. Many Winters have I humbled the storm, but I am an aged tree, and can stand no longer. My leaves are falling, my branches are withered, and I am shaken by every breeze. Soon my aged trunk will be worn out, and the feet of the enemy of the Indian may be placed upon it in safety; for there is none who will be able to avenge such an indignity. Think not I mourn for myself. I go to join the spirits of my fathers, where age cannot come, but my heart fails, when I think of my people, who are soon to be scattered and forgotten. "

His abrasive antagonism toward Christianity mellowed in his last days, and although steadfast to his Longhouse faith, it was his wish to move to a cabin near the Indian Church on Buffum Street near Seneca Street so that his wife and children could be spared long walks to attend school and church services. Red Jacket died in that South Buffalo cabin, and was given a Christian burial in the nearby cemetery (the Old Mission Burial Ground), the present Indian Park at Buffum Street and Fields Avenue, but now lies by his monument in Forest Lawn Cemetery in Buffalo, New York.

The medal which Red Jacket wore was his prized possession. It was a personal gift, made in 1792, from General George Washington, and he was never known to be without it. Red Jacket had studied and comprehended the character of Washington, and placed upon that gift a value corresponding with his exalted opinion of the donor.

Seneca Chief Ely Samuel Parker

Ely Samuel Parker was born near Indian Falls on the Tonawanda Indian Reservation on October 13, 1829, the son of Seneca Chief William Parker. Ely Parker was educated in Law and Civil Engineering, and at the outbreak of the Civil War was employed as engineer at Galena, Illinois, then the hometown of Ulysses S. Grant. They were friends when both joined the Army at the outbreak of the Civil War. Because of Parker's distinguished service at Vicksburg, he was selected to be on General Grant's Staff of Officers. On March 2, 1867, he became a Brigadier General in the Army. By reason of their friendship, as well as of his excellent handwriting, General Grant entrusted him as his personal and official secretary and at General Lee's surrender, Ely Parker drew up the first copy of the Articles of Capitulation. General Parker resigned from the Army in 1869 to accept the appointment as Commissioner of Indian Affairs from General Grant, and held this office until he retired in 1871. He died on August 31, 1895.

Ely Samuel Parker was made a Mason in Batavia Lodge No.88 in 1847 and affiliated with Valley Lodge No. 109, of the same city, on May 6, 1850. He demitted from there on September 6, 1858, to become one of the founders and first Master of Miners' Lodge No.273, in Galena, Illinois, serving from 1858 to 1860. In 1862 he demitted from Miners' Lodge to become the first Master of Akron Lodge No.527 in Akron, NY, under the Warrant dated June 3, 1863. Ely Parker Lodge No.1002 of Buffalo, NY was named for him.

Seneca Chief Cornplanter (John Abeal sometimes spelled Obail)

Chief Complanter, prominent in Seneca Indian affairs of war and peace, was the son of a Seneca Indian woman and a Dutch trader from Albany named Abeal. Chief Joseph Brant and Chief Complanter have been recognized as great Indian leaders and warriors throughout the years. Even though Joseph Brant had more publicity than Complanter, the other chiefs and warriors who were acquainted with both men regarded Complanter as the superior in combat. As a warrior and statesman Complanter's name will endure in Iroquois History. His reservation was on the Allegany River just south of the New York State border. Complanter and Red Jacket were rivals, and each were great orators and leaders. A bitter jealousy existed between the two chiefs. In one incident, Complanter was held responsible for the terms agreed upon by the Treaty at Fort Stanwix, terms which the Senecas detested. Red Jacket would not let anyone forget. Complanter and his half brother Handsome Lake conspired to discredit Red Jacket and after propagandizing the issue, in which they charged Red Jacket for being a witch, a trial was held at Buffalo Creek in 1801, at a Seneca Council House located near today's Seneca Street and Bailey Avenue in Buffalo, N. Y. It was a very serious affair to the Indians, and for nearly three hours Red Jacket spoke in his own defense, and was acquitted. Thereafter the influence of Chief Complanter declined among his people.

Seneca Chief Handsome Lake

Chief Handsome Lake was born in 1735 at Kanawagus (meaning "stinking waters", used by the Indians for curing ills as did the white man at other sulphur springs). The springs were a bit south on the west side of Genesee River from the Indian village (its spelling later changed to Canawaugus) located on a hill before route 5 and route 20 merge into one road to cross the river on the bridge to Avon.

Handsome Lake observing what the European's "fire water" was doing to the Indians and knowing that the strict religion of the Quakers would prove a "bit much" for their temperament, spent most of his life trying to turn them back to their ancient Longhouse religion. Actually it is little different from our Christian religion with only a change of names with their dancing being a very old method of praying. Handsome Lake moved to a Seneca settlement along the Allegany River in 1797. There he became very ill, which was aggravated by excessive drinking of hard liquor. For four years he was bedridden helplessly and without hope for recovery. It had appeared that he had died, and his body was carried back to his Lodge and dressed for burial, but in twenty-four hours he revived from a death like coma. It is said that three strong, quiet and kindly men visited him in a vision. They had been sent to help him regain his strength, so that he could go out among his people to teach. The three men instructed him on how and what he was to teach on his missionary crusade. They then commanded him to go out among his people, preaching the evils of intemperance and encouraging them to return to the faith and ways of their fathers, for the Great Spirit was angry with them for their excessive drinking and lapse in other moral virtues. From that day on he was dedicated to his mission and spent the rest of his life traveling and preaching on the Indian reservations in Genesee Country. The messages he received from the three men are contained in the Code of Handsome Lake, prepared by Dr. Arthur C. Parker. That Code is said to be the basis for the Indian Longhouse Religion. Handsome Lake was modest, quiet and kind, and his religious enthusiasm continued throughout the sixteen years he preached in Genesee Country. During one of his crusades he died among the Onondaga Indians, on their reservation near Syracuse on August 10, 1815.

White Visitors to Genesee Country

Prior to the settling of our area in Genesee Country, we have records of only five white people to have visited here. The first was the "French Invader", the Marquis deNonville, with his soldiers in 1687, who left Montreal by waterway then followed the Iroquois Trail to the Seneca's land, destroying many towns and Indian villages along the way. After his invasion and destruction, deNonville returned to Montreal thinking he accomplished his mission. The Seneca Indians built new towns and villages and returned to their normal living, but vowed vengeance on the French. The French Priests who had been spreading Christianity throughout the Genesee region would no longer enter the area, and all their good work was lost due to deNonville.

Rev. Samuel Kirkland, who visited Buffalo Creek Reservation in June of 1788, was adopted by the Seneca with full formal ceremonies, and gave us a better description of Seneca country. (Rev. Kirkland was a Protestant missionary who had spent many years among the Oneida Tribe and had the confidence of the Seneca Indians. He prepared the first census in the area while doing missionary work).

Silas Loomis, with his father driving cattle from Lewiston to Philadelphia, stayed overnight in the Tonawanda Band's village north of Akron.

Ebenezer "Indian" Allen of Pennsylvania, when fleeing from the British in 1782, became friendly with Mary Jemison's son Thomas, who invited him to stay in their cabin for a while. Allen, being an officer in the British Army with a reputation of violence and cruelty, ended up spending a few years working on Mary Jemison's Gardeau Reservation, but never got very far from the river. Allen ran the saw mill at the Silver Lake outlet, near the river, about five miles away. Mary contended that he had always been honorable, kind and generous with her. Ebenezer Allen was to be the first white settler on the site of today's Rochester.

The French-Canadian soldier William Poudrit, walking home from fighting on the English side in the Revolution, stopped at the Tonawanda Reservation, married a girl there. Descendants of theirs still live on that reservation, but spell the name Poodry, and are Masons.

Mary Jemison—the White Woman and Her Valley

In the Autumn of 1743 on the ship William and Mary sailing from Londonderry, Ireland, heading for Philadelphia, Jane Erwin, wife of Thomas Jemison, gave birth to a baby girl and named her Mary. Mary Jemison had four brothers and a sister. The family lived at Marsh Creek in Adams County, Pennsylvania, known today as Buchanan Valley. In April of 1758, six Indians and four Frenchmen killed the family, but spared the life of Mary. At Fort Duquesne, now the site of Pittsburgh, Mary Jemison was given to two Indian sisters. The three girls traveled by canoe to an Indian village which was 80 miles down the Ohio River. At the Village, they gave her a new name, Dehgewanus, which meant "Two Falling Voices".

Mary Jemison moved to the village of Sciota and married a young, tall, brave, generous and kind, Delaware warrior named Sheninjee. They had a son and named him Thomas, in honor of Mary's father. Nine months after the birth of her son, she traveled six hundred miles on foot to a village on the Genesee River, named Little Beard's Town (the present site of Cuylerville).

After her first husband Sheninjee died, her son Thomas being four years old, she married a six-foot tall, famous and ferocious Seneca chief by the name of Hiakatoo. Although Hiakatoo was 60 years old and she was only 24, her loyalty never wavered throughout his life, which lasted more than 40 years. They had six children—four daughters, and two sons.

Chief Hiakatoo was second in command of the Indian forces under the Mohawk Chief Joseph Brant, and took part In the terrible massacre of white settlers. During the early Autumn of 1779, General John Sullivan's Army was invading the villages in the Genesee Valley, and it was necessary for Mary Jemison and her children to hide from the army of "the Blue Snake" (the name given to General Sullivan). When the family returned to their village, it was found reduced to ashes, so they traveled to the Gardeau Flats where Mary Jemison remained for more than 50 years. In the late summer of 1797, during the Treaty of Big Tree, Mary Jemison was awarded the Gardeau Reservation of 17,297 acres, six miles wide and four and three quarter miles long on both sides of the Genesee River, known as "the White Woman's Tract". Today, most of it is part of Letchworth State Park.

In 1825, the Senecas sold all their land along the Genesee River and moved to the Tonawanda, Cattaraugus, and Buffalo Creek Reservations. Feeling she was hemmed in by the whites, Mary Jemison was determined to move to "Indian country", so upon selling the last of her reservation in 1831, she moved to the Buffalo Creek Reservation instead of joining her own people. It is said that Mary Jemison settled at "Frog Pond" on the bank of the Buffalo Creek near the present intersection of Jamison, Hemstreet & Creek Roads in East Elma.

Reverend Asher Wright and his wife persuaded Mary to attend the Indian Mission School on Buffum Street near Seneca Street in South Buffalo, and in the summer of 1833, she formally joined the Christian Religion. Mary died on September 19th, 1833, at the age of 90 years old and was given a Christian burial at the Indian Cemetery on the Buffalo Creek Reservation. Remarkably the graves of Mary's many Indian friends and acquaintances, including Red Jacket, Young King, Little Billy, Destroy Town, Twenty Canoes, Two Guns, Captain Pollard, John Snow, and Old White Chief, were all buried in the cemetery not far from her. Her marker was a marble slab inscribed "In Memory of the White Woman." If you had visited her grave ten years after her burial you would have found that the marble slab was partly broken and the inscription defaced–for so strange was the story of the old "White Woman" that many strangers visiting the place and wishing a memento had chipped off considerable portions of the marble.

In 1859, William Pryor Letchworth, a wealthy industrialist, established an estate In Letchworth State Park, called "Glen Iris." In 1870, Letchworth moved the old Seneca Council House from Caneadea to Glen Iris. Fascinated by the story of Mary Jemison, in 1874, William Letchworth had Mary's remains brought to Glen Iris. He also transported the log house that Mary had built for her daughter, Nancy, from the old Gardeau Reservation.

On September 19, 1910, the 77th anniversary of her death, a life size statue of a young Mary Jemison, her baby strapped upon her back, was dedicated. Today, in a little corner of Letchworth State Park, is a dedication to Mary Jemison and the Seneca with whom she lived so long. Thousands visit each year to view a log cabin, a statue, and the old Seneca Council House, which Letchworth had moved to that location. Mary Jemison has not been forgotten. Every year, the Castile Historic Society presents a historical pageant on her life in Letchworth Park.

The Early History of the Land West of the Genesee River

Joseph Ellicott, born November 1, 1760, was the son of Joseph and Judith Ellicott. He taught school while still in his teens and with his brother Andrew surveyed the western and northern boundary of Pennsylvania in 1785. Upon his return to Philadelphia after the Treaty of Big Tree he persuaded two of his brothers, Benjamin and David, to help, hired Ebenezer Cary as a surveyor, clerk and generally useful agent, and hired James Brisbane to purchase and bring the supplies which would be needed. They returned in May 1798 and Brisbane brought the first boatload by way of Lake Ontario and the Genesee River, then over land to a stone storehouse the surveying crew had built on their east transit line at Stafford. Later supplies came to Lewiston.

In January 1801, the first office of the Holland Land Company was established. It was located in Asa Ransom's tavern at Clarence Hollow in Erie County where Ellicott started to sell the land. To make travel easier he offered free patches of land along the Iroquois Trail to anyone who would build and operate a tavern about six miles apart, the usual travel distance for one day.

Ellicott finding that the distance to Canandaigua, the distribution point for mail, was too far away, so he decided that the Indians' camping ground at the big bend of the Tonawanda Creek, which was centrally located in the land company's territory, would be a bettor location for an office and capital of the area. The Indian's name for tho bend in the creek was, De-on-qe-we, the Groat Meeting Place, so called because it was the junction of two great Indian trails—one which led from Lake Erie to the Hudson River, and the other from Lake Ontario to the Susquehanna River. In 1801, he ordered the Company to build an office there, and also a dam and a sawmill at the bend of the creek. In March of 1801, Abel Howe came and built a log house that stood nearly opposite the present Holland Land Office Historical Society Building. Ellicott established an office in Howe's log house until the Company's building was erected and completed in 1815, at the "forks of the trail" which lead from Batavia to Lewiston and to Buffalo.

In 1801, Ellicott decided he needed a name for the territory owned by the Company. He wrote a letter to Agent-General Paul Busti, suggesting the name "Busti" or "Bustiville," but Busti refused the honor, and suggested "Ellicott's Town." The name "Batavia" was finally chosen, which was the ancient title of the Kingdom of Holland. On November 7, 1801, the settlement by the name of Batavia was certified.

In 1802, Ellicott applied for a county in Genesee Country to be established, and on March 20, 1802, the original Town of Batavia was born. This territory of the Holland Land Company was soon divided into the present counties of Western New York. The land that contained the bend in the creek became Genesee County and was divided into twelve towns; the center area became known as the Town of Batavia. By 1823, this settlement, at the "bend of Tonawanda Creek" had grown large enough to become the Village of Batavia, and by 1915 the population and industry had increased enough to become the City of Batavia. Thus, the city boundary lines were established, and the remaining area, the Town of Batavia.

Joseph Ellicott had his home built on the north side of today's Main Street at Thomas Avenue, and he wrote in one of his letters of having only to walk diagonally across Main Street in order to reach his Land Company office. While living in that building he gradually enlarged it until by 1818 it became a mansion where he entertained the society of the world.

In 1802, he had Ellicott Hall built at the east end of the Indian campground (today it would be north of Main Street and west of Court Street) to house on the lower floor of its north half the jail, the upper floor the courtroom, and the lower floor of the south half a tavern, with the sheriff living upstairs. He made Aaron Van Cleve the Sheriff and James Brisbane the first Postmaster, also in 1802.

Joseph Ellicott hired Aaron Van Cleve in 1801 as a clerk in the office, who married the sister of Judge James W. Stevens, took the census of all of Western New York in 1810 and 1814, and as a Mason offered the use of his home to Olive Branch Lodge for its early meetings. Also in 1802, Ellicott hired White Chief (or White Feather) who lived north of Indian Falls to lay out a road from Bushville to Clarence. The Iroquois Trail turned north at Bushville and followed today's Kelsey Road to their village in the oak fields, then northwesterly to Lewiston. West of the Town of Alabama the Trail had a branch leading to Clarence.

Being a good Democrat and thinking his job paid well and required little work, Ellicott was chosen as the lector from Western New York for all Presidential elections.

Actually, no one worked harder than he. Even after retiring in October 1821, with Jacob S. Otto of Philadelphia taking his place in the Land Office, he continued trying to interest investors in buying the land areas still unsold. This continuing effort resulted in failing health and in November 1825 he went to New York with his nephews, Ebenezer Mix and Joseph Nixon, for medical treatment, dying there August 19, 1826. He was buried in Batavia Cemetery and his twin sister Rachel had his monument erected. Ellicott never married; his great wealth and his desire to help his relatives encouraged them to reside in and around Batavia. Ellicott's twin sister Rachel's residence was on the north side of Main Street, west of Ellicott Avenue, and his brother Andrew's residence was next to hers.

In 1803, Rachel's son David E. Evans came to work as a clerk in the Holland Land Office, and after his uncle's death became the Company resident-agent and acquired the Ellicott Mansion. From 1818 to 1822 he was a State Senator.

John B. Ellicott, the son of Andrew and Sarah Ellicott, was born in 1795 and became a clerk in the office at an early age. During the war of 1812 he fought at Fort Erie. He and David Evans owned a grist mill in Medina and in 1817, John B. Ellicott sold his half to Evans when he moved to East Pembroke. The house where he had resided is still standing today in the

Town of East Pembroke. In 1851, he moved to Batavia and passed away In 1872, leaving seven children.

James Brisbane and Ebenezer Cary owned the first store in Batavia, with Cary becoming the Postmaster in 1806. His brother Trumbull, born August 11, 1787, in Mansfield, Connecticut, came to Batavia in 1805 as a clerk in their store and by 1810, Trumbull owned it. In 1812, he became Postmaster, then served as a State Assemblyman and Senator, becoming a good friend of Governor Seward. He was the founder of the Bank of Genesee in 1829, the first bank west of the Genesee River, operated the store until 1840, and died in 1869. His grandson, Trumbull, son of Walter, was still in that bank thirty years later.

The Brisbane Mansion which was further east of Evans Mansion (Ellicott Mansion) still stands today, being the City Hall and the Bank of Genesee built in 1831–it is now owned by the Batavia Club and was restored to its original beauty, located today at 201 East Main Street. The William Seaver home was east of the Bank of Genesee, and the Cary Mansion east of the Seaver home, were both destroyed by stupid so-called urban renewal with their paces now occupied by a new YMCA. There are some who feel the Cary Mansion was the most beautiful in Batavia, but I {Bro. Lamkin} favor the Richmond Mansion, possibly because of family friendship. I have a box of camphor wood purchased in China which the Richmonds gave my grandfather. The Richmond Mansion was the larger of the two buildings and was located on the north side of Main Street, in the next block to the east of the Cary Mansion, which was a part of a large tract of land going northward across several of today's streets.

Orphaned at the age of 15, Dean Richmond had inherited his father's salt mining business the year before. Using railroads to transport his salt, he later merged seven of these into the New York Central Railroad System, becoming its founder and president. With added enterprises he became the wealthiest man in the Great Lakes area, and living in Batavia, he maintained an office in Buffalo. Batavia's library was given by the family in memory of Dean, Jr.. Another son, E. Watts Richmond, was a member of a Buffalo Masonic Lodge, and Adelaide Richmond Kenny, the only daughter of Dean Richmond, Sr., inherited the property and was married to William J. C. Kenny, the largest stockholder and treasurer of the Buffalo Courier Express. Four years later, Adelaide, as a widow, moved back to the family home, served as a director of most of Batavia's industries and banks, and was a member of the Board of Education.

St. Joseph's Catholic church was in the northeast corner of Summit Street, and east of the church was the Jerome Girl's home, after whom

St. Jerome Hospital is named. The new St. Joseph's church and its parking area takes up the space once occupied by four homes.

Ebenezer Mix, born in New Haven, Connecticut on December 31, 1789, learned the mason trade under his brother Abiather and studied law under Daniel B. Brown. He came to Batavia in 1809 working as a mason in the summer and teaching school during the winter. He was hired by Ellicott to plaster an arched ceiling by the yard, and his figuring of the yardage was so accurate that in 1811, Ellicott immediately hired him for contracting in the office, where he stayed 27 years. He became the chief salesman and knew every nook and corner of the Holland Land Purchase and was acquainted with nearly all the pioneer settlers. This made him an exceptional authority on the early history and topography of Genesee Country. During the period from 1821 to 1840, he filled the office of Surrogate of Genesee County, and at the request of the Attorney General, codified the laws of New York. As an outstanding mathematician he wrote textbooks on the subject and helped Orsamus Turner write his "History of the Holland Purchase." During the early years he served in the War of 1812. Ebenezer Mix and fifty-one masons applied for a new Warrant for their Masonic Lodge, and when they received it, he became the first Worshipful Master of Batavia Lodge No.88, serving in 1842 and 1843. His home still stands on Mix Place, a short street between Oak Street and Ellicott Avenue. His son was also a Freemason and engineer.

St. James Episcopal Church, one of the oldest in the State, built their building in 1815. The congregation had been served previously by pastors of Ontario County. Trinity Church of New York City donated $1000 toward its construction and almost all of the people I've mentioned belonged. Batavia Lodge No.433 was organized in the building and Lucius Smith, its rector from 1823 to 1833, was an active Mason. Thomas McCully, the builder and a founder of Batavia's Methodist Church, was also a Mason. The building is gone but our Landmark Society was able to save the rectory, the cost being now almost paid off.

Two years later, in 1817, Col. William Seaver, his home having been mentioned before, came to Batavia where he owned a large drug, book and printing business for 50 years. He was Senior Warden of St. James Episcopal Church for 40 years, Postmaster for 29 years, and Master of Batavia Lodge No.433 for ten years. His son Daniel M. Seaver also was a strong Mason and served as Secretary and Junior Warden of Batavia Lodge No.88 until he dimitted from the Lodge on December 14, 1844.

The first building to the east of the Richmond Mansion belonged to Olive Branch Lodge and the next building was the home of Dr. John Z.

Ross, the Lodge's Worshipful Master in 1818. Crossing to the other side of Ross Street was the home of Richard Smith, the virtual father of Freemasonry at Batavia and the Senior Warden of Olive Branch Lodge, U.D. in 1811, and upon the death of their Worshipful Master, Judge Ezra Platt, presided over the Lodge until elected Master in 1812, serving again in 1813 and 1814. Richard Smith was the Worshipful Master named on the Olive Branch Lodge No.215's Charter. He was also Secretary of the Lodge in 1816. When Batavia Lodge No.433 came into being he was Treasurer, remaining so during the Morgan Affair. The building is now a dentist's office. Next to Richard Smith's home was the home of Senator Edward C. Walker, trustee of several universities and a cousin of the Lamkin family. This building has been a funeral home for the past eighty years.

The next building is today's St. James Episcopal Church, with both the Church and the Walker residence using the same driveway. Daniel W. Tomlinson, after making a fortune in cotton in Mobile, Alabama, moved to Alexander and then to Batavia, bringing the Exchange Bank of Attica with him. He gave his first home to the Episcopalians for their present Church, and then he moved to a new home across the street. His descendant, Everett Tomlinson, was still a banker ten years ago.

Col. William Seaver, the first Worshipful Master of Batavia Lodge No.433, had been a doctor before coming to Batavia; Blanchard Powers was the first Senior Warden and Dr. Richard Dibble was the first Junior Warden of Batavia Lodge in 1825. Dr. Richard Dibble's son, Judge Edgar C. Dibble, was Master of Fishers Lodge No.212 in 1853 and in 1857-1858 was appointed District Deputy Grand Master of the counties of Monroe, Livingston, Genesee and Orleans, and most capably discharged the duties thereof.

Other Freemasons during that time were Judge James W. Stevens and his brother, Judge James Taggert, and his son, Judge Moses Taggert—also, Aston W. Caney, the jeweler, Thomas and Tompkins of the clothing store, along with Gad Worthington and his son, Gad B. Worthington. Rear Admiral Ralph Chandler, grandson of Heaman Judd Redfield, was born in father Worthington's home.

Redfield lived at the west end of town on the south side of route 5 at its junction with route 63 and owned land on both sides of West Main Street. As a Democrat lawyer and a Mason, he refused to handle the Morgan trial as District Attorney. He and Jacob Le Roy purchased all the land left when the Holland Land Company went out of business. Redfield was appointed by President Pierce to be the collector of funds at the Port of New York, in which he collected $143.5 million for the government by 1857.

On the north side of Main Street near that entrance to Batavia Downs is a stone marker to show the location of an arsenal built in 1810 for the coming War of 1812, and which was in existence until 1845. Colonel Horace B. Olmsted was its commander along with being the sheriff in 1826. John Eager was a Mason and the owner of the original Genesee Brewery building, which was torn down in 1983.

Such was the situation in 1826. Most of those people were wealthy, most were Masons and many had been running things for a quarter century. Serving in the military was still popular. But the poorer country people were saying, "Some of these big shots bought their rank. We have to do the marching and maybe the fighting. They stand around looking important and continually inspect our work, and we can't get any kind of a higher office. They're all Democrats and if any of them decided to quit, that bunch would get together and pick the man to replace him before election time. That's the reason why our neighbors are picking up their belongings and leaving Genesee County, to start out again in one of the surrounding counties. But there are many of us who don't want to move again. The worst part is that most of the wealthy men are Masons. But, who knows who belongs? We hear some of them travel many miles to go to a meeting, then they stay all night and come home the next day. What farmer can afford to do that? Many of our poorer men feel that even if they had the fancy clothes and could afford to join, the aristocrats would probably turn them down anyway."

Equalitarianism was raising its ugly head, not only among the women, but also with the men who were starting to rebel. Many of us have heard the story of Dr. Daniel White, Master of Pavilion Lodge, leading a St. John's Day parade, with his wife bringing up the rear wearing the oldest clothing she could find and mocking his every move.

"Masons were everywhere."

Early Lodges Around Batavia

The countryside around Batavia in the early 1800's was scattered with tree stumps as more and more pioneers came, cleared the land, and settled in the area. By 1820, about two-thirds of all Lodges in New York State met at country taverns, for the simple reason that suitable rooms and accommodation were not obtainable without great expense. There were neither "high hills" nor "low valleys" in or near Batavia and thus the first Masonic Hall was nothing more or less than a dance hall or a ball room (familiarly called the long room) of one of Genesee County's once famous inns.

In 1802, William Munger put up a large two-story frame building on the north side of Main Street which was a short distance west of the present courthouse. A few years later, it was purchased by William Keyes, who doubled its dimensions by erecting a corresponding addition of equal size on the easterly side. The second story of this easterly portion of the building was set aside for the "long room" to be used for dancing, parties or shows of all kinds that would come around needing a large room for their affair.

Keyes' Hotel later on was called the "Frontier House," and was within a short distance from the winding Tonawanda Creek. It was painted bright yellow, surrounded by tall Lombardy poplar trees, and saw very many golden days. William Keyes died in 1833. Soon after Keyes's death, the Frontier House lost its gilt-edged prestige and acquired a dingy "yaller" hue. In 1854, it was divided and removed to make room for the attractive brick residence erected by George Brisbane. The eastern half of the building was moved to Church Street and the other part moved just west of the old stone Land Office on Main Street. Both were remodeled for homes.

Olive Branch Lodge Under Dispensation

The Masonic Lodge at Canandaigua had to be old; no white family crossed the Genesee until Joseph Ellicott started his work.

Today's Olive Branch Lodge No.39 has the honor of being the oldest Lodge west of the Genesee River. On May 10, 1810, a petition for a Lodge of Freemasons was drawn up by Isaiah Babcock and signed by fifteen brethren. The request was recommended by Genesee Lodge

No.130, at Avon, New York. The petition was presented to Grand Lodge on May 15, 1810, who took the following action: The Lodge was approved to be formed and to hold their meetings in Batavia with the name Fredonian Lodge. After some delay, it was decided to change the name to Olive Branch instead of Fredonian. Dr. Charles Little of Avon, Past Master of Genesee Lodge No.130, was deputized to formally institute Olive Branch Lodge and install its officers. The Olive Branch Lodge commenced a successful career and held sixteen meetings while under dispensation. During the first year, the total membership grew to between forty and fifty members. Its first Master in 1811 under dispensation was Ezra Platt of Bethany, with Richard Smith, mentioned before, as Senior Warden, and Isaiah Babcock, its Secretary for five years. The first meeting of Olive Branch Lodge was on May 11,1811, and was held in Keyes' tavern. Then on September 2, 1811, a plot of ground was purchased by the school board and by the Masons, the sum of $5.00 being paid for Lot number 32 on the north side of Main Street at the corner of an alley (Ross Street) containing 1,500 feet of land. Nathan Rumsey sold it to them with the condition that a brick building was to be built within one and a half years, the lower floor to be used as a school, and the upper for the Masons. The War of 1812 Interfered with construction until February 28, 1814, the date of the first meeting in that building. During the meantime they met with Brother Van Cleve in Ellicott Hall.

Olive Branch Lodge No.215

On May 20, 1813, a Charter was issued to Olive Branch Lodge No.215 at Batavia, in which Richard Smith was named first Worshipful Master, Lemuel Foster was named first Senior Warden, and John Zenas Ross as first Junior Warden. The designated number 215 continued until 1839. During the Anti-Masonic excitement so many Lodges had gone under in the tidal wave of political opinion that the Grand Lodge ordered a thorough consolidation in numbering Lodges, and priority of date of warrant was taken as the basis of seniority. Under said edict, Olive Branch Lodge became No.39 on the present roster. After Richard Smith, Lemuel Foster served as Master in 1815. Blanchard Powers was Master in 1816 and 1817 with John Ross in 1818. Powers again served in 1819 and 1820 with meetings in his home at Bethany.

Compromise of Olive Branch Lodge No.215 & Batavia

Lodge No.433

In 1815, Le Roy Lodge No.260 was formed at Le Roy, and in 1816, Allegany Lodge No.277 was formed at South Pembroke (now Darien); Rising Sun Lodge No.317 was formed at Attica. In addition, Lodges had formed in the towns of Sheldon, Middlebury, and Warsaw, and at a later date in the towns of Alexander, Byron, Stafford, and Covington. These Lodges all drew members from Olive Branch Lodge. In 1820, Olive Branch Lodge No.215's members asked permission of the Grand Lodge to hold meetings In Bethany. Permission was granted and the Lodge assembled in a special communication at Cornelius J. and Jebediah Lincoln's Hall (a public Inn) in Bathany, on April 5, 1821, for its first meeting. The removal to Bethany was originally intended to be temporary, not to exceed three or four years, to awaken new interest in the affairs of Olive Branch Lodge. The Lodge did meet in Batavia on several occasions for burial ceremonies. Between 1820 and 1824, numerous Master Masons who were members of sister Lodges became residents of Batavia. Early in the year 1824, the brethren at Batavia, thinking for the good of the craft that Olive Branch Lodge No.215 should resume its meetings in their old residence, made a formal application to the Lodge but the brethren in Bethany insisted on permanent residence in their own town. By compromise, the Bethany brethren were allowed to retain the old name and warrant, but as an offset, all funds and efforts were given to the Batavia brethren with which to organize a new Lodge under a new name in Batavia. Such then was the end of Olive Branch Lodge at Batavia. On November 8, 1824, at which time the harmonious division of Olive Branch Lodge No.215 took place and on June 8, 1825, Batavia Lodge No.433 received its Charter. During those years, Batavia Lodge No.433 had a membership of 162 and today Batavia Lodge No.475 averages around 680 members.

Olive Branch Lodge No.39

In the Town of Bethany by 1821, Cornelius J. Lincoln owned the tavern which Sylvester Lincoln built back in 1805 and Lodge meetings were held there. The cornerstone of Zion Episcopal Church in East Bethany was laid with ceremony by the members of Olive Branch Lodge No.215 on July 4, 1826, and Calvin Barrows, the first settler of Linden (Bethany Township) told of his attending meetings in Nathaniel Huggins' tavern there after the Morgan troubles subsided. This tavern was built in 1828 and Huggins operated it until he died in 1852. We don't know when Olive Branch No.39 moved to Attica—only that it was there in 1846. In 1844, the members of Olive Branch Lodge No.39 found themselves unable to get enough new members at their present location in the small hamlet of East Bethany, so it was decided to move to Attica in July 1845. No benefit was realized by this change and on December 8, 1846, Olive Branch Lodge No.39 moved to Le Roy where Lucius Parks and a few energetic Le Roy Freemasons, from 1847 to 1857, restored the Lodge to full strength and prosperity.

Batavia Lodge No.88

Bethany in the early years had a Masonic Lodge, No.88, which moved to Batavia for a short time until the entire records of the Lodge burned in a fire—so we don't know much about it. Many Masonic Lodges had gone out of existence during the Morgan Affair and Anti-Masonic period, and Batavia Lodge No.433 went in darkness and finally returned their Warrant to Grand Lodge on June 25, 1839; a period of repose intervened which lasted three years. During the period of darkness of the Lodge the meeting places changed many times. This could be a reason for a Lodge in Bethany by the number 88, meeting there in the early years.

An application requesting a new Warrant for Batavia Lodge No.433 was sent to Grand Lodge by Ebenezer Mix and fifty-one other brethren, and on February 16, 1842, their Warrant was renewed. Grand Lodge changed their numbering system due to the loss of so many Lodges and gave the number 88 to Batavia Lodge. On June 1, 1842, the first meeting of Batavia Lodge No.88 was held at "Holden's upper sitting room" in the village of Batavia. Worshipful Master Ebenezer Mix accepted the suggestion that the Lodge's next meeting would be held at Orange T. Fargo's Tavern, in the Town of Alexander at 2:00 P.M. on June 16, 1842. Batavia Lodge No.88 stayed in existence until November 9, 1847.

On January 4, 1844, tho members of Batavia Lodge No.88 formally voted to change their meeting place from Fargo's Tavern to the Genesee House in Batavia, pending the ability of renting the room, but ended up in renting the Odd Fellows' Cobble Stone block.

In the spring of 1847, Joel Allen, the Lodge's Master, moved to Piqua, Ohio, leaving no experienced
presiding officer. All of the elected officers of the Lodge were young men—good workers but had little
experience in the Ancient Landmarks and usages connected with the

governing of the Lodge. Two of the Lodgos old-time Past Masters, Blanchard Powers and Edon Foster, tried to take over the Lodge, resulting with the two bringing discord into what was then a harmonious Lodge. In this dilemma, Horace M. Warren (acting Master) applied to Grand Lodge for help. The Grand Lodge representative, Ezra S. Barnum, Senior Grand Warden, found it impossible to alleviate the problem, and on November 9, 1847, the Lodge returned their Warrant. Ely Parker was made a Mason in Batavia Lodge No.88 in 1847.

Note: At the December 19, 1844 meeting of Batavia Lodge No.88, their members recommended the

application of several brother masons, living in the Buffalo area, to reestablish Masonry in Buffalo,

and thus the oldest modern day Lodge, Hiram Lodge No.105 came into existence.

On September 2, 1846, the members of Batavia Lodge No.88, voted and gave their consent for Olive Branch Lodge No.39 to move from Attica to Le Roy. (Finally Olive Branch Lodge No.39 found a permanent Masonic home).

Fishers Lodge No.212

The proper moment had finally arrived—the problem that existed due to the two belligerent old Past

Masters had gone away, and the brethren agreed that they should resume the labors of the Lodge. In

December of 1850, a petition to form a Lodge, recommended by Olivo Branch Lodge No.39 at Le Roy, was presented to Grand Lodge.

Fishers Lodge had their first meeting on December 17, 1850, which was held in the room formerly used by Batavia Lodge No.88 in the third story of the eastern end of the Cobble Stone block (now 67 Main Street, Batavia).

The first meeting under the new Warrant on March 4, 1851, started a harmonious and active Lodge. In their first year, they had twenty-one candidates initiated and six Master Masons were affiliated, thus making a total membership of forty-five Masons. For eight year,s Fishers Lodge No.212 had continuous success. In 1859, this success ceased to exist when for some inexplicable reason, candidates for admission were rejected. In this dilemma, it was thought best to dissolve the Lodge. On April 5, 1859, Fishers Lodge No.212 surrendered their Warrant. Within a few days on April 9, 1859, Batavia Lodge No.475 received their Charter.

Further information on Masonry in and about Batavia

Western Star Chapter No.35, Royal Arch Masons, was organized in Batavia on March 29, 1813, where it still exists under that number. Batavia's Fishers Lodge No.212, was named for Lille Fisher, Esq., of Alexander, a very early settler of that area. Bethany formed Lodge No.215.

Le Roy Lodge No.260 was organized under Dispensation on January 7, 1815. The Lodge held the first
meeting February 16, 1815 and had their first candidate on March 6, 1815. By the time its Charter was
presented on June 11, 1816, the Lodge had 150 members, but the Morgan Affair caused its collapse on
September 19, 1827. Walbridge, the tavern keeper of the Morgan incidents, lived in Le Roy. Among the more prominent masons of Le Roy that were preserved included Richmond, Jr. and his uncle Albion D. Richmond, both of Richmond Road west of Fort Hill; also, F. C. Lathrup who lived on the east side of the creek north of Main Street, who owned all the land along the east bank of the Oatka Creek, and Moses Wingate, along with L. F. Wilcox, who lived on the Oatka Trail. A. F. Bartow, Samuel Hall, and Charles N. Vicary lived in Morganville north of Stafford.

In October of the year 1823, Transit Lodge No.363 of Stafford was constituted. Its first Master
was Dr. Samuel Butler, the Senior Warden Edwin Foster, and the Junior Warden Jacob Wade. Rev. Lucius Smith of St. James Church dedicated it when the Lodge received their Charter in September of 1825. The Lodge laid the cornerstone of the Episcopal Church there. The town also had an Odd Fellows Lodge. Masonry seemed to have a rapid growth at this time with the addition of Perry's Constellation Lodge No.404, followed by Arcade Lodge No.419. Hesperus Lodge No.837 (another word for Western Star) of Bergen is also an old Lodge—although we don't know the date of origin, we do know that the Lodges in Bergen and Arcade both built buildings in 1902.

The Town of Pembroke had Allegany Lodge No.225, located on Route 77 south of Corfu, and one Master, Alanson T. Fisher, is reported to have amassed the largest fortune of anyone in the Town of Darien. Pembroke had a Knights Templar organization prior to 1890 with a Templar Hall at Indian Falls, built of material from the mines located there and was replaced less than five years ago by a modern home. As for exact age of the building we find only that the plaster company was in operation in

1876 and that, my wife Ruth Lamkin's grandfather and great-grandfather Were members of the Knights Templar with the older man dying in 1890.

Batavia Lodge No.433, organized in 1824 in St. James Church, held meetings in the Eagle Hotel until it burned in 1833. They surrendered that Charter in 1839 and it wasn't able to renew until 1842. The Morgan Affair disrupted Masonry in the city for 16 years. Pavilion Lodge apparently managed to last at least until 1882 when the Equitable Aid Union held meetings in the Lodge building on the second and fourth Fridays.

An example of the enthusiasm for Masonry can be found in the towns of Caryville and Oakfield, where Masons in both towns petitioned to Batavia Lodge for permission to start Lodges within a three-month period. Both were denied. The Town of Caryville was named for Colonel Alfred Cary, an early settler who founded Cary Collegiate Seminary there. Another relative of mine {Lambkin} attended that school which lasted into this century and I remember one of its buildings next to the Episcopal Church. Cary Seminary had degrees of D.D. and LL.D. with most of his instructors having a D.D.. Charles W. Stickle became Master of Batavia's Lodge and also the superintendent of East Pembroke's Rural Seminary.

In Le Roy, Dr, William Sheldon, the Town's supervisor, and others including Orator H. Kendall, succeeded in having Olive Branch No.39 removed to Attica. At its second meeting in Le Roy in February 1847, under Lucius Parks, it had its first candidate. Worshipful Brother Parks was followed by RW John H. Anderson, who served as Master for 13 years and raised 228 new members during that time. Ho was District Deputy Grand Master for six years, serving Genesee, Wyoming, Monroe, Orleans and Livingston Counties; Phoenix Lodge No.115 in Dansville still is in existence today. Anderson held the offices of Junior Grand Warden, Grand Steward, and Deputy Grand Lecturer of the Grand Lodge of the State of New York. He was also Assistant Grand Lecturer and first High Priest of Le Roy Chapter No.183 of the Royal Arch Masons, the first Generalissimo of Batavia Encampment Knights Templar, and Sovereign Grand Inspector of the 33rd Degree in the Scottish Rite. Two years from now {1986}, Olive Branch Lodge No.39 will celebrate its 175th Anniversary. Rev. Pierre Cushing, Rector of St. Mark's Episcopal Church, and W. P. Simpson both belonged to Batavia's Knights Templar.

Batavia Lodge No.433 renewed again in 1842, held meetings at Orange T. Fargo's Tavern, just inside the Alexander township line on the road toward the Village (Route 98) for 18 months, and then moved to a cobblestone building in Alexander. As it seemed rather unwarranted to have two

Lodges in that village, Batavia Lodge No.433, again surrendered their Charter in 1847 and their members joined Fishers Lodge No.212. After about a year the Lodge moved into the new I.O.O.F. building in Batavia at the corner of Main and Jackson Streets, staying there until April 5, 1859. Dissension between the members of the Lodge had mounted to the point that every candidate petitioning for membership was being rejected and on April 5, 1859 they turned in their Warrant. Four days later, on April 9, 1859, they reorganized as Batavia Lodge No.475, receiving their Charter on July 4, 1859. It is still in existence today.

Today's Attica Lodge No.462 is older than Batavia Lodge No.475, as is Varysburg West Star Lodge No.413. The towns of Warsaw and Castile had Lodges before the Morgan disruption and today Warsaw Lodge No.549 and Oakland Lodge No.379 of Castile are in operation. The only places we know without Masonic Lodges were Alabama and Elba. These Lodges made up one District of our Grand Lodge, just as they were part of one county until May 14, 1841. When the southern part of the Genesee County became Wyoming County and the Genesee-Wyoming District was formed by Grand Lodge, other Lodges were added to the new district, which were also very old.

Akron Lodge No.527, just outside Genesee County limits with several of its Past Masters and many of its members living in Erie County, petitioned in January 1862 to form a new Lodge. They received their Dispensation on August 21, 1862, and their Charter on June 5, 1863. The Lodge's first Worshipful Master was Seneca Chief Ely Samuel Parker, who served two years.

Batavia Commandery No.34, Knights Templar, was organized on September 27, 1865, and is still going
strong.

In 1826, before the Morgan Affair, there were 360 Lodges in New York State with 22,000 members; during the next ten years the total dropped to 75 Lodges with only 4,000 members.

The Story of William Morgan

WIlliam Morgan was born in Culpepper, Virginia, August 7, 1774. Morgan served an apprenticeship as a stone mason at Hap Hazard Mills, Madison County, Virginia. As a young man he went to Kentucky for about four years, returning to Virginia, where he worked on the Orange County Courthouse as a bricklayer. Samuel D. Greene contending that Morgan was a good soldier in the War of 1812, and was advanced to the rank of Captain, but the War Department showed no records of him serving in the Army. In fact, in Robert Morris's book "William Morgan," quoting from his recorded notes containing interviews with hundreds of persons who knew Morgan, there were comments such as, "a worthless fellow," "Iow down white trash," "bankrupt," "an habitual liar," "a hanger on at grog shops," etc.. Morris had classified him as a sot, a bummer, and an ignoramus.

In October of f 1819, he married Lucinda Pendleton, then, in 1821, Morgan went to Batavia, neglectful of his family, never maintaining a home other than a convenient boarding room close to where he would be working. Shortly thereafter, he traveled to Canada, in or about Toronto. According to the Grand Lodge of Canada, there is no evidence that he was a member or was admitted to any Lodge in Canada. After leaving Canada, he headed for Rochester working as a stone mason and then he traveled to Le Roy and Batavia.

In Fairfax, Virginia (some say Richmond—it doesn't really matter), a man opened his store in 1819, who also worked as a stone mason. Richmond was and is the capital of the state of Virginia and greater Washington is only about five miles from Fairfax. While there seems to be no record of William Morgan receiving the first three degrees of Freemasonry, it would have been very easy for him as a stone mason to watch and listen to the Masonic ceremonies, including the Laying of Corner Stones for public buildings and churches. He observed that the men who were involved in such events seemed to enjoy each other's company before and after those ceremonies and he knew that a man had to be wealthy to gain a state or national office. To a poor man with ambition to better himself, Freemasonry appeared to be the answer to Morgan's dreams.

When the English burned Washington, soldiers from Canada told about Toronto. Morgan thought that maybe he could become a Freemason In Canada, as he certainly couldn't in Virginia. Upon his arrival in Toronto in

1821, he invested in a brewery, thereby buying himself a degree of status and was apparently accepted.

While F. W. Beers the historian says, "the Morgan Monument was erected by anti-Masons," the inscriptions on it show many Canadian Freemasons contributing to its expense. Maybe he did receive his degrees in Toronto or as most agree, bluffed his way into meetings using what knowledge he had gained by observation—we really don't know.

The brewery burned down and William Morgan traveled to Lewiston and later on moved to Rochester where he lived next door to Dr. Russell Dyer, nearby Thurlow Weed's home. Although Morgan was very clever, he wasn't quite smart enough to avoid becoming a pawn in Weed's political ambitions.

In May of 1826, leaving his wife and two children in Rochester, he traveled to Le Roy and worked on the Round House next to the Masonic Lodge building. From Le Roy he traveled to Batavia and pretended to be an architect, finding work with Thomas McCully who was building the Eagle Hotel at the southeast corner of Main and Court Streets. He also worked on an old stone building behind the post office. After the Eagle Hotel burned it was replaced by the Richmond Hotel, which is now occupied by our downtown office of the Marine Midland Bank; the old post office that was next to it is now Beardsley's clothing store. Morgan lived for a time in the McCully's home, then moved to the house west of the Holland Land Company's office, and later moved to 72 Main Street on the northwest corner of Russell Place.

Morgan became a member of Western Star Chapter No.35, Royal Arch Mason, on May 31, 1825, in Le Roy, but, as a poor man of questionable character and heavy drinking, was expelled.

On March 13, 1826, Morgan entered into a contract for the publication of his exposé of Freemasonry
with Russell Dyer, John Davids (Morgan's landlord), and David C. Miller, who received his Entered
Apprentice Degree twenty years before, but was prevented from advancement for due cause and held a grudge against the Fraternity. David Miller was also the Editor of the Republican Advocate, the newest of four newspapers in Batavia at the time. Consequently in June or July, with the help of Miller, the partners started to publish a book called, "Illustrations of Freemasonry by William Morgan." The material for the book was obtained largely from an English publication, "Jachin and Boaz." The work was done secretly in the upper floors of the two buildings on Main Street occupied by Miller. Some say rather vaguely that these

buildings were east of the Land Office but it appears more likely they were on the north side of the street opposite today's courthouse and next to John Hamilton's monument works. (Hamilton was a stone cutter of both marble and granite and also an
officer of the Knights Templar.)

On July 25, 1826, Morgan was taken into custody by the sheriff for a debt but was soon released. On August 9, 1826, the "Ontario Messenger", published in Canandaigua, issued a notice warning the people about a man calling himself Captain William Morgan who should not be trusted. This warning was copied by the Batavia papers, and many of the area Lodges were sent this same information, including Lockport Lodge No.73, a Lodge which had several members participating in the "Morgan Affair".

On September 10, 1826, Ebenezer C. Kingsley obtained from Justice Chipman (both living in Canandaigua) a warrant for Morgan's arrest for having stolen a shirt and a tie, which in reality Kingsley had lent to Morgan in May.

Also, on September 10, 1826, a small fire was found in Miller's Printing office, which was extinguished.

The next day, September 11, 1826, the constable of Canandaigua, Holloway Hayward, and five men took the warrant for Morgan's arrest to Le Roy, where it was endorsed by a justice there and then they returned to Morgan's home in Batavia. Morgan offered no objection and went with Holloway Hayward to David Danold's tavern on the northeast corner of Main and Bank Streets, and had breakfast with Hayward and his friends. David C. Miller, as bailor for Morgan, went to Danold's tavern, objecting that Morgan had been taken outside of the Genesee County Jail limits, but constable Hayward felt he was still obligated to carry out his duty and the men left with Morgan.

Reaching Le Roy, Hayward offered to take Morgan to the Justice, Squire Foster, who had endorsed the warrant, so that Morgan might give bail for appearance at the next term of the court. But Morgan declined saying, "he could convince the judge that he did not intend to steal from Kingsley." There had been no forceful action taken that morning in Batavia when he was arrested. When they arrived before Chipman in Canandaigua on September 11, 1826, Morgan proved his innocence but was immediately arrested again for a $2.68 debt he owed Ackley, a tavern keeper in that town. This bill had been assigned to Nicholas G. Chesebro, the Master of Canandaigua Lodge. Morgan offered his coat in payment but this was refused and he was put in the County of Ontario's county jail.

At night, on September 12, 1826, members of the Masonic fraternity called at the jail and in the absence of the jailor, told his wife to release Morgan as the judgement had been paid by Loton Lawson. Lawson lived on the west side of Thomas Avenue in Batavia, north of Joseph Ellicott's Mansion on Main Street.

Morgan was released but upon reaching the street he was suddenly thrust into a closed carriage, gagged, bound and then driven rapidly out of town to the Ridge Road (Route 104), and then continuing toward Lewiston, accompanied by Loton Lawson and two other masons, Colonel Edward Sawyer and John Sheldon. Edward Sawyer lived on the east side of Ellicott Avenue, just about behind Lawson, and Sheldon lived on the west side of State Street.

At the trial for the abductors, some months later, Lawson testified that the Ridge Road was followed to Lewiston and then to Fort Niagara where preparations had been made previously for Morgan's arrival. Near a graveyard the passengers got out, the abductors dismissed the coachman, and William Morgan was then taken into the Fort, blindfolded, bound again and then at 3:00 A.M. on September 14, 1826, he was placed in a vacant magazine until September 19, 1826, at which time he disappeared. No one except masons were allowed to talk to Morgan. It was also revealed that Chesebro had paid for the coach.

Harold August of Middleport tells me that the Wells brothers of that town were forced to leave and moved to Ohio. The sheriff of Niagara County, Eli Bruce, and John Whitney were fined and imprisoned for the part they took in the affair. Other prominent and respected men were convicted, but Chesebro, Lawson, Sawyer, and Sheldon were only indicted for complicity.

Lawson did not say that "he" went the whole distance but simply related what had happened. There is nothing in any of the records to indicate anyone having been murdered. When Morgan disappeared September 19, 1826, he could have easily gone back to Canada, or, as we have all read, possibly to Jamaica where he has been credited with founding Masonry.

After It became known that David C. Miller and William Morgan intended to publish a book, Daniel Johns of Canada came to Batavia. Having lived and become acquainted with some of Miller's friends in Rochester, he offered to advance some money to Miller and was accepted without much scrutiny as to his motives. David Miller supposed that Johns wanted Morgan's manuscript and he certainly wanted John's money. Although Miller had sworn under an oath to protect Morgan's secret, Johns obtained a part of the manuscript for about $30.00 to $40.00, the money being more important to Miller than the manuscript was to Johns.

A warrant in behalf of Johns was issued by justice Bartow (a mason in Le Roy living north of Main Street east of the Oatka Creek) against Miller and his partner Davids to collect the money Johns had advanced.

The warrant was given to constable Jesse French of Stafford who, upon learning that Miller intended to resist, employed several assistants and on September 12, 1826, followed by Roswell Wilcox and Jesse Hurlburt and a large party, went to Batavia to arrest Miller and Davids. Hurlburt lived on the west side of State Street, near John Sheldon of the Morgan business. Wilcox lived on Trumbull Place, and like Hurlburt, was a Mason and also a Knights Templar.

The presence of so many strangers in town excited the citizenry, many of whom offered to resist the attempt to arrest Miller thinking they were after the manuscript. Although Miller had fortified his office with arms, none were used. Wilcox arrested Davids and French arrested Miller. Both submitted and were taken to Danold's Tavern where Davids was soon released. David Miller was taken to the Lodge room in Stafford, kept there two or three hours, and then was taken to Walbridge's Tavern in Le Roy where he was discharged. C. W. Miller, the editor's son, who lived on the east side of State Street and thus a neighbor of Hurlburt, issued the September 15, 1826, edition of the Republican Advocate saying,

> "On Monday two buildings were set on fire and Morgan was seized and carried off some place by a group of ruffians. On Tuesday a mob of more than 100 people came into Batavia to destroy our printing equipment and took our editor, without legal process to Le Roy", etc..

A trial was to be held before four Judges of the Court of Common Pleas including Judges Birdsall, William J. Tisdale of Bethany (mentioned before), James Taggart, a Mason on Summit Street, and Simeon Cummings, another Mason, on Vine Street. French was sentenced to 12 months imprisonment, Wilcox to six months, and Hurlburt to three months.

A tremendous excitement followed the disappearance of Morgan with investigating committees being appointed everywhere. Hostility between Masons and Anti-Masons became bitter. Families and Churches were split. Lodges not only lost members, but also expelled members and some disbanded for years.

The disappearance of Morgan did not halt progress on the publishing of his expose of Freemasonry, and on December 15, 1826, Miller printed the following announcement in his newspaper, "Batavia's Republican Advocate", of the finished work:

Just Published

And for sale at the Advocate Office.

The First Part of Masonry Unveiled, containing a full exposition of the' secrets and ceremonies of that "Ancient and Honorable" Order.

FREE MASONRY

And God Said, "Let there be light and there was light."

The remaining part is now in press and will shortly be published.

Yes, while everybody wasted time and energy on committees or simply argued, Morgan's "Revelations of Masonry" appeared at one dollar per copy. The demand was not as great as anticipated, so the price went down to fifty cents, then to twenty-five cents, and finally the price was reduced to a dime. No profits seem to have been made.

In May of 1827, Batavia Lodge No.433 announced that as usual it would hold its public St. John's Day Celebration. David Miller tried to prevent the celebration but on June 25, 1827, three-hundred Masons assembled along with several thousand spectators, some armed with knives and guns. George Hosmer of Livingston County was the speaker and while the Masons had to endure jeers and insults from the multitude, the day passed without incident. Afterwards, the anti-Masons tried to exclude Masons from the jury.

In October, a dead body was found on the shore of Lake Ontario, brought to Batavia and exhibited on Brisbane's lawn. The anti-Masons formed a great procession with Mrs. William Morgan and Miller as chief mourners to convey the body to Batavia's elite cemetery on Harvester Avenue, where a handsome monument to Morgan's memory was to be placed in a most conspicuous spot at the front, which can be easily seen from Harvester Avenue. This was a golden political opportunity and Thurlow Weed played it to the hilt. Unfortunately for him, it was soon proven without doubt that the body they buried was that of Timothy Monroe, of Clark, District of Newcastle, Upper Canada, who, on September 24, 1827, while returning to Canada in a row boat from the American side, overturned and was thrown into the water and accidently drowned. The anti-Masons, who had been supporting Mrs. Morgan all this time, now dropped her and she turned to the Royal Arch Masons for help.

The story of Morgan's "murder" persisted. Thurlow Weed died in 1882 and on his deathbed he stated that in 1860 (twenty two years before), John Whitney, convicted of conspiracy, confessed to him of the murder, and said he would dictate and sign a statement of confession, but died before he could do so. "But Whitney died in 1869, nine years after, and was buried by Masons in Graceland Cemetery in Chicago, Illinois!"

The story was told to Robert Morris, which seems to be the best attested of any that were told. Whitney told Morris that he had consulted with Governor Clinton, relative to what could be done to prevent Morgan printing the Masonic, expose. Clinton forbade any illegal moves, but suggested purchasing the manuscript for any amount of money up to one thousand dollars (a great sum of money in those days). In Batavia, Whitney summoned Morgan to a conference in which the bribe was presented. Morgan was to receive five hundred dollars if he would go to Canada to "disappear"; his family would be provided for and sent to him later. Morgan agreed. Whitney told Morris that two Canadian Masons received Morgan from the hands of his "kidnappers" at Fort Niagara, traveled with him, a day and a night to a place in Hamilton, Ontario, where they paid him the five hundred dollars, received his receipt for the money and the signed agreement, never to return without permission of Captain William King, Sheriff Eli Bruce, or John Whitney. No man knows where he went from there. Was he murdered or did he travel to some unknown place?

Although Masonry and good people in or out suffered much because of Thurlow Weed and his people, we do have to give him credit for the national political conventions, the two party system, (the Democrats and several small political groups which combined into the Republican Party), but most of all, the little guys today have gained much more say in their local government.

While few of us today have the financial strength of 160 years ago as I illustrated in my hypothetical dialogue earlier, we still retain the values and knowledge, and I hope, the wisdom to serve our fellow man. Or, as Richard Fletcher, the Grand Master of Masons in Vermont, advises, "[M]aybe it's time to move out of the cloistered Lodge room and into the community again." As Masons, have we the privilege of ignoring our local community needs in the drugs, sex and crimes of our juveniles today? Masonry should once again become our Roman Fasces.

Bibliography

Original Bibliography: LaVerne S. Lamkin

F.W.Beers, "County Gazetteer and Directory," June 1890–859 pages.
LaVerne S. Lamkin, "Indian Fails," 1950–253 pages.
O. Turner, "History of the Holland Purchase," about 1850.
Several Township maps of Genesee & Wyoming Counties, 1854, 1866, 1876 and 1900.

Additional Bibliography: Charles L. Ketchum, Jr.

(1) The Morgan Affair and Anti-Masonry by John C. Palmer- 1924.

(2) Freemasonry at Batavia, NY from 1811-1891 by David Seaver- 1991.

(3) Olive Branch Lodge No.39, 150th Anniversary Celebration Pamphlet – Saturday, May 13, 1961.

(4) The History of Freemasonry in the State of New York by Ossian Lang–1922.

(5) History of Lockport Lodge No.73 by R.:W.:Clarence O. Lewis–1964

(6) The First One Hundred Years–A History of the Grand Lodge A.F. & A.M. of
Canada in the Province of Ontario by M.: W.: Walter S. Herrington–1955.

(7) Joseph Ellicott and the Holland Land Company by William Chazanof–1970.

(8) The Hal/and Land Company in Western New York by Robert W. Silsby–1961.

(9) A History of New York State by D. M. Ellis, J. A. Frost, H. C. Syrett and H. J. Carman -1967.

(10) History of the Indian Tribes on North America by Thomas L. McKenney and James Hall–1836.

(11) The White Woman and Her Valley by Arch Merrill-1955.

(12) The Land of the Senecas by Arch Merrill–1949.

(13) Red Jacket, Seneca Chief, 1751–1830, historical collection of Edward A. Waters–1885.

(14) The History of the Seneca Indians by Arthur C. Parker–1926.

(15) The Senecas on Buffalo Creek Reservation by Frank J. Lankes–1964.

(16) Reservation Supplement, Related to Buffalo Creek Reservation by Frank J. Lankes–1966.

(17) An Outline of West Seneca History by Frank J. Lankes—1962.

(18) Sketches of Early Buffalo and the Niagara Region by Sophie C. Becker
_ 1904.

(19) Genesee County, New York edited by Safford E. North—1899.

(20) History of Genesee County 1890–1982 edited by Mary
McCulley—1985.

Appendix: Officers of Former Masonic Lodges at Batavia, N.Y. from 1811 to 1859

{In the format of year, Worshipful Master, Senior Warden, Junior Warden, Treasurer, Secretary}

Olive Branch Lodge Under Dispensation

1811–Ezra Platt, Richard Smith, Lemuel Foster, William Rumsey, Isaiah Babcock
1812–Richard Smith, Lemuel Foster, John Zenas Ross, William Rumsey, Isaiah Babcock

Olive Branch Lodge No.215

1813–Richard Smith, Lemuel Foster, John Zenas Ross, William Rumsey, Isaiah Babcock
1814–Richard Smith, Lemuel Foster, John Zenas Ross, William Rumsey, Isaiah Babcock
1815–Lemuel Foster, John Zenas Ross, Blanchard Powers, William Rumsey, Isaiah Babcock
1816–Blanchard Powers, Edmund Tracy, Charles S. Rumsey, Benjamin Allen, Richard Smith
1817–Blanchard Powers, Charles S. Rumsey, Benjamin Allen, Benj. Porter, Sr., Thomas H. Clark
1818–John Zenas Ross, Eden Foster, Benjamin BLodgett, Abner Ashley, Samuel Lake
1819–Blanchard Power,s Eden Foster, Abner Ashley, Noah North, Samuel Lake
1820–Blanchard Powers, Ephraim Towner, Abner Ashley, Noah North, Samuel Lake

Note: Olive Branch Lodge No.215 moved to Bethany on April 5, 1821.

Early in 1824 the members were thinking of moving back to Batavia, but several members wished to stay in their present location, and a compromise was settled upon. Olive Branch Lodge No.215 would stay in Bethany and retain their Warrant, but the members wishing to return to Batavia would receive the funds necessary to establish a new Lodge. This is the reason for a lapse in the officers listing between 1820 and 1825. Batavia Lodge No.433 received their Warrant on June 8, 1825.

Batavia Lodge No.433

1825—William Seaver, Blanchard Powers, Richard Dibble, Ephraim Brown, Richard Martin
1826—William Seaver, Harry Brown, Jonas S. Billings, Richard Smith, Richard Martin
1827—William Seaver, Harry Brown, Jonas S. Billings, Richard Smith, Richard Martin
1828—William Seaver, Harry Brown, Jonas S. Billings, Richard Smith, Richard Martin

Note: Owing to the Anti-Masonic excitement, Batavia Lodge No.433 was dormant from 1828 to 1829 and had no meetings. Its Warrant was returned in 1839, but did not actively revive until 1842 as Batavia Lodge No.88.

Batavia Lodge No.88

1842—Ebenezer Mix, Thomas McCully, John Allen, Abiel W. Ensign, Daniel M. Seaver
1843—Ebenezer Mix, Eden Foster, John Wheeler, Hector Humphrey, Kelsey Stone
1844—Eden Foster, Joel Allen, Daniel M. Seaver, Hector Humphrey, George G. BLodgett
1845—Joel Allen, Guy B. Shepard, Thomas T. Everett, Hector Humphrey, Eden Foster
1846—Guy B. Shepard, Joel Allen Merrick, C. Townsend, Hector Humphrey, Bradley G. Tisdale
1847—Joel Allen, Horace M. Warren, Hector Humphrey, Stephen A. Wilson, Bradley G. Tisdale

Fishers Lodge No.212

1851–Cyrus Pond, Horace M. Warren, Stephen A. Wilson, Hector Humphrey, John Eager

1852–Horace M. Warren, Edgar C. Dibble, Kimball Ferren, Joseph C. Wilson, John Eager

1853–Edgar C. Dibble, Kimball Ferren, Gad Worthington, Horace M. Warren, Smith Frost

1854–Kimball Ferren, Horace M. Warren, Earl Alex Fargo, George W. Miller, Trumbull C. Kimberly

1855–Gad Worthington, Earl Alex Fargo, Walter Sutherland, Henry T. Cross, David Seaver

1856–Horace M. Warre,n Kimball Ferren, Orrin Dewolf, Henry T. Cross, James A. Olds

1857–Stephen A. Wilson, Orrin Dewolf, Smith Frost, Trumbull Kimberly, James A. Olds

1858–Stephen A. Wilson, Benjamin Pringle, Samuel B. Pierson, Henry T. Cross, David Seaver

1859–Stephen A. Wilson, Orrin Dewolf, Samuel B. Pierson, Albert H. Towne, David Seaver

Note: Dissension in Fishers Lodge No.212 shown its ugly face and on April 5, 1859, the Lodge became dormant. April 9, 1859, Batavia Lodge Under Dispensation was organized and on July 4, 1859, Batavia Lodge No.475 received its Charter and is still in existence today.

SECOND BOOK OF TRANSACTIONS

{*The disclaimer, introduction, et alia, is from the original softcover "Book of Transactions Volume 2". The image of Albert Hoffman as Master of the Lodge could not be adequately reproduced, so one was taken recently for this purpose. The photograph of Brother Fowler could not be reproduced or a substitute found. This was the only book not previously edited for publication or republication by this editor.*}

Disclaimer

The articles or reports in this Book Of Transactions are the viewpoint and opinion of Brother who presented it. They may not be totally factual but they are the authors' interpretations.

In no way does it reflect the beliefs of the Grand Lodge Of New York or of other members of the Craft.

These articles are designed to enlighten and to make the reader ponder over the issues which are contained in this Book Of Transactions.

Editing & Selection Process

The articles in this Book Of Transactions were chosen from the archives of the Lodge. All members were also asked to submit articles if they wished.

The articles were edited by a team of brothers including Brother Mark Robson, W Charles Ketchum and Brother Anthony L Delisi. The Lodge would like to thank these members for their time, work and skill in typing and editing.

The editing was as minimal as possible, changing only glaring errors in spelling and grammar. Old word spelling was left as is and no sentences were edited in a manner that would change the meaning of the words.

The Master's Message

On a snowy Friday, December 29th 1981, a group of Masons were at the Investiture of the 1982 Masters Elect. This ceremony took place at Buffalo Lodge Masonic Temple, 212 Cazenovia St, Buffalo New York.

A few of the Past Masters and interested brethren of various Lodges in the then three Erie Districts gathered to investigate the idea of a Lodge Of Research for Western New York.

Their objectives were to give more light to the Brethren, to encourage the study of all facets of Freemasonry; to read papers and to discuss them in Lodge and in discussion groups. They also thought of building a library where Brothers could do research at a convenient place.

Today, we have that library located at Amherst Masonic Hall and at the Masonic Service Bureau, Inc. Now, twenty-five years since our inception, we have our own web site at www.wnyLodgeofresearch.org where Brothers in Erie County and throughout the internet world can see and read a synopsis of the works of our Brothers from the Western New York Lodge Of Research. Today, our Brothers are often asked to do professional presentations in other local Lodges.

At present, we have over fifty members who are active as well as honorary and corresponding members. Our members have grown into a true family of Brotherly love.

Membership in the Lodge of research is open to all regular Master Masons in good standing.

RW Albert Hoffman
Worshipful Master, 2007-2008

Tribute To RW Bro. Alan G Fowler (1929-2008)

Most of us are aware of the passing of RW Alan G Fowler (or "Brother Alan" as he liked to be called) on Tuesday November 25, 2008. It is good to reminisce.

Alan was born in Bristol, England in 1929 and immigrated to the United States via Canada using his resourcefulness to become a "house painter". Eventually, his background resulted in his becoming a painter at General Motor's Chevrolet River Road facility as well as well as commuting back and forth from GM's Rochester Products Division. He eventually retired from GM.

Concurrently, Bro. Alan's Masonic career was unfolding as he served Nocturnal Lodge No.1137 as master in 1976; 1981; 1989; 2003 and 2004. He was also a Charter Member and the Master of the Western New York Lodge Of Research in 1983; 1984 and 2006.

His appointment as District Deputy Grand Master of the Second Erie District in 1984 did not end his activities in Freemasonry. He also served as Secretary of Nocturnal Lodge No.1137, Amherst Lodge No.981 and The Western New York Lodge Of Research.

None of this data fully describes the merits of Brother Alan. Importantly, he believed in delivering excellent ritual and was willing to perform in any capacity. His generous nature was evident over a long time-frame via his willingness to volunteer in many capacities. The refreshments he furnished at our monthly meetings were well appreciated. Most importantly, he was the communicator via our newsletters and this meant attaining a high degree of proficiency on the computer.

Alan was a person who could be counted on to do an excellent job in a quiet, efficient manner. He exemplified to the highest degree the Masonic principles of friendship, brotherly love and sharing that we strive to achieve. He will be numbered among those rare individuals who left this world a bit better place than they found it. I was fortunate to have been part of his life.

Allen Maull

"Large was his bounty, and his soul sincere ...
He gained from Heaven (t'was all he wished), a friend
no farther seek his merits to disclose ...
The bosom of his Father and his God"

Special Thanks For Our Annual Family Picnic

In August, (just before the start up of the Lodge) we have an annual family picnic. For many years, our Brother and Past Master James Rowe and his wife Joan have opened their home to host this event. The picnic is an informal gathering of Brothers and their wives and guests. On a sunny Thursday in August, 2008, a plaque was presented to Joan and Jim Rowe by RW Albert Hoffman, Master of the Lodge, to thank them for their kindness and hospitality. Flowers were also presented to Joan for her support. They reside in the Town Of Tonawanda.

Did the Morgan Affair Sow the Seeds that Are Strangling Masonry?

By Anthony Delisi 32°
  {Presented September 12, 2008}

Could the Morgan affair have resulted in changes to American Masonry that have caused it to lose members and whither? Many masons today decry the changes in society that are keeping new members from joining the craft and keeping established members from attending more meetings. But, has society changed or have we changed? Did this decline come about as a result of the Morgan Affair?

There are parts of the world where Lodges flourish. In Europe many Lodges have a waiting list of several years for admittance. This article takes a look at the possible cause of the scarcity of membership in American Masonry and what can be done to stem the tide before it is too late.

How The Morgan Affair Changed American Masonry Forever

After the Morgan Affair, Masonry struggled to be acceptable and has never stopped trying to allay the suspicion of outside society. Masons did not want to be labeled secretive or dangerous. We changed our "temples" into "Lodges" in order not to appear like a religion. We stopped studying numerology, ancient civilizations, astrology and most other esoteric subjects at Lodge meetings. We curtailed drinking and fraternal feasts. Over time, we turned instead to barbeques, bowling, raising money for scholarships and charities to occupy our members and to participate in activities that pleased outside society. Masons did tremendous charitable work and continue to do so today. But does the emphasis on charity make the craft interesting and attractive to potential candidates?

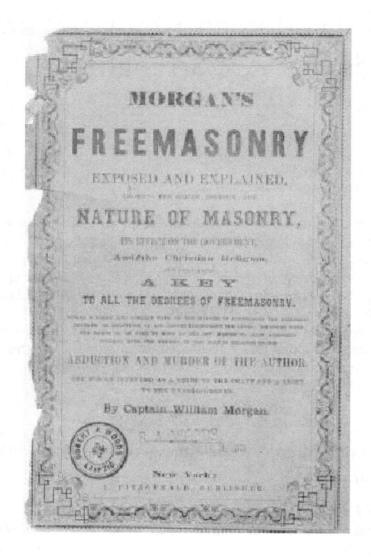

Masonry Won Victories for Democracy & Freedom But Ran Out of Work

Early masons worked for democracy and equality, judging the interior qualities of men. In older times, that was a very radical concept. So was the Masonic concept that men should be free to think and say what they wanted. As masonry spread and great men joined, the world became more democratic. England became a parliamentary monarchy, France experimented with republicanism, the US was born and later, turned away from slavery. All these miracles of human advancement were fomented by good men believing in and embracing Masonic principles. The problem is that once countries became democratic, safe and free of religious intolerance, the need to become a mason became less for society in general and interest waned until a war or crisis loomed.

Toning Down Secrecy and Elitism

Since the dawn of civilization, there have been elite secret societies in almost every culture. Masonry fit the description of an elite secret society. Unfortunately, over the last 50 years, elitism has become very, very unpopular. It is now less popular to try to be richer than others, to try to be better educated than others or to try to get ahead of others through hard work. It is considered "unfair". Society has evolved to pulling down the top instead of pulling up the bottom rungs with hard work, education and perseverance.

The fact that few will discuss is that masonry is an elite society. One of the benefits of membership is the ability to meet on the level with the powerful, the interesting and the patriotic members of our communities with whom we might otherwise never associate.

Secrets also draw interest. In Europe, where masonry is more popular than ever, it is far more secret than in America. The ghost of Morgan has made us too willing to reveal all to show we have nothing to hide. This is a great strategy for acceptance by society except for the fact that it makes us less interesting and makes people less likely to join.

It has been proven throughout history that secrecy generates interest in secret organizations. Whether you agree with secrecy and elitism or not, I think the facts show that in areas of the world where these are emphasized, masonry flourishes. Masonry only departed from these areas as a result of the backlash from the Morgan Affair and the result has been a steady decline in membership.

Could Changes in Society Be the Cause?

Many of us blame declines in membership on less leisure time, declines in morals and other changes in society. But these do not appear to be the cause since society has also changed in Europe and yet they have multi-year waiting lists for men to join.

Building Earthly Lodges

Before the Morgan affair, most Lodges were small and met in taverns. There were very few standing Masonic buildings. Lodges were made up of 20 to 30 men who got to know each other very well and who would do what it took to support their brothers as well as their widows and orphans. These small groups required regular attendance at meetings from all members. The meetings were very fraternal and educational. Great men like Mozart, Voltaire and Benjamin Franklin wanted to attend meetings because they were exciting, moral and stimulating. Since the trend to larger Lodges and buildings things have changed. Lodges are often made up of large numbers of members who do not attend meetings but send in dues to pay for buildings and upkeep. The support of master masons and their families has been watered down by large memberships, many of whom know little about each other and often have not formed a personal fraternal bond. In some cases, this has resulted in the motions but not the substance of the spirit of Masonry.

Opening On The Third Degree Sped Up The Work

Before the Morgan Affair, most meetings opened on the First Degree. Entered Apprentices attended and enjoyed education and fraternity. Later in the meeting, the Entered Apprentices were asked to leave or possibly go to a separate room to do some Masonic work, while the Lodge met on the Second Degree. Here, Fellowcraft business, work and education was conducted. Finally, the Lodge was opened on the Third Degree with only Master Masons in the Lodge.

After the Morgan Affair, Lodges wanted to be sure that men could not join, learn secrets and leave after a few meetings, so we began to open on the Third Degree. The problem was that after men became Entered Apprentices, they could not attend Lodge until they became Master Masons and many lost interest. To keep them interested, Lodges sped up the work. It no longer took a year of hard work and research to move to the next level. The work required dwindled until we finally arrived at one day classes and testing outside open Lodge. It became easy to become a mason, with many candidates pushed ahead past their level of proficiency. Ironically, the easier we made it to move up, the less interested men became in joining, in working and in staying.

The increased speed and ease of becoming master masons also meant men who had not been tested by years of association with the Lodge moved up the ranks as officers, posing a potential problem if men became wardens or masters before their character under all types of situations had been shown in Lodge. It also meant that men who had not had the opportunity to hone their skills through Masonic education, making presentations and leadership skills could become officers and masters of Lodges.

All these factors combined to make Masonry easier to join and move up in but less attractive to many applicants.

Billboards, Low Dues, and "Walmart" Masonry

This "post Morgan" relaxation of standards has continued at some Lodges in order to try and keep membership high enough to pay the expenses of the buildings and to satisfy the statisticians at Grand Lodges. Some Masons have forgotten that Lodges were small and that the goal was to have a great group of good men tied by tight bonds of fraternity. Some Lodges have made dues artificially low and even post billboard ads asking for membership. Many have forgotten that in older times, masons chose the best people in a community and then went out and recruited those whom they had chosen. It wasn't "To Be One, Ask One" it was "To Be One, Be An Outstanding Person And We Will Find You".

The ironic thing appears to be that the easier it is to join an organization and move up its ranks, the less attractive it is to men who are most likely to work hard and raise standards. Hard working men are seeking a challenge. They want value for their time and effort. Groups like MENSA, the Navy Seals, the Olympics all have lots of people who want to join because they are recognized as organizations where it is extremely difficult to be accepted.

What can be done to stem this tide away from the things that attract leaders and workers to masonry?

Top Ten Things that Draw Great Masons

Size Does Not Matter

Masonry needs to return to the belief that it is better to have a small Lodge of superior men than a large Lodge of members who are of lesser moral value or less involved. Many Master Masons say we believe that and yet we sometimes take actions to attract people we barely know and to keep members on the rolls who are not participating.

Recruit the Best

Instead of putting up billboards or using radio advertisements to attract new members, our membership committees should seek out the most upright men in the community and recruit them to join.

Make It Tough to Join

We should return to the days when it was tough to be a Mason. Around the world, it is proven that the harder it is to join and stay, the longer the list of great candidates who wish to join. The jurisdictions that have long waiting lists have serious work candidates must do to join, such as well researched presentations on why they wish to join, or books to be read and understood before joining. Candidates for degrees are tested in open Lodge for proficiency and not promoted without achieving it.

Require a Commitment to Stay

In many parts of the world, you must obtain the permission of the master to miss a Lodge communication. In many jurisdictions, if you miss three meetings without such permission, you are removed from Lodge membership. This keeps Lodges small but vibrant, able to do work and make things happen. This is like pruning a plant to make it stronger. If implemented, our numbers would drop like a rock but we would be left with the members who want to make things happen and have the skills and ambition to do so.

Actual Work at Meetings

Many masons lament that young people are not interested in our meetings. But many meetings have nothing more exciting than paying the light bill. We need to return to itinerant lecturers and interesting presentations of work by members. Is there enough exciting work going on in your Lodge that would make men like Benjamin Franklin, George

Washington, Teddy Roosevelt, Woodrow Wilson and others rearrange their schedule to attend?

Actual Fraternity

Smaller Lodges of about 30 members who are dedicated and active will foster real fraternity. Members will get to know each other well and will become like brothers. Lodge members will know there are 30 men they can trust with their life and their families. That kind of fraternity is what masonry is about, but how can we achieve that will our current structures of 100 to 300 members, most of who we barely know because they do not participate?

Specialty Lodges

In some US jurisdictions, the concept of specialty Lodges has brought members and activity. In Indiana there are Lodges just for cigar smokers, just for Harley Davidson fans, just for antique car buffs, etc. These Lodges draw enthusiastic members to meetings they look forward to attending.

Provide Services Members Want and Need

Lodges should provide services members want and need. Since many of our members are older, perhaps Lodges could provide diet workshops, exercise programs, training for retired men to start new businesses, use the internet, or get jobs. Younger members might be interested in programs that deal with issues that help families or teach parenting methods, how to create and enjoy free time, or other topics important to younger members. Lodges could host Super Bowl parties, rent and show the latest movies, etc.. Having activities that younger members want would be a big step toward attracting them.

Use Modern Communication Tools

We live in an age of instant communications but many Lodges are stuck in the 19th century. Every Lodge should have a webmaster, a website and PowerPoint facilities for presentations. Lodges should be represented on social networking sites like www.myspace.com and www.youtube.com that young prospective members visit for information.

Every Lodge member should have a Lodge email address that can be used for instant communication with members. Lodges should use texting to communicate as well. Would you like to be part of a Lodge that could send an instant text message and have 20 good men come to the aid of a brother in an emergency? Lodges could have a communications officer that creates news for the website and short video clips and articles for the web. Lodge websites should be vibrant and interesting.

These are just a few of the things we could do to attract good men who actively participate. Perhaps the Morgan Affair sent masonry down a road that would lead to fewer members and lowering of standards. Perhaps we have drifted from our roots, Perhaps we have gotten too used to the same old fish fries to keep up with a rapidly changing world.

We can no longer lament that young men are not interested. We have to make it interesting. We can no longer strive for huge Lodges with less than the highest standards in membership, work performed, leadership and participation. We need to look around the world and see what is working in other countries and other states. We need to make changes and good men will once again seek us out.

Masonry and Religion–Are They Compatible?

John Borycki, Master
 {*Presented Nov 18, 1996*}

A leaflet printed in London attacked Freemasonry as being a "devilish sect of men", "anti-Christ", "evil-doers" and "corrupt people". It warned god-fearing people about the "mischiefs and evil practices in sight of God by those called Freed Masons", and to "take care lest their ceremonies and secret swearings take hold of you" and "be wary that none cause you to err from Godliness". The date was 1698, nineteen years before the first Grand Lodge was formed. (Coil, p62) You see, Masonry has always been under attack by the over zealous believer.

Freemasons are easy prey for criticism and attack. Ill treatment is born stoically. It is part of what Masons believe to give the widest latitude to anyone who says anything about them. Freemasons do not practice thought control. However, the challenge of poorly informed detractors who lead their uninformed flocks in search of salvation at the expense of an organization which fails to protect itself is that the attacks become too great. With this in mind, I take this opportunity to speak out, to those who would listen, of my own reaction to the diatribe against the Craft carried on by religious extremists who take on many guises but have several commonalities.

My purpose is to review some of the criticisms against Freemasonry to suggest some reasons behind the attacks and to provide replies which can be used in answering those who ask questions about the Craft. A discussion regarding Masonic precepts is in order.

What makes a Mason? What do Masons believe? Where do Masons come from? The answers to these questions and the information presented will become useful to you in your Masonic travels.

The requirements for becoming a Mason are few, but important, for further Masonic enlightenment must be built on a firm foundation. A petitioner must believe in God and the immortality of the soul, and that's it. That he be of good moral character and sound body is important. However, the foundation is the belief in God and in the immortality of the soul. The form of this belief is left to the conscience of the petitioner and is not a subject for discussion in the Lodge. There is no requirement for the manner of this belief, only that it is held. This is one of the basic tenets of the Craft and one that draws a great deal of criticism. Not only would our detractors have us espouse a particular creed, but further that the creed be theirs. As you can imagine, there would be confusion in the Craft and a complete absence of harmony. "Don't discuss religion or politics" is a phrase familiar to those who are not Freemasons. These topics are not allowed for debate within a Masonic Lodge. This is done for a reason. Religion and politics are divisive forces which have shattered many organizations including some Masonic ones, such as 19th century French Masonry, for example.

The Religious Right as well as other more well-established, traditional religious sects have a point of view which is referred to as *inerrancy*. Inerrancy is the view which holds that their belief is the correct one, the only true one. They view the truth through their own eyes. The inerrantist knows that he is infallible and that all other views are wrong. This, of course, flies in the face of Freemasonry. Freemasons believe that every man is entitled to his own thoughts. In fact, Masons are encouraged to think for themselves and to decide upon what is their truth. The freedoms we enjoy in this country, which are spreading around the globe, are the result of this freedom of thought. The results of free thought were evident by great advances in the arts, in science and in society. We know this period as the Renaissance, the period in which we find the roots of Freemasonry.

Henry Wilson, 33°, in A *Comprehensive View Of Freemasonry* (1973), gives an overview of the literature concerning the origins of the Craft and concludes that the origins lie in the stone-cutter societies of the Middle Ages. He finds that the supposed ancient roots are embellishments in the lore of Lodge formation. He, along with others, like Robert Freke Gould in his epochal and monumental *History Of Freemasonry* (1885), found that the writings of Albert G. Mackey and Albert Pike were fanciful creations within which the detractors of Freemasonry have found much ammunition. These men were sincere Masons and prolific writers. Pike was a student of ancient philosophies and mysteries. He wrote *Morals And Dogma Of The Ancient And Accepted Scottish Rite* in 1871. His addition to the Scottish Rite degrees have produced beautiful symbolism in the further expansion of the Blue Lodge Degrees, Mackey's *Encyclopedia Of Freemasonry* (1874) was still in print in 1924, but Mackey finally joined the "factual school" of reality in his *History* (published posthumously in 1896) in which he realizes the many errors of his prior interpretations. Anyone can write anything about Freemasonry whether he be in the Craft or not, informed or not.

Those who view these writings and ritual with an eye connected to a closed mind will be able to discover enough "paganism" and "Satanism" and "sex worship" to fill many books, and many have done just that. Detractors of the Craft read selectively to choose words and ideas out of context and out of current usage, give material their particular interpretation, and present it as proof against Freemasonry of the most heinous, vile and wretched accusations.

An anti-Masonic book, *The Deadly Deception* by Jim Shaw and Tom McKenny (1988) is the story of a man brought up without the benefit of religion who joins Freemasonry in search of spiritual light. He feels that he has found it and enters into a pact with a Masonic friend. He embraces reincarnation and commits to it as a religious belief. When he finds salvation through the witnessing of an acquaintance, all manner of calumny is heaped upon the Craft. He speaks of conflict with the Bible. He noticed hints of Satanism, demon worship and paganism within the ritual. He found salvation in the New Testament. Good for him, for surely he didn't find it in Masonry. It isn't there. It's not supposed to be! Masonry seeks to take good men and make them better, to improve the human condition and better the lot of man in the world. Shaw's misunderstanding is unbelievable. Many years in the quarries of Masonry, including the coronet of the 33°, crumbled on the poor foundation upon which it was built, having no prior commitment to religion.

Freemasonry encourages, nay, urges its members to be steadfast in the faith of their own choosing. Freemasonry is not a religion and doesn't want to be, according to John J Robinson in A *Pilgrim's Path* (1993). This point is consistently missed by disparagers of the Craft such as John Ankerberg in his series of anti-Masonic videotapes. When I bow my head in prayer, it is my own God to whom I pray, not some sort of Masonic God. The same holds true during a Benediction, Grace, or any other occasion where someone else, "says the words".

Further in this regard is the Masonic recognition and use of a Volume of Sacred Law other than the Book which is sacred to the critic (usually the Bible). Members of the Craft include members of religions whose Sacred Law is not the Bible but the Koran, or the Rig Veda, to name only two. This extension of inerrancy refuses to allow that there are other paths to salvation. Your personal God and Savior better be the one to which the critic subscribes or you will suffer eternal damnation.

There are critics on all sides who argue that there is only one True

Religion and there are—dozens of them. So, who should we listen to? The answer is sensible and obvious. You listen to your own conscience, governed by due inquiry and reasoned thought. This is called toleration, a difficult concept for detractors to grasp.

My *Webster's New World Dictionary, Collegiate Edition*, notes in its definitions that Humanism is a religion. It is defined as having a system of beliefs, practices, and ethical values, resembling, suggestive of, or likened to such a system. Looking up humanism, one finds that it emphasizes the study of human interests rather than that of the natural world or religion. These interests brought about the Renaissance. Freemasonry was founded during the "Age Of Reason" when the human condition was studied and its improvement and development were sought through arts, science, politics and through an expanding and changing economic system. A moral system to meet these changes was needed. One answer on the spiritual side was to change how the established religion functioned. It did not change fast enough and the Reformation took place, followed by the Counter-Reformation, by which time it was too late. Freemasonry was in formation throughout this period. Its purpose was not only one of moral improvement, but one of physical improvement and protection as well. Care for a brother, his widow and orphans is a concept which is part of the original fabric of masonry. It still is.

These programs of moral and physical care for a Brother run counter to many religions who wish to control and be the entire focus of an individual, not allowing any freedom of thought or action. This is extremism. This is the smothering of the soul, not its salvation. A competition is perceived by some religions for not only the soul, but for the whole of one's being.

Masonic Beginnings in New York and the Great Schism 1730–1827

By Jeffrey M. Williamson

{*Presented at The Western New York Lodge of Research*, November 8, 2008. *MW Williamson later became Grand Master of the Grand Lodge of the State of New York in 2016-2018.*}

Historical lineages of "who begat whom" most often tend to be very uninteresting, tedious, and mind numbing. However, I would sincerely beg your patience and perseverance this afternoon as we briefly weave our way through some Masonic history that continues to have a direct impact on our Masonic operations and procedures even up to and including this very day and time!

My goal this afternoon is twofold.

The first part of this presentation will trace our earliest colonial Masonic activities. We will outline our origins from the Première Grand Lodge of the Moderns to the transition of the opportunistic Grand Lodge of the Ancients, and the assimilation of the Modern Lodges into the into the Ancient Grand Lodge authority.

After the birth of our nation, we will continue our studies of the Grand Lodge of the State of New York which will take us up to and including the year 1827 which is just a few months before the start of the Morgan Episode.

The second part of this presentation deals with the Great Schism of the Grand Lodge of the State of New York, and the individuals who were the major characters in resolving the discord. We will also review the unification "Compact" which affects us even to this day.

Masonic Beginnings in Colonial New York

The first Provincial Grand Master of New York, New Jersey and Pennsylvania was Colonel Daniel Coxe (1673-1739) who was nominated, ordained, constituted and appointed Provincial Grand Master by the Duke of Norfolk, Grand Master of the Grand Lodge of England in 1730 in response to a request by the Free and Accepted Masons residing and about to reside in these Provinces. He was born in America but was educated and spent most of his life in England.

Our second Provincial Grand Master was Captain Richard Riggs who was appointed Provincial Grand Master for New York on November 15, 1737 by the Earl of Darnley, Grand Master of England.

Our third was Thomas Goelet who was appointed by Lord Byron, Grand Master of England in 1751.

Note: Little information can be found on either Grand Masters Riggs or Goelet.

Our fourth Provincial Grand Master was George Harison (spelled with one "r") who was appointed June 9, 1753 by Lord Carysfort, Grand Master of the Grand Lodge. Harison was evidently resolved to infuse new life into the Provincial Grand Lodge and stirred the Craft into action. In order to impress the Brethren with the dignity of the undertaking, he called a meeting of the Grand Lodge for the organization of the preparations for a fitting installation.

An advertisement was inserted in the *New York Mercury Newspaper* of November 19, 1753 as follows:

> "The members of the Provincial Grand Lodge of Free and Accepted Masons in New York are desired to meet at the Kings Arms Tavern, on Wednesday, the 19th day of December, on business of importance. By order of the Grand Master."–H. Gaine, Secretary

The installation took place on the festival of St. John Evangelist in December. An article of December 31, 1753 reads as follows:

> On Thursday last at a Grand Lodge of the Ancient and Worshipful Fraternity of Free and Accepted Masons, a Commission from the Honorable John Proby, Baron of Craysfort, in the Kingdom of Ireland, Grand Master of England, appointed George Harison, Esquire, to be Provincial Grand Master, was solemnly published, we hear, to the universal satisfaction of all the brethren present, after which, it being the festival of St. John the Evangelist, service at Trinity Church. The order which they proceeded as follows: First walked the Sword Bearer, carrying a drawn sword; then four stewards with white maces (rods), followed by the Treasurer and Secretary, who bore each a crimson damask cushion, on which lay a gilt Bible; and the Book of Constitution; after these came the Grand Wardens and Wardens; then came the Grand Master himself, bearing a truncheon (baton) and other badges of his office, followed by the rest of the brotherhood, according to their respective ranks- Masters, Fellow Crafts and 'Prentices, to about the number of Fifty, all clothed with their jewels, aprons, white gloves and stockings. The whole ceremony was conducted with utmost decorum, under a discharge of guns from some vessels in the harbor, and made a genteel appearance. We hear they afterwards conferred a generous donation of fifteen pounds from the public stock of the Society to be expended in clothing for the poor children belonging to our charity school; and made a handsome private contribution for the relief of indigent prisoners. In the evening, by the particular request of the brethren, a comedy, called "The Conscience Lovers" was presented in the Theatre in Nassau Street to a very crowded audience. Several pieces of vocal music, in praise of the Fraternity, were performed between the acts. An epilogue suitable to the occasion was pronounced by Mrs. Hallam, with all grace of gesture, and propriety of execution, and met with universal and loud applause(...etc...)

Grand Master Harison labored with untiring zeal and several of the Lodges that he warranted continue to exist to this very day. Had he been able to carry on through the American Revolution, our Grand Lodge would surly have traced it roots to the Première Grand Lodge of England.

Sir John Johnson was the last and fifth Provincial Grand Master and his deputation was issued to him by Lord Blaney, Grand Master of England in 1767. He was formally and installed as Grand Master in 1771.

The struggle for Independence being rife and Sir John being a Tory and Loyalist left for Canada and appointed Dr. Peter Middleton the Deputy Grand Master. Dr. Peter Middleton as Deputy Grand Master issued a warrant to St. John's Regimental Lodge No.1, which was composed of brethren belonging to the Colonial Army who owed their allegiance to Brother George Washington.

Early Lodges in New York City

From the earlier article in the *New York Mercury*, we know that there were at least fifty members of the Craft participating in the Grand Master's Installation, and we could certainly surmise that there existed several Lodges that were active and working.

In 1758, the *Mercury* mentions Temple Lodge celebrating St. John the Evangelist Day. Nine years later the same paper mentions St. John's Lodge No.2, Trinity, Union, King Solomon's, and Hiram Lodges represented at the annual celebration. The only Lodge surviving to this day is St. John's No.2. now renumbered St. John's No.1 on the Grand Lodge register.

St. John's Lodge No.2 hailed from the Première Grand Lodge and their Charter was issued by George Harison in 1757. It was renumbered No.1 and is the oldest surviving Lodge in the City and New York State. *Note: Mackey's History lists St. John's date as 1751.*

Grand Master Harison also chartered Union Lodge. This Lodge was active for a number of years, but suspended its work during the War for Independence as its members were off fighting for independence and could hardly meet in British occupied New York City.

After the war it was renumbered No.8 by the Atholl Provincial Grand Lodge. Robert P. Livingston, who became the first Grand Master of the State of New York, was Master of this Lodge in 1771.

Temple, Trinity and Hiram Lodges were also composed of American patriots and did not survive the war. They most likely were absorbed into the remaining Lodges.

King Solomon's Lodge No.7 was named in a newspaper article as taking a part in the St John's celebration of 1767.

A Lodge which is not mentioned in the published reports of the various St. John's Celebrations during the period of George Harison's Grand Mastership is Independent Royal Arch Lodge No.8 which dates its constitution from December 15, 1760. It has since been renumbered No.2 and it the second oldest Lodge in New York City.

King David's Lodge was issued a warrant on February 17, 1769. This Lodge was composed almost entirely of Jewish Brethren.

Out of all of the early beginnings of the New York City Lodges only St. John's No.1 and Independent Royal Arch Lodge No.2 survive to this day.

Early Lodges outside New York City

At least four of the upstate Lodges can trace their history back to the time before the Declaration of Independence: Mt. Vernon No.3, which was Union No.1 in colonial days, St. Patrick's No.4, Master's No.5, and St. George's No.6. Mount Vernon and Masters are located at Albany; St. Patrick's, at Johnstown; and St. George's at Schenectady. It would sure make an interesting research project to specifically review the status of these long-standing Lodges in the present day.

The oldest Lodge outside of New York City was organized at Albany in 1759, under a copy of the Charter of Lodge No.74, issued by the Grand Lodge of Ireland, in 1737, to the Brethren of the Second Battalion 1st Royals (now Royal Scots), First Regiment of Foot Guards (Infantry). The Battalion was ordered away in 1759 but they left a copy of the warrant with the citizens of the town so they could continue their Masonic labors.

St Patrick's Lodge No.8 (now No.4) of Johnstown was issued a charter May 3, 1766 by Grand Master Harison.

In 1768 George Harison constituted Master's Lodge No.2 at Albany which is at present No.5 in the list of Lodges in the State of New York.

The last known Lodge constituted by Grand Master Harison was Solomon's Lodge No.1 located at Poughkeepsie in 1771. Robert R. Livingston was deputized as acting Grand Master and installed the new officers. On May 16, 1781 an excerpt in the records of this Lodge "obliterated the name of Benedict Arnold from its minutes". George Washington also visited this Lodge on December 27, 1782.

Also, throughout New York were several traveling military Lodges both of British and American origins. American military Lodges include St. John's Regimental Lodge and American Union Lodge No.1.

(Editorial Note: It is important to keep in mind the strong winds of the American Revolution that were sweeping across the entire territory during this era. Co-habitation of villages and towns by both Loyalist and Revolutionary citizens must have been a very daunting and stressful period to the populace.)

The close of the First Provincial Grand Lodge

The first Provincial Grand Lodge of New York derived its power from the Première Grand Lodge of England. It did not survive the shock of the American Revolution chiefly because Grand Master John Johnson saw fit to identify his fortunes with Great Britain. Unfortunately, when he left for Canada he took the deputation giving him authority to direct the Masonic affairs in New York!

If he would have only left the warrant with Dr. Peter Middleton who was the Deputy Grand Master of New York, the tactful leader most likely would have held the Lodges together. And the history of the Grand Lodge of New York might now trace its beginning to the Provincial Grand Lodge of George Harison!

This is a very important note:

Sir John Johnson's withdrawal from New York gave an opportunity to the Ancients.... who took soon took quick advantage and established themselves firmly in the State. The Lodges constituted by the Ancients form the organization from which our present Grand Lodge now officially derives its existence. Nevertheless, it should be acknowledged that we owe a great debt of gratitude to the Première Grand Lodge of England.

The Atholl Provincial Grand Lodge

The Atholl Provincial Grand Lodge ruled New York from 1781 to 1784. It was the Grand Lodge form of government that was derived from the Ancients.

The British Regiments that were sent to America held many Military Lodges that were warranted by the Ancients. Many Military Lodges in occupied New York City were warranted by the Ancients better known as The Atholl Grand Lodge of England. (The Duke of Atholl being Grand Master at the time).

With the Provincial Grand Master of the Moderns fleeing to Canada, the way was now clear for the Ancients to begin their work. Additional British Military Lodges came to New York when Boston was finally evacuated by the British. Before long, seven military Lodges came together and opened a convention and solicited recognition from The Atholl Grand Lodge. Following recognitions and empowered as emergent Provisional Grand Lodge, and with six Lodges of "Ancient York" origins in New York City, A warrant authorizing the Ancient York Provincial Grand Lodge was forwarded from England in the fall of 1782. It bore the date of September

5, 1781. The first meeting, under the authority of the Atholl warrant was held in Roubalet's Assembly Hall, New York City on December 5, 1782. There were present Rev. William Walter Grand Master and the other officers listed in the warrant, together with the representatives of the other nine Lodges, one operating under dispensation. After paying due homage to the new Grand Officers, the Lodges represented surrendered their warrants and received them again as coming from the Provincial Grand Lodge of New York.

Moderns healed by the Ancients

The new Grand Lodge of New York was now official, and of course organized by the Ancients. The rest of the regular Lodges situated throughout New York originated by the Première Grand Lodge of England, which was called the Moderns. Initially they were excluded from membership. In order to provide for their acceptance the new Grand Lodge on January 3, 1783 adopted a resolution healing and admitting the Brethren.

British withdraw from the City

At the conclusion of the war, it was determined that the City of New York would be turned over to the Americans and evacuated by the British on November 25, 1783.

On September 19th the Grand Lodge held a Grand Lodge of Emergency to discuss leaving the Grand Warrant in New York City. It was resolved that the Warrant would remain with the Brethren as may be appointed upon the removal of His Majesty's Troops.

The Rev. Dr. Walter, who was Chaplain of De Lancey's 3rd Battalion, was compelled to leave for Nova Scotia. He presented his resignation from the Grand Mastership on that September day and took affectionate leave of the Lodge and Brethren.

On his nomination, Junior Grand Warden Cock was elected and installed as the new Grand Master. The Grand Lodge Communications met every other month and shortly thereafter met quarterly.

Birth of the Grand Lodge of the State of New York

Robert R. Livingston Grand Master to 1801

At the meeting of February 4, 1784 Grand Master Cock resigned and nominated the Hon. Robert R. Livingston, Chancellor of the State of New York to be Grand Master which **closed** the Provincial Grand Lodge and **opened** the Grand Lodge of the State of New York.

Grand Master Robert R. Livingston continued the challenge of gathering the balance of the "Modern" Lodges into the fold, and the fact that Chancellor Livingston originated from a "Modern" Lodge helped to overcome any obstacles in unifying the Grand Lodge.

The supremacy of Grand Lodge was settled in due time and a new Seal was ordered on September 3, 1788 to bear the legend "**Grand Lodge of the State of New York**"

Grand Master Livingston was only thirty-six years old when he became Grand Master. He was a much respected citizen of the day and was a member of the Continental Congress, served on the committee that drew up the Declaration of Independence, Chancellor of the State of New York, Secretary of Foreign Affairs, Minister to France and successfully negotiated the Louisiana Purchase. He was instrumental in steam navigation and was a partner with Robert Fulton on the Clermont that made its trip up the Hudson River.

At the inauguration of the first President of the Republic it was Robert R. Livingston who administered the oath of Office to George Washington on St. John's Lodge Bible.

Jacob Morton Grand Master 1801–1806

The Grand Line Officers serving with Grand Master Morton were:

- Deputy Grand Master–Edward Livingston- Mayor of New York City
- Sr. Grand Warden–Cadwallader D. Colden–District Attorney and later Mayor of NYC
- Jr. Grand Warden–Phillip S. Van Rensselaer-Albany
- Grand Treasurer–Robert Cocks-Merchant
- Grand Secretary–Daniel D. Tompkins-Congressman, Supreme Ct Justice, Governor of New York & Vice President of the United States of America

The Lodges outside of New York City, particularly at Albany, became disgruntled because it seemed like the New York City Lodges were monopolizing the affairs of the Grand Lodge. With the exception of the Jr. Grand Warden- all of the Officers were from the City Lodges, especially St. John's No.1 and Holland No.8.

In addition, the holding of meetings in New York City imposed considerable hardship on attendance by the rest of the State. A revolt seemed to be brewing and Upstate Lodges were becoming more indifferent to Grand Lodge rules and regulations.

In order to end disputes and establish greater harmony, a resolution was adopted on December 5, 1804 authorizing the Grand Master to appoint Inspectors throughout the State to act as representatives of the Grand Lodge in their respective districts, collecting dues and helping to bring about standardization in the work. The resolution **failed to pass** but the Grand Lodge began to recognize the troubling condition that was developing across the State.

Dewitt Clinton 1806–1820

Grand Master Dewitt Clinton is one of our most prestigious luminaries and hardly needs an introduction to modern day Masons. His accomplishments are monumental and extraordinary.

A brief rehearsal will include Master of Holland Lodge in 1794; Jr. Grand Warden 1795, 1796, and 1797; Sr. Grand Warden 1798; and Grand Master in 1806. He served fourteen successive terms as Grand Master.

Additionally he was Grand High Priest of the Grand Chapter State of New York, General Grand High Priest of General Grand Chapter, Grand Master of the Grand Encampment of Knights Templar of the State of New York, Grand Master of the Grand Encampment of Knights Templar of the United States of America, and also a member of the highest bodies of the Scottish Rite.

He was a State Legislator, US Senator, Mayor of New York City, and Governor of the State. He was the great founder of the Erie Canal which was the largest and most monumental enterprise ever made in the history of mankind at that time. He was active in promoting a free public school system for the betterment and education of the populace.

In 1820 he declined re-election along with several of his distinguished Grand Lodge Officers. Difficulties were beginning to surface and the integrity of Grand Lodge was threatened. Daniel D. Tompkins was then elected and installed the new Grand Master.

Grand Master Tompkins and the Rise of Dissension and the Great Schism

Daniel Tompkins was Vice President of the United States when he was elected Grand Master in 1820. With the retirement of Grand Master Clinton and the strong leadership base of the previous administration, troubles soon began to multiply and the door of dissention and schism swung wide open.

Around 1814, the Grand Visitor concept was adopted. The State was divided into three Grand Masonic Districts for visitation.

The principal duty of the Grand Visitor was to collect outstanding Grand Lodge dues and to bring closer relations between the Metropolitan Lodges and the rest of the jurisdiction.

The three Grand Visitors were divided as follows:

Thomas Lowndes of New York City (First District)—Southern part of the State except New York City, and Putnam, Orange, Ulster, and Sullivan

Ebenezer Wadsworth of Lebanon (Second District)—Middle and Eastern part of the State

Joseph Enos of Eaton (Third District)—Western part of the State including Clinton and Franklin

Country Lodges vs. City Lodges

The three Grand Visitors' main purpose was to collect outstanding Grand Lodge dues. The Upstate Lodges evidently found the arrangement satisfactory; however the City Lodges deemed the plan too expensive.

The two Grand Visitors from the country Lodges districts submitted annual expenses of $1130.00 and $1300.00 while the City Grand Visitor submitted expenses of only $37.00. The fees paid for the collection appeared way too exorbitant by the representatives of Grand Lodge, and the Grand Visitors were abolished. The results were more disastrous than expected.

Grand Visitors Wadsworth and Enos had a large following. The expenses submitted by these Brethren were actually quite valid and their services were wholly devoted to the Craft. The Upstate brethren concluded that the removal of these officers was simply another move on the part of the Lodges of the Metropolitan District to have sole and absolute control of the Grand Lodge.

On September 20, 1820 Grand Master Thompkins called a Lodge of

Emergency to consider the question of Grand Visitations. A committee was formed to create a fair and equitable plan to resolve the differences the report of this committee by December.

With December having come and gone, the Upstate Lodges in the West met in Canandaigua in which a memorial was drawn up complaining of "certain measures and regulations" and proposed a number of recommendations. It was proposed that the State be divided up into eighteen districts and a Grand Visitor to be elected by the votes of the Lodges in their respective districts. They were to attend the meetings of the Grand Lodge and be accredited as representatives of the Lodges in their charge.

Grand Master Tompkins, aware of the danger he was running politically by being involved in the strife that was increasing month by month, declined re-election to the Grand Mastership in 1822. For some unaccounted reason the Brethren elected one of the Past Grand Visitors from the Country Districts– Joseph Enos to succeed Tompkins!

Now the City Lodges felt aggrieved. Seven of the nine committee members chosen to revise the Constitutions and Rules and Regulations of the Grand Lodge were from the Country Districts. The malcontent City Lodges passed resolutions and presented them for adoption which had to be laid over for a year. During the year, the discontent City Brethren set to work to break up the Grand Lodge. The Country Lodges ignored the overtures.

In 1823, the day before the Grand Session, the Upstate brethren were determined not to elect any Brother who was connected with a City Lodge! When the Grand Session opened the meeting got out of hand and Grand Master Enos adjourned the meeting until the following morning.

The City Lodges considered this move to be arbitrary, unconstitutional and a dangerous precedent. Thirty one Lodges proceeded to St John's Hall and elected the Sr. Grand Warden Richard Hatfield as acting Grand Master. The following Grand Officers were elected for the ensuing year:

- John Wells–Grand Master (Who declined the nomination and was replaced by Martin Hoffman)
- Martin Hoffman–Deputy Grand Master
- Richard Hatfield–Senior Grand Warden
- Matson Smith, MD–Junior Grand Warden
- Elias Hicks–Grand Secretary
- Cornelius Bogert–Grand Treasurer

Note: The legitimate Grand Secretary and Grand Treasurer also were a part of this new rebellious Grand Line.

Grand Master Enos ignored the rebellion and called a meeting of the Grand Lodge the next morning. He ordered the Grand Secretary and Grand Treasurer to produce all books, papers, funds and vouchers in their possession. But these Officers paid no attention to the Summons.

A new set of officers were elected, all of them from outside New York City with Joseph Enos as Grand Master. There were now two Grand Lodges each claiming the title of the Grand Lodge of the State of New York. The Schismatic City Grand Lodge and the Lawful Grand Lodge.

The installation of Grand Master Enos was attended by Grand Master Tompkins and Lt. Governor Erastus Root. At that time, about one hundred Lodges comprised the Country Grand Lodge. The leadership of Grand Master Joseph Enos was found wanting and three years later in 1825, Stephen Van Rensselaer III was elected as Grand Master.

Stephen Van Rensselaer III was not present at the Grand Lodge, but Past Grand Master Dewitt Clinton was authorized and requested to install him at Albany. The installation took place on September 29, 1825 and was a brilliant event.

Note: During this period of time, informal meetings were held by representatives of both Grand Bodies endeavoring to seek ways to restore the peace, harmony and re-union of the Brethren.

Stephen Van Rensselaer III

Stephen Van Rensselaer III best known as the "Patroon" and was one of the foremost citizens of the state. He served the Assembly and Senate, was the Lt Governor of the state, Canal Commissioner, member of the United States Congress, Chancellor of the State Agricultural Society and founder of the Rensselaer Polytechnic Institute at Troy. He worked hand in hand with Dewitt Clinton for the opening of the Erie Canal and the establishment of the educational system of the state.

In June of 1826, a resolution was adopted by Grand Lodge empowering Grand Master Stephen Van Rensselaer III and Past Grand Master Dewitt Clinton to meet with the City Grand Lodge and consult with them on all differences on Masonic subjects, and report at the next annual Communication of this Grand Lodge.

That paved the way to heal the schism. In 1827 a committee was formed with five from each rival Grand Lodge who drafted a new compact. The most important items of that compact are presented here below.

The Union

That there ought to be but one Grand Lodge in the State of New York, and that it ought to be held in the City of New York and be considered as a continuation of the Old Grand Lodge. That all allusion to former difference shall be avoided as far as possible.

That the proceedings of the bodies known by the name of the Grand Lodge shall be confirmed and the warrants granted to subordinate Lodges of the two bodies and the proceedings of the said shall be deemed regular.

That the records and archives of the Grand Lodge being in the City of New York, the Grand Secretary shall be chosen from the City.

That the Grand Master or Deputy Grand Master shall be chosen from the City of New York, and the other from the country, the two Wardens from the country, The Grand Secretary and Grand Treasurer from the City.

That the permanent fund shall be managed by five Trustees, viz: The Grand Master, the Deputy Grand Master, the two Wardens and the Grand Secretary, whose duty it shall be to invest all funds over $3000.00 agreeably to the resolutions presented to this committee.

That for the present session the representatives of Lodges shall be entitled to all the rights and privileges to which they are at present, but that it be recommended for the future that the number of Lodges which one Master or Past Master may represent shall not exceed three, and that Past Masters shall not be represented by proxy, and that representatives be paid as heretofore.

That a committee ought to be appointed to revise the Constitution.

The Compact was promptly signed by both Grand Lodge and the schism was ended. On the evening of June 7, 1827, the two bodies met in Tammany Hall as one united Grand Lodge. Great enthusiasm prevailed. Elisha W. King presided as Grand Master, declined re-nomination, and offered it to Stephen Van Rensselaer III, who was elected Grand Master by acclamation.

The official title of the Grand Lodge was declared to be:

"The Grand Lodge of the Most Ancient and Honorable Fraternity of Free Masons of the State of New York"

Summary and Closing

From our early origins of 1730 to the period just months preceding the Morgan episode in 1827, we have delineated our remarkable Masonic ancestry. We outlined our earliest Masonic references and our beginnings in the Première Grand Lodge of the Moderns to the changeover to the

Grand Lodge of the Ancients, and thence to the absorption and assimilation of the Modern Lodges into the Ancient Grand Lodge.

Lastly, we continued our examination of the Grand Lodge of the State of New York which took us through the Great Schism between the City Lodges and the Country Lodges of the Grand Lodge of the State of New York, and the uniting actions of Grand Master Dewitt Clinton and Grand Master Stephen Van Rensselaer III to resolve the rift.

As we look to the future we can only speculate about proposed changes in our Grand Lodge system. In more recent times, there are several Brothers who argue that the old system is no longer needed; that the world about us is smaller; that modern transportation and instant communication have made this "Compact" obsolete and burdensome. Why do we need to alternate Grand Masters or Deputy Grand Masters? Why must the Wardens come from the Upstate? Why must the Secretary and Treasurer come from the City? Is the system broken? Or are these questions a precursor of fanciful legislation yet to be proposed?

Whatever challenge we may face in the future, I am confident that the Brethren of the Grand Lodge of the State of New York will steadfastly work together as Brothers to resolve any and all differences that may challenge our magnificent fraternity. Even the Great Schism was no match for the forceful and unstoppable instincts of Brotherly Love and Affection. The chain that binds the Brethren of this Empire State is a chain not easily broken, it is built to last...to the end of time.

Research and References

Lang, Ossian. *History of Freemasonry in the State of New York.* Grand Lodge of the State of New York, 1922.

Clegg, Robert Ingham. *Mackey's History of Freemasonry, Volume Five.* Masonic History Company, Copyrighted 1898, 1906, 1921

"Old Hickory"—The Man Who Made It Twice

RW Alan G. Fowler PM

{*Presented to The Western New York Lodge Of Research June 17, 1995*}

March 15, 1995 marked the 228th anniversary of the birth of Andrew Jackson, one of the many men from North America who were outstanding Masons. To him, Masonry was something more than beautiful ritual, an impressive ceremony or social order. It was a rule and guide for his life. The term "Old Hickory" was first coined in 1813, when in March of that year he led the Tennessee Troops, under his command, south. In Mississippi, he received the order to disband his troops and send them home. Angered by that order, which would mean leaving his troops stranded with no money or provisions some eight hundred miles from home to find their own way back, he refused to disband and led his troops home. He gained the name "Old Hickory" by defying that order.

The Memorial To "Old Hickory"

If you are a visitor to our national capitol, Washington, D.C., and a mason, it would be fitting for you to look around town for memorials to famous freemasons. One of these memorials is in Lafayette Square, directly opposite the White House. It was the first equestrian statue to be erected in that great city and it was unveiled on January 8, 1853. This is the memorial erected to Andrew Jackson, the seventh President of the United States. There is evidence to show that it was to have Masonic attendance but, apparently the Grand Lodge was not at liberty to appear in Masonic clothing unless Masonic work was to be performed. Somehow, someone had forgotten to make arrangements for that work.

The financial collection started through the efforts of the Jackson Democratic Association who was kind enough to donate the first $12,000. The balance of $20,000 was provided through an appropriation by an Act of Congress.

Modeling of the statue was by Brother Clark Mills. He posed the horse on its two hind feet, and he succeeded in getting a balance. Newspaper accounts of that day say that it "surprised many people, and was much admired". President Jackson was depicted in the uniform of a general officer of the army in the period of 1812. At the time of the dedication of the statue, Washington, D.C. had a population of approximately 50,000. The park where the monument was erected was a commons. The dedication drew a crowd that was estimated and reported as probably the largest and most enthusiastic ever assembled up to that day.

Lineage And Early Days

Andrew Jackson's parents were Scots-Irish from Carrickfergus, in the northern part of Ireland. They took a wagon train from Charleston in 1765 for the southern part of the state, to a place called Twelve-Mile Creek. There was the father, Andrew, mother Elizabeth, and two children, Hugh and Robert. Mr. Jackson tried hard to eke out a living on a very poor tract of land. Two years of labor broke the body and spirit of the man, and early in March of 1767 he died. Just a few days later, on March 15,1767. Mrs. Jackson delivered a son that she named Andrew, after her husband. She abandoned the farm, and went to live with her sister who was an invalid. He was born in the Washaw settlement between North and South Carolina. There has been much discussion over where he was born. It seems that there is as little clarity about his first twenty years as about his early involvement in the Craft. In his will Jackson referred to South Carolina as "my native state". His mother took on the role of housekeeper, and in this manner her children all received the advantages of a well-to-do frontier home.

The early schools did not demand much from the boys. The ability to read, write and make ordinary business calculations was all that was required. It is recorded that he was neither studious nor teachable, and relied strictly upon himself. He was obedient and had a strong natural aptness for knowing exactly what he wanted.

Jackson applied himself to some further learning, and in 1787 in Salisbury, North Carolina, he was admitted to the bar. He then migrated west to Nashville, Tenn. This was where he prepared himself for a political career.

Jackson's Military Record

It is said that Andrew Jackson started out his military career at the age of 13 when, during the Revolutionary War, he and several other young people of the Washaw settlement fought against and were captured by the British. Bro. Philip Roth in his *Masonry in the Formation of our Government* says, "School boys remember this fighting President as an orphan who had his ears boxed by a British officer when a boy. Little did he (the officer) realize that this selfsame boy would become an American General and administer defeat to the British at New Orleans in 1815".

Jackson fought against and defeated the Creek Indians at the battle of Horseshoe Bend in 1814, and was promoted to Major General of the US Army. His assignment then was the defense of New Orleans in the 1812 war. His successful strategy at that time made him a national hero. He added to his fame by operations against the Seminole Indians in 1818, involving the Federal government in an international incident by pursuing them (the Indians) into Spanish Territory.

Jackson's Political Record

- 1795—Member of the Tennessee State Constitutional Convention.
- 1796-97—US Representative from Tennessee.
- 1797-98—US Senator from Tennessee.
- 1798-1804— Judge of the Tennessee Supreme Court.
- 1821—Provincial Governor of the Territory of Florida.
- 1823—US Senator from Tennessee.
- 1829-1837—Seventh President of U.S.

In 1828 Jackson won an easy victory in his campaign to become the seventh President of the United States. He termed it "a victory of the people" and the streets of Washington, D.C. were crowded for the inauguration. He had the doors of the White House thrown open; it was said that the people poured in. But, sadly his victory was tarnished by the death of his beloved wife, Rachel, right after the election. One of his statements was, "To the victor belongs the spoils", and his system of government became known as the "Spoils System". Andrew Jackson's opposition to the U.S. Banking system caused the destruction of many fortunes, and though he believed that he was protecting the interests of the commonwealth, his course was not generally approved. His principle opponent in this case was another Mason, Henry Clay.

Jackson disapproved of the idea that all Federal funds should be kept in the Bank of the United States. He felt that it was unconstitutional, even though the decision had been upheld in the courts by Justice Marshall in the famous McCullough v. Maryland case.

On re-election in 1832, Jackson had the government withdraw all of its funds from that bank; shortly thereafter the bank failed. Many of the prominent people of that time lost money in the failure of that bank, but in 1835 the National debt was paid off, and for the very first time there was a surplus of $35 million in the Treasury.

As President though, he was very easy to fight with. There was the time that he had a serious altercation with Mr. Dickinson, a member of Congress. Dickinson was reputed to be fearless and the best shot in the state. Finally Dickinson became so offensive that Jackson felt obliged to challenge him to a duel. Dickinson won the right to give the word to fire, and at eight paces gave it and fired. Finding that Jackson gave no sign of being hit he cried "My God, I must have missed him!", then Jackson fired, and Dickinson's funeral followed. But Jackson was hit, his breastbone was shattered, a rib broken, and an intestinal injury disabled him for many months.

History is replete with stories of famous people. I came upon one about General Jackson in the *Masonic Outlook*—I think this would be a good place to repeat it.

One evening in the year 1824, a company of English gentlemen, with one American, were assembled at a social gathering in Paris, France. The conversation turned to the coming Presidential election, and fear was expressed that, if Andrew Jackson was elected, the friendly relations then existing between England and the United States might be endangered. The reason for this suggestion was Jackson's implacable hostility to England and his high handed exercise of power during his command at New Orleans.

The one American present was about to reply to these observations, when Colonel Thornton, of the British Army, whose regiment the 85th, had suffered severely at New Orleans, said: "General Jackson showed himself an able and faithful commander during that trying time, had he not used the power confided in him in the 'high handed' manner alluded to, New Orleans would certainly have been captured". As to the charge of 'implacable hostility' in all the intercourse between General Jackson and the British commanders, the American showed peculiar courtesy and was humane in his treatment of the British.

"I beg leave", Colonel Thornton continued, "to mention a single circumstance in support of my assertion. On the day after the battle, we were permitted to bury such of our dead as lay beyond a certain line some two hundred yards in front of General Jackson's entrenchments. All within that line were buried by the Americans themselves. As soon as we had completed that melancholy duty, our General was surprised at receiving a flag, with the swords, epaulets and watches of the officers who had fallen. With them came a note from the American commander, couched in the most courteous of language, and saying that one pair of epaulets were still missing, but that diligent search was being made and when found would be returned. These objects, always considered fair objects of war plunder, had been rescued by General Jackson, and were thus handed over with the request that they be transmitted to the relatives of those gallant officers to whom they had formerly belonged".

This story, and the frank, soldierly way it which it was told, turned the current feeling in favor of "Old Hickory," and drew forth enthusiastic expression of approval.

The American was filled with pride, and he thanked the old General in his heart for proving by his conduct that the defenders of America were not only honorable but chivalrous soldiers.

Jackson's Masonic Record

There is no clear record that I could find as to where and when that he received his degrees. An article on Bro. Jackson published in *The Builder* in 1920, the one that gives a lot of information on just how the statue came to be designed and financed, also listed a few details of his political and personal life but only the accepted belief of where he may have received his degrees is given. In the official Masonic Tribute to General Andrew Jackson, RW Phillip P. Neeley, Grand Chaplain states that, "We have not received information as to the Lodge where he was made a Mason, but learned that he was for some time, during the early part of his life, in connection with a Lodge that met at Clover Bottom", in Davidson County, Tennessee. Another article in the *Builder* in 1925 states "The claim of Greenville Lodge #3 of Tennessee (formerly #43 of North Carolina) seems to be the most weighty. An original transcript of the Lodge record for September 5, 1801 shows that he (Jackson) was a member at that time."

There is clear evidence that he was a member of Harmony Lodge #1 (formerly St. Tammany Lodge #29 of N.C.) in Nashville, as early as 1800. He was present at the first meeting of Tennessee Lodge #2, Knoxville, on March 24, 1800, but that Lodge lost its charter in December of 1808. MW Charles Comstock, PGM of Tennessee and historian, records a visit by Andrew Jackson to Harmony Lodge in Nashville and Polk Lodge UD of Knoxville (dispensation being granted on January 15, 1800).

In 1808, Harmony Lodge #1 lost its charter, and there all record of Jackson's Masonic affiliation ceases until 1822. He evidently kept himself in good standing by paying his dues directly into Grand Lodge, which apparently in those days was permitted. The Grand Lodge of Tennessee proceedings of 1822 credit him with being a Past Master, but no other record can be found to corroborate this. It is interesting to note those proceedings of October 7, 1822, for it records as present "the following brethren, Past Masters, and admitted to seats as members: to-wit James McComb, Andrew Jackson and thirteen others, together with sundry 'Brethren visitors'".

Jackson was unanimously elected as Grand Master of the Grand Lodge of Tennessee on that same day, and installed into office after the Grand Lodge had been opened on the Past Master's degree. He was elected again in 1823, serving until October 1824. He was known to be a Royal Arch Mason, (the custom at that time was that the Royal Arch degree was conferred by the Blue Lodge), as he served the Grand Chapter of Tennessee as Deputy Grand High Priest at it's institution on April 3, 1826. On June 8, 1845, he attended Cumberland Chapter #1 R.A.M. and assisted in the installation of Officers of that Chapter. MW Andrew Jackson was also elected an honorary member of Federal Lodge #1 in Washington, D.C. on January 4, 1830, and Jackson Lodge #1 of Tallahassee, Florida. While he was serving his first term as President of the United States, he was elected a member of the Grand Lodge of Florida. One of the things that we do know for sure is that Andrew Jackson contributed $35.00 in 1818 to the erection of a Masonic Temple in Nashville, in which edifice he requested two Lodges to perform funeral rites.

One of the first things that Jackson did was to secure the uniformity of work in that jurisdiction. He called a special session of the Grand Lodge from April 7 to 12, 1822 to consider that issue. He said "To your discretion is submitted the preservation of the unswerving characteristics and unchangeable purity of an Order, which has enabled it to survive the persecutions of bigotry, the enmity of the ignorant, and the force of the wicked who view, every new or novel elucidation of the leading points in the first three degrees with jealous doubt". The future President visited the Grand Lodge only once after his terms were over—in 1839, when he once again presided over it's deliberations.

It is peculiarly appropriate that we should honor Andrew Jackson, because "Old Hickory" of all the many Presidents of our country who have been members of our great fraternity, is the only one whose Masonry was put to the test in a great political campaign. Bigotry and intolerance were signs in his day that were much greater than our own, but, his triumphant victory over William Wirt the nominee of the Anti-Masonic party in 1832 effectively, and we hope finally, ends all involvement of strictly fraternal questions in partisan battles. It is said that he neither altered his position for political motives nor equivocated on his stand. He stood tall, while the membership in the craft was decimated in the aftermath of the Morgan affair. Andrew Jackson and Henry Clay were the two prominent Masons who defied the Anti-Masonic Party, which of course had its origins in the "alleged" disappearance of William Morgan at Batavia, New York. These people attempted to make the Morgan affair a "Party Issue" during Jackson's campaign, but "Old Hickory" stood pat and was elected President. Until his death in 1845, he continued to be an active Brother in the Craft.

Here are Andrew Jackson's own words in reply to Anti-Masonic writers.

> "I have been unjustly accused of extending our Order and our principles into a neighboring country with a view of converting them into an engine of political influence. In the presence of this respectable assembly of my Brethren, and on the symbols of our order spread around me and the sacred book which is open before me, I solemnly aver that this accusation is false and unfounded, and that Masonry has nowhere been converted to any other than pure and philanthropic purposes."

His death took place June 8,1845. He was buried in Nashville, Tennessee, with Masons taking part in the ceremonies. Funeral corteges were held in other cities, among them Buffalo and New York, in which Brethren of the Craft also participated. Jackson is revered by the Craft for his devotion to Masonry during those trying times of 1826–1840. Any public clamor against the Craft did not cause him to change his position.

To the best of my knowledge Andrew Jackson was the only Mason to be elected twice as President and Grand Master.

Bibliography

Baird, George (PGM, D.C.). *Memorials to Great Men who were Masons* "The Builder". 1920: p48

Bargee (GM. PA) *"An Affectionate Tribute to Andrew Jackson"* G.L. A.M & F.M. PA : July 7,1845

Bassett, John Spencer. *The Life of Andrew Jackson.*

Denslow, William R. *10,000 Famous Freemasons.* Vol 1 A–D

Rothwell, C.L. *A Look at old Hickory.* Masonic Americana

"Knights Templar Magazine" 4th P Dec. 1974

James, Marquis. *Portrait of a President*

Logan, Henry. *Andrew Jackson's Faith in Masonry.*

"*Masonic Outlook*": March 1925

McClanahan, Arch Erwin (PGM. Tenn.). *Grand Masters of Tennessee, 1813-1992*

G.L. Tennessee. 1993

Proceedings, Grand Lodge of Tennessee: October 1845

Remi, Raymond. *Andrew Jackson*

Shepherd, S.H.. A *Study of Old Hickory's Craft Activities*

"*Masonic Tidings*": April 1930

Neeley, Phillip P.. "*Grand Chaplain Tribute to General Andrew Jackson: The Ante-Bellum Period*". Grand Lodge F.& A.M. State of Tennessee

"*Masonic Presidents of the United States*". A Souvenir of the Exhibition Library & Museum.

RW Grand Lodge State of Pennsylvania – I received information from Mr Stuart A. Schaeffer.

Chancellor R. Livingston Masonic Library, Grand Lodge, F.& A.M. State of New York.

A thank you is also extended to Cherry Todd, an assistant in the Grand Secretary's office,   Nashville, Grand Lodge F.& A.M. State of Tennessee

Masonic Interest in the Saints John & the Fate of Others who Shared this Interest

By Anthony L Delisi 32°
{Presented March 2008}

Author's Note: This paper is not a scholastic paper. The points raised cannot be proven. It is written to raise our awareness of things we see but do not see. This paper is designed to raise questions, not to provide answers. Our forefathers in Masonry were masters of hiding mysteries in plain sight. This paper is part of my campaign to ask Grand Lodges and Supreme Councils not to change ritual and degrees because any word changed may eliminate clues to our past so well hidden as to seem unimportant and worthy of change. To illustrate this point we will look at the unusual association of the Saints John and Masonry.

We masons are very interested in preserving the memory of the Saints John. It is so important to us that even though we are not part of any specific religion, nor allowed to discuss religion in our Lodges, we make an exception for the Saints John and we refer to them early and often.

As soon as a poor blind candidate knocks at the inner door, he is told that the Lodges are dedicated to the memories of these men. Oddly, even though the name of Christ has been eliminated from Masonic ritual and even though the name for God has been carefully chosen to offend no member of any religion, it seems odd that we would expect Jewish, Moslem, Hindu and all other non-Christian masons to keep the memories of these Christian saints top of mind. The conundrum thickens when you realize that these saints, while important in the life of Christ are certainly not as important as Christ himself, or as Mary the Virgin or Mary Madeleine to Christians and yet none of these are mentioned in Masonic rituals—only the Saints John.

Why are the Johns so important to us? Through the years, if Masons caused the evolution of ritual to exclude Christ and any specific name for God, why were the references to John allowed to remain?

This paper will look at some of the possible explanations for this phenomena as well as the curiously harsh fate of other societies who shared an interest in the saints John, right up to the extermination and execution of every member that could be found by the Church.

The Pagans & The Sun

The first group that had to be dealt with to make room for Christianity and Western beliefs was the pagans. To do this, the Church made pagan beliefs seem childlike or evil. Even what we have been taught about the great civilization of Egypt shows a great people with a pretty weak religion. We have glorified the Egyptian contribution to building, writing and civilization but we have left their religious beliefs in the dark. This is especially interesting because the Egyptian concept of Ma'at matches closely with Masonic moral beliefs. We have been taught that the Egyptians spent millions of man-hours building the pyramids as tombs for vain Pharaohs. There is actually very little evidence that the Pyramids were primarily tombs, just as if future archaeologists uncovering St Paul's Cathedral in London might conclude it is a tomb just because many people are buried there.

This same pattern is true of Druids, Celts and many other pagan religions. Many pagan religions worshiped and were centered around the Sun or "most high" and there are several references in our ritual that have a definite "Sun" flavor including the ritual spoken by the Junior Warden at open and close of every Lodge, references in the Hiramic legend, and the fact that all Lodges are said to operate at "high noon".

The Sun & The Saints John Connection

Many people forget that until fairly recent times, if you openly believed anything that was against official Church beliefs, you would be killed. Even if you looked like you were meeting secretly, you could be arrested and killed. If you were involved in a religion that was based on the sun, you would have to mask your meetings and purpose. There may be an interesting connection to the sun under the noses of the authorities.

As we know, all Masonic Lodges face (actually or metaphorically) east to west. Churches have traditionally been built so that the main entrance to the church faces the point on the horizon where the sun first appears above the horizon on the feast day of the saint to whom the church is dedicated. On the feast of John the Baptist (June 24th) the sun rises due east and so churches dedicated to him would face due east. If a building was dedicated to St John the Evangelist, whose feast is December 27th, the building would face due west. That means a Lodge could be dedicated to either St John. These two feast days are highly significant to sun worshipers since they are the days of the summer solstice and the winter solstice, days important to pagan sun worshippers as the birthday and death of the sun. But they are significant to masons as well. In fact, the Grand Lodge Of England was founded on the Feast of St John in 1717.

Remember that for 1500 years, if you met to celebrate the birth of the sun, it meant losing your life, your families' lives and your possessions. However, if you met to honor the Saints John, you were a good Christian and member of the community. Could our brothers have used this interest in the Saints John to cover an interest in the sun that may have been dangerous and irregular in the eyes of the Church?

Which John Are We Talking About?

It has also struck me as odd that Masonic references almost always mention the "Saints John" without separating them as if they were connected. There is no connection. John The Baptist was the prophet who baptized Christ and John The Evangelist was the Beloved Apostle who is credited with writing the Gospel of John. The Church has always been suspicious of people too attached to John the Baptist for a reason we shall touch on in a moment. Many heretics seem to have had an attachment to John The Baptist and it may be that to confuse authorities, our forefathers thought it best not to reveal which John was being talking about. I have not found any other logical reason to always connect these two saints without identifying them.

A Question Of Degree

It is interesting to note that underground or irregular organizations had degrees of membership as do Freemasons. The initiates or apprentices might have been told the Lodges were dedicated to The Saints John and only when the apprentice had been tested and initiated might it have been revealed what the true meaning was. This true meaning may have been kept so secret that over many years, the true meaning was lost and all degrees believed the exoteric message and not the esoteric one. This is exactly why changing rituals and degrees may wipe out forever the esoteric meaning "hidden in plain sight".

Groups Dedicated To John The Baptist & Their Extermination

Throughout European history, groups associated with John The Baptist have faced unusual fear and anger from the Church and have been harassed and exterminated. Why has an attachment to John The Baptist been so dangerous?

John The Baptist

John the Baptist appears to have been a member of an Egyptian mystery school who came to Israel to convert Jews. The Bible marginalizes John and this is a often a hint that a person like John was too well known to leave out, so the best thing was to put them in the story but make their role small. Some authors, such as Dr. Morton Smith, believe there had been a conflict between Christ and John and that Christ may indeed have been responsible for John's death. If this were true, the Church would not want anyone to study or be dedicated to the Baptist in case such study and interest revealed facts best left unknown.

The Mandaeans

This little known group of "St. John Christians" are Gnostics who survived by living in secluded parts of Iraq that were not visited by outsiders until recently. They believe St. John The Baptist was God's prophet or messenger. They have baptism and degrees of initiation. They have a secret handshake, or "kusta", that they use to identify members. They survived by being away from Europeans for centuries but now face extinction at the hands of radical Moslems.

{The Mandaeans}

The Templars

Since we are so familiar with the Templars, I will not go into details here. Remember that they were particularly fond of John The Baptist, held meetings that were tiled and were accused of worshipping a bearded head. The entire order was arrested, tortured and disbanded beginning in 1307 in an unusual run of cruelty even for cruel times.

The Cathars

The Cathars were a group of Gnostics declared to be heretics by the Church. The lived mainly in the mysterious Languedoc area of France and they were horribly and cruelly wiped out by the Church in the only crusade ever aimed at fellow Christians (the Albigensian Crusade) even though they posed no apparent threat. They had a special reverence for St. John the Baptist and this area of France has an unusually large number of churches dedicated to St. John that face due east and west. This is also part of the area that has a large number of Black Madonnas, which includes Lorraine and Toulouse, where many early Templars and

St. Bernard, their patron, were from. The Cathars had two degrees of membership and secret recognition signs. The level of cruelty and desire to exterminate this harmless group was unusual. When the crusaders reached Beziers in France, there were about 200 Cathars in the town and a few thousand Catholics who refused to identify the Cathars. The commander ordered ever man woman and child in the town killed saying, "Kill them all, God will recognize his own"

Leonardo Da Vinci & The Underground Stream

As you can imagine, anyone who had Gnostic, John-based, or sun based beliefs knew they were in serious danger if discovered. From about 1200 to 1700, these beliefs were revealed and passed on through hidden meanings in things like ballads such as "grail stories", playing cards, alchemy and art. These were ways to meet with others, exchange views and identify yourself without arousing suspicion or courting arrest and death. Remember that at this time, most people were illiterate, as education was reserved for the very rich and the Church, so paintings and symbols were very important to them.

To give a local and modern example of hiding messages in plain sight, I am including here two photographs I took of local businesses. Their signs appear to display the square and compass. Is it or is it a coincidence that the name of the gallery is Avenue? Have you noticed these signs before? Would an uninitiated person make the connection? If it were illegal to be a mason, would these businesses be arrested? Would fleeing masons go to these businesses to see if they might be a safe haven? This is exactly the kind of message that was passed on, hidden in art by Gnostics and followers of John until it became safe to reveal oneself. Let's look at a few examples hidden in plain sight.

Da Vinci is now well known for his paintings that seem to glorify John, showing him superior to Christ and using the famous "John gesture" of the finger angrily pointing up. This gesture appears to be a way of Da Vinci and a surprising number of others to this day identifying themselves as Gnostics and followers of John hidden in plain sight in paintings paid for by the Church. Could the references to John in our rituals and dates be the same kind of hidden references?

In his painting of the Last Supper, Da Vinci left many clues. Notice the John gesture and the fact that John the Disciple appears to be a woman and is leaning away from Christ so as to seem to be trying to distance himself. This may be a hidden message from a follower of John, many of whom accuse Christ of having John killed. Notice the person making the menacing "John gesture" at Christ.

The following were self-portraits of Nicolas Poussin created in 1649 and 1650. The 1650 portrait shows him surrounded by right angles and he is deliberately showing his right hand which appears to have a ring with a symbol on it. Could he be trying to tell us he was a Freemason without revealing it to the uninitiated?

One final painting to study to show how Masonic messages have been hidden in plain sight for a very long time is "The Pilgrim" by Hieronymus Bosch.

Notice the square on the building at the top of the roof and another on the gate to the pen. Notice the unusual footwear and pant leg, similar to the clothing of candidates for degrees. Notice an unusual rope or cable tow around the chest. Notice that even though he is carrying a hat, he is wearing a hood or blindfold on his head. He is turning his back on a building that is falling apart and has people in debauched activity that may represent the Church. This was painted in the late 1400s, long before historians say Freemasonry existed. Could the similarities to our ritual be mere coincidence?

Freemasons Survive

The Church wanted to destroy Masonry just as they did other John-based societies, Gnostics and Humanists. This is clear from a reading of the various encyclicals against the Craft and the wording used. The underground stream may have allowed our beliefs to exist until the power of the Church diminished and they were no longer able to kill those opposed to their views. By 1717, the Church was so diminished in power and it was finally clear that no Catholic would ever again sit on the English throne, and so on the Feast of St John The Baptist in 1717, modern Masonry came out of the closet and acted as if it were just invented.

The Challenge

The challenge we all face is keeping the secrets that were hidden in plain sight alive. The degree of Masonic education has dwindled. For example, in the book *The Secret Architecture Of Our Nation's Capital*, David Ovason discusses the knowledge of astronomy and symbolism that Masonic leaders of the United States processed, far beyond anything most Masons ever come across today. The unusual times for the laying of cornerstones to important buildings was based on astronomy. Because we are no longer in danger of death because we are members of the Craft, many of us have abandoned our quest for knowledge and more light in favor of chicken dinners and social events. Further, in an effort to be politically correct and non-controversial, many of the terms, ritual and other facets of masonry have been changed. There are many mysteries hidden in plain sight in our rituals and degrees that give us clues to our past, the beliefs of our brothers, and our purpose.

Where's The Proof?

Many Masonic historians are looking for proof that will never be found. In my opinion, that does not mean that anything that cannot be proven by original written documents is not true. Remember that our past may cover a time from about 300 CE to 1500 CE when people were largely illiterate and anything written could cost you and everyone you know their lives. During the Inquisition, it was common practice to torture someone in a town and only let him live if he accused others of heresy. This meant anyone could be accused and investigated. Because of these reasons, even the people who could write did not write anything down that could instead be memorized. But the secrets we memorize can die with us if we do not pass it on before death to another initiated person. Since death can come quickly and unexpectedly, many secrets committed to memory are hidden so well, they disappear over time. The true history of a secret, and the persecuted organization that took pride in its ability to hide them in plain sight, will never be revealed in normal ways and may defy the research of academics. One of our quests should be to look at the ritual and other Masonic traditions with an open mind and look for things, like the unusual mention of the Saints John, to look for clues for hidden meaning. For future generations of Masons to do this, we need to preserve rituals in their original form and look for the meanings and treasures our brothers left for us hidden in plain sight.

Two Grand Lodges in New York

Written by Charles L Ketchum, Jr.
{Presented to the Lodge August 10, 2004}

The Beginning

DeWitt Clinton was Grand Master in the State Of New York from 1806 to 1820. In 1820 at the annual communication, he declined reelection, along with Deputy Grand Master Martin Hoffman and Senior Grand Warden Cadwallader Colden, Mayor Of New York City. This was a serious loss to the fraternity as problems were arising within the Grand Lodge. Jealousy had become apparent with the success of Clinton's political endeavors, dissensions went out of control, and schisms and persecutions continued for many years.

Daniel Tompkins Elected Grand Master

Daniel Tompkins was the vice-president of the United States when he was elected Grand Master to replace Clinton. Troubles increased from the start. After being elected Grand Master, a resolution was adopted to terminate the Grand Visitor appointments under DeWitt Clinton.

During Clinton's tenure, he established three Masonic Districts for visitation under the control of District Visitors. The first district consisted of the southern portion of the state except New York City and the counties of Putnam, Orange, Ulster and Sullivan. The Second District covered the middle and eastern section of the state except Clinton & Franklin counties. The Third District encompassed the western part of the state and Clinton and Franklin counties. The primary duty of the Grand Visitors was to collect the delinquent Grand Lodge dues from the Lodges. The office of Grand Visitor had appeared entirely necessary to the upstate Lodges, but the New York City Lodges thought differently.

At the Annual Communication in 1820, the New York City Lodges regarded the expense accounts of the Grand Visitors as too costly, especially after reports from Ebenezer Wadsworth, the Second District Grand Visitor being allowed $1,130.00 for expenses and Joseph Enos of the Third District allowed $1,300.00. When the Grand Lodge Representatives voted to abolish the Grand Visitors Office, the results were more disastrous than expected. Grand Visitors Wadsworth and Enos had a large following and the upstate brethren believed that the elimination of this office was simply another maneuver on the part of the Metropolitan Lodges to exercise exclusive and complete control over the Grand Lodge.

Grand Master Tompkins, realizing the seriousness of the situation, summoned a "Lodge Of Emergency" on September 20, 1820, to evaluate the dispute over the Grand Visitors. The Grand Lodge admitted "the system of visitation" was essential to the preservation of all Lodges under the jurisdiction of New York State. A committee was appointed to determine a fair and satisfactory plan to reestablish harmony between the Lodges and report back at the December quarterly communication. There was no report in December by the committee, so the representatives of the western Lodges in the state held a meeting at Canandaigua and drew up several recommendations. It was proposed that the state be divided into eighteen districts, with a Grand Visitor elected by the Lodges in their respective districts. These officials were to attend the meetings of the Grand Lodge as the accredited representatives of the Lodges in their charge.

The Schism Begins

Grand Master Tompkins recognized his political jeopardy and decided in 1822 not to seek re-election to the Grand Mastership. Past Grand Visitor Joseph Enos was elected to succeed him.

Discord was evident after Joseph Enos was installed as Grand Master. The New York City Lodges were aggravated because only two of their representatives were appointed to the committee on revising the Grand Lodge Constitution and all the Rules and Regulations. Just before the conclusion of the meeting, the Master of Benevolent Lodge No.142 presented the following preamble and resolution to Grand Lodge:

> Whereas, serious dissensions have arisen in this Grand Lodge, calculated to impair the dignity and respectability of our Order; and, whereas, these dissentions are wide-spread in their dire consequences are fraught with mischief, the termination of which cannot be foreseen; therefore,
>
> Resolved, that it is expedient to form in the State Of New York two Grand Lodges, one to be located in the City Of New York and the other in such town or place as a majority of the Lodges out of the city may designate.
>
> Resolved that the Lodges out of the city be permitted to select the Grand Lodge under whose jurisdiction they will hail.
>
> Resolved that the mode and manner of dividing the fund be submitted to the decision of the Grand Lodge of ....

According to the Constitution, the resolution had to be laid over until the following year. On the day before the Annual Communication of 1823, the delegates from the upstate Lodges met in a caucus and resolved not to support any man for Grand Lodge office who was associated with a city Lodge. The session of the Grand Lodge commenced with a united effort by the upstate delegates to elect a complete line of officers from their members. Grand Master Enos recognized the situation was getting out of hand and adjourned the meeting until the following day.

Action Taken By Grand Master Enos

The action taken by the Grand Master was considered irregular, unconstitutional and a threatening precedent to the Grand Lodge and the representatives of the thirty-one Lodges, most of them from New York City. These proceeded to St John's Hall to reorganize, with senior Grand Warden Richard Hatfield presiding. The representatives elected the following Grand Lodge Officers for the ensuing year:

John Wells—Grand Master
Martin Hoffman—Deputy Grand Master
Richard Hatfield—Senior Grand Warden
Matson Smith, MD—Junior Grand Warden
Elias Hicks—Grand Secretary
Cornelius Bogert—Grand Treasurer

Grand Master Enos summoned a meeting of Grand Lodge for the next day, but Hicks, Grand Secretary, and Bogert, Grand Treasurer, paid no attention and did not show up. A new slate of officers was elected to the Lawful Grand Lodge and all were from outside New York City as follows:

- Joseph Enos—Grand Master
- John Brush—Deputy Grand Master
- Nathaniel Allen—Senior Grand Warden
- Thomas Barker—Junior Grand Warden
- Charles G Haines—Grand Secretary
- Welcome Esleeck—Grand Treasurer

Schismatic City Grand Lodge

John Wells, who had been elected Grand Master by the thirty-one Lodges representing the Schismatic City Grand Lodge, rejected the office of Grand Master, because of his professional obligation as a distinguished jurist. Three months later, he died and Martin Hoffman was elected Grand Master by a unanimous vote.

During Grand Master Hoffman's tenure, a memorable event in the history of the City Grand Lodge took place, adding greatly to their image throughout the country. It was the reception of the Marquis and Brother Lafayette of France, when he revisited the United States in 1824. Grand Master Hoffman remained in office until June 7, 1826, when he declined reelection and Elisha W. King was elected Grand Master.

The Schismatic City Grand Lodge numbered only thirty-one Lodges but was in procession of the records, archives and funds.

The Lawful Grand Lodge

The Lawful Grand Lodge commonly called "the Country Grand Lodge" had about one hundred Lodges pledging their allegiance to them, with about one hundred thirty upstate Lodges remaining neutral. In spite of constant agitation from the members to have the Headquarters of the Grand Lodge relocated to Albany, the Country Grand Lodge held all their meetings in New York City. Grand Master Enos was not an effective leader—he was reelected Grand Master in 1824, but not unanimously. He received two hundred and twelve votes; Steven Van Rensselaer received seventy-one votes; twenty-one votes were cast for John Brush. Enos's character and honesty were questioned and he never presided over another meeting of the Grand Lodge. During his last year as Grand Master, informal meetings were being held by representatives of both Grand Lodges to find ways of restoring harmony.

The Return To One Grand Lodge

In 1825, the Country Grand Lodge held its Third Annual Convention, which was attended by representatives of 116 Lodges. A sincere desire for consolidation of the two rival Grand Lodges was predominant. Stephen Van Rensselaer of Albany, an outstanding resident of the State, was elected Grand Master but was not present. Past Grand Master DeWitt Clinton was empowered and requested to install him in Albany. The installation took place on September 29, 1825.

On June 12, 1826, a resolution was adopted by the Country Grand Lodge, requesting Grand Master Van Rensselaer and Past Grand Master DeWitt Clinton to receive all correspondence offered by any of the Lodges of

New York City and to confer with them on all differences and to present a report at the next Annual Communication of Grand Lodge. An understanding was reached and recommendations were prepared to reunite the two groups.

The Compact

The two Grand Lodges appointed a committee, consisting of five representatives from each body, and on June 6, 1827, met and agreed upon terms of an agreement. The "Compact" as it was officially called, read as follows:

> That there ought to be one Grand Lodge in the State of New York and that it ought to be held in the city of New York and be considered as a continuation of the old Grand Lodge.
>
> That all allusion to former difference shall be avoided as far as possible.
>
> That the proceedings of the bodies known by the name of the Grand Lodge shall be confirmed and the warrants granted to subordinate Lodges of the two bodies and the proceedings of the said bodies shall be deemed regular.
>
> That the records and archives of the Grand Lodge being in the city of New York , the Grand Secretary shall be chosen from the city.
>
> That the Grand Master or Deputy Grand Master shall be chosen from the city of New York and the other from the country, the two Grand Wardens from the country, the Grand Secretary and Grand Treasurer from the city.
>
> That the permanent funds be managed by five Trustees, viz: the Grand Master, the Deputy Grand Master, the two Grand Wardens and

the Grand Secretary, whose duty it shall be to invest all funds over $3,000 agreeably to the resolutions presented to this committee.

That for the present session, the representatives of Lodges shall be entitled to all rights and privileges to which they are at present, but that it be recommended for the future that the number of Lodges which one Master or Past Master may represent shall not exceed three, and that Past Masters shall not be represented by proxy and that representatives be paid as heretofore.

That a committee ought to be appointed to revise the Constitution.

This agreement was promptly ratified by both Grand Lodges and the schism was ended. On the evening of June 7, 1827, the two bodies met as one united Grand Lodge, in Tammany Hall. Grand Master Van Rensselaer was elected Grand Master by acclamation, and a feeling of satisfaction and joy was felt by everyone in attendance.

Robert B. Fogler said it best in his *Recollections Of A Masonic Veteran*, Part 6, June 29, 1873,

> "The excitement of feeling was intense. Hand joined hand with a warmest grasp, and if ever the beautiful Psalm Of David, 'Behold how good and pleasant it is for brethren to dwell together in unity' was to be delivered in a Lodge with feeling, with joyous laughter, and with affected tears, such was the case on that occasions when the Grand Master read it in the East to that assembled throng."

The official title of the Grand Lodge was declared to be "The Grand Lodge Of The Most Ancient And Honorable Fraternity Of Free Masons of the State of New York."

Bibliography

Lang, Ossian. *History Of Freemasonry In The State Of New York*. 1922

Coil's Masonic Encyclopedia. (Henry Wilson Coil 33°) 1962

Fogler, Robert B.. "Recollections Of A Masonic Veteran" (parts 2 through 6 of the 40 parts) published in the New York Dispatch in 1873 & 1874

Astrology: As Above, So Below

By Phillip G. Beith 33°

{*Biography given: Phillip G. Beith is an Illustrious 33rd degree Mason and Secretary of the Valley of Buffalo. He is also an Astrologer, Lecturer and Freelance Writer. He has been published in Buffalo Magazine and New York Alive Magazine. He is a 40-year member and past Regional Monitor of the Rosicrucian Order AMORC. He is a retired Service Manager from Monroe Systems For Business, (the old Monroe Calculating Machine Co.)*}

Several years ago, I wrote an article about a dull subject and made it interesting. Buffalo Magazine, the magazine section of the Buffalo News, bought the story and published it. Today, I'm going to try to take, what may be for some of you a bunch of hooey and try to make it interesting.

Is Astrology fact or fiction? As Above, So Below. What is a Horoscope? You have in your hands a chart wheel.

There, that's a Horoscope–a wheel with a lot of silly looking symbols and numbers. That wheel and those symbols are an astronomical configuration of the orbiting planets, against the backdrop of the Zodiac, frozen in a time and place. And, throughout history, for thousands of years, meanings have been interpreted from those symbols.

The science of astrology, which sets forth in mathematical terms, the relation of the heavenly bodies to things on earth, has mostly been handed down to us from the ancient magi. Not that we merely accept what they have stated; but, using statistical methods upon observed results, we have found their statements and interpretations amazingly accurate.

As a herdsman, our early forefather watched the shortening and lengthening of the days; and when the Sun in its annual pilgrimage entered a certain cluster of stars, he knew from experience that the green grass soon would be starting on the mountain side, and he drove his flocks from the valley to those more luxurious pastures.

So, also the rose with the morning sun. The time of harvest was at hand when certain other groups were seen, and winter's bleak scarcity was heralded by the wending southward of the orb of day.

Thus, early man became the astronomer, his sustenance depending in great measure upon his ability to interpret, upon climate and the denizens of the earth, the effects of celestial phenomena.

There is a peculiar sympathy, between the thoughts of man and actions for which he finds no rational motive.

That is, the same sympathy that exists between the happenings on earth and the positions of the planets in the sky also manifests through the unconscious mind.

Having seen what powerful influences were exerted by the heavenly bodies upon all things external to himself, it was only natural that those studiously inclined should wish to ascertain their influence upon man himself.

As a general rule, it was found that people born in the spring, just after the days and nights became of equal length, were more energetic and had more initiative than people born at some other times of the year.

People born with the same group of stars rising upon the horizon were observed to possess characteristics in common. Likewise, the portion of the heavens occupied by the Moon was found to influence the brain capacity.

These were the Magi, the original Masons.

Therefore, in whatever era of the dim prehistoric past the first Masons lived, it follows from the very meaning of the word that they were the wisest, holiest, most revered of men. If true to their principles, there can be no more exalted souls upon this planet than are to be found among Freemasons.

Now remembering that Mason and Imagination are derived from the same root-word, a little light begins to dawn upon our perplexity. The very early Mason was not a worker in stone, but a mental builder, in whose work Imagination played the most important part.

A mason now is considered to be a builder – one who constructs. Likewise were those Wise Men of the East; but in their work the sound of neither hammer nor saw was heard; for they were mental builders.

The Masons, as a class separated from the populace and became the sages, philosophers, scientists, the spiritual advisers and priests.

These Masons early perceived a sympathetic relation existing between the organism of man and the fiery points in the firmament above, a definite correspondence between certain sections of Solomon's Temple and the human body. They found that there are certain principles pervading nature that express themselves in the influence of the stars, on the earth, in the sea, in the air, and in the body of man.

Therefore, the early Masons sought out the correspondences in nature, and built their pictured symbols into the sky, as the Temple of Solomon, Grand Architect of the Universe. And this grand edifice, erected by the

Ancient Masons; is of most perfect design, revealing as it does to the discerning, the Will of Deity; for what wiser thing could man do than to imitate the building of this ancient structure, and build for his own indwelling soul a mansion as perfect in its proportions, and as harmonious in its arrangements, as the Temple of King Solomon!

From these observations, covering immense periods of time, whose aim was to ascertain the relation existing between man and the stars, arose the sublime science of Astrology.

Through the ages they discovered that the Zodiac is made up of twelve signs. Each sign has a unique meaning.

In this modern world some say Astrology is a weird subject. When the Sun is in Capricorn, it is winter and it is cold. When the Sun is in Cancer, it is summer and it is hot. There's nothing weird about that!

History has assigned basic keywords for the 12 signs of the Zodiac.

The basic keywords for the 12 signs are:

Aries–Aggressive and Pioneering

Taurus –Down to Earth

Gemini–Intellectual and Communications

Cancer–Love of home

Leo–Proud Authority

Virgo–Precision and health oriented.

Libra–Diplomatic and peaceful

Scorpio–Secret, psychic and sexual

Sagittarius–Aspiration and philosophy

Capricorn–Responsible, punctual, ambitious and thorough

Aquarius–Humanitarianism, science, universal friendship, and new systems

Pisces–Nebulous and sensitive to the unknown

When someone asks, "What is your Sun Sign?" that means where was the sun in relation to the zodiac, from your viewpoint on earth, when you were born. Most people know it as their Birthday Month.

The Sun is your basic vitality. The who you are.

But there is more to it then your Sun Sign. There are nine more planets, each with another unique meaning that also travels through the signs.

The Moon is your emotions.

Mercury is your thinking

Venus is how you love and the things that you love. Whatever is precious in your life.

Mars is your aggressiveness.

Jupiter is your abundance. Anything to do with expansion. Some call Jupiter the good guy.

Saturn is the teacher. The constrictor. They call Saturn the bad guy.

Uranus is the sudden and unexpected. The new and original.

Neptune is inspirational and Idealistic or Self defrauding and chaotic

Pluto is chaos and reform, death and regeneration.

HOUSES

There are 360 degrees in a circle. Divide twelve signs into 360 and you get 30 degrees per sign. The Horoscope chart is divided into twelve sections. The sections are called houses—Houses of affairs. Each house is related to a sign.

1st house—Self Awareness, approach to life, early life. How you look at the world.

2nd house—What you earn through your own efforts. Your self worth.

3rd house—Communication, short travels, close relatives, early education.

4th house—Home, house and property.

5th house—Creativity, children and gambling. Anything speculative.

6th house—Health and Service.

7th house—Partner, how the world looks at you.

8th house—Sex and death, occult, what you don't earn through your own efforts.

9th house—Higher thinking, higher education, long distant travels, Inspiration.

10th house—Career, those in authority.

11th house—Hopes and goals, friends and wishes. Groups.

12th house—Hidden and confined.

A keyword for the house and sign:

I am, I have, I think, I feel, I will, I analyze, I balance, I desire, I see, I use, I know, I believe.

Let's take a Sun trip through the Zodiac.

SUN IN SIGNS

The Sun takes one year to travel around the zodiac. So it spends one month in each sign.

I know, you're going to say, "wait a minute, the Sun doesn't go around the earth, the earth goes around the Sun." That's right. But, when you view the Sun from earth, as the earth travels around the Sun, what part of the Zodiac are you viewing.

These meanings are the best and the worst of the Sign.

Sun in Aries (March 21–April 20)

You are either ambitious and assertive or impulsive and hot headed. You can be kind or cruel. Want to be first. Can't be Idle. They're the ones that honk their horns in traffic. Aries is the first sign, and the beginning of Aries is the first day of Spring, the start of the seasons.

Temperamental Aries

> Who works from morn to set of Sun,
> And never likes to be outdone?
> Whose walk is almost like a run?
> Who? Aries.

Sun in Taurus (April 21–May 21)

You are either thorough and harmonious or stubborn and possessive. You like to pick up the check. You are fond of food and comforts. Slow to Anger but never forgets.

Headstrong Taurus.

> Who smiles through life–except when crossed?
> Who knows, or thinks he knows, the most?
> Who loves good things: baked, boiled or roast?
> Oh, Taurus.

Sun in Gemini (May 22–June 21)

You are either spontaneous, dexterous and alert or scattered brain, fickle and babbling. You are fast talking and live by your wits. Tendency not to follow through and tend to skim their reading.

Worrisome Gemini.

> Who's fond of life and jest and pleasure;
> Who vacillates and changes ever?
> Who loves attention without measure?
> Why? Gemini

Sun in Cancer (June 22–July 22)

You are either sympathetic, domestic and maternal or moody lazy and gluttonous. You tend to hoard You like to have two of everything, one for later. You have a hard shell on the outside, but crying on the inside.

Hard-shelled Sympathetic Cancer.

Who changes like a changeful season:
Holds fast and lets go without reason?
Who is there can give adhesion
To Cancer?

Sun in Leo (July 23–August 21)

You have leadership, dignity and loyalty or you are arrogant egotistical and self-centered. You are theatrical forever on stage. You talk about your exploits. And you can crawl with a child and make faces with them.

Loving Leo.

Who praises all his kindred do;
Expects his friends to praise them too–
And cannot see their senseless view?
Ah, Leo.

Sun in Virgo (August 22–September 23)

Either you have discrimination and hygienic purity or you're a criticizing cynical hypochondriac. Hypercritical of others and themselves. The lint pickers of the Zodiacal.

Critical Virgo.

Who criticizes all she sees:
Yes, e'en would analyze a sneeze?
Who hugs and loves her own disease?
Humpf, Virgo

Sun in Libra (September 24–October 23)

You are balanced, courteous and harmonious or indecisive, wishy washy and inconsistent. You always see the other persons viewpoint. Upset by the lack of harmony.

Introspective Libra.

Who puts you off with promise gay,
And keeps you waiting half the day?
Who compromises all the way?
Sweet Libra.

Sun in Scorpio (October 24–November 22)

You are either courageous and resourceful or vindictive and sarcastic. You can be sensual or spiritual. A Taurus never forgets but a Scorpio gets even.

Ultimate Scorpio

Who keeps an arrow in his bow,

And if you prod, he lets it go?
A fervent friend, a subtle foe–
Scorpio.

Sun in Sagittarius (November 23–December 22)

You are either generous, love the outdoors and sports or you are over confident, fanatic and tactless. You study in depth. You are so honest you put your foot in your mouth quite often.. Constantly asking Questions and before you get the answer you're on the next question.

Pursuing Sagittarius.

Who loves the dim religious light;
Who always keeps a star in sight?
An optimist, both gay and bright–
Sagittarius.

Sun in Capricorn (December 23–January 20)

You have organization and justice with authority or you are resentful, pessimistic and unforgiving. You are the goat that climbs the highest mountain or goes in circles around a stick.

Relentless Capricorn

Who climbs and schemes for wealth and place,
And mourns his brother's fall from grace–
But takes what's due in any case?
Safe Capricorn.

Sun in Aquarius (January 21–February 19)

You are progressive, co-operative and have diplomacy or you're an opinionated flighty unreliable perverse dictator. You are twenty years ahead of your time. Feel you know best. Eccentric temperament.

Deliberate Aquarius.

Who gives to all a helping hand,
But bows his head to no command–
And higher laws doth understand?
Inventor, Genius, Superman–Aquarius.

Sun in Pisces (February 20–March 20)

You are either intuitive, have inspiration and compassion or procrastinating, sorrowful, confused, gullible, heavy drinker. Some say it's the dustbin of Zodiac. Skip the rules and regulations. Can't take stress, too sensitive and tend to drink.

Soulful Pisces.

Who prays, and serves, and prays some more;
And feeds the beggar at the door–
And weeps o'er loves lost long before?
'Poor Pisces.

Here is a little Biblical tidbit.

It is commonly considered from the many New Testament pronouncements of astrological doctrine, that the Twelve Disciples were chosen, each to represent a different one of the twelve fundamental types and qualities. The disciples considered this order so important that after Judas's betrayal Mathias took his place as one of the twelve.

Was it a coincidence that there is 12 signs in the Zodiac and 12 Biblical disciples?

Peter**the Aries**: the fiery, impulsive, changeable, pioneering leader, who eventually became the rock upon which was founded the New Church "of the Lamb."

Aries, 1st house pioneers.

Simon**the Taurus**: the dogmatic, determined zealot; who was concerned with property and finances, rebelled against the payment of taxes, and received from Jesus the admonition–"Render unto Caesar the things that are Caesar's."

Taurus, 2nd house of money and possessions.

James, "the lesser**Gemini**:" Slow to accept the authenticity of the Messiah, but became the eloquent preacher of the church in Jerusalem, and an active evangelist.

Gemini 3rd house communications.

Andrew**the Cancer**: the sympathetic home body, a follower of John the Baptist, whose first thought when he discovered the Messiah was to run quickly and fetch his brother Simon.

Cancer, 4th house, home and family.

John**the Leo**: the most beloved apostle.

Leo, 5th house, on stage.

Philip, **the Virgo**: always precise, calculating, enquiring, and practical.

Virgo, 6th house, analytical skeptic.

Bartholomew, **the Libra**: the innocently pure one. The tactful, persuasive evangelist.

Libra, 7th house, peacemaker.

Thomas**the Scorpio**: the doubting skeptic, yet bold and courageous.

Scorpio, 8th house, prying secrets.

James, **the Sagittarius**: the great teacher, who with Peter and John became the spiritual leaders of the early church.

Sagittarius, 9th house, inspiration.

Matthew, **the Capricorn:** the tax gatherer, the politician, the one in authority in the governing seat in Rome

Capricorn, 10th house, Authority.

Thaddeus, **the Aquarius:** who considered the lot of the peasant, and sought to better the living and working conditions of the masses.

Aquarius, 11th house, Humanitarian.

Judas Iscariot, **the Pisces:** who when he succumbed to temptation suffered severe pangs of remorse.

Pisces, 12th house, Sensitivity.

Was that a coincidence?

Oh! Incidentally, I understand that one of the versions of the Bible refers to the three Wise men as the three Astrologers!

The Moon

Let's take the Moon through the Zodiac. Where is your Moon?

The Moon is your emotions.

Moon in Aries—Desire to be strong and independent. Love is a chase

Moon in Taurus—Slow to fall in love, but they love forever. Like their comforts.

Moon in Gemini—Restless, constantly seeking without knowing what you want.

Moon in Cancer—Feelings are easily hurt. Go into a shell and clam up. Should follow your own intuition and don't listen to Mother.

Moon in Leo—Are not happy taking orders. Find it difficult to lie, cheat, or steal.

Moon in Virgo—Often in conflict with themselves. Love with the mind rather than the heart.

Moon in Libra—Defends people under attack. Strong sense of Justice. Will not compromise their principles.

Moon in Scorpio—The spirit is willing but the flesh is weak. A strong drive to be spiritual and feel ashamed of things sexual.

Moon Sagittarius—Always striving for something better. Must learn to accept life for what it is and people as they are.

Moon in Capricorn—Goal minded. Can't stand defeat. Become Bitter.

Moon in Aquarius—Feel people need them. Hang on the telephone in an endless effort to run people's lives.

Moon in Pisces—Dwell in misty perfection of and for themselves. Psychic

Sponge. Develop their own code of laws, your laws are not necessary. Greatest unhappiness is to violate their own principle.

Mercury

Let's try one more planet through the signs of the Zodiac.

Mercury is your thinking.

Mercury in Aries–Sound is important. Unhappy in a raucous atmosphere. Loud noise gives headaches.

Mercury in Taurus–Need a physically beautiful partner. Attracted to superficial beauty. Good observers but don't listen well.

Mercury in Gemini–Know a little bit about everything a great deal about nothing. Seldom stop to think things through.

Mercury Cancer–Forever discussing their own feelings. Over react personally to everything. Beauty or ugliness.

Mercury Leo–Hear a conversation change the words around and take credit.

Mercury Virgo–Dissect their impressions to death.

Mercury Libra–Everything has to be "Just Right."

Mercury in Scorpio–Intensely critical of anything improper. Have a 6th sense and can see through a phony.

Mercury Sagittarius –Miss things under their nose cause their eye is on the mountain.

Mercury Capricorn–Doesn't miss a thing.

Mercury Aquarius–See things in terms of the good it will do others.

Mercury in Pisces–See and hear what they want to. Personal bias gets in the way of their judgment.

There's seven more planets. But I think you get the picture.

You can see how just knowing a birth date can divulge your emotions, your thinking, your loves, your aggressiveness, your abundance, your constriction, your unexpected and your inspiration and reform.

If you kept track of the numbers, when we dealt with just the Sun Sign, we divided the world into 12 groups of people.

Not too impressive. You have met many Aries, Sage's or Libra's who were quite different.

Then, we delineated the different planets in the Signs of the Zodiac. This narrowed the search for an individual to a 24 hour period. A lot of people are born around the world on the same day. You know they are not all alike.

So how do we distinguish you as an individual? How about the time you were born?

Okay, so maybe a couple hundred babies were born around the globe at that same moment.

Where were you born? Now we pin point your location, your spot on earth, by Longitude and Latitude.

Now we have an individual, born at that particular place at that particular time.

Where were you—where were the planets—when you inhaled your first breath, the breath of life and became a living soul? At that time and place, the magnetic imprint of the Universe was recorded in your DNA. And now we can map the pattern of the moment—The Horoscope.

The earth turns one degree every four minutes. What was the degree of the Zodiac rising in the East when you inhaled your first Breath? Now we have a unique chart. There is no other pattern like yours unless they were born in the next hospital room. Even twins are 30 minutes apart.

Remember those houses of affairs? Now we plot the planets in the houses.

If you have Mars in the 1st house, you're a fighter. Someone born two hours later would have Mars in the 2nd house of money. Mars is go-go-go. They would be a spend thrift.

What is important, you now know your Ascendant or Rising Sign. This sign is how you look at the world. Your **Rising Sign** is as important as your **Sun Sign**.

The newspaper Horoscope columns don't know when you were born. So they assume that everyone was born at sunrise. If you read the horoscopes in the newspapers or magazines, read your **Rising Sign**. It will fit you better.

Do the Planets influence your life? I didn't say control, I said do they have an influence?

The planet Neptune has to do with your inner thinking. The down deep hard to reach thought patterns.

Let's take a trip with Neptune through some of the Signs.

Neptune is pretty slow. It takes 164 years to go around the Zodiac. It spends about 14 years in each Sign.

At the beginning of the century, Neptune was in the Sign of Cancer. Cancer is the home. That was a time of dinner around the table. Father knows best.

Then around 1915, Neptune entered the Sign of Leo. Leo is on stage, the spotlight. This was the era of the great Broadway plays.

Fourteen years later Neptune entered the sign of Virgo. Virgo – the sign of Health and service. This was when penicillin was discovered. Prescriptions became prominent.

Neptune was in the Sign of Libra from 1943 to 1956. Libra the balance, the pretty the nice. This was the age of the flower children and the love one another.

In 1956 Neptune entered the sign of Scorpio. Scorpio represents the sexual influence. This was when pornography came out in the open. Up until then, it was a big hidden product.

When Neptune entered the inspirational sign of Sagittarius in 1970, this was the great spiritual upsurge. Some were branded Jesus Freaks. Oral Roberts, and Jimmy Swigert were popular.

The Sign of cold calculating Capricorn was next in 1984. Businesses started to crumble.

Then from 1998 to 2012, Neptune resides in the humanitarian universal friendship sign of Aquarius. Time to get back to brotherly love. What a time for fraternal brotherhood to open its doors. If the world lived what Masonry taught, what a beautiful world it would be.

Kind of makes you wonder–doesn't it?

It seemed that whenever man discovered something new that would benefit mankind, so too did they discover a new planet. New Planets Usher in New Periods in World Affairs.

After the collapse of the stock market in 1929 and the commencement of the greatest financial depression the world has ever known, the discovery of the disastrous planet Pluto was officially announced. It was also when man discovered atomic energy.

In the 1846 when man discovered the nebulous Neptune, he also discovered how to make the gaseous either. It ushered in the period of oil and gas which prepared the way for our present means of locomotion. It also brought into the world the new religion of spiritualism.

In the 1781, when Uranus was discovered, so too was electricity discovered. Uranus, the planet of invention and independence, ushered in the machine period. England transformed from an agricultural into an industrial nation. The republican form of government came to be a dominant factor in the Western Hemisphere.

Maybe if you go back far enough in time, when Mars was discovered he probably discovered fire.

Kind of makes you wonder–doesn't it?

The first six houses represent Me, My money, My relations, My family,

My children, My health. The 7th to 12th represents all the other affairs in life.

A lot of Planets on the top—extrovert, Planets below—introvert.

Planets in the East—Go-getters, opportunities will present themselves.

Planets in the West—Few opportunities. Followers, but good followers..

Interpreting the signs, the planets, the houses, and the aspects. You get a pretty good picture of the tendencies of an individual.

Oh! The aspects. That's the geometric angle of one planet to another. If two planets are 90° apart, that's a square. That's a collision like two cars at an intersection.

120° apart, that's a trine, that's the luck in your life.

60° apart, that's called a sextile, that's the opportunities that present themselves, but you have to take advantage of them.

180° opposition, pulls apart, and 0° a conjunction combines the power.

A chart with a lot of squares is a life of trials and tribulations. A chart with a lot of trines, is a life filled with luck. Everything goes their way. A chart with no aspects, well, you've met those kind of people!. No problems, no calamities, and no successes. Their just there.

Remember when we read the best and the worst? The squares are the worst and the trines are the best.

The terminology can describe a person. Instead of saying, "She's a hot headed red head," you could say, "She has Mars in Aries, what do you expect."

Do the stars control you? No, no no. But they might create an influence in your life.

The more highly evolved you are the less you are influenced by it. The less evolved you are, the more you follow the crowd, you don't make waves, you ride the waves.

The lower evolved plant life is 100% controlled by the seasons.

As the Sun passes through the different signs in the course of the year, the climatic and other changes affect man and his activities in different ways.

The law of cause and effect, what you sow, so shall you reap, also works in harmony with the universe, so that a man is born at the time when the positions of the bodies in the solar system will give the conditions necessary to his experience and advancement in the school of Life.

How do they predict the probability of the future?

Your birth chart froze and recorded a moment in time. But the planets keep revolving. As the planets conjunct, square, trine and sextile your Natal planets, so too does your life tend to go.

The **emotional Moon** goes around once per month and your moods tend to change for no reason. We know the Moon affects the tides. The tides are volumes of water. The human body is 61% water.

The **powerful Sun** goes around once per year and keeps you healthy or sick depending on the aspects it makes in your chart. Hippocrates, the most revered name in medicine, said: "A physician, tending a patient, without a knowledge of Astrology has no right to call himself a physician."

The **communicating Mercury** takes 88 days to go around, and when it goes retrograde, letters get lost, phone calls aren't made, and words are misinterpreted.

The **lovely Venus** takes 225 days, the **aggressive Mars** about a year in a half. The male and female. The love and anger.

Abundant Jupiter takes 12 years and spends one year in a sign. **Constricting Saturn** 28 years, a little over two years in a sign. When the transiting Saturn is in your 2nd house of money—your finances are tight. When Jupiter goes through they tend to increase and when the go-go Mars passes through you spend more.

Shattering Uranus spends seven years in a sign and disrupts your life accordingly.

Illusive Neptune 14 years, and depending where it hits, beware of pie-in-the-sky deceptions. **Revolutionary Pluto**, 248 years to go around your chart. Never make it in a lifetime. The slower the planet the more intense the influence. It's like taking a magnifying glass focusing the Sun on an object. The longer you hold it steady—the hotter it gets.

Studying Astrology can be fun.

The astrologer acts according to mechanical rules, sometimes called the grammar of astrology. He considers the signs of the zodiac, the sun, moon and planets, their natures, aspects and relations as they appear in the figure of the heavens, which he erects.

The conclusions he draws there from are sometimes wrong, sometimes vague, sometimes right. They are usually right if he reads from the event after it has happened.

The Horoscope is not only the birth of a child. It can be the birth of an event. The signing of a contract, the beginning of a trip.

When the Titanic departed from Southampton, the departure time indicated a void-of-course Moon—What is planned will not complete.

When John F. Kennedy was sworn in as President, an Invalid Ascendant indicated nothing ventured nothing gained.

When the spacecraft Columbia blasted off the pad at Cape Canaveral at 10:39 in the morning it also indicated an Invalid Ascendant plus the accident pattern of piercing Mars squaring shattering Uranus.

The planets do not make something happen. They just indicate that if something is going to happen, that is the probable time. If you're going to slide off the road, it will probably be when the road is icy.

The planets promise, they do not provide.

The Grand Architect of the Universe did not bring us here without a plan.

The greatness of the universe, the magnitude of the divine scheme, becomes understandable if we but consider man merely a segment of the whole, instead of an especially blessed and segregated part of the plan.

Do not think that mere "floating balls of matter" affect ones destiny from distant regions of space, but, rather know that the Unity of the Supreme Architect, in His ineffable splendor and Mystery, constituted man as a microcosm, of the vast universe, and reflects "below" in the material world, that which occurs "above" in the Celestial World. As above – so below.

It kind of gives new meaning to "*Thy Will Be Done On Earth As It Is In Heaven.*"

The Pillars, in the dark North of Lodge, represent the polarity of all life. The Positive/Negative, Male/Female, Black/White, Light/Dark, Above/Below. You can't have one without the other. The two globes are the celestial sphere–a globe mapping the constellations, and the terrestrial sphere–a globe mapping the earth.

For astrological purposes it is necessary to map the heavens at any instant of time in reference to any specific point on the surface of the earth. The latitude and longitude of birth must be known before a birth-chart may be erected, and the longitude and declination of the planets must be calculated. Thank GOD for computers. It used to take three hours to calculate a horoscope. The data of one is obtained from a map of the earth–the terrestrial globe, and the data of the other is obtained from a map of the heavens–or celestial globe.

The whole of Masonry, as well as the whole of human life, is contained with these two spheres, for they symbolize astrology.

The Mystery is that all is One, connected, and events that occur synchronistically, are according to the Laws of Nature.

The universe sprang into existence in conformity to the law of numbers. In their interaction with one another they form by a principle similar to that giving musical overtones. In the chromatic scale, the interval is divided into twelve tones, illustrated by the 7 white keys and the 5 black keys of a piano.

Every known object in the Universe has been assigned a planet, sign or house. Everything we contact corresponds to one of the ten planets or twelve Zodiacal signs. From Angels, Colors and Flavors—to Forms, Jewels and Metals. Psychology, Physiology, Pathology and Physiques—Agriculture, Vocations, Meteorology, and Medical. All have a place in the Grammar of Astrology.

These, manifesting as the 12 zodiacal signs and 10 planets of the chain, together with the 10 original numbers, form the 32 paths of evolution, which really are the 32 factors of all manifested existence.

Each of the first thirty-two degrees is founded upon one of the thirty-two most important principles in nature, Each represented by either a number, a planet or a Zodiac Sign, the thirty-third degree being a seal showing that earth's mission has been accomplished.

In natal astrology we find that the sun actually rules the individuality, the moon the mentality, and the ascendant the personality. In actual astrological practice the sun is considered as ruling the ego, the moon as ruling the mind and the ascendant as ruling the body.

Pluto, Neptune and Uranus have an influence over the highest ideals of man.

Jupiter, Saturn and Venus have an influence over man's moral nature, his reflective powers and his affections.

Mercury, Mars and the Moon image, construct and mold the products of man's genius.

The Lodge, of course, represents the human temple. The Blazing Star of the Masonic Lodge, the compass joined to the square typifies both higher and lower union.

The Blue Lodge, the blue represents the sky above. The Masonic Temple thus is the mansion of the Sun; the universe itself; a spangled canopy of blue, so situated and so arranged as to prove the most suitable Lodge room for the initiation of the candidate: the Human Soul.

The square, being an instrument suited to the measurement of plane surfaces, embodies the idea of a vertical line, or positive force, meeting a horizontal line, or negative force at an angle which is measured in a single plane.

In practical astrology this is the first step, the zodiacal positions of the Sun, Moon and planets are found, and their aspects calculated. Strange as it may seem to the uninitiated, it is these aspects that are found potent in the affairs of life.

In fact, the policy of the Ancient Masons was to make every discovery of importance relative to the development of human character and the attainment of immortality with an appropriate symbol. One of the ten numerals, to one of the ten planets, or to one of the twelve zodiacal signs. A symbol is that which stands for something. As thought is impossible without the use of symbols.

As Masonry is a study of symbols, they even assigned a symbol to the officers of the Lodge.

The treasurer in the Lodge typifies the acquisitiveness of Saturn, as does his place in the Lodge, which is north of the Master. Jupiter expresses the qualities of warmth, expansion, and geniality. It rules the secretary of the Lodge to the south of the Master. Venus the Junior Deacon, Mars the Senior Deacon, Mercury is the Junior Warden, the Moon facing the Sun is the Senior Warden facing the Master and The sun is the Worshipful Master the rising sun and rules the Lodge.

When the Sun rises in the East to open and govern the day, so too the Zodiac Sign rising in the East at your moment of birth opens and governs your viewpoint of the World.

When we have the astrological birth-chart of an individual we possess a positive map of his various important vibratory rates and how they are related to each other.

From the astrological birth-chart and the progressed aspects we can plot the invisible influences operative in the life of the individual at any given time, and thus have a positive way of mapping the probable events and the time they will happen, in the individual's life.

The chart of birth is a map of the soul's need for expression and outlines unerringly the course it should follow.

When he conforms his life to the music of the spheres as sounded at his birth, and either avoids the discords, or transmutes them into harmonies, that he lives to his best and reaches the highest degree of soul initiation.

When you concentrate on a horoscope, it's just like dipping a photographic raw film in a pan of developer, a picture slowly starts to develop.

In Modern Masonry, as well as in that more ancient, we find closely associated with the common gavel the 12-inch gauge and the 24-inch rule. The factors that gauge the tone quality of the forces reaching man and expressing through his organism are the twelve zodiacal signs. They are the chief gauges of his life, character, and efforts.

The sign the sun is in at birth is the gauge of his personality. They gauge his thoughts, his speech his actions, and the events which enter his life.

They gauge the strength and the harmony of the influence of such planets as may be within their bounds.

But the particular department of life influenced by each zodiacal sign, by each section of the twelve-inch gauge, must be ascertained by the application of the 24-inch rule. This rule embraces the 24 hours of the day. All the zodiacal signs rise, culminate, and set, within the limit of this 24-inch rule—can the astrological influences affecting it be learned. Furthermore, this rule of 24 sections measures out to man the time when each of the important events of his life will take place; for each 24-hour cycle after birth, according to the most approved astrological practice, actually releases forces that bring to pass the major events that transpire during the corresponding year of life.

The 24-inch rule, then, is the 24-hour day, during which the signs of the zodiac, bearing with them all the planets, rise and set. By its proper use as a time measuring instrument the exact position of all the signs and planets at any moment of time may be known. Such a chart erected for the moment of birth, is the best possible road map to a successful life, and to the goal of complete initiation.

It is said that the Masonic Lodgeroom is as long as from east to west; as wide as from north to south; as high as from the surface of the earth to the highest heaven; and as deep as from the surface of the earth to the earth's center.

Only one thing has such dimensions. That thing is the universe as mapped by the Mundane Houses of a horoscope. Therefore, the Lodgeroom is the universe considered from the point on the earth where the candidate stands.

The third dimension of a horoscope is always considered to reach from the center of the earth beneath the observers feet to the zenith directly over his head. From the standpoint of astrology it would be difficult to give a better definition of the dimensions of the stellar universe than this one formulated by the Ancient masons.

The First House of the celestial map, the place where the sun is each day at dawn when it awakens the sleepy world into a fresh period of activity, in natal astrology rules birth. This house of birth is the northeast portion of the birth-chart. Therefore, in absolute conformity to astrological correspondences, when the candidate for the Entered Apprentice degree, that is, the candidate for initiation on the physical plane, has been reinvested with his clothing he is placed in the northeast corner of the Lodge room and caused to stand upright like a man. Even as the sun after its daily birth ascends to a vertical position, so does the candidate stand upright like a man, by his position indicating the will to strive for higher things.

Not only is the First House, or northeast corner, of a celestial chart, the house of birth of man, but it marks the birth, or commencement of each new enterprise. This explains why,

> "The first stone in every Masonic edifice is, or ought to be, placed at the northeast corner, that being the place where an E.A. mason receives his first instructions to build his future Masonic edifice upon."

The trestleboard is man's consciousness, where the soul drafts the plans for the actions of life.

The ornaments of the Lodge are: the checkered pavement, or mosaic; the blazing star in its center; and the indented tassel, or beautiful tessellated border that surrounds the pavement.

About this star, which on earth represents man and in the sky represents Polaris, is a mosaic of black and white checks. The movement of the planets through the zodiac causes their rays to converge to form squares, trines, sextiles, semi-squares, and other geometrical figures. The influence of some of these is harmonious, corresponding to the white checks. The influence of others is discordant, corresponding to the black checks. They well represent not only the geometrical designs of the birthchart, which predisposes him to certain experiences. They are Archives of Masonry in which the records are kept written in the divine language of celestial correspondence.

What is one primary benefit of the Horoscope? Take a child's chart. Decipher his natural tendencies, and lead him in that direction.

As a twig is bent, so shall the tree grow.

Get astrology out of the hands of wizards and charlatans and let academic professionals see the possibilities of the patterns set by the Grand Architect of the Universe. Nothing is by accident. All things have a time and a season. Read the 3rd Chapter of Ecclesiastes in the Holy book upon our alters.

> To everything there is a season and a time to every purpose under the heavens.
> A time to be born and a time to die.
> A time to plant
> A time to heal, a time to break down and a time to build up.
> A time to weep and a time to laugh.
> A time to mourn and a time do dance.
> A time to get and a time to lose.
> A time to reap and a time to sew.

A time to keep silence and a time to speak.
A time to love and a time to hate.

When Sir Isaac Newton, entering Cambridge, was asked what he desired to study, he replied: "Mathematics—because I wish to test Judicial Astrology." In later years, when he was chided for his belief in the validity of astrological principles, he replied: "Evidently you have not looked into Astrology; I have."

> One ship sails east and another sails west
> With the self-same winds that blow.
> "Tis the set of the sail and not the gale
> Which determines the way they go.
> As the winds of the sea are the ways of fate
> As we voyage along through life,
> "Tis the act of the soul that determines the goal,
> And not the calm or the strife.

As above, so below. Astrology—fact or fiction? You decide.

Visiting English Lodges

John Comstock

{The author's biography was submitted for Volume 3 and can be found there preceding his two articles.}

For the last year of my career I was very fortunate in that I was able to work and live in England. I spent most of that year in the city of Southampton which is near the central southern coast, about an hour and a half by train southwest by London.

On one of my days off I went to London and took a tour of the Grand Lodge of England. The next day at work, one of my British co-workers asked me what I had done on my day off. When I told her, she said her father in law was a mason and she would let him know that I was one too. Then next day she told me her father in law would like me to visit his Lodge. That had a snowball effect, because during my first visit several other brothers approached me and invited me to their Lodges. I often attended Masonic get together every week, and once made four in one week. While I was in England I was able to see each degree several times, an installation, and an 18th degree of the ancient accepted rite.

After attending Lodge, I would return to my apartment and write down my impressions of the evening. Although there are many similarities between the English and US versions of masonry, there are also many differences. I found the differences very interesting, and that's what I will focus on In this paper.

The Grand Lodge of England has authority over Masons in England. The Grand Master is a member of Royalty and holds the position for life, or as long as he desires to hold it; right now the Grand Master is the Duke of Kent. The hierarchy is broken down further into 47 provinces and the city of London. Each province has its own Provincial Grand Master. The Lodges I attended were all in the Province of Hampshire and the Isle of Wight, this province has 256 Lodges. The Provincial Grand Master attended most of the meetings I was at.

There is no one specific ritual in the Grand Lodge of England—There are several commonly used ones, and others that are not so common. Individual Lodges are allowed to choose the one they want to use. I was told that many Lodges originally had royal sponsors who would make whatever adjustments to the ritual they wanted. I saw work done from four different rituals, and although they were very similar they did have their differences.

The Grand Lodge of England had many ritual variants for sale In its shop, and I purchased a copy of what is known as the Emulation Ritual, which is said to be the oldest variation. Unlike at our own Masonic Service Bureau, I was able to purchase the ritual without even showing a dues card. I also purchased the Scottish Ritual at the Grand Lodge of Scotland without showing any proof of membership. I was not even asked if I were a Mason. Neither ritual is written in code.

In fact, I never had to show a dues card or my Masonic passport or work my way into any Lodge. I was just accepted at my word that I was a Mason. I asked a couple of times why they didn't verify that I was a Mason, and the response was the same both times, "Why would anyone want to attend these meetings if he weren't a Mason?" I was, however, always asked what Grand Lodge I was under, and they were satisfied when I told them New York, as they knew it was one that the Grand Lodge of England Recognized. The one problem they do run into is visitors from unrecognized grand Lodges, especially from France and Italy.

I was impressed by the numbers in attendance at the meeting. Usually there were around 100, even though Lodge membership was limited in size. A couple of times there were many more in attendance, and they were worried about having enough seats for everyone. I saw a lot of the same faces at the different Lodges, as many brothers belong to more than one Lodge, and there is a lot of visitation between the Lodges. Members not able to attend a meeting are required to call the Master and give an excuse for not attending. At the beginning of the business portion of the meeting, the Master reads what are called the "regrets"–the names of the members who were unable to attend, and he states that he has accepted their reasons for not attending. I never saw this involve more than four people.

The Lodges have waiting lists of prospective candidates desiring to join; it is not unusual to take four to six years from the time an application is made until the time a candidate takes his First Degree. When a prospective candidate asks to join, his sponsor usually checks with all the local Lodges to see which one has the shortest waiting list and then proposes him at that Lodge. Because of this there are often friends in different Lodges who attend each other's Lodge regularly. All the Lodges I visited put on two sets of degrees each year. Only one candidate was allowed for each degree, so there would only be two new brothers added every year.

The dress code is different from ours. Before my first visit I was told to wear a black tie, which I took to mean wear a tuxedo. It didn't mean wear a tuxedo—it just meant that the necktie had to be black, and is worn with a dark suit. A Grand Lodge or Provincial Grand Lodge tie could also be worn. Tuxedos are never worn; the formal clothing worn by Lodge officers is a morning suit, a black jacket, and black or grey vest and grey-striped trousers. White gloves are always worn by all and are as mandatory as wearing the Apron. The Master never wears a hat.

Aprons are not provided for visitors, and there was some scrambling to find one for me to wear. Later I made a special trip to London to buy one for my next meeting. The Grand Lodge of England has its own souvenir and regalia store right in the building, and directly across the street from the Grand Lodge are two other stores that sell Masonic Regalia.

The Apron differs for each degree.

The Apron for the Entered Apprentice is a white lambskin apron worn [as we wear them for that Degree]. The White Aprons we use in Lodge are what they would consider Entered Apprentice Aprons.

The Fellowcraft Apron is white lambskin, similar to the Entered Apprentice, with the addition of two sky-blue rosettes at each corner of the bottom. It is not worn [with the flap as we do for this Degree].

The Master Mason's Apron has three rosettes and two ribbons. There are seven metal tassels at the end of each ribbon. Those of you who have been to Ontario Lodges may recognize it because it is identical to the Aprons worn there. This Apron came into standard use in England around 1815. The rosettes symbolize the Three Degrees. The two ribbons represent the pillars [in ritual]. The seven metal tassels represent the seven Liberal Arts and Sciences and also the number of brothers that make a Lodge perfect. In their Second Degree lecture, it states, "Three brothers rule a Lodge, five hold a Lodge, seven or more make it perfect."

The Master and Past Master Aprons are the same and replace the rosettes with metal upside down "T"s forming three sets of right angles. There are no special Aprons for the officers; they are differentiated by their jewels.

The Lodge rooms were all very beautifully furnished. The carpeting, which they referred to as the "checquered pavement" is actually indented and tessellated. It is checkered black and white. I was told that the checkering
represented opposites in our lives such as good and evil or joy and sorrow. One of the brothers told me he often used the symbolism of the carpet to contemplate his life. He said that while Eastern Mysticism had its symbol

for opposites in yin and yang, Western Mysticism, or Freemasonry, has its checkered carpet symbolizing the same thing.

The stations and places of the Master, Wardens, and Deacons were the same as ours. However, next to the Deacon was an Inner Guard who dealt with the Tyler, or as he was sometimes called, the Outer Guard. The six or more Stewards sat on the sidelines. There was no Marshal, but the person who occupied that chair was called the Master of Ceremony. The Treasurer and Secretary sat at desks along the north wall. Next to the Treasurer was the Almoner who took a collection at every meeting for the Masonic charities supported by the Lodge. There were rows of seats on each side of the East for Grand Lodge Officers, Past Masters, and Masters of other Lodges. They were always filled. On the Master's left sat the immediate Past Master.

There was usually no Chaplain; all the prayers were led by the Master. However, the Master did have the option of appointing a Chaplain if he chose to. The Bible was on a pedestal directly in front of the master, and the candidate would kneel before the pedestal when obligated. The three candles representing the Lesser Lights were placed next to the chairs of the master and wardens.

In the center of the Lodge where our altar is located was what looked like a low table and was called the Tracing Board. On this Tracing Board was a picture relating to the degree the Lodge was working in, and it was used as a prompt in giving the lecture of the degree. It also would let a person entering the Lodge late know which degree the Lodge was working in. The Tracing Board for the First Degree showed the Greater and Lesser Lights in Masonry. The Board for the Second Degree showed a curving staircase and the middle chamber, and that for the Third showed a skull and coffin.

All business is done in the first degree. Entered Apprentices could participate and vote in the meetings. The only time a Lodge is raised to the Second or Third Degree is when that degree is conferred.

When the Lodge opens, the Brothers stand and sing a hymn while the officers march into the Lodge room in a procession. After the Lodge is closed, the officers march out while the Brothers sing a closing hymn.

There are no due guards in English masonry, and the signs are different from ours. Our Sign of Fidelity is not used, but the sign for the degree that the Lodge is working in is used in its place.

There are also slight differences in the degrees. The candidate does not change into a costume. He will have his suit coat removed and his shirt unbuttoned and the appropriate trouser leg rolled up. He will have a slipper on one foot but will keep his shoe and sock on the other. He is only blindfolded in the First Degree.

In the First Degree, when the candidate starts to enter, the Inner Guard holds a dagger to the candidate's naked left breast and says, "Do you feel anything?" When the candidate says yes, the Inner Guard holds the dagger in the air and the candidate is brought into the Lodge. Later the candidate is told that the reason for this was to imply that had he rashly attempted to rush forward he would have been an accessory to his own death by suicide whilst the brother who held the dagger would have remained firm and done his duty.

For me, the first part of Third Degree was the most impressive, because it was done in almost complete darkness except for one candle burning by the Master. The darkness alludes to the darkness of death, and represents a "journey through the dark depths of spiritual night to the brightness of the eternal stars."

I was also able to attend a Rose Croix Chapter's 18th Degree. Being the English variation of our Ancient and Accepted Scottish Rite, in England it is called the Ancient and Accepted Rite of England and Wales. The degrees have the same names but are very different. In England, the candidate is brought into a room in the Lodge that is painted all black. There the candidate takes an obligation and is given the 4th through the 17th Degree. The Brothers reverse their collars and move through a doorway into a room that is painted red. The candidate is blocked from entering the room and taken to what is called a chamber of darkness where he is left for a while to contemplate his life. Then he is brought into the red room and given the 18th Degree. Unlike our Scottish rite where everyone becomes a 32nd Degree Mason, most English Masons stop at the 18th Degree, with very few continuing to the 32nd.

The Lodges usually opened at 6:00pm. There was a festive board after every meeting. Since the Lodge halls were busy every night of the week, they would sign yearly contracts with caterers who would furnish the food and the support staff.

The festive board was always a full meal, served by waitresses. It started with an appetizer or soup. Next would be salad and rolls, and then the main course—often roast beef, roast pork, or roast lamb, and with at least three vegetables. Next would be desert, coffee, tea, and chocolate mints, and they would finish with crackers and cheese. Wine was served throughout the meal, and the Stewards would constantly make their rounds to ensure your glass was full. The cost of the dinners was usually 13 pounds, which was just under US$26. Since I was always a guest, I was never allowed to pay for my meal, so I used to try to make it up by buying rounds of drinks afterwards.

During the festive board the Master gave a series of seven toasts starting with "To the Queen and the Craft" and working his way through all the Grand Lodge Officers and Provincial Grand Lodge Officers to the new Brothers. Then someone would rise and toast the Master. Then the Master would toast the visitors, and the visitors would toast the Lodge. Each toast ended with a ritual that came originally from military Lodges and represented a 21-gun salute.

At 9:00pm the Tyler would rise and state "The hour is nine, when the hands of the clock form a square." And he would give the final toast, known as the Tyler's toast,

> "To all poor and distressed masons, wherever dispersed over the face of earth and water, wishing them a speedy relief from all their sufferings, and a safe return to their native country, if they so desire."

I was very impressed by Masonry in England. I was impressed by how beautiful their Lodge rooms were, by their attendance, and by how well their degree work was done.

I was mostly impressed at their courtesy, fellowship and brotherly love. They really treated me like a Brother. I was invited everywhere and treated wonderfully everywhere I went. They inspired me to become a better Mason, and I hope one day to return the favor.

THIRD BOOK OF TRANSACTIONS

The Master's Message, 2013 Publication of the Third Book of Transactions ("Volume 3")

It's been my privilege and honor to sit in the East this year. I love being in a room full of my brothers while one of them presents his latest work. Especially I love the discussion we always have afterwards. (Usually that's when I finally figure out what the guy was talking about.) I will be the first to admit that I'm not such a scholar myself. I'm more of a man of action. It was my strong desire upon taking up this gavel to raise the profile of the Western New York Lodge of Research in the region.

Last October we honored a number of Distinguished Masons who have served the Lodge well over the years. We are at a point where our roster of Charter Members is diminished from the original 25 to roughly a half dozen. I hope we can replenish the ranks with men as distinguished as those sorely missed forebears. These last five years or so have seen a revival of interest and energy resulting in the affiliation of many new and curious brothers along with just as many experienced brothers. We even have several brothers from across the state and the country that have affiliated. The more the merrier.

Our first book of transactions came out 25 years ago, followed by a long stretch of discussion and fellowship without a lot of finished work. In 2009 a second book was published, raising the bar for our current effort. We have had many more presentations than are represented here, of course. Some were ready to print almost un-edited. Some were composed to be read aloud to the room, so needed a little editing to fit in a book.

Some were so graphical or multimedia-based they could not be rendered on these pages at all. Some were excellent, challenging, and worthy, yet for one reason or another did not get finished by their authors. For that reason, I challenge future Masters to develop a plan to put a Book of Transactions together in their own years.

Meantime, I wish to thank the brothers who took my vision of publishing this year and made it happen. We are lucky to have some very talented writers and editors who put this together in a very short period of time. We are certainly going to have the opportunity to recognize more Distinguished Masons in the years to come.

Fraternally,
Wor. John Haslam, Jr.
Master, 2012-2013

Introduction and Disclaimer

It is our pleasure to present this third volume of our "Book of Transactions" on behalf of the Western New York Lodge of Research. The articles contained herein represent recent papers and presentations by members and guests in our own meetings or those of a local Lodge or concordant body. Individual copyrights are maintained by their authors and are used here by permission.

Minimal editing has been done for the sake of consistency and accuracy, with every intention to preserve the style and intention of the author. Articles are listed in alphabetical order according to author.

As with most written works of brethren within the Fraternity, the ideas and opinions presented here are that of their respective authors. They do not necessarily reflect the position of the Grand Lodge of the State of New York or other Masons in general.

Though laden with researched facts, the articles are open to the interpretation of both writer and reader. Within the Lodge of Research, we explore, debate, and encourage each other to draw our own often contrasting conclusions. We encourage you to do the same with this Book of Transactions.

We wish you the benefits of speculation on these topics and the desire to seek further light, herein and in all things.

Submitted 1 May 2013,

Bros. *Mark Robson and Kenneth JP Stuczynski*
Editors

Spiritual Alchemy

Phillip G. Beith 33°
{*A biography was previously given in Volume 2.*}

Introduction

The subject of Alchemy is one of great interest and it is well to approach the consideration of the science from the standpoint of Western Occult Philosophy, handed down to us from the Sages.

Alchemy has two aspects: the material Alchemy and the spiritual Alchemy. Material Alchemy deals with Chemistry, the science which investigates the construction of material substances. It treats the essential nature of Matter, of the Elements, of metals, of minerals, and of Transmutation.

The material alchemist works with the common minerals, such as copper, lead, tin, and iron, in the endeavor to change them into a metal more valuable. The ancients attempted to transmute base metals into gold.

Spiritual Alchemy deals with human nature. Spiritual Alchemy is what we are all about. So what can spiritual gold be? This we must find out by applying the law of correspondences.

Astrology and alchemy arrived in Europe together. A language that was applicable to one was likewise applicable to the other.

Astrology teaches that everything on earth has its correspondence in the sky, and everything in the sky has its correspondence on earth.

Anything and everything on earth is ruled by a planet or sign in the sky. Thus did the alchemists write and talk and think in the language of celestial correspondence.

The law of correspondence states:

- Gold itself vibrates to the Powerful Sun;
- Silver vibrates to the Emotional Moon;
- Metallic Mercury vibrates to the planet Thinking Mercury;
- Copper vibrates to Loving Venus;
- Iron vibrates to Aggressive Mars;
- Tin vibrates To Abundant Jupiter;

- Lead vibrates to Constricting Saturn.

Seven metals—seven planets.

It is said that gold is the most perfect of all metals. Therefore, spiritual gold, as applied to man, must be the most perfect part of his constitution.

Gold is extremely malleable and ductile. Consequently we must seek a human principle that adapts itself to numerous states and conditions.

Gold is practicably indestructible, so that which we seek in man must be eternal. Gold is not tarnished, nor is it readily attacked by other chemical elements. Gold is a precious metal that is used as a standard of value.

Let us then explore human existence for an unchangeable element that remains pure and resists the acids of criticism and the fire of affliction. What is the standard of value in man?

The standard value in man is—The Ego. The Ego answers all requirements. What the Sun is to astrology, and what gold is to economics and industry, the ego is to individual man.

Sunlight is not complete unless it contains the seven rays of the solar spectrum, nor is the musical gamut as it should be unless there are seven tones within the octave.

Thus also, a little study of astrology will demonstrate, there are seven lower-octave planets the influences from which are felt by every living being.

If we apply the law of correspondences it brings the conclusion that there are seven of these necessary factors: seven colors of the solar spectrum combine to produce white light; seven tones of the scale combine in the production of music; seven planets constitute the septenary scale of astrological influences; and seven expressions of form in the constitution of man.

The seven expressions are:

1. Without a heart, representing the Powerful Sun and untransmuted gold, the physical body of man cannot function;
2. Without a skeletal structure, representing Saturn and lead, a material organism suggests the resistance of a jelly-fish;
3. Without a venous system, representing Venus and copper, higher forms of life cannot function on the external plane;
4. Nor do they function energetically without an arterial system, representing Jupiter and tin;
5. A nervous system, represented by Mercury both as planet and metal, is essential to any worth-while thinking on the material plane;

6. A muscular system, representing aggressive Mars and iron, is essential for such physical movement as enables man to work;
7. And all organisms on earth depend upon a fluidic system, represented by the Moon and silver, for growth and the replacement of worn out tissues.

Yet however pure the metals, no complete transmutation is possible unless all seven are at hand in ample quantity. And thus, as seven is present in those things expressing perfection of form, even in the septenary constitution of man, we may safely conclude it enters into the composition of gold.

This is the key to alchemical synonyms.

"As above, so below."

Spiritual Alchemy

The laboratory of any alchemist is determined largely by the kind of work at hand.

The *material* alchemist must have a place where he may keep his furnace, chemical reagents, retorts, crucibles, test tubes, fluxes, and the metals upon which he experiments.

The *mental* alchemist follows similar principles; but the elements with which he works are his thoughts. He seeks to flux them one against the other, and recombine them in a mental gold that will attract to him ability, wealth, power and success.

To make gold not only must all the materials of which it is composed be present, but before the transmutation is perfected all must be there in proper proportions.

Within these seven are the qualities developed by all metals, the qualities that enter into the composition of gold. Therefore, if they are combined in proper proportion, and properly acted upon alchemically, the product is transmuted gold.

The *spiritual* alchemist needs a more comprehensive laboratory. The metals with which he works are the experiences of life. His materials he collects from the whole domain of nature. These he converts to his uses in the laboratory of his own soul.

So likewise, if man is to have transmuted gold, the ingredients of which it is composed must all be there. A spiritual body is not a fit vehicle for the soul if some of its essential organs are wanting. To provide these there must be adequate experiences of all seven types.

Therefore, in the processes of spiritual alchemy, it is well to give due regard to this principle of flux. Care should be taken when it is apparent that there is beginning to be an excess of some particular metal, even though thoroughly purified, that a similar amount of the metal of opposite polarity be sought out, purified, and added to the transmuting composition.

To recognize the proper flux for each alchemical metal, although there are other methods of determination, the one most convenient is to use the test of astrological correspondences. Take the solar system as our model. Thus, as a little study of astrology will demonstrate, there are seven lower-octave planets the influences from which are felt by every living being.

The Powerful Sun, representing Gold, needs no flux

On one side of gold we find lead, tin and iron—Saturn, Jupiter and Mars. On the other side we find copper, mercury and silver—Venus, Mercury and the Moon.

Constricting Saturn is a masculine planet and must be balanced by the feminine Loving Venus, that is, copper and lead should be present in equal volume.

Abundant Jupiter must be balanced by Thinking Mercury. Thus tin should equal in volume the amount of Thinking Mercury.

Aggressive Mars is a masculine planet and must be balanced by the feminine Emotional Moon. Iron and silver should be acquired in like amounts. Any excess of positive metal over negative metal, or any predominance of negative over positive, offers resistance to raising the vibratory rate, and consequently hinders transmutation.

Transmuting Lead that vibrates to Constricting Saturn

Because selfishness is so strongly entrenched in human nature lead is difficult to purify. Heavy responsibilities, monotonous labor, financial loss, disappointments, prolonged sickness, are some of the more common forms of lead. But even when so purified, in some lives there tends to be an excess of lead. As a consequence, in order to melt it, or dissolve in the spiritual light, an adequate flux becomes necessary. This flux is furnished by an equivalent amount of copper. Copper vibrates to Loving Venus.

Heavy work and responsibility should be balanced by amusements and relaxation. Sickness and sorrows should find solace in love and affection. These provide the opposite polarity which overcomes the resistance of lead to transmutation.

Therefore, whenever the alchemist has on hand a superabundance of lead, let him energetically cultivate the affections, compassion, refinement and sympathy. When lead is pure, material motives give place to those more spiritual. Why would spiritual lead and spiritual copper when combined in equal quantities have an intensity of vibration that imparts organized spiritual substance?

It must be answered that it is through the same principle that enables a metallurgist to reduce an acid mineral when united to an alkaline mineral to a molten state from the solid form with a temperature that would not perceptibly affect either alone. In the molten state both minerals have attained to a markedly different molecular vibration, and their glow indicates there has been set up in the electromagnetic field a finer-than-material substance of intense vibratory rates that previously had no existence.

Transmuting Tin that vibrates To Abundant Jupiter

Genial warmth, financial gain, religion, philosophy, conceit, sports, wealth, optimism, and a hearty constitution are common forms, or ores, of tin.

Tin, because it normally has a rather high vibratory rate, is not difficult to transmute. Religious aspirations, actions of good will, devotion to charity, the reverence of the mighty works of Deity, all have a vibratory rate sufficiently intense to require very little acceleration to complete their transmutation.

Yet at times there is an excess of tin that should be fluxed with an adequate amount of thinking Mercury. Good fortune and opulence should never be divorced from the exercise of intelligence.

Abundant Jupiter Wealth gives opportunity for dissipation, but thinking Mercury reveals its folly. Every condition that confronts you is a problem to be solved. There is a right way to meet each event of life, and the effort adequately to solve these problems is a fruitful source of alchemical thinking Mercury.

Transmuting Thinking Mercury

Intellectual activities, teaching, writing, travel, mathematical work, accountancy, stenography, are the more common ores of Thinking Mercury.

Unless it is present, even lead is frustrated. For plotting and scheming, either constructive or destructive, comes to naught unless carried out intelligently. Iron needs it also, for combat and building alike depend for effectiveness upon intelligence. Nor can we live in a truly religious manner, or otherwise cultivate tin properly, without the exercise of reason.

The gold of power, the silver of domestic responsibility, and the copper of worth-while friendships, alike are made more valuable by the presence of the mental keenness of Thinking Mercury. We can not have too much intelligence, nor can we overdo the exercise of reason.

But it becomes arrogant in the belief that thinking Mercury alone is capable of rightly directing the conduct of men, and of solving the problems of the universe. When intellect presumes too much, or whenever there is excessive mental activity, before the Thinking Mercury will transmute it becomes necessary to supply an equivalent flux of tin.

This tin may be had anywhere. A smile of kindness, a story that will evoke a laugh can readily be picked up and passed on, although remembering and telling it is an art to be cultivated. Prayer, now and then, even though silently uttered, costs little in the way of effort.

Therefore, if nature has brought you tin in abundance, see to it that you gain an equal amount of Thinking Mercury. Analyze closely your own actions, learn to discriminate between the true and the false, and exercise resolutely your intelligence in all matters that you do. Thus do you acquire the proper flux for an excess of tin.

Transmuting Iron that vibrates to aggressive Mars

Accidents, fires, courage, energy, desires and passions, and acute illnesses are some of the common kinds of iron. Iron, while one of the most useful metals, unless fluxed with an equal amount of silver, determinedly resists being dissolved in the spiritual light.

No matter how impoverished the circumstances, no matter how restricted the circle of friends, there is always opportunity to acquire adequate silver. Enjoy your home and provide your food. Acquire, cherish and painstakingly take care of your dependents.

Transmuting Copper that vibrates to Loving Venus

The gain or loss of a spouse, relations with friends, love affairs and scandal, social advancement or disgrace, jealousy, beauty, artistic appreciation—the expression of the affections are some of the more common kinds of copper. Copper, like tin, when once purified is one of the easiest of metals to transmute. Love is convertible. It is desire, passion, attraction, and enthusiasm for the God of your Heart. It is the attractive force that manifests throughout nature, and that holds the form together.

Nevertheless, there can easily be an excess of copper. It manifests chiefly as a tendency to seek the line of least resistance. Disagreeable duties are shirked. Problems are avoided rather than faced. Hard work of all kinds is avoided, and there is a tendency to spend too much of the life pleasure seeking rather than in the accomplishment of worthy enterprise. Joy and amusement have their place, but such excess of copper must be balanced and fluxed with an adequate amount of lead.

Lead is not hard to find. There is always work to be done by those with the will to do it, especially hard, disagreeable, and monotonous work.

Transmuting Silver that vibrates to the Emotional Moon

Domestic relations, the home, children family, dependents, food, shelter and the various commodities that make life endurable furnish those experiences that are the commonest forms of silver.

Not only is iron everywhere present, but more often than not it is forced upon us by others.

To permit others to impose upon us unduly not merely weakens our power of resistance, but through building up the habit of taking advantage of people, actually injures the character of the person doing the imposing. Yet in energetically struggling to advance those causes that are for universal welfare, in protecting the weak, and in repelling invasion, neither anger nor the desire for destruction should actuate the person, but instead there should be present an energetic determination merely to establish conditions that are for the betterment of society. This furnishes an ample flux for silver.

Transmuting Gold

Honor, position, station, employment, leadership, power, the relation to boss or employer, and political efforts are the more common contacts of life that furnish those experiences that may be classified as untransmuted gold.

Some opportunity to exercise an influence for the betterment of human life is ever present, and when grasped and such power as at hand is exercised, gold is quickly transmuted, and together with the other six transmuted metals completes the building of an imperishable and perfect spiritual form.

Correlations in the Lodge

Seeing that man is a seven-fold creature, being incomplete and incompetent when any of the seven expressions are absent, so too the Masonic Lodge room, typifying man on the physical plane also is incomplete and incompetent unless at least seven officers are all present.

The physical laboratory of instruction is the Masonic Ritual of the Lodge room. The Lodge room being a ground plan of King Solomon's Temple indicates the material plane where all receive their first initiation—where they encounter the tests and trials of everyday life.

The Pillars of Boaz and Jachin, in the dark North of Lodge, represent the polarity of all life—positive/negative, male/female, black/white, light/dark, above/below. You can't have one without the other. Even today's computers are binary—ones and zeros.

The two globes are the *celestial sphere*, a globe mapping the constellations, and the *terrestrial sphere*, a globe mapping the earth. The whole of Masonry, as well as the whole of human life, is contained with these two spheres, for they symbolize astrology.

The Mystery is that all is One, connected, and events that occur synchronistically, are according to the Laws of Nature. These, manifesting as the 12 zodiacal signs and 10 planets of the chain, together with the 10 original numbers, constitute 32 symbols.

As thought is impossible without the use of symbols and Masonry is a study of symbols, they even assigned a symbol to the officers of the Lodge. The study of Masonic Symbolism, then, becomes the study of the thoughts and ideas of the ancient Master Minds as expressed by them in the language of universal symbolism.

And according to the laws by which the Ancient Masons worked—which are also the famed laws of the Medes and Persians—that which is above has an exact correspondence to that which is below, and Solomon's Temple was actually constructed to serve as a model after the design of which each Mason should strive to erect his own physical tenement.

Consequently, as there are seven chief planets in the heavens above, there must be, and are, exact correspondences to these in man's domain. In the heavens, then, the seven Masons required to open a Lodge are the seven lower-octave planets. These embrace man's seven-fold constitution.

We have before us, then, the problem, though not a difficult one, of ascertaining the office in the Lodge room corresponding to each of man's seven chief components. Such a problem is most easily approached by first studying the correspondence between the sections of man's constitution and celestial influences, and the correspondences between the officers of the Lodge and celestial influences; and then, from this knowledge, arriving at the correspondences and their meaning between the officers and the sections of man's domain.

The **Powerful Sun** is the planet expressing power and royal dignity. The Powerful Sun is the Worshipful Master rising to open and govern the Lodge. When the Powerful Sun rises in the East to open and govern the day, so too the Zodiac Sign rising in the East at your moment of birth opens and governs your viewpoint of the World.

Therefore, the **Worshipful Master** corresponds to the ego in man's hermetic constitution. The Master, represents the human ego.

The duties of the Master are to set the craft to work. The temple in which he dwells must not be profaned by vicious thoughts or unseemly fantasies. Constructive work in the human edifice demands only pure and elevated thinking. In this edifice there are many workmen—organs, cells, and thought-cells. Little progress can be made if there is antagonism between them. Disorderly conduct upon the part of one of these is like a small rebellion. All must perform their tasks in harmony, and in obedience to the true Master, the deific ego.

The **Emotional Moon** facing the Powerful Sun is the **Senior Warden** facing the Master. The Senior Warden does assist the ego in its work, even as the Emotional Moon assists the Powerful Sun in bringing forth life on earth, or as in a birth-chart, assists in governing the life forces.

In a similar manner natal astrology teaches that the influence of the Powerful Sun, ruling the individuality, is transmitted to the Emotional

Moon, ruling the mentality, and thence to find expression is directed by Thinking Mercury, the messenger of the gods.

The **Treasurer** in the Lodge well typifies the acquisitiveness of **Constricting Saturn**, as does his place in the Lodge, which is north of the Master, in a region, therefore, of coldness. These values so received are then paid out, that is, they are transformed into mental and physical actions.

Constricting Saturn is the planet expressing coldness, contraction, and concreteness. The physical body is the most gross and concrete section of man's constitution.

Abundant Jupiter corresponds to the **Secretary** who sits at the south of the Master. Abundant Jupiter expresses qualities the antithesis of those expressed by Constricting Saturn.

The function of the Secretary is to record every experience of life. Every thought, every sensation, every emotion, is retained. Each event is recorded in the astral body either as a credit or debit. Every thought and emotion is accompanied by a change in the physical body, these values, either as assets or as liabilities, are actually turned over to the Treasurer, or physical body.

Loving Venus, in astrology, rules the sign Libra, the sign that governs open enemies. Therefore, it is quite fitting also that the Master should appoint Loving Venus, the **Junior Deacon**, to station the outer door.

The business of the **Junior Warden – Thinking Mercury** – is said to be observing time, calling the craft from labor to refreshment, watching them through this period that they may not give way to intemperance and excess Man's most vital refreshment is the period of sleep.

The gavel represents the human will. Will power, as indicated by the use of the gavel, is energy directed persistently to some purpose. How then can we develop will power? How can we develop the first implement of a Mason? Only by practice – there is no other way.

Such a development of the will is, therefore, according to the ancient sages, the first implement of a Mason. Every man, according to the Ancient Masons, has a definite constructive work in the world.

The **Senior Deacon**'s place in the Lodge is that of the active **Aggressive Mars**. The welcoming and clothing of visiting brethren refers to the circumstance that while man occupies a physical body he must subsist to an extent on other forms of organic life. Man's animal soul and physical requirements demand the co-operation of these cosmic brethren, and they are welcomed as food to build up the physique of man.

The **Tyler** symbolizes man's thoughts. The duty of the Tyler is said to be to keep off all cowans and eavesdroppers. This Tyler represents objective consciousness, chiefly the reason that guards the threshold of the mind and determines what thoughts shall, and what thoughts shall not, be allowed entrance to man's domain.

These eavesdroppers and cowans are all unworthy thoughts and inharmonious attitudes toward life. Only thoughts that are constructive in quality, and emotions that are harmonious, are duly qualified, and only to such does the Master, the human ego, if he performs his duties properly, grant permission to enter. Very few people realize how very important this work of the Tyler is. Thus is it that the only way man can change his destiny and make it better is through cultivating appropriate thoughts and emotions

Man must act under a **warrant** or **charter** from the Grand Lodge of the solar system. This warrant, or chart of birth, is a map of the soul's need for expression, and outlines the course it should follow. This chart(er) indicates just the work you must perform to make progress and receive initiation within the Lodge of life. Your charter is the chart of the heavens present at the time of your birth.

It is only when you conform your life to the music of the spheres as sounded at your birth, and either avoid the discords then sounded, or transmute them into harmonies, that you live to your best and reach the highest degree of soul initiation.

Each Soul Is Responsible for Its Own Destiny

Only through experience are Love, Wisdom, and Self-Consciousness acquired; and only through the conscious application of love, guided by wisdom, is the soul able to win its way homeward again to realms of infinite light, a self-conscious, immortal being. Such is the glorious destiny of man as taught by seers and sages and as revealed by the ritual of Ancient Masonry. Ancient Masonry teaches that each soul is a responsible entity working out its own deliverance from a voluntary and purposeful incarceration in matter. Freedom can be obtained only through knowledge of the laws of nature, and conformity in thought and deed to them.

It is the exemplification of these laws relating to the development of the body, of the intellect, and of the soul, that constitutes the paramount message of Ancient Masonry to the Twentieth Century world.

This outline of incomparable value is the ritual of Masonry.

You are the Lodge. You are the Master of your destiny. The entrance to your thoughts is guarded by your tiler. Your furnace of experience is the furnace of brotherly love.

The chart of birth is a map of the soul's need for expression and outlines unerringly the course it should follow. An astrological chart is the Grand Architect's trestle board of your life.

The ancient Masons, or Magi, specialized in acquiring knowledge that would enable Man to live to his highest and make the most rapid spiritual progress. This information was passed on to posterity in the language of universal symbolism.

The Lodge room is your laboratory; the officers are the symbolic metals.

These Magi emphasized these four things, that: (1) the soul survives physical death; (2) energies from the planets exert an influence over human life and destiny; (3) love is a powerful constructive agent; and (4) thought is a powerful influence to shape human life and destiny.

As spiritual alchemists, we take good men and make them better. We are striving for perfection—That Spiritual Alchemy transmuted into Spiritual Gold.

Arthur Conan Doyle and Sherlock Holmes: Their Western New York Legacy

By John W. Comstock

{*Biography given: Wor. John W. Comstock is a Past Master of the Western New York Lodge of Research. He is also a member of the Maine Lodge of Research. He has been a collector of the writings of Sir Arthur Conan Doyle for over forty years. He is also a student of labor history and has made pilgrimages to the village of Tolpuddle and related martyr's sites for his study of the Tolpuddle Martyrs.*}

Arthur Conan Doyle was a Freemason and a writer who created a fictional character in 1887. That fictional character appeared in four novels and 56 short stories and is known the world over. Not only have these novels and stories been translated into more than 200 languages, but they have never been out of print since they were first published over a hundred and twenty years ago. This fictional character has appeared in plays, movies, on the radio and on television. He has been in comic strips and cartoons, and although he is only a fictional character many people think that he once actually lived. As you will see later he even showed up in Buffalo a few times. Even if you have never read any of the original stories, I am absolutely certain you know who this character is and would identify Sherlock Holmes immediately from his deerstalker cap, magnifying glass and meerschaum pipe.

There are many Sherlock Holmes fanatics who are organized into dozens of societies devoted to the study of Sherlock Holmes—the most famous being the Baker Street Irregulars who meet yearly in New York City. Many of these groups take their names from things mentioned in the stories, such as The Red Circle of Washington DC, Mrs. Hudson's Cliff Dwellers of New Jersey, The Bootmakers of Toronto, The Trained Cormorants of Long Beach California, The Baritsu Society of Japan, and of course An Irish Secret Society at Buffalo whose name comes from the story, "His Last Bow."

In this story Holmes goes undercover as an Irish American Motor expert named Altamont who is aiding German spies in England during World War I. When asked how he infiltrated the group Holmes says "I started my pilgrimage at Chicago, Graduated in an Irish Secret Society at Buffalo, gave serious trouble to the constabulary at Skibbereen and so eventually caught the eye of a subordinate agent of Von Bork, who recommended me as a likely man."

These organizations have newsletters and journals that discuss many of the idiosyncrasies found in the stories, such as: Was Dr. Watson wounded in the leg or the shoulder? Did Holmes go to Oxford University or Cambridge University? How many wives did Watson have? Some writers have even speculated that Watson was actually a woman. This all prompted one critic to say, "Never has so much been written by so many about so little."

Sherlock Holmes has become much better known than the man who created him, Sir Arthur Conan Doyle. But Arthur Conan Doyle was an amazing man in his own right.

Arthur Ignatius Conan Doyle was born into a poor family in Edinburgh Scotland in 1859. He put himself through medical school with money earned by working on a whaling ship in the Arctic Ocean. His first short story was published in 1879 when he was only 20 years old. Although the Sherlock Holmes stories made him famous they were really just a small part of his literary output. He wrote over 60 books which included historical novels, adventure novels, science fiction novels, travel books, a history of the Boer War, a six volume history of World War I and three books of poetry. He also wrote books on Spiritualism, dozens of short stories, and several plays.

Phoenix Lodge No.257 in Portsmouth England.

In 1887, he became a Mason in Phoenix Lodge No.257 in Portsmouth England. One of his brothers in the Lodge was Dr. James Watson, whom he later named the character Dr. Watson after. In 1901, he became a member of Mary's Chapel Lodge No.1 in Edinburgh Scotland. He had many Masonic friends, among them Harry Houdini, Teddy Roosevelt, and Rudyard Kipling. Conan Doyle and Kipling both attended a military Lodge, Rising Star Lodge No.1022, in South Africa, during the Boer War.

Sherlock Holmes was not a Mason, but Freemasonry is mentioned in several of the stories. In the Adventure of the Norwood Builder, Holmes says to one of the characters "You mentioned your name as if I should recognize it, but beyond the obvious facts that you are a bachelor, a solicitor, a Freemason, and an asthmatic, I know nothing whatever about you. And in the story The Red Headed League, Holmes talks about another character, "Beyond the obvious facts that he has at some time done manual labor, that he takes snuff, that he is a Freemason, that he has been in China, and that he has done a considerable amount of writing lately, I can deduce nothing else."

Conan Doyle volunteered to fight in the Boer war but was told he was too old, so he worked as a volunteer doctor in an army field hospital. Bothered by international criticism of British treatment of prisoners during the war, he wrote and privately published an influential pamphlet, The War in South Africa: Its Causes and Conduct, strongly defending British behavior. This pamphlet was translated into several languages and was distributed worldwide. Because of this pamphlet he was knighted by King Edward VII in 1902.

Arthur Conan Doyle was also a sportsman. He played cricket, he was the first goaltender on what has become the Portsmouth England professional soccer team. He drove in one of the first automobile races in Europe. He golfed and played rugby. He was the first to introduce cross country skiing in Switzerland. He was a boxer and was asked to referee the heavyweight championship fight in 1910 between Jack Johnson and Jim Jeffries but he refused because he felt the fight promoted racial bigotry.

He was a war correspondent in the war between Britain and the Dervishes in Egypt, after which, in 1898, he wrote a novel called the Tragedy of the Korosko, which is about Muslim terrorists kidnapping a boatload of tourists. He was also a war correspondent in Europe during World War I.

He ran for Parliament twice and lost both times. He personally investigated two closed criminal cases which led to two wrongly imprisoned men being released.

Doyle wanted to make a lasting name in English literature and felt that Sherlock Holmes was holding him back, so in 1893, he killed Holmes by having him fall over the Reichenbach Falls in Switzerland in a fatal struggle with Professor Moriarty. When Doyle first visited Niagara Falls the next year he told reporters that if he had known how spectacular Niagara Falls was, he would have used it instead. Holmes came back to life in 1901 when Doyle was offered too much money to refuse for more stories. He continued to write new adventures about the detective until his death in 1930.

Doyle's first wife passed away in 1906. In World War I he lost his brother, a son, two brothers in law and two nephews. Long interested in psychic phenomena, Conan Doyle announced in 1916 that he would dedicate the rest of his life to the Spiritualist religion and launched a campaign to convince the world that the dead actually communicated with the living.

He began to write extensively on the subject, and to travel the world with his family promoting his beliefs. From those who had lost loved ones during the First World War he found a ready acceptance for his arguments, but his beliefs were to bring him into conflict with many people during the course of the final thirteen years of his life.

Spiritualism became Conan Doyle's religion and his driving force, taking him around the world for lecture tours. He was referred to as the Jesus Christ of Spiritualism. His beliefs often made him the subject of ridicule, this ridicule increased when he wrote a book called The Coming of the Fairies in which he expressed his belief in fairies and claimed real ones had actually been photographed by two little girls.

His beliefs hurt his reputation. Instead of being buried in the poets corner of Westminster Abbey with his Masonic brother Rudyard Kipling, he was buried in the garden of his home, and when the family sold the home in 1955 his body was moved to a country churchyard over a hundred miles away and re-buried early in the morning before anyone could object to him being buried in consecrated ground.

There are statues to Sherlock Holmes in London, Edinburg, Moscow, and Meiringen, Switzerland. There were none to Conan Doyle until just five years ago when one was finally erected to him in the village of Crowborough, England, where he last lived.

Arthur Conan Doyle came to Buffalo twice. On November 27, 1894, he read from his writings at the Women's Union New Hall in Niagara Square. The tickets cost 50 cents and a dollar. The Buffalo Express the next day said "the hall was filled with people, all of whom listened to him with eager attention. The evening will be remembered with pleasure a long time by all who were present." The Buffalo Evening News said "in addition to three readings from Sherlock Holmes, Doyle charmed the audience with a narrative of his life."

Conan Doyle returned to Buffalo on May 12 1922, when he gave a talk on Spiritualism called "Recent Psychic Evidence" and showed examples of spirit photographs. It was at the Teck Theatre on Main and Tupper, and admission ranged from 55¢ to $2.75. His talk was sold out and The newspapers all reported it in depth. The Courier commented on the absence of youth in the audience saying it was "an audience of grey heads and wrinkles."

Overriding the story of Conan Doyle's speech was another story that day. The Buffalo Courier had a huge 3 inch headline, "*Lady Conan Doyle Lost Six Hours*" and underneath that "*Frantic Enquiry on US Side*." The Buffalo Commercial put it a little differently "*Sherlock's Dad Finds Missing Family Quickly*," and "*Wife and Children Disappear but Can't Escape Father of Deduction*." Despite the wild headlines the story was simple. Doyle stopped in Buffalo to give his talk, but his wife and children continued on to Niagara Falls. When they got there they checked into the wrong hotel. Doyle couldn't reach them by telephone, so the authorities were contacted. The problem was quickly resolved but it made great headlines.

Conan Doyle also visited Rochester, where Spiritualism started, but it was reported in the Buffalo Times that "The noted author incurred some displeasure among Rochester Spiritualists when he made the statement following his visit there that while Rochester was the birthplace and actual world center of his faith, Buffalo is situated in the most advantageous geographical position to be the psychic center of the world."

On October 23, 1899, six years after his apparent death over the Reichenbach Falls, Sherlock Holmes stepped out onto the stage of the Star Theater on Pearl Street in Buffalo. In those six years Arthur Conan Doyle had been busy. He had completed a successful American lecture tour (which included Buffalo). His play Waterloo was regularly being performed by the famous British Actor Henry Irving. He had written and published several books. Into this fray would step William Gillette. At this time Gillette was one of the most popular actors in the United States, comparable to John Wayne or Tom Cruise at the height of their popularity.

William Gillette had been born in Connecticut in 1853 to a very wealthy family. His father was a U.S. Senator. His family had hoped William would follow in his father's footsteps, and when he became an actor they were horrified and disowned him. He first appeared on the stage in Boston in 1875. In 1886, he brought a civil war drama called Held by the Enemy to the stage. It became a smash hit by 1887, helping make William Gillette one of the richest and most famous actors in America. Gillette had a formula for his success. His plays were known for spectacular stage effects and for starring some of the most well known actors of the day.

Arthur Conan Doyle had written a Sherlock Holmes and was looking for someone to produce it. The script found its way to one producer who suggested to Gillette that it be his next play. Gillette put his own finishing touches on Doyle's play, but the script burned in a hotel fire in San Francisco. Gillette re-wrote the play from memory, and on October 23, 1899, it played for the very first time at the Star Theater in Buffalo. The reviews the next day were full of praise. The Buffalo Commercial called it "Mr. Gillette's Triumph." The Courier said that Gillette "took a hypodermic of cocaine so artistically as to make it one of the finest hits in the whole performance." The Enquirer said "its success was instantaneous."

The Star Theatre was the most luxurious Theatre in Buffalo. Its construction started August 1887 and it opened on Christmas Eve, 1888. The Star cost $225,000 to build, and although it was a gloomy looking building in the gothic style, its claim to fame was that with its steel and brick construction it was fireproof. The citizens of Buffalo were afraid of fires—in 1888 alone, The Banner Milling Company, The Genesee Oil Works, The Barnes Hengerer Co. Dry Goods Store, several Buildings on Exchange street and St. Paul's Episcopal Church had burned down.

The Star Theatre, Buffalo, N.Y.

For 30 years, The Star was one of the leading theatres in the country, hosting famous actors such as Lillian Russell, Henry Irving, Ellen Terry, Lilly Langtree, Lionel Barrymore and Masonic Brother George M. Cohan. When the play Sherlock Holmes opened, the Star was managed by Peter Cornell, whose young daughter Catherine became enamored with Theatre.

Catherine Cornell grew up to become known as the "first lady of theatre" in the 1930s and 1940s, and the theatre at the University at Buffalo is named after her. It is an interesting coincidence that in 1933, Catherine Cornell played the role of Juliet in Romeo and Juliet at the Erlanger theatre in Buffalo. Playing Romeo was Basil Rathbone who went on to play Sherlock Holmes in a dozen movies that are still shown on late night TV.

On March 19, 1920, the last newspaper ad appeared for a Star Theatre that had obviously gone downhill, offering "Continuous Vaudeville, and Ali Rajah the master mind reader, seats for 10 and 20 cents." In September 1920 the theatre reopened as Shea's Criterion, a movie theater, but finally closed in December 1923. The Building was demolished in 1925 for the Mercantile Exchange Building, which was later demolished for the Buffalo Convention Center.

In January 1901, after a successful run on Broadway, Gillette returned to the Star theatre as Sherlock Holmes again. The reviews were even better. The Buffalo Enquirer said, "The performance was perfect in every detail." The Buffalo Evening News, which had given it rave reviews the year before, said that this was superior to the earlier production.

William Gillette would go on to play Sherlock Holmes over 1,300 times. He appeared on Broadway, in London, and in several tours throughout the United States. In London, one of the characters, Billy the page boy, was played by a young Charlie Chaplin. Gillette's farewell tour as Sherlock Holmes brought him back to Buffalo to the Erlanger theatre in February 1930, where at 67 years of age he played to packed houses with rave reviews. Gillette lived until 1937.

Perhaps the best tribute to William Gillette was by Chicago reporter Vincent Starrett, who said "I would rather see William Gillette Play Sherlock Holmes than be a child again on Christmas Morning."

William Gillette wasn't the only Sherlock Holmes to play at the Star. In August 1905 a minstrel show called *The Ham Tree* had a juggling detective called Sherlock Baffles. That juggler was Freemason, W.C. Fields.

In April 1977 a Touring Company brought Gillette's play back to Buffalo. One of the stars was Kathleen Gaffney, a young actress from Niagara Falls. She was the CEO and artistic director of Studio Arena Theatre at the time it closed. The last time Gillette's Sherlock Holmes played locally was in 1994 at the Shaw Festival at Niagara on the Lake, where it got 4 ½ stars out of five in the Buffalo News Review.

In January 1978 history repeated itself when Studio Arena Theatre presented the first performance of a new Sherlock Holmes Play called the Crucifer of Blood, starring Paxton Whitehead and Glenn Close. Like the original Sherlock Holmes, Crucifer of Blood became a success both on Broadway and in London.

Sir Arthur Conan Doyle died from a heart attack on July 7, 1930. All the Buffalo papers carried his death as front page news, but an editorial from the Buffalo Times the next day expressed the feelings of many of his fans, saying:

> "We first made the acquaintance of Sir Arthur Conan Doyle when we were ten, when his first Sherlock Holmes stories began to appear. We still think his detective stories were the best that ever appeared in the English language. He not only could mystify his readers, but he had the power to harrow up the emotions. In the flesh we met him when he must have been an old man. His son had been killed in the war, and he had turned to Spiritualism for consolation. He not only believed that he would see the boy again, he knew that he already was with him in the room, perhaps at that moment standing at his elbow.
>
> He believed in fairies too. He had seen the little creatures dancing on the lawn, clamoring over the buttercups. He had gotten hold of some photographs of fairies. He had seen fairies. Who were we to dispute it? Artists, they say, see purple shadows. Some have vision so keen that they notice things that escape the rest of us.
>
> We went away thinking. And we envied the old gentleman. For we never saw fairies, with gossamer wings, dancing in a circle in the mottled moonlight.
>
> We wish we could see them [too]."

A Short Historical Introduction to the Scottish Rite

By W. Bruce Renner, 33°

{*Biography given: RW D. Bruce Renner is a Past Senior Grand Warden of the Grand Lodge of New York, and is the president of the board of trustees of the Chancellor Robert R. Livingston Masonic Library. In the Scottish Rite of Freemasonry, Bro. Renner holds memberships in several Valleys in upstate New York; he holds the 33°, and he currently is working on a comprehensive history of the AASR in New York from the Union of 1867 to the present. In the York Rite, he is a Past Grand High Priest of the Grand Chapter of New York, and holds both the KYCH and the Order of the Purple Cross.*}

Introduction

Whenever the actual beginning of Freemasonry occurred, it was apparent by the late 17th or early 18th Century that the organizational model was very successful. The most important reason perhaps was the erosion of a class-based society and an emerging middle class which amassed wealth from capitalistic ventures rather aristocratic inheritance. The opportunity for once highly differentiated people to meet in less formal circumstances was a perfect fit for the Lodge based organization.

There was also a general interest in esoteric subjects. Today, esoteric study is undertaken by a relatively small number of people, even within Freemasonry. Most Masons are like Sunday morning Christians who like to sing hymns but have a limited grasp of theology. In the formative years of Freemasonry, by contrast, there was a broader interest in and acceptance of the esoteric, albeit on a more emotional level. There was also a propriety that required such interest not be merely eccentric. Freemasonry gave just the right balance—a touch of the mysterious in a perfectly proper and enjoyable setting.

A successful business model always attracts imitators. In Freemasonry's case both external and internal communities imitated its organizational model. Externally, many organizations wrapped the Masonic model around their own mythology. Thus we have The Oddfellows, The Knights of Columbus, and the Knights of Pythias, among many others.

The expansion internally can be seen as a result of the open-ended allegory of the third degree, and of a desire to expand the Masonic metaphor into other settings. A Christian setting, leading to integration with the Templar story, is one example. The fundamental driver was an ever-increasing demand for Masonic outlets. What follows is a short summary of the early history of the Scottish Rite, one of the most successful extensions of Symbolic Lodge Masonry.

There are records of Lodges conferring the degree of "Scots Master" or "Scotch Master" as early as 1733. A Lodge at Temple Bar in London is the earliest such Lodge on record. It was in France, however, that there was the greatest interest in what became to be known as high degree Freemasonry, degrees beyond the three craft degrees. Many rites were penned as high degree Freemasonic content. In general, these degrees provided a more romantic vision of Freemasonry, interwoven with the ideas of knighthood and a particular fascination with Scotland.

Estienne Morin, Henry Andrew Francken, and the New World

A French trader, Estienne Morin, had been involved in high degree Masonry in France from 1744. In 1747 he founded a Scots Masters Lodge in the French colony of what is now Haiti. Over the next decade, high degree Freemasonry continued to spread to the Western hemisphere as the high degree Lodge at Bordeaux warranted or recognized seven Ecossais or Scottish Lodges there.

In Paris in the year 1761, a patent was issued to Estienne Morin creating him "Grand Inspector for all parts of the New World." This patent was signed by officials of the Grand Lodge at Paris and appears to have originally granted him power over the craft Lodges only, and not over the high, or "Ecossais" degree Lodges. Later copies of this patent appear to have been embellished, probably by Morin to improve his position over the high degree Lodges in the West Indies.

Early writers long believed that a "Rite of Perfection" consisting of 25 degrees, the highest being the "Sublime Prince of the Royal Secret", a predecessor of the Scottish Rite, had been formed in Paris by a high degree council calling itself, "The Council of Emperors of the East and West". It is now generally accepted that this Rite of twenty-five degrees was compiled by Estienne Morin and is more properly called "The Rite of the Royal Secret", or "Morin's Rite". However, it was known as "The

Order of Prince of the Royal Secret" by the founders of the Scottish Rite, who mentioned it in their "Circular throughout the two Hemispheres" or "Manifesto," issued December 4, 1802.

While Morin had assumed the power to establish Scottish Lodges throughout the new world, his personal activity was centered on the West Indies. It fell to a naturalized French subject of Dutch origin named Henry Andrew Francken to spread the high grade Freemasonry to North America. Morin appointed him Deputy Grand Inspector General as one of his first acts after returning to the West Indies. Francken worked closely with Morin and in 1771 produced a manuscript book giving the rituals for the 15th through the 25th degrees. Francken produced at least two more manuscripts in 1783 and about 1786. These manuscripts included all the degrees from the 4th through the 25th.

A Lodge of Perfection was chartered in April 12, 1764 in New Orleans, becoming the first high degree Lodge on the North American continent. Its life was short, however, for the Treaty of Paris (1763) had ceded New Orleans to Spain. The Catholic Spanish crown had been for decades hostile to Freemasonry. Documented Masonic activity resumed in the Delta in the 1790s.

Francken travelled to New York in 1767 where he granted a Patent dated December 26, 1767 for the formation of a Lodge of Perfection at Albany. This marked the first time the Degrees of Perfection (the 4th through the 14th) were conferred in one of the thirteen British colonies. This Patent and the early minutes of the Lodge are still extant in the archives of The Supreme Council, Northern Jurisdiction.

Although most of the thirty-three degrees of the Scottish Rite existed in parts of previous degree systems, the Scottish Rite did not come into being until the formation of the Mother Supreme Council at Charleston, South Carolina, in May 1801.

Isaac De Costa, one of the deputies commissioned to establish Morin's Rite of the Royal Secret in other countries, formed constituent bodies of the Rite in South Carolina in 1783, which eventually became, in 1801, The Supreme Council of the Ancient and Accepted Scottish Rite, Southern Jurisdiction. All regular Scottish Rite bodies today derive their heritage from this body.

On May 1, 1813, an officer from the Supreme Council at Charleston initiated several New York Masons into the Thirty-third Degree, and then organized a Supreme Council for the "Northern Masonic District and Jurisdiction." On May 21, 1814, this Supreme Council reopened and proceeded to "nominate, elect, appoint, install and proclaim in due, legal and ample form" the elected officers, "...forming the second Grand and Supreme Council." The charter of this organization, written January 7, 1815, added, "We think the Ratification ought to be dated 21st day May 5815."

Presently the Supreme Council, 33°, Northern Masonic Jurisdiction, dates itself from May 15, 1867, when it merged with the competing Cerneau "Supreme Council" in New York.

Albert Pike

We now come to the important personage of Albert Pike. Born in Boston, Massachusetts on December 29, 1809, Albert Pike is asserted within the Southern Jurisdiction as the man most responsible for the growth and success of the Scottish Rite from an obscure Masonic Rite in the mid1800s to the international fraternity that it became.

Pike received the 4th through the 32nd Degrees in March 1853 from Dr. Albert G. Mackey, in Charleston, S.C., and was appointed Deputy Inspector for Arkansas that same year. At this point, the degrees were in a rudimentary form, often only including a brief history and legend of each degree, and some other brief details without a workable ritual for their conferral. In 1855, the Supreme Council appointed a committee to prepare and compile rituals for the 4th through the 32nd Degrees composed of Albert G. Mackey, John H. Honour, W. S. Rockwell, C. Samory, and Albert Pike. Pike did all the work of the committee.

In March 1858, Pike was elected a member of the Supreme Council for the Southern Jurisdiction of the United States, and became its Grand Commander January 1859. The American Civil War interrupted his work on Scottish Rite rituals. In 1870 he and the Supreme Council moved to Washington, DC, where he finally completed his revision of the rituals in 1884. Pike also wrote lectures for all the degrees, which were published in 1871 under the title Morals and Dogma of the Ancient and Accepted Scottish Rite of Freemasonry.

Pike's ritual has been reworked by countless ritual committees over the intervening years, and the Northern Masonic Jurisdiction, in particular, has made an effort to move away from Pike's dense and esoteric approach to a lighter one focused on expanding the symbolic Lodge's lessons of morality and the importance of character, often illustrated through events in American history.

The Scottish Rite Today

The Scottish Rite continues to provide two important functions beyond the Symbolic Lodge. First, it possesses a rich ritualistic tradition that enhances the knowledge and insight of a Master Mason, and second, it provides a venue beyond the scope of what an individual Lodge can provide that allows a common meeting place for Masons from different Lodges.

The Scottish Rite is organized into local units called Valleys. In our Northern Masonic Jurisdiction, several charitable activities are conducted by the Valleys. The flagship is the 32° Masonic Learning Centers for Dyslexic Children. In addition we have a scholarship program, and The Museum of Our National Heritage and the John Van Gorden Library located at the headquarters of the Supreme Council in Lexington, Massachusetts.

Addendum I: The Valley of Buffalo—A brief early history

The Valley of Buffalo has four bodies operating under it: The Palmoni Lodge of Perfection; The Palmoni Council, Princes of Jerusalem; The Buffalo Chapter of Rose Croix; and the Buffalo Consistory. They are severally empowered to confer the 29 degrees from the 4th to the 32nd. The 33° can only be conferred by The Supreme Council.

Prior to 1867 there was no Scottish Rite presence west of Rochester. In early 1867 ten Buffalo Masons who had received their Scottish Rite Degrees in Syracuse petitioned the Supreme Council for a patent to establish a Lodge of Perfection and a Council, Princes of Jerusalem in Buffalo which was duly granted. Palmoni Lodge of Perfection and Palmoni Council were born. For several years their continued existence was tenuous due to the limited time of its members, the lack of facilities and equipment, and the curious fact that to be a member one had to be first a Knight Templar.

A fire in 1882 cost the Lodge all of its records and its Charter. Some reorganization occurred and they eventually received a duplicate charter. Through the efforts of a brother, Abram Oppenheimer, the Lodge finally began to grow, and a commitment was made to do excellent ritual in full form, a tradition that has been largely keep until the present. The

Council's history isn't as well documented, but it appears that its activity or lack thereof was very much consistent with the Lodge.

By 1892, the Lodge and Council were on such good footing that many felt it was time to add a Chapter of Rose Croix and a Consistory, thus making it a complete Scottish Rite Valley. At the meeting of the Supreme Council held in September of that year Ill∴ Charles W. Cushman, 33°, then Thrice Potent Master of Palmoni Lodge, accompanied by a lesser known, but equally distinguished Mason, Ill∴ David L. Day, 33°, urged the granting of a dispensation for a new Chapter and Consistory in Buffalo. Buffalo Chapter Rose Croix and the Buffalo Consistory were established. The growth of these two bodies was rapid and they received their Charters on September 21, 1893.

The Valley had one member who achieved the highest rank in the Scottish Rite—that of Sovereign Grand Commander. That man was Ill \ George A. Newbury, 33° SGC, who served in that role from 1965-1975.

Addendum II: Recommendations for further reading

You may have difficulty in finding A History of The Supreme Council, 33°, AASR, NMJ—USA by George Newbury and Louis L. Williams, but although dated (it was published in 1987) it is the best history available for The Supreme Council of the Northern Masonic Jurisdiction.

A far rarer book is the History of Buffalo Consistory AASR, by James Leroy Nixon. Published in 1915, it gives a fascinating glimpse into not only the early days of the Scottish Rite in Buffalo, but also of Buffalo itself during the transition from the 1 9th to the 20th century. A few copies exist in the Valley Library for study.

The Lodge of the Double-Headed Eagle by William L. Fox (1997) and The Valley of the Craftsmen edited by William L. Fox (2007) are both valuable histories of the Southern Jurisdiction.

There is currently no overview of the Northern Masonic Jurisdiction's ritual, but Rex R. Hutchen's A Bridge to Light gives an excellent short introduction to the degrees of the Southern Jurisdiction, which have largely held to the Pike ritual.

A far more comprehensive view is given in the newly released Scottish Rite Ritual Monitor and Guide by Arturo De Hoyos. Weighing in at just under a thousand pages, it provides a complete text of all the degrees minus the secret work, and many additional commentaries, making it the most detailed guided on ritual of any Masonic organization to date.

For those willing to make the effort and like original source material, there is Albert Pike's *Morals and Dogma of the Ancient and Accepted Scottish Rite of Freemasonry*, a dated and difficult, but rewarding read.

To learn more about Albert Pike the man, there is Jim Tresner's *Albert Pike, The Man Behind the Monument*.

Finally, for a view into the history of the Scottish Rite's unique theatrical approach to degree presentation, there is *The Theatre of the Fraternity* edited by C. Lance Brockman.

The Tolpuddle Martyrs

By John W. Comstock

{*Biography given: Wor. John W. Comstock is a Past Master of the Western New York Lodge of Research. He is also a member of the Maine Lodge of Research. He has been a collector of the writings of Sir Arthur Conan Doyle for over forty years. He is also a student of labor history and has made pilgrimages to the village of Tolpuddle and related martyr's sites for his study of the Tolpuddle Martyrs.*}

Freemasonry has had an influence on much of our society. It had a tremendous effect on the mutual benefit societies that proliferated in England in the mid 18th Century and in the United States after the Civil War. Mutual benefit societies have been around since the beginning of Western Civilization. In classical Greece and Rome, artisans, soldiers and tradesmen would form clubs where a subscription was paid in and the member would receive benefits if they needed them. Usually the benefits included burial costs, sickness benefits, and pensions for widows and children.

In the Middle Ages in Europe, these needs were often filled by the guilds, which usually had a charitable fund for ill members and members' dependents. Many Medieval guilds were craft-based, regulating craft trades; others were lay religious fraternities with no ties to the crafts.

In the late 1600's Daniel Defoe wrote about these mutual benefit societies and suggested that a national friendly society be created in England that all working people would be required to join and pay into. The friendly society would then provide assistance in time of sickness or unemployment, and take the responsibility of poor relief away from the local governments. It was seen as a way to induce the lower classes to practice self help.

Without these mutual benefit societies if a man died poor he would be buried in an unmarked grave in a potter's field. His wife and children would wind up at a poor house, or work house where they would have to perform hard labor to survive.

The Freemasons of the time were composed of the middle and upper classes in Britain. Although there were requirements to help distressed brethren, their widows and orphans, Freemasonry was not, nor ever was intended to be a benefit society.

Freemasonry was one of the principal drivers of the 18th Century Enlightenment. A high proportion of the scientists, scholars, statesmen, and artists of that era were Freemasons. Because all masons were equal within the Lodge, relationships between men who held different social statuses became possible. Men with political and religious beliefs that would normally keep them separated could now meet and have friendly discussions. Because what was said in the Lodge was considered secret, it was safe to discuss new or radical ideas.

The Freemason framework or model of an organization was very flexible, and was adopted by many of the fraternal and friendly organizations. In that framework there was a foundation legend or metaphor, usually claiming ancient origins of the organization. The legend would give the society its nomenclature, symbols, and a story to expound moral teaching. Candidates would be put through an initiation ceremony which included blindfolding, some form of ordeal or fright, and an oath of secrecy. Initiated members would identify themselves to each other with passwords, handshakes and gestures.

Many of these organizations freely took symbols and regalia from Freemasonry and made it their own. While the apron is the badge of a Mason and symbolizes the aprons worn by the masons at the building of King Solomon's Temple, many organizations in the 18th and 19th Centuries wore aprons.

The Oddfellows wore aprons into the late 19th Century but then abandoned them for collars representing the various degrees. The aprons are explained in a description of the English initiatory degree from 1797. In that degree the Lodge room was in darkness lit by only a single candle. Loose, rough planks representing a road were set around the Lodge room. The candidate was blindfolded, naked, and had his hands tied behind his back. He had to make three circuits around the Lodge room where he was pushed off the road, made to walk through brushwood, burned with a taper, and drenched with water. He then swore an oath of secrecy; the blindfold was removed to reveal a skeleton in front of him and a lecture on the inevitability of death was delivered. Finally the candidate was given a white lambskin apron to cover his nakedness. He was told that the apron symbolized the covering of Adam and Eve when they lost their innocence, as well as the sacrifice of the Lamb of God atoning for Adam and Eve's sins.

Other groups, such as the Royal Antediluvian Order of Buffaloes, wear aprons and other regalia similar to that worn by Masons. They still have a large membership in England and Australia, and there are several Lodges in Canada including four near Hamilton, Ontario. Although they claim to be Antediluvian, or existing from before Noah's flood, they were actually founded in 1822 by two music hall artists who were excluded from a Stage Guild. Their name comes from a music hall song, *"Chasing the Buffalo."*

The Ancient Order of Free Gardeners used a square, compasses, and a pruning knife as their symbol. They also wore aprons with the All Seeing Eye on it. The Ancient Order of Druids also wore lambskin aprons.The Grand Alfred Order of Old Friends used many Masonic Symbols including the All Seeing Eye, the square, and Jacob's Ladder. They, too, wore aprons. Their motto was: "We relieve a distressed brother." The Independent Order of Mechanics freely use the square and compasses today even though they are not connected to the Freemasons.

The French Revolution lasted 10 years from 1789-1799; 1793 and 1794 was a time known as the "reign of terror" in which as many as 40,000 men and women were executed. Most of them were aristocrats or from the upper class. The French Revolution terrified the British Aristocracy because they knew the same type of revolt could happen in Britain. In 1799 the British Parliament passed the Combination Acts which included The Unlawful Societies Act, an act "for the suppression of societies established for seditious and treasonable purposes"; once enacted, the act affected all societies whose members were required to take an oath. Before the act passed, in an unusual display of Masonic solidarity, the Grand Master of the Antients, the Grand Master of the Moderns, and the Grand Masters of the Grand Lodges of Scotland and Ireland met with the Prime Minister and had Masonic Lodges exempted from this legislation. The Combination Acts were repealed in 25 years later in 1824.

Tolpuddle, England is a small village in the county of Dorset near the English Channel. It was a rural, farming area with most of its inhabitants being farm laborers who worked the farms of wealthy large landowners. In 1834, the pay for the farm laborers was standard and controlled by the landowners. For a workweek of more than 70 hours, a laborer was paid 9 shillings, which is the equivalent of $22 in today's money. If his wife worked she usually could earn only an extra shilling. Younger sons could earn a shilling a week, while older sons could earn up to four shillings. The average farm family expenditure per week at this time for very basic rent, food, and necessities was slightly over 13 shillings. If a farm laborer died, injured himself or became sick his income stopped and his family became destitute. The friendly society was the insurance policy of the time.

George Loveless was what was called at the time a religious dissenter, meaning that he did not follow the Church of England. He was a Methodist lay preacher. He was also a farm laborer, and in 1832 he and a group of farm laborers met with the local landowners and the vicar of Tolpuddle asking for wage increases to 10 shillings a week. The landowners agreed, but later reneged on the deal, and lowered the wages to 6 shillings a week. The Church of England vicar, who was there to be a witness, denied that there had been any agreement.

George Loveless made a decision to start a friendly society, and at the first meeting 40 men showed up. The organization was called The Tolpuddle Friendly Society of Agricultural Laborers, and dues were set at one shilling to join and a penny a week. The fund was to be used to help members in distress.

On December 9, 1833, three candidates were initiated into the Tolpuddle Friendly Society. All were blindfolded and taken to an upstairs room of a cottage. There they took an oath: "I do before Almighty God and this loyal Lodge do solemnly swear that I will not work with any illegal man or men, but I will do my best for the support of wages, and most solemnly swear to keep inviolate all the secrets of this order. I will not write, or cause to be wrote, print, mark, either on stone, marble, brass, paper or sand, any thing connected with this order. So help me God and keep me steadfast in this my present obligation. I further promise to do my best to bring all legal men whom I am connected with into this order. If ever I reveal any of the rules, may the drawn sword before me plunge my soul into eternity, and may I be disgraced in every Lodge in the kingdom." After taking the oath the candidates kissed a bible that was in front of them and had their blindfolds removed. Two six foot drawings hung on the wall in front of them: one was a skeleton; the other a representation of death with the words "Remember thine end" above it.

Two of those new candidates were actually spies for a wealthy landowner, James Frampton. Frampton was also the Chief Magistrate of Dorset. After the initiation he had a flyer bearing the date February 22, 1834, printed and distributed. The flyer warned that any person taking part in an oath to enter into an illegal society would be guilty of a felony and subject to transportation to Australia for seven years. The alleged purpose of the flyer was to give everyone in the county due notice of what might happen if they did take part in an illegal oath. Two days later on February 24, 1834, George Loveless and five others were arrested for giving an illegal oath, and taken to Dorchester, the county seat, for trial. Loveless wasn't too concerned because he knew the illegal societies act had been repealed 10 years before.

However, when the men were charged, they were charged under the 1797 Mutiny Act which made it a felony to administer an oath. The law had been created to deal with mutiny in the military but was used in this case because it had such a severe penalty. The two spy candidates testified against the six men. The judge and the jury were clearly against the men from the start. George Lawless wrote, "The greater part of the evidence against us was put into the mouths of the witnesses by the judge." The six were all found guilty and sentenced to the maximum punishment of seven years transportation. At the sentencing the judge said he felt that the sentence shouldn't be just a punishment, but an example and a warning for others. Others did take the warning, and many groups changed their ritual. The Oddfellows in England removed the oaths from their ritual. The Oddfellows in the United States were angered with this because they weren't consulted. So they split with the English Grand Lodge and renamed themselves the Independent Order of Oddfellows, eventually becoming much larger than their British parent.

Transportation to Australia was a horrible thing. Although the British had outlawed slavery, the transportation ships were no better than the slave ships of the time. The prisoners were kept shackled in cramped quarters and let out onto the deck for less than two hours a day. The food was usually bad and in small quantity. Ship captains would hold food back so that they could sell it when they arrived in Australia, causing many starvation deaths on the voyages. This stopped after the British Government started paying the captains based on the number of prisoners that reached Australia alive.

Once the prisoners arrived in Australia they were forced to endure hard labor. George Loveless worked on a chain gang on the roads. The others worked on farms under horrible conditions. When a prisoner finished his sentence in Australia he would be set free but was unable to return to England unless he paid for his own voyage home. Few could ever do this because work was scarce and often done by newly arriving convicts. For those that did get work, the low pay kept them at subsistence level.

Four of the Tolpuddle men were married, with twelve children between them. The families were left destitute with no income at all. Magistrate James Frampton refused their application for Parish Relief, saying "You shall suffer want, you shall have no mercy, you should have known better." He said if they could afford to pay their friendly society's entry fee of one shilling and then a penny every week then they did not need parish relief. He told them, "Go to your club and see if they will assist you now."

The courtroom at Dorchester had a newly added feature that was until then not seen in British Courts. It was a press gallery, and it was filled with newspaper reporters during the trial. Within days the story had circulated around England and protests from other friendly societies and trade unions started. Uproar greeted the news of the verdict and sentence when it reached London. Before the six men had even left for Australia, a mass rally of 35,000 people was held in London. Petitions with over 800,000 signatures demanding the pardon of the men were presented to the government. At the rally a fund to sustain the wives and children of the men was started, and money poured in from friendly societies, trade unions, and individuals from all over the country. Ironically, the man chosen to distribute the money to the women had been rejected as a juror for the trial because he was a Methodist.

Several members of Parliament worked hard to get pardons for the men. King William IV was not too concerned about giving anyone pardons until the more radical members of Parliament put pressure on the King. King William's brother, the Duke of Cumberland, was the Grand Master of the Orange Order, a fraternal society for Protestants that started in Ireland and spread to the rest of Great Britain. Indictments were written against the Duke of Cumberland for being the head of an illegal order, but before the case could proceed to court, the King pardoned the laborers.

Although the men received pardons and free passage home, governmental incompetence was not finished with them. The Governor of Australia was notified about the pardons for the 6 men, but he said nothing. George Loveless didn't find out about his pardon until months later when he read about it in an old newspaper. Loveless contacted the other men and all except James Hammett returned home to England in 1837. Hammett was serving time in prison for assault and did not return until 1839, three years and 5 months after his pardon.

A nationwide collection was taken up for the men, now called the Tolpuddle Martyrs, and two large farms were leased for them, but they didn't stay out of trouble. They became marked men once again by becoming vocal supporters of the Chartist movement which pressed the British Government for a vote for every man 21 years of age, a secret ballot, removal of property qualifications for members of Parliament, and other rights now taken for granted.

Realizing they were again in danger, five of the men and their families emigrated to Canada, where they lived the rest of their lives quietly as farmers near London, Ontario.

James Hammett stayed in England working as a builder's laborer. Hammett was the only martyr not related to the other five men; he was also not a Methodist, but a member of the Church of England. It was not until 1875 that the final secret was discovered. Although he was a member of the Tolpuddle Friendly Society, James Hammett had not been at the meeting where the illegal oaths were given. The spies had mistaken him for his younger brother John Hammett. James Hammett took the fall for his brother because his brother's wife had been pregnant with their first child at the time of the arrest. Hammett is buried in Tolpuddle where a monument to the martyrs was erected and every July the British trade unions have a weekend festival to remember them.

History repeated itself in the coalfields of Pennsylvania in 1877. Ten men, members of the Ancient order of Hibernians, an Irish Catholic fraternal organization still in existence, were executed by hanging because it was claimed they were criminals known as the Mollie Maguires.

Many friendly societies evolved into labor unions or insurance companies, those that didn't either changed into solely fraternal organizations or disappeared completely once governments started providing services such as Social Security in the United States and the National Insurance Act in Great Britain. Freemasonry was the model for all these groups, showing people how to organize and manage groups before degrees in management or business administration existed. But most importantly Freemasonry showed people they could take care of each other.

The Cities of Rome and Jerusalem and the Foundations of Christian Theology: How the Craft's use of the Temple Legend Has Lead to 'Unspeakable' Things

Mark J. Robson

{Presented to The Allied Masonic Degrees March 31, 2010. Biography given: Bro. Mark J. Robson was raised in 2007 and become the Secretary of the WNY Lodge of Research in 2008. He has a B.A. in Religion and Philosophy from Roberts Wesleyan College, and an MBA from St. Bonaventure University. He is a 32° member of the Valley of Buffalo, Illustrious Master of Buffalo-Keystone Council #17 currently, an MSA recipient from Tonawanda Commandery #78, a member of the Iroquois Chapter, AMD, and belongs to the Thomas Smith Chapter of Research. He is a Financial Mediary practicing in Buffalo, NY, having spent the previous ten years as a Financial Planner.

Editor's Note: At the writing of this book, Wor. Robson has sat as Master of Hiram Lodge No.105, the oldest Lodge in Erie County.}

Introduction

I shall demonstrate what I think is the unconscious source of some Christians' opposition to Freemasonry by comparing historical surveys of Rome, Jerusalem, and Christianity: The Church has always been philosophically opposed to the rebuilding of King Solomon's Temple in Jerusalem. And furthermore, that the Church's position on this was a rooted in an earlier Roman position. Finally, that this opposition is so embedded in the foundation-story of the Church that they can never be comfortable with the Craft so long as the building of King Solomon's Temple is central to our ritual.

A History of Rome from Empire to Ecclesia

The history of Rome begins with a band of villages on the Seven Hills, near the Po River. Following the decline of Egypt and Mycenae and the Hittites around 1200 BCE, Rome became one of many communities to rise up in the ensuing vacuum. The Republic became the Empire, in tandem with the rise of Athens, Thebes, Sparta, Israel, and others. Socrates and Plato taught them how to govern. Euclid taught them Geometry, which they used to become Builders. Because they learned to build, like the Egyptians before them, the Romans became the Masters of the Known World. As they spread out, they incorporated the Teachings of the Ages taught in each conquered region into the Roman religion. Easily seen religious and cultural influences come from Egypt, Babylon, Celt/Druids, Hebrews, Greeks, Germania, Gaul, and the Moors. They were all permitted, even embraced, so long as the populace cooperated with the Roman rulers on civil matters. So much so that it is a contradiction in terms to refer to a Roman religion beyond this collection of foreign religions, and the worship of the Emperor. When the legions destroyed a city during conquest, they would always first rebuild the temple of the local religion, whatever it was. (Goodman 2008)

Consider conditions at the end of the Empire. The Jews have been banned from Jerusalem since 135 CE because they would not worship the Emperor and they constantly rejected Roman rule. Constantine adopts Christianity 200 years later, and moves the capital of the Empire to the East. The Bishop of Rome effectively becomes the representative of the Empire in the West. The end of the Empire comes with the northern tribal invasions in the 5th and 6th Centuries.

Now consider conditions during the Holy Roman Empire. Constantinople is surrendered to the Muslims in 1453. The Pope has had the final say in royal successions for a millennium. The Church has become the only place to get an education, power and prestige. Europe has a new Pax Romana. It can truly be said that the Popes have replaced the Emperors both politically and culturally. The Jews, however, still do not worship him.

Consider at last the Papal Bull In Eminenti issued in 1738 where Clement XII condemns secret societies for the first time. Whatever motives conspiracy theorists may find in the politics of the time, Clement says plainly that he condemns Secret Societies for fomenting Revolution and for hating the Catholic Church. How did we become enemies of the Church that had employed our operative brethren and predecessors for the 500 years prior? Was it contemporary politics only, or were ancient politics at play as well?

A History of the Hebrews in Jerusalem

With the decline of Syria, the Hittites, and Canaan after 1200 BCE, the nation of Israel also rises to fill the ensuing vacuum. The stories of Babel, Abraham, Lot, and the descendants of Seth, the son of Noah, are formed. The Egyptian 'captivity' ends as Moses leads them back to the Jordan River. Joshua takes Jericho. David and Solomon establish their Royal House, and the First Temple is built. From 1000-700 BCE Israel is ruled by Kings and Judges, ending with the Babylonian captivity. Around 565 BCE the First Temple is destroyed. Zerrubbabel rebuilds the Temple with the support of Cyrus the Persian. Dynasties of Ptolemys and Seleucids reign as Kings from 330 BCE.

The Maccabees/Hasmoneans drive out the Assyrians and 'purify the Temple' about 165 BCE, and ally with Rome about 150 BCE in a mutual protection treaty. About 65B CE Ptolemy destroys or ravages the Temple in a pacification, after which Herod the Great is installed by Rome in 36 BCE. He rebuilds what Pompey destroyed, resulting in the Second Temple remarked on in the Gospels as so beautiful. This conforms to the Roman tradition remarked on earlier. Herod Antipas, the 'Herod' of the Gospel, co-rules with Pontius Pilate through thru 36CE in a relatively amicable relationship with Rome. Roman society has by this time adopted a 'Sabbath' day in many cities, and was becoming somewhat Monotheistic with the Emperor as the God of Gods.

So-called messiahs abound in and around Jerusalem for 200 years before and after the Christian Advent. Yeshua ben Joseph was neither the first, nor the last. Titus, the son of Emperor Vespasian, puts down 'another messianic rebellion' in 66-72 CE, which tragically ends at Masada in a Jewish mass suicide. Vespasian then removes the Temple treasury and all it's gold (Menorahs, tables, ornamentation, altars, etc.). Such is the value of this taking that he later uses it to pay for the building of the great Coliseum back in Rome. This is celebrated on The Arch of Titus in Rome, and a recently deciphered dedication sign found in the foundation of the arena.

Hadrian finally puts down one last Messiah named Simon Bar Khosiba in

135 CE. At this point the Temple is completely and finally destroyed, and Jews are forbidden to enter Jerusalem ever again. Hadrian enforces this by building a Roman city, Aelia Capitolina, on the ruins of Jerusalem, and a temple to Jupiter on the former site of King Solomon's Temple. The Tenth Legion garrisons there to keep order and prevent Jewish resettlement. Rome eventually learns to distinguish between Roman-born Christians, Gentiles who are willing to submit to the Empire in all other ways but their worship, and their Jewish peers who want to return Jerusalem to rebuild their Temple in defiance of Roman rule. One wonders what happened to the stories of Jewish martyrs in the Coliseum; there were surely as many of them as there were Christian martyrs.

By the time Helena, mother of Constantine arrives in Jerusalem about 320 CE in search of artifacts and sacred sites, it has become a desolate backwater of the Empire, with no economic or cultural life. The Xth Legion soon leaves, their job done. Jerusalem remains this way for hundreds of years, until the advent of Islam. The Temple bedrock becomes holy to Muslims as a result of Mohammed's visionary ascension. They build the Dome of the Rock over the Temple site around 900 CE.

The Crusades are fought from about 1100 to 1300 CE at the urging of the Roman Church, but clearly not in order to restore the Temple. The Knights of the Temple of Jerusalem stabled their horses there. Jerusalem remains in Muslim control after the Crusades up to the rise of Zionism in the late 19th Century. Anyone who advocates returning Jerusalem to the Jews in order to rebuild the Temple is not taken seriously. From 1900 to 1940 huge numbers of Jews arrive in a Jerusalem under British rule. Having defeated Hitler's attempt to create a New Rome, the Allies in 1948 create a New Jerusalem, and an Israeli government. Masonry meanwhile is accused by some in the Catholic Church of being run by 'the Jews'. Catholics are strictly forbidden to join the Craft. What is it we do that so deserves this enmity?

Jesus founded a Jewish sect that is the Jews' nemesis.

The Theological history of the Hebrews runs from Creation to Noah to Abraham to Moses to David to the Prophets and the Temple to their ultimate transformation from a country and a place into a People Chosen by God. This is sometimes called the Haggadah and the Halakhah, meaning the Stories of God's active demonstration in history of His Love for His Chosen People.

Rabbinic writings started around 200 BCE to gradually introduce the idea that Jerusalem and the Temple were not any longer the physical manifestations of God's presence. This was a good thing, since they kept getting conquered and demolished. The Jesus Movement was originally one of several sects within Jewish society working out this idea. The Essenes at Qumran were another. These were often in contrast to the Pharisees, famous in the Gospels. This is the reason why the Church later became predominantly gentile, although they had some trouble explaining why Jesus' message was first delivered to the Jews. The fact that Rome prevented the Jews from rebuilding their Temple was taken as proof that God had abandoned Israel as a nation.

The Early Church Fathers said that Jesus came out of Hebrew history as God's messenger for all mankind, not just the Hebrew Nation. About 150 CE the Founder of the Roman Church, Justinian, took this one step further and wrote a book, "Against The Jews", detailing how the Church was now the legitimate heir to God's Favor. Jesus' gentile followers worked on many different paths to bring God's message to the Gentile world. Discoveries of previously unknown gospels and writings in the last 50 years have shown that the early church took its lead from the Roman approach to religion—borrow freely from here and there, as long as you worship the right Leader. In 325 CE, Constantine called all the Bishops together and forced them to define their Creeds and the Books in the Two Testaments at the Council of Nicaea. Gnostic gospels and other texts were buried at Nag Hammadi, Egypt, some 100 years later, apparently for safekeeping.

Jesus' divinity was debated back and forth for these 300 years because the Church didn't know how to say the Jews were no longer God's chosen People. Hebrew Scriptures were widely used as proofs of God's approval of what Jesus did and who He was; the Gentile Christians were caught in a logical trap. The First Proof of Jesus' Divinity and the validity of the Church that worships Him was the certainly the Resurrection. The destruction of the Temple of Jerusalem, proving God had left the physical Temple and now lived on in our spiritual Temples, became the Second Proof. So once it was plain that Rome would never allow the Temple to be rebuilt, the Church could claim to be the New Israel, the Chosen People of God.

So long as there is no Solomonic Temple in Jerusalem...

What does all this have to do with Masonry?

Speculative Masonry derives from operative traditions that were tied to the Church significantly. What did our operative ancestor brothers build? Castles and Cathedrals. The Church and the Nobility were their only employers. Harmony and peace prevailed back in the day. So what turns the Church against the Craft in 1738?

Anderson's Constitutions of 1725 and 1736 are a systematic response to confusion over the many legends, rituals, and allegories in use at the time. Many innovations must have occurred during the transition from Operative to Speculative Masonry. Ramsay's Oration first ties the Craft to the Templars in 1736. Sir Isaac Newton secretly obsessed with the dimensions of the Temple and a New Jerusalem before he died in 1727. The Temple Legend of the Craft prevails over other allegories like Noah, Isis, Hermes Trismegistus, among many others. English and Scottish Grand Lodges were asserting their authority and becoming 'regular' in their use of rituals around King Solomon's Temple.

Each Papal Bull can and should be debated on its unique merits and circumstances, but they all speak of a 'hatred of the Church' by the Craft and it's kindred societies. That just sounds strange to me. Masonic adherence to the principles of equality, tolerance and fraternity simply do not justify that accusation. Is it possible that our allegorical use of King Solomon's Temple is too easily misunderstood? If we honor the ancient Temple as our Great Work, can it also be seen as a repudiation of this 'unspoken proof' of the Church's preferred status in God's eyes? When a good Christian person asks a Mason to explain himself, he doesn't give a full and detailed answer, and he shouldn't. I think many good Christians do not wrestle with the mystery of how the People of Israel become the People of the Church. The premise that the Temple of Jerusalem has been made unnecessary is essential to Christian Theology. It is so deeply held that it is almost 'unspeakable'.

I propose that when we as Masons are asked to explain Masonry, and say, "It's about building King Solomon's Temple, but I can't tell you any more", we make the hearer uneasy without either of us knowing quite why. If we consider the story of these two cities and of Christian Theology, proven by the destruction of the Temple that must not be rebuilt, we might be able to give account of ourselves without raising the distraction of Religion unintentionally.

Source

Goodman, M.. *Rome and Jerusalem : the clash of ancient civilizations*. New York: Vintage Books, 2008

The Ancient Landmarks: Our Indefinite Boundaries

Wor. Nathan A. Shoff, Past Master, Harmonie Lodge No.699, F. & A. M. of the State of New York

{© 2007-2011 Nathan A. Shoff. This paper was originally presented before the brethren of Harmonie Lodge No.699 on November 28, 2007. Presented in its currently edited and updated form at the Western New York Lodge of Research on October 8, 2011.

Biography given: Wor. Nathan Shoff was raised in 2005 in Harmonie No.699, and ascended to the East there in 2010. He is a graduate of UB Law School and lives in Canandaigua, NY, where he has a private law practice and is a Senior Legal Editor for Thompson Publishing.}

I. Introduction & Importance of the Ancient Landmarks

Although they may be respected and admired throughout Masonry, one of the least understood concepts within the Craft is that of the "Ancient Landmarks." While all Freemasons are in agreement with regard to the importance of fidelity to these guiding principles, just what the Landmarks are, the prohibition of their alteration, and the universality of their adherence, have remained vague and elusive throughout the history of modern Freemasonry.

Various authorities of the Craft have consistently held—in ritual, in jurisprudence, and in commentary—that the Ancient Landmarks are of the utmost importance to Freemasonry. For example, the Charge to the newly raised Brother in the third degree ceremony states, in part,

> "The Ancient Landmarks of the Fraternity, entrusted to your care, you are carefully to preserve, and never suffer them to be infringed, or countenance a deviation from the established usages and customs of the Fraternity."[1]

In the early eighteenth century, English Grand Master George Payne, in compiling his General Regulations, determined that "[e]very annual Grand-Lodge has an inherent power and authority to make new Regulations, or to alter these, for the real benefit of this ancient Fraternity: Provided always that the old Landmarks be carefully preserved ..."[2]

The New York Grand Lodge Constitutions, rules, and regulations, stress the importance of these Landmarks to an even greater degree than is found in the previously cited English Constitutions. Section 101 of the Constitutions of the Grand Lodge of Free and Accepted Masons of the State of New York affirms that Grand Lodge

"is the supreme and sovereign Masonic authority, executive, legislative and judicial. Its powers are inherent and are subject only to such limitations as the Grand Lodge may impose upon itself or which are imposed by the Ancient Landmarks of Freemasonry or by the law of the land."[3]

Furthermore, Section 116 of the Constitutions states

"it shall be the duty of the Grand Wardens to assist in the affairs of the Grand Lodge and diligently to endeavor to preserve the Ancient Landmarks throughout the jurisdiction."[4]

Thus, even the supreme governmental authority of Freemasonry in New York recognizes that its actions must be subordinate to, and protective of, these Landmarks. Indeed, the rules of construction maintain that the very Constitutions themselves must be interpreted "upon the theory that their provisions were intended to be in accord with the Landmarks."[5]

The tenor of Masonic law in New York demonstrates the reverence which the Fraternity holds for these Landmarks, as shown by the most serious consequences faced by a Lodge which fails to adhere to them. A Lodge, "once chartered . . . is subject to all the obligations . . . such as are defined in its charter, by the Constitutions, and by the Ancient Landmarks"[6] and "may forfeit its charter by . . . [d]eparture from the original plan of Masonry and Ancient Landmarks."[7] Section 1180 of the Handbook of Masonic Law clearly states that "departure from the original plan of Masonry and the Ancient Landmarks on the part of a Lodge constitutes a Masonic offense."[8] The available penalties for such offense can be reprimand, fine, payment of trial costs, or, as previously stated, forfeiture of the Lodge Charter.[9]

Interestingly, although the Code of Procedure and Handbook of Masonic Law both list a number of Masonic Offenses which are capable of being committed by an individual brother, including "acts or conduct tending to impair the purity of the Masonic institution or its usefulness

. . ."[10], there is no explicit reference to adherence to the Ancient Landmarks in this context. Nevertheless, the previously quoted Charge clearly renders it incumbent on all Master Masons to strictly adhere to the Ancient Landmarks of Freemasonry and protect their perpetual purity with the utmost care.

Viewing the Ancient Landmarks through this lens of sanctity, one could expect a clear and unambiguous list of what things do, and do not, constitute the Ancient Landmarks. However, in the jurisdiction of the Grand Lodge of the State of New York, there is no official list of the Ancient Landmarks. There is a list printed as an Appendix to the New York Constitutions, but said list is prefaced with the statement: "The following list was prepared by M∴W∴ Joseph D. Evans, Past Grand Master, but has never been accepted by Grand Lodge."[11]

The 24-Inch Gauge Masonic Resource Guide goes even further, in pointing out that "[t]he Grand Lodge of New York has never formally accepted any of the versions of the Landmarks that are accepted by many other jurisdictions."[12]

Thus, although fidelity to the Landmarks has been of great importance to all Freemasons, it is not entirely clear exactly what is and what is not included as an Ancient Landmark.

II. Definition of "Ancient Landmarks"

Before embarking upon an historical analysis of the various lists of Ancient Landmarks, let us first approach a basic definition of the term "Ancient Landmark." Starting with the Holy Bible, we learn that

> "[i]n ancient times, it was customary to mark the boundaries of lands by the means of stone pillars or heaps of stones. The removal of such landmarks was a grievous crime and an evidence of fraudulent intent by the offender."[13]

It is written in Deuteronomy 19:14 that "thou shalt not remove thy neighbor's landmark, which they of old time have set in thine inheritance." And in chapter 27, verse 17 it is written "[c]ursed be he that removeth his neighbor's landmark". Further, Proverbs 22:28 states "removeth not the ancient landmark, which thy fathers have set."

These quotes are taken from biblical books written subsequent to the Hebrews' Exodus from Egypt and their conquering of Israel, and show that the principle importance of landmarks to the ancient Hebrews was to demarcate where one person's lands stopped and another's began.

Presumably, setting such boundaries was essential to encouraging increase in agricultural production and the development of commerce once the Israelites settled in the "Promised Land." Even today, many modern legal descriptions and surveys of real property in rural areas of America make use of certain large trees, stones, waterways or boulders as landmarks to illustrate where the property's metes and bounds are to begin and end. These landmarks are thus seen as ancient, and organic, divisions between people and places.

Additionally, landmarks can be utilized to point the way *toward* someone or something. One of the term's standard definitions is "a . . . structure used as a point of orientation in locating other structures"[14] or "an object or feature of a landscape or town . . . that enables someone to establish their location."[15] We use landmarks in such a context in our everyday lives quite frequently. For example, when giving a friend directions to a place you are familiar with but they have never been, how often do we tell them to "turn right at the old cemetery", or "don't go past the monument", etc.?[16]

In relation to speculative Freemasonry, the Ancient Landmarks have been defined by some sources as those universal customs of the Order which have gradually grown into permanent rules of action, and originally established by competent authority, at a period so remote that no account of their origin is to be found in the records of Masonic history, and which were considered essential to the preservation of integrity of the institution to preserve its purity and prevent innovation.[17]

The distinguished legal scholar and Freemason, N. Roscoe Pound, described the Landmarks as

> "certain universal, unalterable, and unrepealable fundamentals which existed from time immemorial and are so thoroughly a part of Masonry that no Masonic authority may derogate from them or do aught but maintain them."[18]

They may be further characterized as those ancient, immutable traditions which clearly define and separate the Craft from other forms of religious, political and civil society. The Ancient Landmarks are those things which set Freemasonry apart, and which, within Freemasonry, point toward our philosophic ideals.[19]

The noted scholar, Dr. Albert G. Mackey, set forth three essential characteristics of the Ancient Landmarks: "[1] immemorial antiquity; [2] universality; and [3] absolute irrevocability,"[20] which some scholars have reduced to a two-pronged test: "(1) a landmark must have existed from the 'time whereof the memory of man runneth not to the contrary'", and "(2) a landmark is an element in the form or essence of the Society of such importance that Freemasonry would no longer be freemasonry if it were removed."[21]

In my opinion, the necessary qualities of the Landmarks proposed by the scholar John S. Simons are the most succinct but comprehensive available. They are, first "[The Landmark] exists from time immemorial; second, it expresses the form and essence of the Craft; and third, it is agreed that it can never be changed."[22] As will be explained more thoroughly in subsequent sections of this paper, I believe that the most important of these elements is the second – that the Landmark is something which "expresses the form and essence of the Craft."

There are literally dozens of lists of Ancient Landmarks that have been compiled by Masonic Lodges, poets and scholars throughout the centuries. As an appendix to this paper {found at the end of this article}, I have attached an assortment of many of these lists with the quote (if sufficiently brief) or paraphrase of each of the Landmarks they describe. It is important to remember in reviewing the following analysis that, in New York State, there is no official list of Ancient Landmarks. Interestingly, The Grand Lodge of New York is not unique in this fact, as the Grand Lodges of twenty-five other states also do not seem to have an officially sanctioned list of Landmarks.[23]

III. Historical Review and Analysis of Various Lists of Ancient Landmarks

Whether comprised of three or fifty-four enumerations, I have found that the Landmarks listed by various sources can be generally classified into four basic categories: (1) Landmarks relating to candidate qualifications; (2) Landmarks relating to moral rules and the individual conduct of brethren; (3) Landmarks relating to Masonic secrets and ritual; and (4) Landmarks relating to the administrative rules and bureaucratic functioning of the Craft. While there may be substantial overlap with certain Landmarks, these categories have proven helpful for conceptualizing and analyzing the various lists.

Some of the earliest lists of rules and regulations governing Freemasonry, many of which later became incorporated as Landmarks of the Craft, are documents known as the "Old Charges" composed for the operative Masons of the Fourteenth through early Seventeenth Centuries.

It is important to note that, strictly speaking, the Old Charges are not enumerations of Landmarks, as they were merely the rules—or "charges"—of the inner organization of operative Masons many years prior to the development of a predominantly speculative Freemasonry.[24]

Additionally, the manuscripts of the Old Charges are conceived of as part of the written laws of Masonry, while the Landmarks are thought more akin to the unwritten, or common, law of Masonry.[25] Nevertheless, I believe that the principles written in the Old Charges meet many of the previously-described requisites of being considered Landmarks, insofar as they (1) are ancient in origin; (2) relate to and describe the essential beliefs and rules of the Craft; and (3) were / are considered unchangeable. Also, many of the duties listed in the Old Charges have close correlation to the items in the Nineteenth and Twentieth Century lists of Ancient Landmarks. Therefore, I have included some of the Old Charges in the Appendix to this paper, and will briefly describe them here.

Upon reviewing these ancient manuscripts, it appears that the Old Charges emphasize candidate qualifications and the rules of conduct for craftsmen, with very little, if any, treatment of ritual work or Craft bureaucracy. It is from these ancient Charges that we have the first exposition of the candidate qualifications—namely, that he be a man, free-born, of lawful age, of good parentage, that he be a law-abiding gentleman, and without maim or defect in his body.[26] These basic qualifications of candidates to Masonry have remained largely unchanged throughout the past six hundred years, with a few notable exceptions which shall be explained later.

The Regius Manuscript and Cooke Manuscript also list admonitions to the brethren to perform, or to avoid, certain specific conduct. These admonitions had largely to do with moral rules, the purpose of which could be no less than to ensure a harmonious and efficient workplace for the operative Mason (and more importantly, to ensure the same for the Master's employer). For example, a Master Mason must not supplant another in his work, he must not harbor a thief or dishonest man, nor may a Mason have sexual relations with his Master's wife, daughter or concubine.[27] All of such conduct, if done, may have instilled dissention amongst the Craftsmen, or even worse, distrust of the Master of the work. Such discord and contentiousness would have created the potential for slowing down the work and lowering its quality and efficiency.

Most interestingly, the Mason's duties to love God and the Church, and to swear allegiance to the Crown, are phrased in these early manuscripts as duties of a Mason, rather than as pre-requisite qualifications for an apprentice. Presumably, in Fourteenth and Fifteenth Century Britain, atheists and irreligious libertines were largely non-existent, and so it may have been unnecessary to prove one's religious fidelity prior to being made a Mason. Aside from the obvious moral import of these duties, such rules of conduct may have had an additional significance to the operative Mason. That is, the Catholic Church and regent were, at that time, the primary employers of the operative Free-stone Masons, since the Church and Crown were the only institutions with the financial ability and political authority to erect large stone buildings, cathedrals and castles. To ensure a continuing source of work, it must have been imperative for the operative Masons' guilds to give due respect and homage to the civil and religious authorities which were the source of their livelihood.

Although some of the moral duties and rules enumerated throughout the Old Charges do not have obvious parallels in the Ancient Landmarks (for example the mandate to always pay for one's food, or the prohibition from drinking after eight o'clock at night or playing cards or dice[28]), they do, generally, support the fundamental characteristic of Freemasonry as being a moral institution which "makes good men better."

The first time in the historical record that we find a term similar to "Ancient Landmarks" used to describe unalterable rules of the Fraternity, is in Anderson's Constitutions of 1723. Regulation XXXIX states, in part:

> Every Annual Grand Lodge has an inherent Power and Authority to make new Regulations, or to alter these, for the real Benefits of this ancient Fraternity: Provided always that the old Land Marks be carefully preserv[e]d, and that such Alterations and new Regulations be proposed and agreed to at the third Quarterly Communication preceding the Annual Grand Feast.[29]

As this was the only reference to the "old Land Marks" in the entirety of the document—without any definition or exposition thereof—this allusion has resulted in the ensuing centuries of confusion concerning the Landmarks' exact content.[30]

Nevertheless, as the Craft of Freemasonry moved from being primarily a Guild for the promotion of an operative science to a Fraternity dedicated to the speculative art, the Old Charges—listing requirements and duties at least analogous to the Ancient Landmarks—showed a significant shift in focus. Although such things as the qualifications of a candidate remained important, and largely unchanged, the Landmark lists of the Nineteenth century seem to have done away with many of the enumerated rules of conduct prescribed for the operative Mason, and instead placed greater emphasis upon the ritual content and bureaucratic workings of Freemasonry.

This transition in emphasis appears to have begun after the formation of the Grand Lodge of England in the early Eighteenth Century, as can be seen by a review of James Anderson's "Old Charges of Free and Accepted Masons," published along with the Grand Lodge Constitutions of 1723. While Anderson's "Old Charges" continued to include many rules of conduct for the brethren, gone is the duty to have allegiance to one particular religious sect or Church. Instead, the first charge states only that a Mason

> "is obliged, by his Tenure, to obey the moral Law . . . and 'tis now thought more expedient only to oblige them to that Religion in which all Men agree, leaving their particular Opinions to themselves . . ."[31]

Anderson's Old Charges also include such specifically administrative material as the qualifications for Wardens, Masters, Grand Wardens and Grand Masters, a rule against employing unskilled laborers, as well as an admonition that "all the Tools used in working shall be approved by the Grand Lodge."[32]

Additionally, we can find some of the first references to Masonic secrecy and ritual in the directives of Anderson's Old Charges. Under the heading "Of Behaviour", Anderson writes "[Masons] are to salute one another in a courteous manner, as you will be instructed, calling each other Brother, freely giving mutual Instructions as shall be thought expedient . . ." and further

> [Masons] shall be cautious in [their] Words and Carriage, the most penetrating Stranger shall not be able to discover or find out what is not proper to be intimated . . . [Masons] are . . . particularly not to let [their] Family, Friends, and Neighbours know the concerns of the Lodge.[33]

Finally, Anderson states that, when meeting a strange Brother, "[a Mason is] cautiously to examine him, in such a Method as Prudence shall direct . . ."[34] Thus, the modes of recognition and secrecy of the Fraternity—considered by many later writers as Ancient Landmarks of the Craft—were recognized as important components of Freemasonry from at least the early 18th Century. Indeed, there is evidence that operative Master Masons in Scotland and Northern England developed a secret

"Master's Word" as long ago as 1550 in order to strengthen the Masons' Guilds in those areas of Britain.[35]

Dr. Albert Mackey compiled one of the most famous and enduring lists of the Ancient Landmarks in 1858. Published in the *American Quarterly Review of Freemasonry*, and later in his book "Text Book of Masonic Jurisprudence", Mackey's list of 25 Ancient Landmarks was one of "the first attempt[s] to codify the Landmarks of Freemasonry" in written form.[36] Mackey's list of Landmarks include many of the "ancient" rules and customs of Freemasonry already described, such as the use of modes of recognition, secrecy of the Craft work, examination of visitors, the duty of the Mason to be subject to the civil law of his country, and the candidate's qualifications (being a man, free-born, un-mutilated and of mature age).[37] While three of Mackey's Landmarks seem to deal with candidate qualifications (numbers 18-20), and approximately two of the Landmarks are strictly moral exhortations to the brethren (numbers 17 and 22), the vast majority of Mackey's Landmarks deal exclusively with the form and character of Masonic ritual, and the administrative functioning of the Craft.

For example, Mackey's second Landmark limits Freemasonry to the three degrees of Entered Apprentice, Fellow-Craft and Master Mason, and his third Landmark is the perpetuation of the Hiramic Legend of the third degree ceremony.[38] Furthermore, at least five of his Landmarks concern the governing of Freemasonry by a Grand Master, and the Grand Master's various rights, or "prerogatives." [39] Finally, Dr. Mackey concludes his list with Landmark 25, which states that "the last and crowning Landmark of all is that these Landmarks can never be changed."[40]

Dr. Mackey's list – perhaps due to it being one of the first attempts at codification of the Landmarks – has enjoyed vast acceptance by many Masonic Lodges in North America since its writing. Many Grand Lodges in the United States utilize Mackey's list, if not as their officially sanctioned list of Ancient Landmarks, at least as a reference for their brethren.[41]

However, I assert that many of these "Landmarks" included by Dr. Mackey should not qualify as such according to the definition we adopted earlier (the Landmarks as fundamental principles which demarcate the bounds of Freemasonry as a unique society), nor by Mackey's own definition. That is, many of these "Landmarks" did not exist from time immemorial, and may not be considered universally accepted, or necessarily irrevocable.

For example, although the Old Charges do mention the selection of a temporary Grand Master to preside over the Craft's annual or triennial

Assembly,[42] some scholars have pointed out that a standing Grand Master of Freemasons did not exist prior to the institution of the Grand Lodge of England in 1717, and thus any of the standing Grand Master's prerogatives listed in Mackey's Landmarks 5 through 8 are strictly creatures of the Grand Lodge.[43] Said Landmarks thus have not existed from time immemorial, and could be easily changed by an alteration in the Grand Lodge's Constitution.

Furthermore, having a single executive officer, elected by the members of the Grand Lodge, can hardly be thought to be a feature unique to Freemasonry today. Nations, states, counties, towns, other civic societies, and even corporations all elect their executive officer for a set period of time, from amongst the members of the respective group or jurisdiction, and empower that officer with certain general authorities during their tenure.

Similarly, the right of every Mason to send instructed representatives to Grand Lodge meetings (Mackey's Landmark 12), and the right of every Mason to appeal their subordinate Lodge's decision to Grand Lodge (Mackey's Landmark 13)[44] are not, despite their possible antiquity, exclusive characteristics of Freemasonry. Even in Dr. Mackey's time, such things as a republican form of government and appellate review of a subordinate tribunal's decision were existent in English and American society as a whole, as well as in the Fraternity.

The "Landmark" that a Lodge must be governed by one Master and two Wardens is similarly lacking in historical pedigree insofar as the earliest sources recount that there must be one Master of the work and one Warden which he may appoint.[45]

Even some of the ritual principles listed by Mackey do not issue from "time immemorial." While Mackey's second Landmark restricts Freemasonry to three degrees, there is scant evidence for the existence of any more than two degrees in the Craft until the 1730s.[46] The third Landmark, concerning the Legend of the Third Degree, while integral to the Craft ritual today, did not appear in early Freemasonry until after the establishment of the Grand Lodge in the early 1700s.[47] Again, such Landmarks could not be sustained as "ancient" under Mackey's definition.

Finally, Mackey's 25th Landmark, which states that it is an Ancient Landmark that the Landmarks cannot be changed, is perhaps the least justifiable. This, of all the proposed Landmarks, is most offensive to the art of logic insofar as it is a tautology: one cannot alter the Landmarks, because it is a Landmark that the Landmarks cannot be altered; or, put another way, it is a Landmark that the Landmarks are unalterable, so a distinguishing feature of the Landmarks is that they cannot be changed. Of course, as described above, there are a host of Constitutional and legal regulations which militate against one's modification of the Ancient Landmarks, such that a Masonic scholar of Mackey's caliber need not resort to such dearth of reasoning. This Landmark again seems to have no basis in antiquity, is actually antithetical to some of the principles of the speculative Craft (logic, as one of the seven liberal arts), and is not itself immune from change.[48]

For its many faults, we Masons owe a debt of gratitude to Dr. Mackey for his efforts to create a comprehensive list of Ancient Landmarks, as his List of 25 generated a renewed interest in the Landmarks during the Nineteenth and Twentieth centuries, and produced a host of other proposed lists. Some of these lists delved into even further jurisprudential and administrative minutia, such as H. B. Grant's list of 54 Landmarks officially accepted for some time by the Grand Lodge of Kentucky, or the 31 enumerations of the former (Nineteenth Century) New York Grand Lodge Constitutions.[49] On the other hand, the Twentieth Century lists of Landmarks tend to be much more concise, such as that of the Grand Lodge of Massachusetts (1918), or more notably, Roscoe Pound's list of seven Ancient Landmarks (1925).

Pound, a noted legal scholar as well as Master Mason, posited that the following should consist of the Ancient Landmarks:

1. The Belief in The Great Architect Of The Universe.
2. The Belief in the persistence of personality (immortality of the soul).
3. The Volume of Sacred Law as an indispensable part of the Lodge furniture.
4. The Hiramic Legend of the third degree.
5. The obligation of secrecy and modes of recognition.
6. The symbolism of the operative art as used for the purposes of moral and religious teachings.
7. That a candidate must be a man, freeborn, and of mature age.

I consider Pound's list to be one of the better lists, insofar as it largely contains only those fundamental principles of Freemasonry which distinguish it as a social institution; many of which (numbers 1, 2, 5, and 7) can properly be said to have their origin from "time immemorial."

Proposed List of Ancient Landmarks for Freemasonry

in the Twenty-First Century

Notwithstanding the traditional three elements of which the Landmarks must consist, I contend that the Ancient Landmarks have been, and should continue to be, fluid concepts which may be altered to a certain extent in recognition of the changes in the non-Masonic world, so long as they continue to clearly mark the distinction between Freemasonry and other forms of society, as well as point toward Freemasonry's ultimate aims and ideals.

To which end, I humbly propose the following as a Twenty-First Century list of the Ancient Landmarks, with a brief explanation of the reasoning for each:

1. That all Masons must believe in a Supreme Deity. Freemasonry's ultimate goal is the construction and perfection of the individual Mason's spiritual Temple, and, as such, the Fraternity's members must recognize the existence of a Deity which created our world, spiritual and physical (The Great Architect Of The Universe). This Landmark properly distinguishes the Fraternity in two important ways. First, Western civil society is largely secular and makes little acknowledgement of Deity except in certain holiday or ceremonial contexts. Second, and as importantly, most religious groups or quasi-religious philosophical organizations mandate that a particular sect, denomination, or creed be adhered to by their members to the exclusion of all other faiths or practices. Thus, Freemasonry is unique in requiring that brethren have a belief in a Supreme Deity, but affording each member the freedom to practice his faith in whatever manner he sees fit.

2. That all Masons must believe in the persistence of the personality after death, as illustrated by the Hiramic Legend of the Third Degree. Many religions throughout the world hold a belief in the continuity of one's spiritual life after physical death. What makes this Landmark unique to Freemasonry, however, is that this belief is again couched in the universal language of symbolism, such that it can be accepted by reasonable men of all faiths. This belief is illustrated by the Hiramic Legend of the Third Degree. The life, betrayal, death and raising of Hiram Abif is a re-telling of the ancient mythos of the dead god returning to triumphant life. Osiris, slain by his brother Seth and resurrected by Isis, and Jesus Christ betrayed by Judas, crucified and resurrected, are but two of the most well known examples of this

sacred mystery. Freemasonry is one of the last organizations in modern civil and religious society to perpetuate this ancient teaching through the regular enactment of this dramatic mystery.

3. That membership in Freemasonry is limited to adult men who are found to be moral and capable of understanding its teachings. Outside of the Roman Catholic clergy, there are few, if any, spheres of modern life that are exclusive to men by rule or regulation. Today, women are involved in virtually all aspects of civil, political, economic, professional, leisure, and religious society. That Freemasonry is limited to men is an accident of history, insofar as this regulation has its origin in the operative Freestone Mason guilds of medieval Europe. While I cannot vouch for the motivations of our Eighteenth and Nineteenth Century forebears, I think that the perpetuation of this rule as a Landmark in the Twenty-First Century is not out of any disrespect for women. To the contrary, I consider it to be merely the recognition that the natural tendencies of the sexes when in a communal atmosphere—especially in the highly sexualized atmosphere of modern Western culture—are to be distracted by each other's guiles and flirtations. However, as stated above, the fundamental aim of Freemasonry is to promote the moral growth of its members and erection of each Mason's Spiritual Temple. When in the process of building the Spiritual Man, one should not pose undue temptation to the Natural Man.

You may note that I did not include the phrase "free-born" in this proposed Landmark. That is because, today, the serfdom and slavery which were the foundation for the ancient requirement that an apprentice be "free-born" have largely been eradicated. The Enlightenment ideals promoted by many of our Masonic brethren in the past centuries have thankfully relegated these evils to the dustbin of history, and require that we now regard every man for his own worth, regardless of the accident of his circumstances of birth. Some Old Charges and Ancient Landmarks state that "no bondsman" may be made an apprentice. While the speculative as well as the operative Craft may have legitimate, practical reasons for wishing to avoid allowing debtors to join the Fraternity, even a liberal application of this rule would have substantially negative effects on the acceptance of new brethren. After all, there are very few men who have no mortgage, car loan, student loan, or other form of debt for which he is responsible.

Finally, one will note that I proposed a variation in the qualification that a candidate be not "maimed or deformed" to that he be "capable of understanding its teachings". The requirements of physical perfection noted in the Old Charges, and maintained in many of the lists of Ancient Landmarks, are mostly vestiges of the needs of the operative Stone Masons. While said physical qualifications were important to ensure that apprentices were capable of performing the operative labor of the Craft, I believe that, today, the basic qualification that the candidate be intellectually capable of understanding the teaching of Freemasonry is as important to the speculative science in which we have been predominantly engaged since the Eighteenth Century. It is true that certain physical requirements are practically necessary to perform the modes of recognition. But, as described more fully later, for almost a century some Masonic bodies have permitted modification of these requirements so as to allow good men, although maimed, to enter our Lodges.

4. That all Masons, in meeting on the Level, are equal to one another as Brothers. Despite the many social changes in England and the United States within the past one hundred years, it is axiomatic that many people continue to be discriminated against for no sensible reason. However, in my experience, I have found that Freemasons treat each other with reciprocal respect, kindness and brotherly love, regardless of each other's socio-economic status, race, national origin, or religious denomination. Such true equality between men is both an ideal, and a unique characteristic, of Freemasonry.

5. That Freemasonry teaches the speculative sciences of Morality, Natural Philosophy, and Mystic Spirituality through symbolic and allegorical use of the history, legends, and tools of the operative art of free-stone masons.

Although extremely rare in religious and civil society today, Freemasonry is not alone in history as being an initiatic school of sacred mysteries. The ancient Greeks and Romans taught spiritual and philosophic truths to their initiates in the Pythagorean School, the Orphic Rites, the Dionysian Mysteries, the Delphic Mysteries, and the Cult of Mithras. The Egyptians and Greeks initiated many into the Mysteries of Isis. The ancient Hebrews sought spiritual enlightenment through the Qabbala, the Merkabah, and the teachings of the Essenes. And Western civilization is crowned by the sacred mysteries of early Christians, the Gnostics, and the Corpus Hermitcum. However, only the Craft of Freemasonry utilizes Geometry,

Architecture, Biblical texts, and the Working Tools of the operative Masons in an allegorical and symbolic fashion to communicate and impart these important moral, philosophical and religious truths.

In the preceding proposed list of Landmarks, I suggest certain alterations or changes to what have hitherto been inviolable principles of the Craft, namely the candidate qualifications. This raises the questions: are not the Landmarks by definition unchangeable and are they not universally accepted in their present form?

The Unchangeable Nature and Universal Acceptance of the Ancient Landmarks

Two problems presented in the preceding sections are that: (1) there are many different lists of Ancient Landmarks, all of which proclaim their own accuracy and exclusivity; and (2) few Grand Lodges in North America have given any particular list of the Ancient Landmarks their imprimatur by officially adopting one list over another.

First, when reviewing the development of the Ancient Landmarks in Masonry – especially during the transition from operative Masonry to speculative Masonry – it becomes relatively clear that many of the Ancient Landmarks can be, and have been, altered. For example, the Old Charges in the Regius Manuscript and Cooke Manuscript require that a Mason "love [be loyal to] the Church."[50] Of course, when written in the late Fourteenth and early Fifteenth centuries, this rule could have no other meaning in England than that the apprentice must be loyal to the Roman Catholic Church.[51] However, in Anderson's "Old Charges" of 1723–after nearly two centuries of bloody civil war and division over the issue of religious denominations in England–we find a clear alteration of this Landmark. Not only is the duty of loyalty to the Catholic Church removed by Anderson, but such adherence to sectarianism is clearly repudiated by his first Charge:

> "to obey the moral Law . . . and . . . only to oblige them to that Religion in which all Men agree, leaving their particular Opinions to themselves . . ."[52]

This is undeniably a significant change in the previously accepted Mason's duty of fidelity to the Church, and now represents the "modern" conception of the role of religious fidelity in Freemasonry. Perhaps the change of that Landmark was necessary or only expedient, but if nothing else, it was a *change*.

Somewhat less apparent of a change in the Landmarks has to do with the issue of loyalty to the civil authorities and countenance of treason. Again, the Regius and Cooke Manuscripts, the Old Constitutions, and Anderson's Old Charges, all demand that a Mason be loyal to the King of England and his subordinate civil magistrates, prohibiting treason or the aid of another in treason or rebellion against the Crown.[53] Despite these ancient rules clearly forbidding it, many Freemasons in the American Colonies were instrumental in the planning, preparation and execution of the rebellion against King George III. The most celebrated hero of the Revolutionary War, General George Washington, was a noted Freemason throughout his service to the United States. While many modern lists of the Ancient Landmarks continue to insist that Freemasons remain loyal and subject to the laws of the country they inhabit, one cannot discount the fact that the original prohibition of rebellion against the British Regent—as the supreme civil authority in the American Colonies—was conveniently ignored by some Masonic colonists in America.

Another most interesting revision of the Ancient Landmarks has occurred in more recent history in the Masonic jurisdiction of New York. For many years, part of the requisite candidate qualifications included the need for physical perfection; that is, being "hale and sound, not deformed or dismembered."[54] As described previously, the existence of this Landmark had almost certainly to do with the need for operative Masons to adequately perform their physical labors, and, later, to ensure that a brother could perform the modes of recognition properly. However, in response to the number of injured and disabled veterans returning from World War I who wished to become Freemasons, in 1922 the Grand Lodge of New York "amended the Book of Constitutions by authorizing a waiver in individual cases of physical disqualifications resulting from service in the World War."[55]

Furthermore, probably in response to a similar situation stemming from the aftermath of World War II, in 1945, Grand Lodge

> "adopted a still further amendment authorizing the Grand Master 'by dispensation in individual cases to waive disability to conform to the ritual' declaring that it 'recognized physical qualifications as a regulation rather than a Landmark'"[56]

Undoubtedly, the physical qualifications of a candidate for Masonry existed since the very beginning of the Fraternity, giving them the requisite antiquity to be considered a Landmark. However, the Grand Lodge of New York in the first half of the Twentieth century, by merely amending the Constitutions, accomplished the same thing that Anderson achieved by drafting his "Old Charges" in the Eighteenth Century – they altered an "unalterable, immutable" Ancient Landmark to conform to the needs of modern society and the preservation of the higher aims and principles of the Craft.

The second issue to be addressed is the "universality" of these Ancient Landmarks. While all Masonic bodies admit the existence of the Ancient Landmarks, there seems to be little agreement regarding of what specific principles and rules the Landmarks should be composed. Despite this confusion and variety of opinion, Grand Lodges do not frequently refuse to recognize other Grand Lodges because that particular jurisdiction fails to agree that one of Mackey's administrative "Landmarks," such as the Grand Master's prerogative to make Masons at sight, is an immutable Landmark. However, there is at least one very significant example of a major rift in the Masonic family due, in part, to the significant alteration of a Landmark.

In the latter part of the Nineteenth century, the Grand Orient of France, in the development of what it considered liberty of conscience, discontinued its acknowledgement of the existence of a Supreme Being; and, as a consequence, in 1878, relations were ruptured between the Grand Orient of France and the Grand Lodge [of England], which remained true to its original principle and reaffirmed that a belief in TGAOTU is the first and most important of the Ancient Landmarks.[57]

The Grand Orient of France continues to overlook the Landmark requiring members to maintain a belief in The Great Architect Of The Universe to this day, because the Grand Orient claims that it is a

> "'liberal' and 'non-dogmatic' Freemasonry; bringing together believers and nonbelievers alike and guaranteeing its members absolute freedom of conscience and research. ... The Lodges within the Grand Orient de France . . . follow a humanistic approach."[58]

Although Grand Lodges in the United States refused to recognize the authority or legitimacy of the Grand Orient of France prior to this development,[59] it is probable that such a remarkable change to this important Landmark only solidified American Grand Lodges' resolve to oppose the recognition of the Grand Orient of France.[60]

The Ancient Landmarks thus cannot be considered "universal" per se, so long as there are a substantial number of Masonic Lodges in France and elsewhere – once in amity with Anglo-American Grand Lodges – that now ignore the "first and most important" Ancient Landmark. The standard answer to such an argument is that those Lodges which issue from the Grande Orient de France are "irregular", and thus are not recognized as legitimate Masonic bodies by the Anglo-American Grand Lodges that do hold true to the "universal" Ancient Landmarks.

Nevertheless, there is little, if any, consistent agreement between the British, Canadian, and American Grand Lodges relative to what is and what is not an "Ancient Landmark". As alluded to previously, virtually every Grand Lodge jurisdiction maintains a slightly different list of Ancient Landmarks – many of which are "unofficial."[61] As adherence to the Ancient Landmarks are often prerequisite to recognition of one Grand Lodge by another, it is instructive to review some of the Landmarks specifically listed by a sample of Grand Lodges and Masonic conferences in their standards for recognition. While there are many additional requirements that can be determinative of whether a particular Grand Lodge recognizes another (i.e. if the other Grand Lodge has exclusive jurisdiction, or whether it was established by three or more regularly constituted Lodges, etc.)[62], I have limited the present analysis to those matters already described as possible "Landmarks."[63]

The Commission on Information for Recognition of the Conference of Grand Masters of Masons in North America, held in the 1950s, determined that all recognized Grand Lodges must

> "subscribe fundamentally . . . to the Ancient Landmarks, Customs and Usages of the Craft. This requires adherence to the following: (1) Monotheism – An unalterable and continuing belief in God; (2) The Volume of Sacred Law – an essential part of the furniture of the Lodge; (3) Prohibition of the discussion of Religion and Politics."[64]

The Grand Lodge of California states that other Grand Lodges are recognized as "regular," if they "confine their authority . . . to the three degrees of Craft or Symbolic Masonry" and "[r]ecognize and support the Ancient Landmarks which include, particularly, the Three Great Lights and belief in a Supreme Being and the immortality of the soul."[65]

The Grand Lodge of Virginia, although not mentioning a required belief in immortality, does maintain that

> The Grand Lodge may extend . . . recognition [to a foreign Grand Lodge] if it appears to its satisfaction . . . [that i]ts ritual is fundamentally in accord with the Ancient Landmarks, customs, and usages of the Craft. This involves: (a) monotheism; (b) The Volume

of Sacred Law, a part of the furniture of the Lodge; (c) Secrecy; (d) The symbolism of the operative art; (e) The division of Symbolic Masonry into the three degrees of Entered Apprentice, Fellowcraft, and Master Mason; (f) The legend of the Third Degree. It makes Masons of men only [and] it is non-sectarian and non-political . . .[66]

One of the most interesting list of requirements for Grand Lodge recognition is found in the Masonic Code of Wyoming, wherein, in addition to only admitting men and being non-sectarian and non-political, a foreign Grand Lodge must also "adhere in principle to the Ancient Landmarks, traditions, customs and usages of the Craft as set forth and adopted by the Grand Lodge of England in 1723."[67] Presumably this refers to Anderson's Constitutions and Old Charges of 1723, which, as was already noted, failed to specify exactly of what the Ancient Landmarks consist. Perhaps in recognition of this difficulty, the Grand Lodge of Wyoming states that the Ancient Landmarks involve a belief in one God, a belief in immortality, the display of the Three Great Lights while a Lodge is at work (especially the Volume of Sacred Law), that Masonry is limited to three degrees, and a "belief in secrecy."[68]

Lodges outside of North America have had very similar "Landmark" statements contained in their recognition requirements. The United Grand Lodge of England, in 1929, determined that, among the "Basic Principles" which are required of a Lodge to receive the United Grand Lodge's recognition are: (1) belief in the Great Architect of the Universe; (2) that all initiates take their obligation on the Volume of Sacred Law; (3) that the membership is limited to men; (4) that the Three Great Lights are always to be displayed during working; (5) that religious and political discussion is prohibited in Lodge; and (6) "That the principles of the Antient [sic] Landmarks, customs and usages of the Craft shall be strictly observed."[69] These "Basic Principles" were changed somewhat in Great Britain in 1938, when the Grand Lodges of England, Ireland and Scotland issued a joint statement relative to certain "fundamental principles" which are required of other Grand Lodges who seek "fraternal accord" with the Grand Lodges of England, Ireland and Scotland. These "fundamental principles" still include the belief in the Great Architect of the Universe, reverence for the Volume of Sacred Law, and prohibition of sectarian religious or political discussion, but the limitation of membership to men is noticeably absent. Instead, the 1938 Statement (officially adopted by the United Grand Lodge of England in 1949) emphasizes the requirement that all Freemasons be obedient to the civil authorities of the land in which they inhabit.[70] The Grande Loge Francaise mirrors many of the

"Landmark" requirements expressed by their English and American brethren, but, similarly to the Grand Lodge of Wyoming, has the mandate that, to be recognized, "a Grand Lodge must [c]onform itself to the Old Charges from Anderson's Constitutions."[71]

Therefore, based upon the foregoing analysis, it appears that the concept of Ancient Landmarks is universal, but the specific items composing the Ancient Landmarks are not. Discounting the aberration – though significant in number – of Masons under the Grande Orient de France and that Lodge's subordinates, we may say that these two Landmarks are "universal" amongst Anglo-American Grand Lodges, insofar as the adherence to each is required for most other Grand Lodge recognitions: (1) A belief, usually phrased as monotheistic, in The Great Architect Of The Universe; (2) The necessity to display the Volume of Sacred Law in Lodge while at work as the most important of the Three Great Lights of Freemasonry.

Therefore, it seems that if the Landmark relates to one of these most fundamental beliefs or basic ritual customs of the Fraternity, other Masonic bodies would more readily show their approbation for the failure to adhere to said Landmark. Thus, Anglo-American Grand Lodges refuse to recognize the Grand Orient of France due to the latter's violation of the Landmark pertaining to a belief in the Great Architect of the Universe.[72] It is possible that a similar rift might develop if one Grand Lodge were to do away with the need to display the Volume of Sacred Law on the Altar during the candidate's obligation. But, if a Grand Lodge were to allow a Master to be elected who did not serve as Warden first, I doubt any other Grand Lodge would publicly disdain such a minor alteration to a purely administrative "Landmark".

Conclusion

The subject of the Ancient Landmarks has been unsettled since their first veiled mention in Anderson's Constitutions of 1723. In sum, the Ancient Landmarks should be considered not only widely accepted ancient rules, but those rules and customs so fundamental to the character and nature of Freemasonry that they clearly demarcate the boundaries between the Craft and the profane world, and such as mark the path toward the prevailing aims of our Fraternity—Light in Masonry. So long as the average Mason recognizes that there is no one "official" list of Ancient Landmarks, he may be comfortable in, and encouraged to, reflect on what he perceives to be the core principles of Freemasonry, so that he may establish for himself those Ancient Landmarks which he is "carefully to preserve, and never suffer . . . to be infringed, or countenance a deviation from the established usages and customs of the Fraternity."

Appendix: Compilation of Selected Lists of the Ancient Landmarks [73]

I. "A POEM OF MORAL DUTIES" (REGIUS MANUSCRIPT) (c. 1390 AD)

The Fifteen Articles:

1. The Master Mason must be steadfast, trusty and true; and be perfectly just in his treatment of his workmen, and in his conduct to his employer.
2. The Master Mason must be punctual to the general congregation [meeting] unless he is taken ill or has some other reasonable excuse.
3. The Master Mason must not take an apprentice for less than seven years.
4. The Master Mason must only take free-born gentlemen as apprentices.
5. The Master Mason must not accept a maimed or deformed man as apprentice.
6. The Master Mason must not accept craftsmen's wages for his apprentice's labor.
7. The Master Mason must not harbor a thief, murderer or immoral man.
8. The Master Mason must not suffer an incompetent workman to be employed.
9. The Master Mason must be wise and undertake no work that he cannot complete.
10. A Master Mason must not take away a job from another Master Mason.
11. Masons must not do work during the night, unless it be academic / intellectual labor.
12. Masons must not speak badly of their fellows' work.
13. The Master Mason must fully instruct his apprentice in all matters of the Craft.

14. A Master Mason must not take an apprentice unless he knows he will be able to fully instruct him during the seven-year term.
15. A Master Mason must not lie, bear false witness, or aid any of his fellows in sinning.

The Fifteen Points:

16. The Craftsman must love God, the (Catholic) Church, his Master, and his fellows.
17. The Craftsman must put in an honest day's work on the workday.
18. The Craftsman must keep his Master and fellows' secrets, wherever imparted.
19. The Craftsman must not make false statements about the Craft, or lie to his Master or fellows.
20. The Craftsman must accept the pay given by the Master Mason, but the Master must inform the Craftsman before noon if his services are no longer needed.
21. There must be no envy or dissention amongst the Craft that would impede the workday.
22. A Mason must not commit adultery with his Master's wife, his fellows' wife, or fellows' concubine.
23. The Craftsman should always strive to be a mediating force between his Master and his fellows, and always be true to both his Master and his fellows.
24. Craftsmen must serve one another equally, as brothers, pay all non-Masons fairly, and provide an accounting to any fellow who demands the same.
25. A Mason must live a good and honest life, but any Mason that is wicked must be tried at assembly, and, if found guilty, duly punished.
26. A Craftsman must not allow a fellow to spoil a stone by his poor work, but should teach him the proper methods with "fair words".
27. The non-Masonic civil authorities are empowered to enforce Masonic ordinances and rules on the Craftsmen.
28. The Craftsman must swear never to be a thief, or provide aid to any thief.
29. The Craftsman must swear an oath of allegiance to his Master, his fellows, to Masonic law, to the King, and to the Fourteen Points (landmarks).
30. If any Craftsman is found guilty of trespass against Masonic ordinances before an open assembly, he must swear to never again

practice the Craft, under pain of imprisonment and forfeiture.

II. MATTHEW COOKE MANUSCRIPT (c. 1450 AD)

The Nine Articles:

1. A Master Mason must be wise and truthful to his employer, and honest in paying the craftsmen according to the work performed.
2. A Master must always attend the annual congregation unless he be gravely ill, in which case due notice of his illness must be given to the Master serving as President of the congregation.
3. A Master Mason must not take an apprentice for a period less than seven years.
4. A Master Mason must only take a free-born man as apprentice.
5. A Master Mason must not pay his apprentice more than the apprentice truly deserved.
6. A Master Mason must not accept a maimed or deformed man (or any man that is incapable of doing a mason's proper work) as an apprentice.
7. A Master Mason must not employ or maintain a thief as apprentice.
8. A Master Mason must always employ the most skilled workmen (and discharge the incompetent workman).
9. A Master Mason must never supplant another Master in his work.

The Nine Points:

10. A Mason must love God and the (Catholic) Church, the Saints, his Master and his fellows.
11. A Mason must give a fair day's work for his pay.
12. A Mason must keep his fellow's secrets communicated in Lodge, chamber or other Masonic meeting.
13. A Mason must maintain the honor of the mason's art, and do no harm to it.
14. A Mason should not gripe about his pay, and must fulfill his work duties to his Master.
15. A Mason must unquestioningly obey the Master's determination of his disagreement with his fellows while at work.
16. A Mason must not covet the wife or daughters of his Master, or his fellow workmen, and must not take concubines.
17. If picked to be a Warden by his Master, a Mason must be a true

mediator between the Master and his fellows, and honorably discharge his duties.

18. A Mason must prevent an unskilled fellow workman from spoiling a stone, and must lovingly instruct him in the craft.

III. EUCLID'S ADMONITIONS [74]

1. Masons must be true to their King.
2. Masons must be true to their respective Master.
3. Masons must be true to each other and love one another.
4. Masons must not speak ill of one another.
5. Masons must perform a fair day's work for their pay.
6. Masons must ordain the wisest among them to be their Master.
7. Masons should be paid reasonable enough wages that they may live honestly.
8. Masons must assemble once a year to discuss and learn the Craft, and correct any offending Brethren.

IV. "SAYING THUS BY WAY OF EXHORTATION" (CHARGES) [75]

1. A Mason must honor God and His Church.
2. A Mason must be loyal to the Sovereign, never commit Treason or a Felony, and never countenance another in Treason.
3. A Mason must be loyal to fellow-Masons, and treat them as he would want to be treated.
4. A Mason must keep the science of Masonry (Geometry) secret.
5. A Mason must faithfully do his work to the profit of the employer.
6. A Mason must avoid foul language, and call his fellow workmen Fellows and Brethren.
7. A Mason must not commit adultery with his neighbor's wife, daughter, maid or servant.
8. A Mason must not commit adultery with any woman of the house wherein he is a guest.
9. A Mason must always pay for his meat and drink in the house wherein he is a guest.
10. A Mason must not take on a job which he knows himself unable to expertly finish.
11. A Mason must only charge a reasonable fee for his work.

12. A Mason must take on a job that pays well enough that he may live honestly, and fairly pay his Fellows.
13. A Mason must never supplant a Fellow in his work.
14. A Mason must not take an Apprentice for less than seven years, and said Apprentice must be born of good parents.
15. A Mason cannot make another person a Mason without the consent of at least five or six of his Fellows, and not unless that person is freeborn, of honest parentage, and of sound and able body.
16. A Mason must not pay any of his Fellows more wages than they deserve.
17. A Mason must not slander any of his Fellows.
18. A Mason must not slight his Fellows, without very urgent cause.
19. A Mason must revere his Fellows in brotherly love.
20. A Mason must not play cards or dice, except during Christmas time.
21. A Mason must not frequent prostitutes, or promote prostitution amongst his Fellows.
22. A Mason must not go drinking at night past eight o'clock, and then only in the company of at least one of his Fellows.
23. A Mason must come to the yearly assembly to submit to the censure of his Fellows, if said Assembly is within ten miles of his home.
24. A Mason must not make a Mould, Square or Rule, except as are allowed by the Fraternity.
25. A Mason must, if he employs strangers, set them to work at least two weeks and pay their wages fairly.
26. A Mason must faithfully perform and complete the work agreed to with the employer.

V. "THIS CHARGE BELONGETH TO APPRENTICES" [76]

1. An Apprentice must honor God, the Church, the King, his Master and Dame, and must not be absent from his Master or Dame except by permission from one or both of them.
2. An Apprentice must not steal, and must not be an accessory to theft from his Master or Dame to the value of six-pence.
3. An Apprentice must not commit adultery or fornication in his Master's house, with his wife, daughter, or maid.
4. An Apprentice must not disclose his Master's or Dame's secrets, nor the secrets of any Free Mason.

5. An Apprentice must not argue with his Master, Dame or fellow mason.
6. An Apprentice must act reverently toward all fellow Free Masons, and must not use dice, cards or other unlawful games except during Christmas time.
7. An Apprentice must not frequent taverns, except to do the Master's or Dame's errands, or with their consent.
8. An Apprentice must not commit adultery or fornication in any man's house wherein he is a guest or in which he performs work.
9. An Apprentice must not marry, or contract to marry, during his apprenticeship.
10. An Apprentice must not steal his Master's or any fellow Mason's goods, nor allow another to do so if in his power to prevent.

VI. ADDITIONAL ORDERS & CONSTITUTIONS MADE AND AGREED UPON AT A GENERAL ASSEMBLY HELD ... ON THE EIGHTH DAY OF DECEMBER, 1663 (c. 1663 AD) [77]

1. No man can be made an accepted Free Mason unless there is a Lodge constituted of at least five Free Masons; one brother of which is a Master or Warden, and one of which is an operative Free Mason.
2. No one can be an accepted Free Mason unless he is of able-body, honest parentage, good reputation, and obeys the civil laws.
3. No accepted Free Mason may be admitted into any Lodge or Assembly without a Certificate proving the time and place of his acception, from the Lodge that accepted him.
4. Each Free Mason shall bring a note to the Master of the time and place of his acception.
5. The Fraternity shall be governed by one Master, with as many Wardens as are determined at the yearly Assembly.
6. No person shall be accepted as a Free Mason unless he is at least 21 years old.
7. No person shall be accepted as a Free Mason without taking an oath of secrecy.

VII. JAMES ANDERSON ("OLD CHARGES OF FREE AND ACCEPTED MASONS") (1723 AD) [78]

1. ("Concerning God and Religion") A Mason must obey the Moral Law, be a good man, true, honorable and honest, and should practice religion of whatever denomination his conscience obliges.
2. ("Of the Civil Magistrate Supreme and Subordinate") A Mason must be loyal to the civil authorities, and should not countenance a brother his rebellion against the State.
3. ("Of Lodges") Every Mason should belong to a Lodge, and be subject to its By-Laws and Regulations; however, all persons admitted to the Lodge must be good and true Men (no women), free-born (no bondsmen), of mature and discreet age, and of good Report.
4. ("Of Masters, Wardens, Fellows and Apprentices") Masters and Wardens are chosen only based upon their merit. An Apprentice must be without maim or defect in body, and descended of honest parents.
5. No Brother can be a Warden until he has been a Fellow-Craft;
6. No Brother can be a Master without serving as a Warden;

iii. No Brother can be a Grand Warden without serving as a Master of a Lodge;

1. No Brother can be a Grand Master without being a Fellow-Craft, and be a noble gentleman or distinguished artist, architect or scholar.
2. ("Of the Management of the Craft in working")
3. All Masons must work honestly on working days;
4. The most expert Fellow-Craft is to be appointed Master;

iii. Masons must avoid all foul language and behave courteously at all times;

1. The Master must be loyal to his employer and pay no more wages to the Brethren than they truly deserve;
2. All Masons must be faithful to their employer;
3. Masons must not supplant another Mason in his work before it is finished;

vii. The Fellow-Craft chosen to be Warden must be loyal to both his Master and his Fellows;

viii. Masons must not gripe about his pay, and must not desert the Master;

1. A younger (less-skilled) Brother should be properly instructed so as to prevent spoiling the materials;
2. All the tools used in working must be approved by the Grand Lodge;
3. Free and Accepted Masons should not work with unskilled laborers and must never teach general laborers the lessons taught to Brothers and Fellows;
4. ("Of Behaviour")
5. Masons should not hold private conversations, interrupt the Master or use foul language during Lodge;
6. The Lodge members are the proper judges of all cases and controversies betwixt Masons, and no Mason should sue a fellow unless absolutely necessary;

iii. Masons should avoid excess, controversy, and should not create arguments about Religion, Nations, State Policy, or politics;

1. Masons should courteously salute each other as Brother, and freely instruct each other without being overseen or overheard;
2. Masons should be cautious in their words and actions when amongst strangers;
3. Masons must keep the Lodge concerns secret, always act morally, support their families, and avoid gluttony and drunkenness;

vii. A Mason must test a strange Brother, and all true Brothers he must respect and give aid to if able.

VIII. LAURENCE DERMOTT ("PRINCIPLES OF THE CRAFT," AHIMAN REZON) (1756 AD) [79]

1. A Mason must believe in, and worship, "the eternal God."
2. A Mason must believe in sacred scripture ("all those sacred Records which the Dignitaries and Fathers of the Church have compiled and published").
3. A Mason must be submissive / loyal to the civil authorities (a "Lover

of Quiet").[80]

4. A Mason must avoid intemperance and excess.
5. A Mason must abide by the Golden Rule ("treat his inferiors as he would have his Superiors deal with him").
6. A Mason must come to the relief of the poor; especially fellow-Masons.
7. A Mason must obey his Master and presiding Officers, and act courteously and seriously in Lodge.
8. A Mason should study the Arts and Sciences diligently.
9. A Mason should always do Justice and love Mercy.
10. Only those men who are free-born, of mature age, "upright in Body and Limbs," and "endued with the necessary Senses of a Man" may be made a Mason.

IX. MW JOSEPH D. EVANS (NEW YORK, 1854) [81]

1. The distinctive ritual points: the signs, tokens, words, and the Hiramic Legend.
2. That every candidate must declare his belief in one God and the immortality of the soul.
3. That every candidate must be a man, free born, of mature age, of good repute, and having no physical or mental defect.
4. That every Mason must obey the civil authorities and the Masonic regulations of his jurisdiction.
5. That no specific religious sect or political opinion can be required of a Mason, and that sectarian religious or political discussion is banned in Craft assemblies.
6. That an individual Lodge has the final authority to determine who is initiated or affiliated therein.
7. That the ballot for candidates must always remain secret.
8. That a Master's final decision cannot be appealed to the Lodge.
9. That a Lodge cannot try its Master.
10. It is the Grand Master's prerogative to preside over any Masonic assembly in his jurisdiction, and to exercise the executive powers even while Grand Lodge is in recess.

X. ALBERT G. MACKEY, M.D. ("THE FOUNDATION OF MASONIC LAW," *AMERICAN*

1. The modes of recognition (due guards, signs, tokens and words).
2. The existence of only three degrees of symbolic Masonry: (1) Entered Apprentice; (2) Fellow–Craft; (3) Master Mason (inclusive of Holy Royal Arch).
3. The Hiramic legend of the third degree.
4. The Fraternity is governed by a Grand Master, elected from the body of the Craft.
5. The Grand Master's prerogative to preside over every assembly of the Craft, wherever and whenever held.
6. The Grand Master's prerogative to grant dispensations for conferring degrees on candidates / brothers at irregular times.
7. The Grand Master's prerogative to grant dispensations for the opening and holding of special Lodges.
8. The Grand Master's prerogative to make Masons at sight by the convening of an "occasional Lodge".
9. The necessity of Masons to congregate in Lodges.
10. That a Lodge must be governed by one Master and two Wardens.
11. The necessity that every congregated Lodge must be duly tiled.
12. The right of every Mason to be represented, and instruct his representatives, at the yearly General Assembly (Grand Lodge).
13. The right of every Mason to appeal a decision of his brethren in their subordinate Lodge, to Grand Lodge.
14. The right of every Mason to visit and sit in every regular Lodge.
15. Strange visitors cannot enter the Lodge before passing a test or examination to prove that they are Masons, unless said visitor is known to be a Mason by one of the brothers present.
16. No Lodge can interfere in the affairs of another Lodge, nor give degrees to brethren who are members of other Lodges.
17. Every Freemason is amenable to the laws and regulations of the Masonic jurisdiction in which he resides, regardless of whether he is a member of any Lodge therein.
18. A candidate for Freemasonry must be a man, unmutilated, free-born, and of mature age.
19. A candidate for Freemasonry must believe in the existence of Deity, as the Supreme Architect of the Universe.
20. A candidate for Freemasonry must believe in his resurrection to a

future life.
21. A "Book of Law" is an indispensable element of the furniture of a Lodge.
22. All Masons are equal; all Masons meet upon the level.
23. That Freemasonry is a secret society.
24. That Freemasonry is a speculative science, founded upon an operative art, which explanation of the symbolic use of the terms of that art teaches moral and religious lessons.
25. That the Landmarks can never be changed.

XI. GEORGE OLIVER, D.D. (early Nineteenth Century AD) [83]

1. The Lodge must be opened and closed with all the specific ceremonies and rituals, such as properly tiling the Lodge, making the invocation to the Great Architect of the Universe, and having the proper number of officers.
2. Masons meet on the Level and part on the Square; meaning that Masons are equal to one another only while in Lodge.
3. A Mason must never invite his friend to petition to become a Mason, and all candidates must declare that they were not solicited by their friends, or by any mercenary or unworthy motive.
4. A candidate must be freeborn, of good morals and have full and proper use of his limbs. To ensure these qualifications are met, the candidate must be strictly researched, with inquiry made of his friends and neighbors, before the ballot is taken.
5. Before a candidate can be initiated, he must be proposed in open Lodge, with a notice of the proposal sent to each brother of the Lodge. The ballot for the candidate cannot be taken sooner than the next regular Lodge meeting after the proposal.
6. The preparation of the candidate and initiation ceremonies, which teach scientific beauties and moral truths.
7. The white apron as a mark of innocence and badge of a Mason.
8. The tests of industry of the candidate in the First Degree, which are intended to convey some preliminary insight into the allegorical system of Masonry.

XII. JOHN W. SIMONS ("PRINCIPLES AND

1. Masons must believe in the existence of a Supreme Being and the immortality of the soul.
2. The moral law is the rule and guide of every Mason.
3. Masons must respect and obey the civil law and Masonic regulations of his country and jurisdiction in which he resides.
4. That "new-made Masons" must be free-born, of lawful age, and "hale and sound at the time of making".
5. The modes of recognition (due guard, signs, grips, and words) and the ceremonies of the three degrees.
6. That the Master's final decision (or the Warden's in the Master's absence) cannot be appealed to the Lodge.
7. That a Mason cannot be made a Master of a Lodge until he has served at least one year as Warden.
8. That every Mason has a right to visit every regular Lodge, unless, in doing so, it would disturb the harmony or working of the Lodge he wishes to visit.
9. The Grand Master has the prerogative to preside over every assembly in his jurisdiction; to make Masons at sight; and to grant dispensations for the formation of new Lodges.
10. That a candidate cannot be made a Mason without submitting a petition and being accepted by unanimous ballot of a regular Lodge, unless he is made a Mason "at sight" by the Grand Master.
11. That the ballot for candidates is strictly and inviolably secret.
12. That a Lodge cannot try its Master.
13. A Mason must be amenable to the laws of the jurisdiction in which he resides, even if he is a member of a Lodge in a different jurisdiction.
14. A Mason has the right to be represented in Grand Lodge, and to instruct his representatives.
15. The general aim and form of the society must be preserved inviolate and transmitted to our successors.

XIII. ROBERT MORRIS ("CODE OF MASONIC LAW") [85]

1. The Ancient Landmarks are unchangeable and imperative.
2. Masonry is a system which symbolically teaches piety, morality,

science, charity and self-discipline.
3. The Law of God is the rule and guide for Masonry.
4. A Mason must submit to the civil law, "so far as it accords with the Divine Law."
5. The Masonic Lodge and the Masonic institution are one and indivisible.
6. The qualifications of a candidate regard his mental, moral and physical nature.
7. Personal worth and merit are the basis of official worth and merit.
8. The official duties of Masonry are esoteric.
9. The selection of Masonic material and the general labors of the Masonic Craft are exoteric.
10. The honors of Masonry are the gratitude of the Craft and the approval of God.
11. Masonic promotion, both private and official, is by grades.
12. The Grand Master may have a Deputy.
13. The Master, as head of the Lodge, is elected by the Craft.
14. The Wardens transmit communication between the Master and the body of the Lodge, and are also elected by the brethren.
15. The members of the Lodge must obey the Master and Wardens.
16. Secrecy is an indispensable element of Masonry.
17. The Grand Lodge is the supreme authority in its jurisdiction, but subject to the Ancient Landmarks.

XIV. FORMER CONSTITUTIONS OF THE GRAND LODGE OF FREE AND ACCEPTED MASONS OF THE STATE OF NEW YORK (1856 – 1869 AD) [86]

1. All candidates must believe in the Supreme Architect of the Universe.
2. That all Masons must conform to the moral law, as the rule and guide of every Mason.
3. That all Masons must obey Masonic law and authority.
4. That the rites and ceremonies of the degrees, including the Ancient York Rite, are immutable and no man can make innovations in them.
5. That contention and lawsuits between Masons are contrary to Masonic law and regulations.
6. That charity to a poor brother, his widow and orphans, is a right of him to demand, and the duty of his brothers to provide.

7. That Masonic instruction is the right of every brother to receive, and duty of every brother to bestow.
8. That Masons have the right to visit other Lodges, but said right may be forfeited or limited by particular regulations.
9. Candidates for Masonry must be a man, at least 21 years old, free-born, of good report, hale and sound, and not deformed or dismembered.
10. A man can only be made a Mason in a regular Lodge, except when made at sight by the Grand Master.
11. That the Grand Master may make Masons at sight, and grant dispensations to do the same, but otherwise a candidate must be voted in unanimously.
12. The ballot for candidates or for membership is strictly and inviolably secret.
13. A petition for membership, once presented and referred to committee, cannot be withdrawn.
14. When demanded, a candidate has the right to be balloted for each degree separately.
15. A man must raise a Master Mason and sign the By-Laws before he is considered a member of the Lodge.
16. That it is the duty of every Master Mason to be a contributing member of a Lodge.
17. A Lodge under dispensation is only a temporary body, and thus cannot be represented in Grand Lodge.
18. The Master and Wardens of a Lodge are elected once a year, and, if selected, cannot resign during their term, and are, of right, the representatives in Grand

Lodge unless they decide to send a proxy.

19. No Mason may be elected Master of a Lodge unless he is a Master Mason who has served as Warden.
20. No appeal of the Master's (or Warden's acting as Master) final decision may be made to the Lodge membership.
21. That every Mason must be tried by his peers; and hence the Master cannot be tried by his Lodge.
22. That a Mason must not have contact with a clandestine or expelled Mason.
23. That, even if Grand Lodge restores a man to membership, it does not automatically restore his membership to a subordinate Lodge.

24. Even a Mason unaffiliated to a particular Lodge is still subject to the disciplinary power of Masonry.
25. A Mason must be admonished by the Master or Wardens three times before he can be tried for a breach of the moral law.
26. That a failure of a Lodge to meet for one full year is cause for the forfeiture of the Warrant.
27. That it is the right, as well as the duty, of every subordinate Lodge to be represented at Grand Lodge at its annual assembly.
28. That a Grand Lodge has supreme and exclusive jurisdiction over Ancient Craft Masonry within its territorial limits.
29. That no appeal lies from a final decision of the Grand Master (or Deputy or Warden occupying the chair of Grand Master in his absence).
30. That the office of Grand Master must be annually elected by the Grand Lodge.
31. That the Grand Lodge must meet at least once each year.

XV. DR. MITCHELL ("HISTORY OF FREEMASONRY") [87]

1. The "unwritten Landmarks" consist of all the essential rituals and teachings of the Lodge-room, and can be learned nowhere else.
2. The "written Landmarks" are the six enumerated Landmarks found in the Old Charges of Free and Accepted Masons (1723).[88]

XVI. LUKE A. LOCKWOOD ("MASONIC LAW AND PRACTICE") [89]

1. The belief in the existence of a Supreme Being; that his Will is revealed to humanity; the resurrection of the body, and the immortality of the soul.
2. The obligations, modes of recognition, and Hiramic legend.
3. The inculcation of the moral virtues, of benevolence and of the doctrines of natural religion by means of symbols derived from the building of the Temple of King Solomon and the operative craft of masonry.
4. That Masons must obey the moral law, and the civil law (government) of the country they inhabit.

5. That the Grand Master is head of the Craft.
6. That the Master is head of the Lodge.
7. That the Grand Lodge is the supreme governing body within its jurisdiction.
8. That every Lodge has a right to be represented in Grand Lodge by its first three officers or their proxies.
9. That every Lodge has power to make Masons and to administer their own affairs.
10. Every candidate must be a man, of lawful age, free born, under no restraint of liberty, and "hale and sound."
11. That no candidate can be received except by unanimous ballot, after due notice and inquiry into his character.
12. That the ballot (for candidates) is inviolably secret.
13. That all Masons are peers (equality in the Lodge).
14. That all Lodges are peers.
15. That all Grand Lodges are peers.
16. That no one can be Master of the Lodge unless he is first a Warden (unless with the dispensation of the Grand Master).
17. That the obligations, modes of recognition, forms and ceremonies of initiation are secret.
18. That no innovation can be made upon the body of Masonry.
19. That the Ancient Landmarks are the Supreme Law, and cannot be changed or abrogated.

XVII. GRAND LODGE OF MASSACHUSETTS (1918 AD) [90]

("The (following) list of Landmarks is not declared to be exclusive")

1. Monotheism, the sole dogma of Freemasonry.
2. Belief in immortality, the ultimate lesson of Masonic philosophy.
3. The Volume of Sacred Law, an indispensable part of the furniture of the Lodge.
4. The Legend of the Third Degree.
5. Secrecy.
6. The Symbolism of the Operative Art.
7. A Mason must be a freeborn male adult.

XVIII. Wor. ROSCOE POUND (1925 AD) [91]

1. The Belief in The Great Architect of the Universe.
2. The Belief in the persistence of personality (immortality of the soul).
3. The Volume of Sacred Law is an indispensable part of the Lodge furniture.
4. The Hiramic Legend of the third degree.
5. The obligation of secrecy and modes of recognition.
6. The symbolism of the operative art as used for the purposes of moral and religious teachings.
7. A candidate must be a man, freeborn, and of age.

XIX. COMMISSION ON INFORMATION FOR RECOGNITION OF THE CONFERENCE OF GRAND MASTERS OF MASONS IN NORTH AMERICA (1950 AD)

1. Monotheism – an unalterable and continuing belief in God.
2. The Volume of Sacred Law – an essential part of the furniture of the Lodge.
3. Prohibition of the discussion of Religion and Politics.

Citations

[1] "Master Mason Degree, Third Section, Part III," in *The Standard Work and Lectures of Ancient Craft Masonry*, ed. Gary A. Henderson (New York: Grand Lodge of Free and Accepted Masons of the State of New York, 2001) 218-19.

[2] George Payne, "General Regulations Section 39," in *The Constitutions of the Free-Masons* ("Anderson's Constitutions"), ed. James Anderson (London: Anderson, 1723; reprinted Philadelphia: Benjamin Franklin, 1734).

[3] Wendell K. Walker, et al., comp., "Book of Constitutions Section 101," in *Masonic Law of New York*, (New York: Grand Lodge Free and Accepted Masons, 1977), 4. See also, Wendell K. Walker, et al., comp., "Handbook of Masonic Law Section 82," in *Masonic Law of New York*, (New York: Grand Lodge Free and Accepted Masons, 1977), 23 ("The powers of Grand Lodge are, however, subject to such limitation as . . . are imposed by the Ancient Landmarks of Freemasonry") and Wendell K. Walker, et al., comp.,

"Handbook of Masonic Law Section 180," in *Masonic Law of New York*, (New York: Grand Lodge Free and Accepted Masons, 1977), 49 ("The Grand Master cannot determine the physical qualifications of a candidate and cannot issue a dispensation allowing a Lodge to disobey a Landmark").

[4] Wendell K. Walker, et al., comp., "Book of Constitutions Section 116," in *Masonic Law of New York*, (New York: Grand Lodge Free and Accepted Masons, 1977), 10. See also, Wendell K. Walker, et al., comp., "Handbook of Masonic Law Section 250: Duties and Powers of Grand Wardens," in *Masonic Law of New York*, (New York: Grand Lodge Free and Accepted Masons, 1977), 61.

[5] Wendell K. Walker, et al., comp., "Handbook of Masonic Law Section 26: Rules of Construction," in *Masonic Law of New York*, (New York: Grand Lodge Free and Accepted Masons, 1977), 8. See also, Wendell K. Walker, et al., comp., "Handbook of Masonic Law Section 768," in *Masonic Law of New York*, (New York: Grand Lodge Free and Accepted Masons, 1977), 197 ("The legislative powers of a Lodge . . . must not be in derogation of the Constitutions, Ancient Landmarks or its own particular by-laws").

[6] Wendell K. Walker, et al., comp., "Handbook of Masonic Law Section 585: Duties, Powers and Privileges," in *Masonic Law of New York*, (New York: Grand Lodge Free and Accepted Masons, 1977), 155.

[7] Wendell K. Walker, et al., comp., "Book of Constitutions Section 336," in *Masonic Law of New York*, (New York: Grand Lodge Free and Accepted Masons, 1977), 49.

[8] Wendell K. Walker, et al., comp., "Handbook of Masonic Law Section 1180: Departure from Ancient Landmarks,"in *Masonic Law of New York*, (New York: Grand Lodge Free and Accepted Masons, 1977), 304.

[9] Wendell K. Walker, et al., comp., "Handbook of Masonic Law Sections 1402 – 1405," in *Masonic Law of New York*, (New York: Grand Lodge Free and Accepted Masons, 1977), 340.

[10] Wendell K. Walker, et al., comp., "Code of Procedure of the Grand Lodge of Free and Accepted Masons of the State of New York Section 5: Enumerations of Masonic offenses by individual," in *Masonic Law of New York*, (New York: Grand Lodge Free and Accepted Masons, 1977), 4; and Wendell K. Walker, et al., comp., "Handbook of Masonic Law, Section 1134: Unmasonic Conduct," in *Masonic Law of New York*, (New York: Grand Lodge Free and Accepted Masons, 1977), 297.

[11] Wendell K. Walker, et al., comp., "Book of Constitutions: Appendix," in *Masonic Law of New York*, (New York: Grand Lodge Free and Accepted Masons, 1977), 88.

[12] R. W. Gilbert Savitzky, ed., *The 24-Inch Gauge Masonic Resource Guide*, (New York: Masonic University of New York, 2006), 18.

[13] *Freemasonry and the Holy Bible: The Great Light in Masonry, according to the authorized or King James' Version*, (Wichita: Heirloom Bible Publishers, 1991), 70.

[14] "Landmark," Merriam-Webster Dictionary online edition, http://www.m-w.com/dictionary/landmark (accessed October 1, 2011).

[15] "Landmark," Oxford English Dictionary online edition, http://oxforddictionaries.com/definition/landmark (accessed October 1, 2011).

[16] Athena Stafyla, "The Masonic Landmarks," Pietre-Stones Review of Freemasonry, (2003),

http://www.freemasons-freemasonry.com/athena1.html (accessed October 1, 2011). In her article, Ms. Stafyla also considers the term "landmark" to have a similar architectural significance; "(a) similar practice has resulted in the allegorical use of the word landmark in Masonic philosophy, marking a cathedral point in the inner organization and way of thinking in Masonry, without which it would be impossible for a Lodge to be characterized and seen as such".

[17] Robert Macoy, "Landmarks, Masonic," A *Dictionary of Freemasonry*, ed. Robert Macoy (New York: Gramercy Books (reprint) 2000), 216.

[18] R. W. Gilbert Savitzky, ed., *The 24-Inch Gauge Masonic Resource Guide*, (New York: Masonic University of New York, 2006), 18. Aside from being dean of Harvard Law School, Nathan Roscoe Pound was a Past Master of Lancaster Lodge No.54 A.F. & A.M. Lincoln, Nebraska, and helped to found The Harvard Lodge A.F. & A.M., "Roscoe Pound," Wikipedia, http://en.wikipedia.org/wiki/Roscoe_Pound (accessed October 1, 2011).

[19] Daniel Doron, "Landmarks and Old Charges," Pietre-Stones Review of Freemasonry, (2004), http://www.freemasons-freemasonry.com/doron.html (accessed October 1, 2011). "In other words, the Landmarks of Freemasonry are established usages and customs which serve as boundaries both inwards as well as outwards of a Masonic organization. If we examine this definition closely, it will be apparent that it contains a goal; not only boundaries but such that conform to the goals of Speculative Freemasonry."

[20] Michael A Botelho, "Masonic Landmarks," http://www.srmason-sj.org/web/journalfiles/

Issues/Feb02/botelho.htm (last accessed October 10, 2007); see also

"Masonic Landmarks", Wikipedia, http://en.wikipedia.org/wiki/ Masonic_Landmarks (accessed October 1, 2011).

[21] Percy Jantz, "The Landmarks of Freemasonry," Grand Lodge of British Columbia and Yukon, (2004), http://freemasonry.bcy.ca/texts/ landmarks.html (accessed October 1, 2011).

[22] Daniel Doron, "Landmarks and Old Charges," Pietre-Stones Review of Freemasonry, (2004), http://www.freemasons-freemasonry.com/ doron.html (accessed October 1, 2011); citing John W. Simons, "The Principles of Masonic Jurisprudence".

[23] Paul M. Bessel, "Landmarks," (2007), http://bessel.org/ landmark.htm (accessed October 1, 2011); such states lacking an official Landmarks List include Alabama, Alaska, Arizona, Arkansas, California, Colorado, Idaho, Illinois, Indiana, Iowa, Missouri, Montana, Nebraska, New Jersey, New Mexico, North Carolina, Ohio, Pennsylvania, Rhode Island, Texas, Utah, Virginia, Washington, Wisconsin and Wyoming.

[24] Daniel Doron, "Landmarks and Old Charges," Pietre-Stones Review of Freemasonry, (2004), http://www.freemasons-freemasonry.com/ doron.html (accessed October 1, 2011); Athena Stafyla, "The Masonic Landmarks," Pietre-Stones Review of Freemasonry, (2003), http://www.freemasons-freemasonry.com/athena1.html (accessed October 1, 2011).

[25] Anonymous, "The Laws of Masonry," Short Talk Bulletin, Vol. VII, No.12, (1929),
http://www.masonicworld.com/education/files/artnov01/ The%20Laws%20of%20Masonry.htm (accessed October 1, 2011).

[26] Anonymous, A Poem of Moral Duties (Regius Manuscript), Articles 4, 5, and 7, (England, 1390); Anonymous, Matthew Cooke Manuscript, Articles 4, 6, 7, (England, 1450); J. Roberts, ed., "The History of Free Masons, etc.", "Saying Thus By Way of Exhortation," Charges 14 and 15, "Additional Orders and Constitutions . . .," numbers 2 and 6, in The Old Constitutions Belonging to the Ancient and Honorable Society of Free and Accepted Masons (London: Roberts, 1722).

[27] Ibid.

[28] Ibid.

[29] George Payne, "General Regulations Section 39," in The Constitutions of the Free-Masons ("Anderson's Constitutions"), ed. James Anderson (London: Anderson, 1723; reprinted Philadelphia: Benjamin Franklin, 1734).

[30] Unfortunately, the 1738 edition of Anderson's Constitutions was no

more helpful in this regard, as it merely repeated the same reference to "Old Land Marks" in Regulation XXXIX, without further explanation.

[31] James Anderson, *The Old Charges of Free and Accepted Masons* (London: Anderson, 1723).

[32] Ibid.

[33] Ibid. (emphasis added)

[34] Ibid.

[35] Jasper Ridley, *The Freemasons: A History of the World's Most Powerful Secret Society* (New York: Arcade Publishing, 2001) 6-8.

[36] Anonymous, "History of the Landmarks of Freemasonry", Grand Lodge of British Columbia and Yukon, (2004), http://freemasonry.bcy.ca/grandLodge/landmarks_history.html (accessed October 1, 2011); see also, Anonymous, "The Ancient Landmarks of Freemasonry", Trinity Valley Masonic Lodge No.1048 A.F.&A.M. (Texas, 2007); but see Daniel Doron, "Landmarks and Old Charges," Pietre-Stones Review of Freemasonry, (2004), http://www.freemasons-freemasonry.com/doron.html (accessed October 1, 2011) ("According to MacBride, the Landmarks listed in Dermot's 'Ahiman Rezon' (1756) about a hundred years before Mackey's Encyclopedia was published . . ."); see also R. W. Gilbert Savitzky, *The 24-Inch Gauge Masonic Resource Guide*, (New York: Masonic University of New York, 2006), 17, which dates M∴ W∴ Joseph D. Evans' list to 1854, fully four years before publication of Mackey's list.

[37] Albert G. Mackey, "The Foundation of Masonic Law", American Quarterly Review of Freemasonry, volume II

(1858): 230. See Landmarks 1, 15, 17, 18, and 23.

[38] Ibid., Landmarks 2 and 3.

[39] Ibid., Landmarks 4 – 8.

[40] Ibid., Landmark 25.

[41] Paul M. Bessel, "Landmarks," (2007), http://bessel.org/landmark.htm (accessed October 1, 2011). The following Grand Lodges reference Mackey's list: Delaware, Washington DC, Georgia, Maine, Maryland, North Dakota, Wisconsin; The following Grand Lodges have adopted Mackey's list as official: Kansas, Oklahoma, Oregon, South Carolina, South Dakota.

[42] Anonymous, A Poem of Moral Duties (Regius Manuscript) (England, 1390); Anonymous, Matthew Cooke Manuscript (England, 1450).

[43] Daniel Doron, "Landmarks and Old Charges," Pietre-Stones Review of Freemasonry, (2004), http://www.freemasons-freemasonry.com/doron.html (accessed October 1, 2011). See also, Percy Jantz, "The Landmarks of Freemasonry," Grand Lodge of British Columbia and Yukon,

(2004), http://freemasonry.bcy.ca/texts/landmarks.html (accessed October 1, 2011).

[44] Albert G. Mackey, "The Foundation of Masonic Law," American Quarterly Review of Freemasonry, volume II (1858): 230.

[45] See, e.g., Anonymous, Matthew Cooke Manuscript (England, 1450), Point 8. See also Percy Jantz, "The Landmarks of Freemasonry," Grand Lodge of British Columbia and Yukon, (2004),

http://freemasonry.bcy.ca/texts/landmarks.html (accessed October 1, 2011).

[46] Daniel Doron, "Landmarks and Old Charges," Pietre-Stones Review of Freemasonry, (2004), http://www.freemasons-freemasonry.com/doron.html (accessed October 1, 2011). See also, Percy Jantz, "The Landmarks of Freemasonry," Grand Lodge of British Columbia and Yukon, (2004), http://freemasonry.bcy.ca/texts/landmarks.html (accessed October 1, 2011).

[47] Ibid.

[48] Daniel Doron, "Landmarks and Old Charges," Pietre-Stones Review of Freemasonry, (2004), http://www.freemasons-freemasonry.com/doron.html (accessed October 1, 2011) ("In my opinion, the last Landmark can hardly be regarded as a Landmark at all, since all it stipulates is that these Landmarks can never be changed. Certainly not when we know the self same Landmark was changed in 1823").

[49] Robert Macoy, "Landmarks, Masonic," A *Dictionary of Freemasonry*, ed. Robert Macoy (New York: Gramercy Books (reprint), 2000) 216.

[50] See, Anonymous, A Poem of Moral Duties (Regius Manuscript), (England, 1390) Point 1; Anonymous, Matthew Cooke Manuscript, (England, 1450) Point 1.

[51] See also, J. Roberts, ed., "The History of Free Masons, etc.," "Saying Thus By Way of Exhortation" Charge 1, "This Charge Belongeth to Apprentices" Charge 1, in *The Old Constitutions Belonging to the Ancient and Honorable Society of Free and Accepted Masons*, (London: Roberts, 1722).

[52] James Anderson, *The Old Charges of Free and Accepted Masons*, (London: Anderson, 1723).

[53] Ibid.

[54] See, e.g., Anonymous, A Poem of Moral Duties (Regius Manuscript), (England, 1390) Article 5; Anonymous, Matthew Cooke Manuscript, (England, 1450) Article 6; J. Roberts, ed., "The History of Free Masons, etc.," "Saying Thus By Way of Exhortation" Charge 15, "Additional Orders and Constitutions . . ." number 2, in *The Old Constitutions Belonging to*

the Ancient and Honorable Society of Free and Accepted Masons, (London: Roberts, 1722); James Anderson, The Old Charges of Free and Accepted Masons, (London: Anderson, 1723) Charge No.4; Joseph D.Evans, (1854) No.3; Albert G. Mackey, "The Foundation of Masonic Law," American Quarterly Review of Freemasonry, volume II, Number 18, (1858): 230; "Old Constitutions of the Grand Lodge of New York," Landmark No.9, in Robert Macoy, "Landmarks, Masonic," A Dictionary of Freemasonry, (New York: Gramercy Books (reprint), 2000), 216.

[55] Wendell K. Walker, et al., comp., "Handbook of Masonic Law Section 92: Disturbing Requirement of Physical Soundness," Masonic Law of New York, (New York: Grand Lodge Free and Accepted Masons, 1977) 26.

[56] Ibid. (emphasis added). No doubt, logically, the Grand Lodge of Free and Accepted Masons of the State of New York had to add this clarification. After all, if a hallmark of an Ancient Landmark is that it cannot be changed (by even Grand Lodges), then anything that is changed, must not really be an "Ancient Landmark".

[57] William Preston Campbell-Everden, Freemasonry and Its Etiquette, (New York: Gramercy Books (reprint), 2001), 9.

[58] Grand Orient of France, "History", http://www.godf.org/index.php/pages/details/slug/the-grand-orient-de-france-1 (accessed October 1, 2011).

[59] See Wendell K. Walker, et al., comp., "Handbook of Masonic Law Section 38: Source of Masonic Authority," Masonic Law of New York, (New York: Grand Lodge Free and Accepted Masons, 1977) 15, Footnote 5 ("One hailing from the Grand Orient de France could not be affiliated in any Lodge in this jurisdiction, unless his dimit was granted before the June Communication of the Grand Lodge of 1869"); see also Paul M. Bessel, "U.S. Recognition of French Grand Lodges in the 1900s," (1998) http://bessel.org/masrec/france.htm (accessed October 1, 2011) originally published in Heredom: The Transactions of the Scottish Rite Research Society, volume 5, (1996): 221-244. W∴ Paul Bessel recounts how Grand Lodges in the United States withdrew their recognitions of the Grande Orient de France at the behest of the Grand Lodge of Louisiana after the former "recognized a Masonic group called the 'Supreme Council of the A. and A.S. Rite of the State of Louisiana'", which the Grand Lodge of Louisiana considered a "strange perversion" and "an invasion of its territory" by the Grande Orient.

[60] Paul M. Bessel, "U.S. Recognition of French Grand Lodges in the 1900s," (1998) http://bessel.org/masrec/france.htm (accessed October 1, 2011)

originally published in *Heredom: The Transactions of the Scottish Rite Research Society*, volume 5, (1996): 221-244. Although many United States Grand Lodges began limited recognition of the Grande Orient in the early 20th century – in a show of solidarity with their French brethren during World War I – and the Grand Lodge of the State of New York ratified inter-visitations with the Grande Orient de France and Grande Loge Francaise in 1917, the Grande Orient has not been formally recognized by New York State Grand Lodge.

[61] Paul M. Bessel, "Landmarks," (2007), http://bessel.org/landmark.htm (accessed October 1, 2011).

[62] Paul M. Bessel, "Masonic Recognition Issues," (1998), http://bessel.org/masrec/recstand.htm (accessed October 1, 2011).

[63] For a fascinating and illuminating discussion of the issues surrounding inter-Lodge recognition see Paul M. Bessel, "Masonic Recognition Issues," (1998), http://bessel.org/masrec/ (accessed October 1, 2011).

[64] Paul M. Bessel, "Masonic Recognition Issues," (1998), http://bessel.org/masrec/recstand.htm (accessed October 1, 2011).

[65] Ibid.

[66] Ibid.

[67] Ibid.

[68] Ibid.

[69] Ibid.

[70] Ibid.

[71] Ibid.

[72] It is important to note however, that there is currently in existence a Grande Loge Francaise and a Grande Loge Nationale Francaise, which do conform to the Anglo-American Landmarks relative to the belief in TGAOTU, as well as some others not maintained by the French Grand Orient. The Grand Lodge of New York, among many other Anglo-American Grand Lodges, recognizes and is in comity with the Grande Loge Nationale Francaise.

[73] Due to the limitations of space, the Landmarks listed here are most often paraphrased from the original sources. Citations to the full text of the originals are given when possible.

[74] As listed in J. Roberts, ed., "The History of Free Masons, etc.," in *The Old Constitutions Belonging to the Ancient and Honorable Society of Free and Accepted Masons*, (London: Roberts, 1722).

[75] Ibid.

[76] Ibid.

[77] Ibid.

[78] James Anderson, *The Old Charges of Free and Accepted Masons* (London: Anderson, 1723).

[79] Laurence Dermott, *Ahiman Rezon: Or A Help to a Brother*, pp. 14–24 (London: James Bedford, 1756). This Ahiman Rezon served as the Constitutions of the Antient Grand Lodge of England (a 1751 competitor to Anderson's Grand Lodge at London).

[80] Interestingly, Dermott has a more liberal interpretation of submission to civil authority than his compatriot Anderson, insofar as this Principle is qualified "provided they (the civil powers) do not infringe upon the limited Bounds of Religion and Reason."

[81] As listed in Wendell K. Walker, et al., comp., "Book of Constitutions: Appendix," in *Masonic Law of New York*, (New York: Grand Lodge Free and Accepted Masons, 1977), 88.

[82] Robert Macoy, "Landmarks, Masonic," *A Dictionary of Freemasonry*, ed. Robert Macoy (New York: Gramercy Books (reprint) 2000), 216-221.

[83] As listed in Robert Macoy, "Landmarks, Masonic," *A Dictionary of Freemasonry*, ed. Robert Macoy (New York: Gramercy Books (reprint) 2000), 221-224.

[84] Ibid. 224.

[85] Ibid. 224-225.

[86] Ibid. 225-226.

[87] Ibid. 226.

[88] See Section III above, and Anderson's Old Charges set out at Appendix VII.

[89] Ibid. 227.

[90] Percy Jantz, "The Landmarks of Freemasonry," Grand Lodge of British Columbia and Yukon, (2004), http://freemasonry.bcy.ca/texts/landmarks.html (accessed October 1, 2011).

[91] See, generally, Michael A. Botelho, "Masonic Landmarks," http://www.srmason-sj.org/web/journalfiles/Issues/Feb02/botelho.htm (accessed October 10, 2007); Daniel Doron, "Landmarks and Old Charges," Pietre-Stones Review of Freemasonry, (2004), http://www.freemasons-freemasonry.com/doron.html (accessed October 1, 2011).

[92] "Masonic Landmarks," Wikipedia, http://en.wikipedia.org/wiki/Masonic_Landmarks (accessed October 1, 2011).

The Arabic Cipher Hypothesis: Was Banking the Holy Grail and Numerals Its Keeper?

Ken JP Stuczynski

{Biography given: Bro. Kenneth JP Stuczynski, raised in 2012, is a business owner, interfaith minister, writer, and martial artist. With a degree in Philosophy (concentration in Ethics) and a minor in Psychology, his scholastic interests span nearly all arts and sciences, and enjoys research and writing on myriad topics, including world faiths and culture, past and present. He is currently Tyler of West Seneca Lodge #1111, Flag Bearer for Pond Chapter No.853 OES, and Junior Deacon for the upcoming year at the Lodge of Research.

Editor's Note: At the time of this printing, he is serving for the first time as Worshipful Master, for Ken-Ton Lodge No.1186, installed by MW Jeffrey M. Williamson and taking his obligation on the Bible used by the Western New York Lodge of Research. In 2018, he finished his year as Patron with his wife as Matron of Pond Chapter No.853 OES. He also serves as webmaster for NYMasons.Org on the Communication Committee for the Grand Lodge of the State of New York.}

Introduction

There has always been speculation about what the Knights Templar may have discovered in the Holy Land. Legends depict scenes of horses and men rushing back to Europe under cover of night, with news or evidence of some great discovery. The perceived sins of omission of historians have become assumed hidden treasures and power cached within the priories of secret orders. These were the Grail stories, written and rewritten, told and retold over the first few centuries after the crusades.

In modern times, the object of Grail mythos transformed from the "cup of a carpenter" to the bloodline of the Christian Christ. The idea that knowledge is power, and such great knowledge would have meant great power, has been proffered as a main cause to the prosperity of the Knights

Templar. This implies monetary support as protection of such secrets at best, blackmail of the Holy See at worst.

But what if the great discovery, upon entering the Temple in Jerusalem, was as mundane and unpretentious as a banking ledger? The Arabs had preserved much knowledge from their Hellenistic Roman predecessors, and no banking beyond Jewish lenders and money changers had been seen in Europe since the Fall of Rome. Would such a tool show such advantage to account for the Templar's wealth? And may Arabic numerals—not in popular use until centuries later—have been a cipher, their means of encrypting their records and practices?

To explore these questions we must do several things: (a) review the banking practices before, and during, and after the crusades; (b) review the wealth of the Knights Templar and other factors that would account for it; and (c) determine the extent of knowledge in Europe of Arabic numerals at the time, ideally including the existence of bank drafts or other records showing their use.

The Templar's Inheritance

Economic transactions are as old as Mankind. Currency transactions stretch back to the edge of history, facilitated by and necessitating the widespread use of writing and numeric systems. Even lending and credit is far older than the Classical World[1], the last power of which, Rome, had a well-documented and extensive practice.

How extensive? The Empire had money-changers, money-lenders, insurance, joint-lending capital for government contracts and individual bank investments for private enterprises, even the issuing of stock shares. Interest was paid on deposits and they cashed checks.[2] Banks issued travelers checks, bills of exchange, and even bought and sold realty.[3] Like today, loans were backed by collateral, secured by liens, and regulated by the state in not just practice but consequence of non-repayment.[4] To see that banking was pervasive in Roman life, all one must do is consider the very existence of a bank "panic" of 33 AD.[5]

Like all things Roman, banking originated from elsewhere, in this case the conquered Greeks, whose culture in turn conquered the Empire. Thirty-three Hellenistic cities had private banks before the time of Christ.[6] Syria was so known for its banking that the words for "Syrian" and "banker" were synonymous in Gaul.[7]

When the Western Roman Empire fell, it was understandable that whole industries and economies failed and coinage became scarce, resulting in a "massive simplification of the economy".[8] From that time until the Crusades—where the Templars and Lombards emerged—the most complex commercial activities were commercial trade fairs that transcended political boundaries.[9]

But the achievements of classical civilization were not lost. Economic historian Peter Heathers writes of the Arabic world during Europe's "Dark Ages":

> "Early medieval Islam was at the height of its prosperity and political cohesion. It was a world of extravagant wealth and lavish court life, where scholars had an interest in preserving the ancient traditions of Greek and Roman learning, not least in science and geography, subjects which had largely fallen into abeyance in Christendom."[10]

And like the writings of Plato, it is easy to see that banking systems may also have been recovered through the interactions of pilgrims and knights with the peoples and powers of the Levant, who further advanced them (along with mathematics) in their own right.[11]

We know that inroads had already been laid in terms of trade. Volga Bulgars had trade alliances with the Caliphs since the 7th Century, and in the 10th converted to Islam. Islamic explorers and merchants even ventured North beyond the Bulgars to establish trade relations with the Ar-Rus (forerunners of the Russian people), ruled by a powerful mercantile class. European goods were exchanged for Islamic silver "flowing into the North" no later than 800 CE, with routes becoming established via the Dnieper and Volga rivers. It increased through the 9th Century, Islamic coins reaching Scandinavia and the Baltic.[12]

Arabic coin influx decreased between 870-900 CE during political chaos in the Caliphate, disrupting the Slavic economies for a time. By 920, most trade with the Rus was done indirectly in the land of the Volga Bulgars, connecting Islamic and Viking merchants. Approximately 80% of all the silver entering the North did so between 900-1030 CE, after which "supplies dwindled to virtually nothing".[13] The point here is the lack of direct economic interaction between the East and West during those centuries.

The end of this intermediary paradigm was marked by the Crusades, where we find the Knights Templar given the Temple of Solomon, five years after the founding of the Order in 1113 AD. Oddly noted in 1185, a Temple's mosaic displayed its founder and "cost of undertaking".[14] And it is in precisely this place they may have found numismatic secrets. Early Rome used temples as banks and treasuries, and in later years, in Ephesus, the Temple of Artemis was the chief bank.[15] And at the time of Josephus and Herod, the Jewish Temple itself was a national bank.[16]

In other words, texts one would expect to find would not be limited to scripture, but scrolls or tomes of ledgers. Ledgers were part of the basic tools of previous bankers, and ranged from a simple list of transactions to extensive records in larger banking networks, such as the Bank of the Ptolemies.[17]

Such a discovery may explain why the "Poor Fellow-Soldiers of Christ and of the Temple of Solomon" became prolific bankers so quickly, and not by novel invention. The most common textbook lesson we learn about the Templars is their development of a system of deposits and withdrawals by bank note that allowed a travelers money to be "moved" great distances at little risk and as fast as the traveler could journey. What is forgotten or omitted is that this system had been prolific in the Classical world. States and wealthy families used such book transfers, and multinational publican societies has "a similar service to that of ATMs".[18]

The Templars quickly adopted Arab dinars, Byzantine hyperpera, and silver drachmas, and loans were made to Aragon as early as the 1130s.[19] King Louis writes in 1146, "I have to inform you that they have lent me a considerable sum of money, which must be paid to them quickly, that their house may not suffer, and that I may keep my word."[20] They had competition with Italian bankers, also new to the scene and also having direct contact with the Islamic World. However, there is evidence of Templar activity pre-dating them.[21]

A century or so later, according to Addison,

> The King of England borrowed money in France "upon the security of his regalia and crown jewels, which were deposited in the Temple at Paris", a "long list of golden wands, golden combs, diamond buckles, chaplets and circlets, golden crowns, imperial beavers, rich girdles, golden peacocks, and rings innumerable, adorned with sapphires, rubies, emeralds, topazes, and carbuncles ... inspected in the presence of the Treasurer of the Temple at Paris, and that the same were safely deposited in the coffers of the Templars.[22]

He further writes, "The wealth of the King, the Nobles, the Bishops, and of the rich Burghers of London" was deposited and kept in the Temple of London, making it a "storehouse of treasure." By the 13th Century, the Temple at London managed the money and affairs of the Queen (widow to Richard Coeur de Lion), as well as various other business affairs and diplomacy.[23]

Thus the handling of money had been intertwined with power from the start until DeMolay relinquished the Order's treasury and power to the Pope and King Philip IV of France in 1307.[24] And money-lending was likely their undoing, as it was Philip "The Fair"—who was in debt to them—expelled the Templars from France in 1304, and perhaps not coincidentally also took the property of the Italian bankers.[25]

The Balance Sheet

The question now arises as to how much banking was responsible for the rise and wealth of the Knights Templar. There is perhaps no way to see the complete picture because of the sheer scope of such an undertaking. According to William of Tyre, writing in 1185, "their possessions indeed beyond the sea, as well as in these parts, are said to be so vast, that there cannot be a province in Christendom which does not contribute to the support of the aforesaid brethren, whose wealth is said to equal that of sovereign princes". Annual income for the Order in Europe was estimated at $30,000,000 (at the time of Addison in 1852, equivalent to over $800,000,000 in 2012), possessing 9,000 manors or lordships that provided rents, corn, cattle, and other agricultural products. In addition to this, they received "immense riches ... obtained from pious and charitable people all the advowsons within their reach, and frequently retained the tithe ... deputing a priest of the Order." By the end of their prowess, the property possessed by the Templars was "astonishing", a litany of estates, farms, and other properties of rent, each including a priest who acted as almoner.[26]

We have touched upon their significant banking prowess, and use of their Temples as treasuries in style of earlier times, but the above speaks of much income unrelated to banking. From the very start, they were endowed with "much treasures in gold and silver" from Normandy and Scotland and in their first hundred years "the Order continued rapidly to increase in power and wealth in England, and in all parts of Europe, through the generous donations of pious Christians".[27] But it hints of trade and commerce and not merely the result of the excesses of charity when we hear King Henry say to them in 1255 "[Y]ou are said to possess a well-equipped fleet" and requested use of it and provisions from the Templars and Hospitallers for an expedition to the Holy Land.[28] And there were other sources of income. The Knights were the agents of ransom payments in the Holy Land[29] and received tribute from the Assassins.[30]

Therefore, they produced goods, perhaps to near-total agrarian self-sufficiency. They dealt in real estate, specifically in the collection of rents. And all the while, so much support from princes and paupers came in that Hugh de Payens placed a "prior" in England specifically to "transmit the revenues to Jerusalem", followed by "heaping gifts and benefits", wills, and so forth. As an added advantage, they were given blanket exemptions from taxes. King Henry III, "one of greatest benefactors", held a fair at Walsenford (County of Essex) every three years on anniversary of death of St. John the Baptist, the Patron Saint of the Order, and gave them rights of judiciary over their lands and manors. [31]

Therefore, whatever advantage they gained in reviving ancient banking is not apparent because of the vast wealth gained by other means. Further riches and sources from banking may have been concealed, which seems consistent with the fact they were so industrious yet made their case of self-imposed poverty such that even Kings spoke of the Order's wealth and power being derived from alms. And one cannot deny they held a near monopoly on banking, displacing a half millennium of Jewish-only money-lending, not bound to the Christian prohibition of usury.

The only rival of the Templars were the Genoese, those Italians known as the "Lombards" by the North, who with their "bancherii" (benches, by which the work "bank" is derived) would in the end inherit the market share of the disbanded Knights ad not simply bankrolling Italy and the Papacy. By 1200 AD, the Italians were doing inter-bank transfers, creating a marketplace, rather than a monolithic institution such as the Templars crafted. [32] Though granting that the Templars had the know-how before them, Durant speaks of the Lombards as the definitive modern bankers of their time, to an extent that banking terms in almost all European languages are derived from Italian terms[33]–that is, except the word "check" or "cheque", which may have come from the ancient word "*chek*" that likely became "*saqq*" in Arabic.

Trade Secrets

If the Knights Templar did discover banking methods, it would appear they kept it to themselves, as apart from the Lombards some time later, they were the only Gentile game in town. One possible way they could preserve the secrecy of their records was to place them in cipher–and what better way than to use the numeral representations of the Saracens? Arabic numerals afforded them easier accounting, first of all with the existence of a character for "zero". Secondly, the mathematics of a decimal system with single digits per place value was simpler to manage, unlike the constant additive and subtractive place values of leftover Phoenician letters that was passed down to Europe, through Rome, from the Etruscans. With the exception of grandfather clocks and movie credits, "Roman" numerals have been displaced by Hindu-derived "Arabic" ones to this day. But to White Men at the time of the Crusades, it was an utterly unfamiliar script.

But it is not the number zero but the word of which it was called in Arabic that may be the smoking gun of a secret code. The placeholder for a null value was a circle, "*sifr*" in Arabic, by which the modern word "cipher" is derived.[34]

Another question—if we assume the Knights Templar did indeed use Arabic numerals as a cipher—is if it afforded them enough advantage by virtue of being unknown. When were they introduced? On an expedition c.1130 to translate Arabic works of philosophy and science, John of Spain introduced the astronomy tome "*al-Khwarizmi*" (a corruption of which became the word "Algorithm"), and with it the new numbers.[35] In 1202, Leonardo Fibonacci published "Liber Abaci", widely presenting the new numbers and sparking a "rebirth of mathematics in Latin Christendom", followed closely by the introduction of algebra and its application to geometry. But intellectual and commercial realms may as well have been different continents, because both the numbers and their written manipulations were resisted by merchants, who favored the abacus to the point of outlawing them in Florence in 1299. This indicates the figures and figuring was there, but only scholars—and perhaps Templar bank staff—could read and use them. It was not until the 16th Century that the old was thoroughly displaced by the new. [36]

In other words, an old, ciphered Templar ledger would seem plain enough to modern eyes to not realize its nature, or power at the time. All that needs to be done to close the case is to find a Templar bank draft or ledger using Arabic numerals. As of this date, this author has been unable to find one, but again, it may be somewhere in some museum case or photo book, in plain sight.

Conclusion

We have established the foundations of banking in the Ancient and Classical Worlds. We have exposed the lack of such economic edifices in the Dark Ages of Europe, while maintaining their prosperous preservation in the East. We have declared the assets and profits of the Temple's keepers for two centuries after contact with Arabic culture and numerals.

The circumstantial evidence is strong that Templars using Arabic numerals is plausible in geography, time, and advantage. It may or may not have been the primary source of their economic and political prowess. To make profit from it, they had to creatively overcome the scriptural taboo against usury by means similar to modern Islamic Banking.

And then there is another possibility they may have employed: lending of promissory notes greater than the amount kept in a treasury—a practice used by modern banks—would have been better than Alchemy, making gold not from lead, but from numbers on a ledger. This also could account for their skyrocketing wealth, but without a more comprehensive account of their finances, we may never know the role or extent by which banking was a Holy Grail worth protecting by foreign symbols.

Citations

[1] Roberts, Keith. *The Origins of Business, Money, and Markets*. (New York, NY: Columbia University Press, 2011), 22-23. Clay promissory objects date back to at least the third millennium BC in Mesopotamia, where interest was already an established custom.

[2] Durant, Will and Ariel Durant. *Caesar and Christ*. (New York, NY: MJF Books, 1944), 79-80, 88

[3] Durant, Will and Ariel Durant. *Caesar and Christ*. (New York, NY: MJF Books, 1944), 331

[4] Roberts, Keith. *The Origins of Business, Money, and Markets*. (New York, NY: Columbia University Press, 2011), 238-239

[5] Durant, Will and Ariel Durant. *Caesar and Christ*. (New York, NY: MJF Books, 1944), 331-332

[6] Roberts, Keith. *The Origins of Business, Money, and Markets*. (New York, NY: Columbia University Press, 2011), 130

[7] Durant, Will and Ariel Durant. *Caesar and Christ*. (New York, NY: MJF Books, 1944), 331

[8] Heather, P. J. *Empires and barbarians: the fall of Rome and the birth of Europe*. (New York, NY: Oxford University Press, 2010), 380

[9] McDonald, Scott B. and Albert L. Gastmann. *A history of credit & power in the Western world*. (New Brunswick, NJ: Transaction Publishers, 2001), 67

[10] Heather, P. J. *Empires and barbarians: the fall of Rome and the birth of Europe*. (New York, NY: Oxford University Press, 2010), 465

[11] El-Ashker, Ahmed Abdel-Fattah and Rodney Wilson. *Islamic Economics : a short history*. (Leiden, Netherlands & Boston, MA: Brill,

2006). The contributions of Early Islamic Civilization to banking and economics in general, as well as its decline by the time of the Crusades, are just outside the scope of this introductory paper.

[12] Heather, P. J. *Empires and barbarians: the fall of Rome and the birth of Europe.* (New York, NY: Oxford University Press, 2010), 465-467, 474-475

[13] Heather, P. J. *Empires and barbarians: the fall of Rome and the birth of Europe.* (New York, NY: Oxford University Press, 2010), 477-478. At this point, the centers of economic power in Islam had moved farther East from Iraq and Iran to the home of the Samanid dynasty in Eastern Iran. Their Khurasan solver mines were at peak production, estimated at 40-45,000,000 coins (120-150 tons) per year.

[14] Addison, C.G. *The Knights Templars.* (London, Longman, Brown, Green, and Longmans, 1852), 145-146

[15] Durant, Will and Ariel Durant. *Caesar and Christ.* (New York, NY: MJF Books, 1944), 79, 515

[16] Durant, Will and Ariel Durant. *Caesar and Christ.* (New York, NY: MJF Books, 1944), 536. This perhaps places Jesus of Nazareth's overturning of the tables in a more revolutionary context.

[17] Roberts, Keith. *The Origins of Business, Money, and Markets.* (New York, NY: Columbia University Press, 2011), 130

[18] Roberts, Keith. *The Origins of Business, Money, and Markets.* (New York, NY: Columbia University Press, 2011), 238

[19] McDonald, Scott B. and Albert L. Gastmann. *A history of credit & power in the Western world.* (New Brunswick, NJ: Transaction Publishers, 2001), 68, 69

[20] McDonald, Scott B. and Albert L. Gastmann. *A history of credit & power in the Western world.* (New Brunswick, NJ: Transaction Publishers, 2001), 190

[21] McDonald, Scott B. and Albert L. Gastmann. *A history of credit & power in the Western world.* (New Brunswick, NJ: Transaction Publishers, 2001), 69

[22] Addison, C.G. *The Knights Templars.* (London, Longman, Brown, Green, and Longmans, 1852), 374, 497

[23] Addison, C.G. *The Knights Templars.* (London, Longman, Brown, Green, and Longmans, 1852), 348

[24] Addison, C.G. *The Knights Templars.* (London, Longman, Brown, Green, and Longmans, 1852), 406

[25] McDonald, Scott B. and Albert L. Gastmann. *A history of credit & power in the Western world.* (New Brunswick, NJ: Transaction Publishers,

2001), 70. Earlier, King Philip exiled the Jews from France, among whom were the lending predecessors of the Templars and Lombards.

[26] Addison, C.G. *The Knights Templars*. (London, Longman, Brown, Green, and Longmans, 1852), 479, 488

[27] Addison, C.G. *The Knights Templars*. (London, Longman, Brown, Green, and Longmans, 1852), 153-154, 192

[28] Addison, C.G. *The Knights Templars*. (London, Longman, Brown, Green, and Longmans, 1852), 370

[29] McDonald, Scott B. and Albert L. Gastmann. *A history of credit & power in the Western world*. (New Brunswick, NJ: Transaction Publishers, 2001), 68

[30] Addison, C.G. *The Knights Templars*. (London, Longman, Brown, Green, and Longmans, 1852), 370

[31] Addison, C.G. *The Knights Templars*. (London, Longman, Brown, Green, and Longmans, 1852), 154, 351, 250. Not only were Templar lands and endeavors exempt from taxation, they often handled taxation of the tenants in their lands on behalf of the crown.

[32] McDonald, Scott B. and Albert L. Gastmann. *A history of credit & power in the Western world*. (New Brunswick, NJ: Transaction Publishers, 2001), 75.

[33] Durant, Will and Ariel Durant. *The Age of Faith*. (New York, NY: MJF Books, 1944), 628-629

[34] Durant, Will and Ariel Durant. *The Age of Faith*. (New York, NY: MJF Books, 1944), 241. The Italians shortened the number from the Latinized Arabic "zephyrum" to "zero".

[35] Durant, Will and Ariel Durant. *The Age of Faith*. (New York, NY: MJF Books, 1944), 910-911. The title of the book "al-Khwarizmi" was later corrupted to become the word "Algorithm".

[36] Durant, Will and Ariel Durant. *The Age of Faith*. (New York, NY: MJF Books, 1944), 990

Works Cited

Addison, C.G. *The Knights Templars*. London: Longman, Brown, Green, and Longmans, 1852.

Durant, Will and Ariel Durant. *Caesar and Christ*. New York, NY: MJF Books, 1944.

Durant, Will and Ariel Durant. *The Age of Faith*. New York, NY: MJF Books, 1944.

El-Ashker, Ahmed Abdel-Fattah and Rodney Wilson. *Islamic Economics : a short history*. Leiden, Netherlands & Boston, MA: Brill, 2006.

Heather, P. J. *Empires and barbarians: the fall of Rome and the birth of Europe*. New York, NY: Oxford University Press, 2010.

McDonald, Scott B. and Albert L. Gastmann. *A history of credit & power in the Western world*. New Brunswick, NJ: Transaction Publishers, 2001.

Roberts, Keith. *The Origins of Business, Money, and Markets*. New York, NY: Columbia University Press, 2011.

Western New York Lodge of Research Under Dispensation By-Laws

ARTICLE I—NAME

Sec. 1: This Lodge shall be known and distinguished as "WESTERN NEW YORK LODGE OF RESEARCH," and is held by virtue of a Dispensation granted by the Grand Lodge of Free and Accepted Masons of the State of New York, dated on the 21st day of October 1982.

ARTICLE II—OBJECT

Sec. 1: The object of Western New York Lodge of Research shall be to promote and advance the interests of Free Masonry through study and research, and to encourage Masonic education.

ARTICLE III—MEETINGS

Sec la: The Annual Stated Communication of Western New York Lodge of Research shall be held during the month of December, and at that meeting Lodge Officers shall be elected and installed for the ensuing year.

Sec 1 b: There shall be at least two (2) other meetings of Western New York Lodge of Research each year, one in Spring, preferably in March and one in Autumn, preferably in October.

Sec. 1 c: The date for each meeting shall be selected by the Elected Officers, and written notice of each meeting shall be given to the members.

Sec. 2a: The place of the Stated of Summoned Communication shall be the Buffalo Consistory.

Sec. 2b: The hour of the meeting shall be 7:30 p.m., provided that the Master may, by notice to the members, designate another hour whenever in his judgment, the work before the Lodge may require it.

Sec. 3: At any Stated or Summoned Communication of the Lodge, no business shall be transacted unless there shall be a quorum present and that such quorum shall consist of at least five (5) Active members of the Lodge.

ARTICLE IV—MEMBERSHIP

Sec. la: Membership in this Lodge shall be by affiliation only.

Sec. lb: All Petitioners must be Master Masons in good standing of Lodges in jurisdictions recognized by the Grand Lodge of the State of New York.

Sec. 2: The membership of Western New York Lodge of Research shall consist of three classes as follows: (1) Active Member. (2) Corresponding Member. (3) Fellow.

Sec. 3: ACTIVE MEMBER

(1) Active members shall be elected by unanimous secret ballot at a Stated Communication of the Lodge subsequent to the proposal in open Lodge, of which proposal all Active members shall be notified.

(2) Active members shall have the right to vote, ballot and be eligible for office.

(3) Active members shall be entitled to receive all communications of the Lodge and a copy of the published proceedings or transactions of the Lodge.

Sec. 4: CORRESPONDING MEMBER

(1) Corresponding members shall be elected at a Stated Communication of the Lodge by a majority vote by a show of hands, without notice in a call for the communication.

(2) Corresponding members shall be entitled to receive a copy of the published proceedings or transactions, in accordance with Article X Section 2.

(3) Corresponding membership in the Lodge is open to Master Masons in good standing, Masonic Lodges, and Concordant Masonic Bodies recognized by the Grand Lodge of the State of New York.

Sec. 5: FELLOW

(1) A Fellow must be a Master Mason in good standing of a Lodge in any jurisdiction recognized by the Grand Lodge of the State of New York.

(2) A Fellow shall be elected by unanimous ballot at a Stated Communication of the Lodge subsequent to their proposal in open Lodge, of which the Active members shall be notified.

(3) A Fellow shall have all the rights, privileges and benefits of Active

membership and shall be exempt from the payment of fees and dues to the Lodge.

(4) Fellowship is an honor to be conferred upon Master Masons for outstanding achievement in Masonic research and publication.

ARTICLE V—OFFICERS

Sec. 1: The elective officers shall be a Master, a Senior Warden, a Junior Warden, a Treasurer, a Secretary and three Trustees one of whom shall be elected annually for a three year term.

Sec. 2: The Master shall appoint a Senior Deacon, a Junior Deacon, two Masters of Ceremony, two Stewards, Chaplain(s), a Marshal and a Tiler.

Sec. 3: The Master shall appoint such committees as may be necessary for the conduct of the business of the Lodge.

ARTICLE VI—TREASURER

Sec. 1: The Treasurer shall receive from the Secretary all monies paid into the Lodge and shall give his receipt therefore; keep a just and regular account thereof; and deposit the same in such bank, trust company, or savings institution as the Lodge may designate. All monies shall be deposited in the name of the Lodge, and no withdrawals shall be made except by check signed by any two of the following officers, upon authorization by the Lodge: Master, Treasurer, Secretary.

ARTICLE VII—SECRETARY

Sec. 1: The Secretary shall record the proceedings of the Lodge under the direction of the presiding officer; shall receive all monies paid into the Lodge and pay the same to the Treasurer, taking his receipt therefore; and shall keep accurately such books of records and perform such duties as prescribed by the Grand Lodge.

ARTICLE VIII—CERTIFICATE OF ELECTION

Sec. 1: The Lodge shall file a certificate of election of Trustees in accordance with the Benevolent Orders Law of the State of New York;

and the manner of electing Trustees and their terms shall conform to the requirements of the Law.

ARTICLE IX—FEES AND DUES

Sec. 1a: Petitioners for Active membership shall pay as affiliation fee of twenty-five dollars ($25.00).

Sec. 1b: Petitioners for Corresponding membership shall pay an affiliation fee of ten dollars ($10.00).

Sec. 1c: A Corresponding member petitioning for Active membership shall pay a fee of fifteen dollars ($15.00).

Sec. 1d: The current years dues are included in the affiliation fee.

Sec. 2a: Active members shall pay dues of fifteen dollars ($15.00) per year.

Sec. 2b: Corresponding members shall pay dues of ten dollars ($10.00) per year.

Sec. 2c: Annual dues are payable in advance on or before the beginning of each calendar year.

ARTICLE X—PUBLICATIONS

Sec. 1: The Lodge may, at convenient intervals, publish proceedings or transactions containing such portions of the addresses in the Lodge and such germane material as may be desirable to print. It may also publish new Masonic books of outstanding merit, reproduce or print Masonic documents of historical importance, and reprint scarce Masonic books and pamphlets.

Sec. 2: The compilation, manufacture and distribution of all publications of the Lodge shall be in the charge of a Publications Committee appointed by the Master. The Lodge may, in its discretion, establish rules and regulations concerning the publication and sale of articles and books to individuals and bodies including the classes of membership mentioned in Article IV Section 2.

ARTICLE XI—AMENDMENTS

Sec. 1: These By-Laws may not be amended except by a proposition in writing and adopted by a vote of the majority of the Active members present at a subsequent communication summoned for that purpose.

Submitted to the Lodge for approval on September 22, 1982 by Wor. Charles L. Ketchum. Jr.

Approved by the Lodge on December 6, 1982 under Worshipful Master Alan G. Fowler.

Founding Members, Charter Members, and Worshipful Masters

There were twenty-one founding members of the Western New York Lodge of Research No.9007 F&AM Grand Lodge of the State of New York, and 25 charter members the following year (1983). The title and Lodge listed is the respective current title and affiliation or that of the time of their passing. Of particular note is Nocturnal Lodge No.1137, which merged in 2008 and its descendant Lodge is now Ancient Landmarks Lodge No.358—we have used their altar cloth for many years at our stated communications. The years for Masters are listed as the calendar year in which they started their term, and does not include subsequent partial calendar years (where the Masonic year was shifted to begin in May some years ago).

Founding Members

Wor. Alan G. Fowler—Nocturnal No.1137

Wor. Lewis E. Newman—Nocturnal No.1137

Wor. Charles L. Ketchum, Jr.—Tyrian No.925

Wor. Donald C. Markham—Erie No.161

Wor. Eugene E. Compton—Master Builder No.911

Wor. John Borycki—Washington No.240

Wor. John P. Fulciniti—Tyrian No.925

Wor. David W. Jamison—Occidental No.766

Wor. Joseph E. Smeller, Jr.—Harmony No.699

Wor. Herman T. Black—Queen City No.358

Wor. Jack Jensen—Christopher G. Fox No.1021

Wor. David L. Beu—Occidental No.766

Wor. Irwin Cole Stickle—Christopher G. Fox No.1021

Bro. Melvin H. Levy—DeMolay No.498

Bro. Ned T. Elliott—Nocturnal No.1137

Wor. George H. Freiberg, Sr.—Nocturnal No.1137

Wor. Ronald S. Januszkiewicz—Buffalo No.846

Wor. Lavern S. Lambkin—Akron No.527
Wor. George E. Strebel—Kenmore No.1132
Wor. Frederick W. Leisinger, Jr.—Washington No.240
Wor. Raymond E. Terwilliger—Akron No.527

Charter Members

Bro. Louis A. Alphonsetti, Sr.—Nocturnal No.1137
Wor. Weston H. Carter—Springville No.351
RW Edward G. Eschner—Emulation No.1022
Wor. Stuart M. Farmer—Master Builder No.911
Bro. Graham L. Fox—Nocturnal No.1137
RW Harold T. Gerlach—Buffalo No.846
RW Albert E. Hemstreet—Occidental No.766
Wor. Ward A. Peterson—Cheektowaga No.1163
RW R. Kerford Wilson—DeMolay No.498
Wor. Max Winklhofer—Emulation No.1022
Bro. Robert J. Parks—Washington No.240
RW Charles T. Dale—Christopher G. Fox No.1021
Wor. Kenneth Perry—Eggertsville No.1157
Wor. Julius C. Roese—Ely Parker No.1002
Bro. Louis A. Alphonsetti, Jr.—Johnson City No.970
MW Ernest Leonardi—Floral City
Wor. Robert B. Wolcott, Jr.—Occidental No.766
Wor. H. Curtis Buffum—Highland No.835
RW Frank H. Anderson—Mystic Art No.899
Bro. Joseph Evans—Eggertsville No.1157
RW Carl Luther—Harmony No.699
Bro. Morris Smith—Fortune No.788
RW Robert J. Zolczer—Tyrian No.925
Wor. Henry J. Meyer Jr.—Living Stone No.255
RW Robert D. Mulholland—Living Stone No.255

Worshipful Masters of the Lodge

1982-1984—RW Alan G. Fowler—Nocturnal No.1137
1985—RW Charles L. Ketchum, Jr.—Tyrian No.925
1986—RW Donald C. Markham—Erie No.161
1987—Wor. David W. Jamison—Occidental No.766
1988—Wor. Joseph E. Smeller, Jr.—Harmonie No.699

1989 Wor. Stuart M. Farmer–Master Builder No.911
1990-1991–RW Jack Jensen–Christopher G. Fox No.1021
1992–Wor. Frederick W. Leisinger, Jr.–Washington No.240
1993–RW Max Winklhofer–Emulation No.1022
1994–Wor. Irwin Cole Stickle–Christopher G. Fox No.1021
1995–Wor. Donald H. Davis–Perseverance No.948
1996–Wor. Courtney G. Kerruish–Concordia No.143
1997–Wor. John Borycki–Washington No.240
1998–Wor. Robert B. Wolcott, Jr.–Occidental No.766
1999–RW Edward L. Meyers
2000–Wor. James A. Rowe–Queen City-Christopher G. Fox No.358
2001-2002–Wor. Allen E. Maull–Amherst No.981
2003-2004–Wor. Norman G. Walker–Master Builder No.911
2005–Wor. John R. Eggen–Fortune No.788
2006–RW Alan G. Fowler–Nocturnal No.1137
2007-2008–RW Albert W. Hoffman–Millennium No.1179
2009–RW Brian Singer–Millennium No.1179
2010–Wor. John W. Comstock–Emulation No.1022
2011–RW Paul S. Sabo–Eggertsville-Grand Island No.1138
2012–RW John Haslam–Western Star No.1180
2013–RW Robert Drzewucki–Living Stone No.255
2014–RW Daniel DiNatale–Harmonie No.699
2015–Wor. Myron Deputat–Hiram No.105
2016–Wor. E. Walter Cook IV–Ken-Ton No.1186
2017–RW Peter Filim–Hiram No.105
2018–RW David Bindig–Fortune No.788

About the Editing of this Book

A Diverse Ideal

The various contents of this book were written, published, edited, and republished over a period of roughly 30 years. The writing style and degree of scholarship is therefore diverse. We may find one author to be casual and contemplative, while another adheres strictly to a formal tone and meticulous citations. All of these have a welcome place in the inclusive intellectual milieu of Freemasonry. A Research Lodge ought be no different, deferring judgment on those men without letters, to inspire each to progress in those skills necessary to convey higher thoughts and claim higher achievements.

General Style Considerations

There is currently no standard style guide for writing and research in Masonic endeavors, though there are more and less common conventions that have evolved over the years. Many publications in the United States use *The Quarry Project Style Guide* by the Masonic Research and Preservation Conference. This urges the standard convention of capitalizing most words referring to specifically Speculative Masonic uses, such as Lodge, Degree, Apron, Mason, etc., while omitting others in various cases. These rules are not strictly obeyed here, but attempts at consistency are made unless otherwise noted. Logic also prevails over some of the style's details in punctuation. Some conventions are outright contradicted, as "No." preceding Lodge numbers is forbidden in the guide, but is the only proper choice for practice in the jurisdiction from which our Research Lodge hails.

We have simplified titles by omitting the difficult-to-format "three dots" character. In other words, "M∴W∴" and "R∴W∴" are rendered "MW" and "RW" respectively, except in quotations. This is standard for publications such as the "Empire State Magazine", in which this editor is a regular columnist. As further editor's prerogative, the title Worshipful is abbreviated as "Wor."; the title Brother is generally spelled out at the beginning of sentences and abbreviated otherwise as "Bro.".

The choices of Brothers or Brethren has been preserved. It is often used interchangeably or without intention of specific nuance, but an important distinction can be made. Brethren refers to a group of Masons as a body, such as those present at a communication; Brothers refers to each of them as individuals. This is lost on most Brothers, or the Brethren in general, but adds much power to words when wielded with intention. I found a perfect example in my travels with MW Jeffrey Williamson, who will most often address an assembly of Masons at informal gathering as "My Brothers"–speaking endearingly at once to each person in the room, rather than broadcasting collective instruction as would be transmitted from behind the hat and gavel in the East to no one in particular.

The Turabian method of citations (which the *Quarry Project* is promoted as an extension of) is a natural contender as a standard for citations in this field. It is here not meticulously followed, and authors in some cases have insufficient details on sources to have given "proper" citation.

In view of all the above, most of the content has been edited to conform, but much has been kept–especially with regards to historical passages. If there is an inconsistency, it is either with reason or begs a forgiveness or error due to solitary, voluntary efforts in editing over long periods.

In all cases, rewriting broadly was avoided in favor of preserving the spirit of the presentations.

Content History

This book is divided into sections denoting separately published volumes in chronological order. However, the order itself is not an honest narrative.

The articles in *Works Under Dispensation* include the history of the Lodge, published 25 years after the fact (2008), with sections repeated in the original and cleaned up when republished as a composite tome with *Volume 1* in 2014. This latter version did not contain minutes and bylaws found in the original, some of which may be considered inappropriate to publish (such as the names of those petitioning to affiliate). Only a few omissions are here re-published for the first time.

The work *The Morgan Affair, Why?* was recently rediscovered during the compilation of this book. It was a composite of an article written on or before 1985 and extensive edits and additions made in 1997, the year it was spiral bound similar to *Works Under Dispensation* and *Volume 1*. The unique challenges in editing it for use here are outlined in the introduction to that section, and the work exactly as it was originally presented is available from this editor and publisher.

Volume 2 was printed in 2009 and contained an article previously in *Works Under Dispensation* ("The Early History of Freemasonry in Erie County"), which will only be found in *Under Dispensation* in this composition. There was also an article, "*The Sacred Lodge*", found in the development notes that did not make it in but most of the content was also found in "Astrology: *As Above, So Below*", and in a later volume, "Spiritual Alchemy", all by the same author. Also, edited versions were found of most of the articles and apparently not used–the printed version of articles contained all the errors of the originals. In such cases, the corrections and suggestions were considered, adjusting clear errors without pause, but being conservative in making only stylistic changes that bring necessary clarification to the author's intent.

Volume 3 followed the format of *Volume 2* and was printed in 2013. What you see does not mean there were not other works in or before 2013. Some were not ready by this deadline and so may be published in a *Volume 4* when they become available as written works rather than notes or a slideshow. This work is already in progress, but is not included here so that we can put a definite limit on the size and time spent crafting this bound work.

Each section (book) keeps its "Message from the Master" and editor's introductions from the softcover versions, there being none in earlier printings. The order of the articles was preserved unless otherwise noted, but no clear purpose can be clearly construed, except to find that Volume 3 was ordered alphabetically by the author's last name.

Author Honorifics

Another challenge from the spread of works across these decades is the titles and biographies of the contributing authors. Many honorifics of authors have changed or been added since the writing or publication of their articles. Such titles are fully omitted in the Table of Contents and headings of chapters, but will be given in bylines of their respective works as they first appeared as publication. Some articles are further prefaced as to changes to the author's titles and biographical details as of the writing of this book.

Redactions

Secrecy in Masonic knowledge is broadly subjective in the extreme–some jurisdictions only recently use written, ciphered ritual books while others have them in plain view online. Some of us in New York were shocked at how much was revealed in a recent BBC documentary on Freemasonry in the United Grand Lodge of England. Others only insist on secrecy with regards to grips and words.

There were a very few cases that details of ritual and symbolism were redacted or replaced (substituted text in square brackets). The general intention, as in most of what we speak in daily life, is that we can refer to things that will make sense to us, but not register on the radar of the "profane" mind in any way that would break the confidence we have made between ourselves. Our words, like our symbols or the number of steps leading up to a building, are hidden in plain sight. Saying a pant sleeve is rolled up is hardly an infraction without giving the additional context, that which we know having experienced it. Such things shall remain illegible and unintelligible, and therefore not a violation.

Copyrights & Images

It is assumed that those who contributed to the content contained herein did so willingly, knowing it could be republished at some future time. Every reasonable effort had been made in previous editions to ensure this, and there have been no objections over these years. This is not a for-profit endeavor, and we can assure ourselves that our purpose in publishing this is consistent with the values and intentions of such Brothers as have openly shared their work. We give each author credit for their contribution, and if any content here does not make it clear its authorship, it is because it is not known.

There may be instances where words are borrowed and citation is lacking. We are aware of none and did not find any upon inspection, but there is always a chance. Any such instance would be minute and unintentional and should not be construed as plagiarism.

The images here are all public domain, or the property of the Lodge or its contributors, to the best of our knowledge. Images that were uncertain or ornamental alone were replaced or omitted.

A Final Note

This is not a perfect work. None of the articles were untouched from their original versions. Adjustments were made respectfully and with deliberation, but we accept responsibility for errors or unwanted changes and welcome criticism to help us endeavor to do better in future publications.